Road Atlas 2016

WHAT'S INSIDE

Best of the Road® Trips

Our editor's six favorite road trips from our Best of the Road® collection.

Mileage Chart

Driving distances between 90 North American cities and national parks.

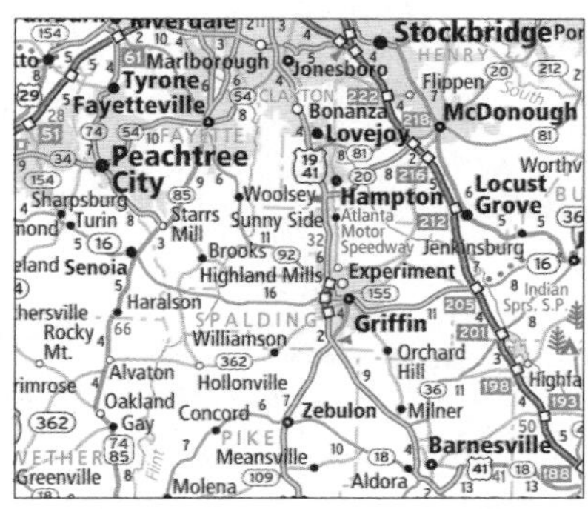

Maps

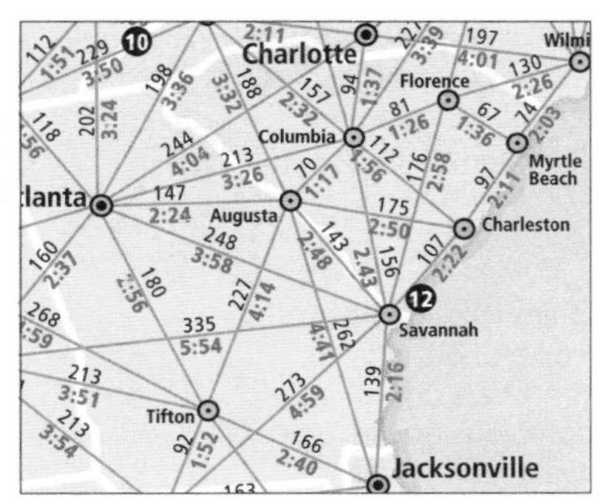

Mileage and Driving Times Map

Distances and driving times between hundreds of North American cities and national parks.

If you have a comment, suggestion, or even a compliment, please visit us at randmcnally.com/contact or write to:
Rand McNally Consumer Affairs
P.O. Box 7600
Chicago, Illinois 60680-9915

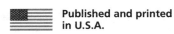

Published and printed in U.S.A.

1 2 3 VE 16 15

The Sustainable Forestry Initiative® (SFI) program promotes responsible environmental behavior and sound forest management.

Printed by Quad Graphics

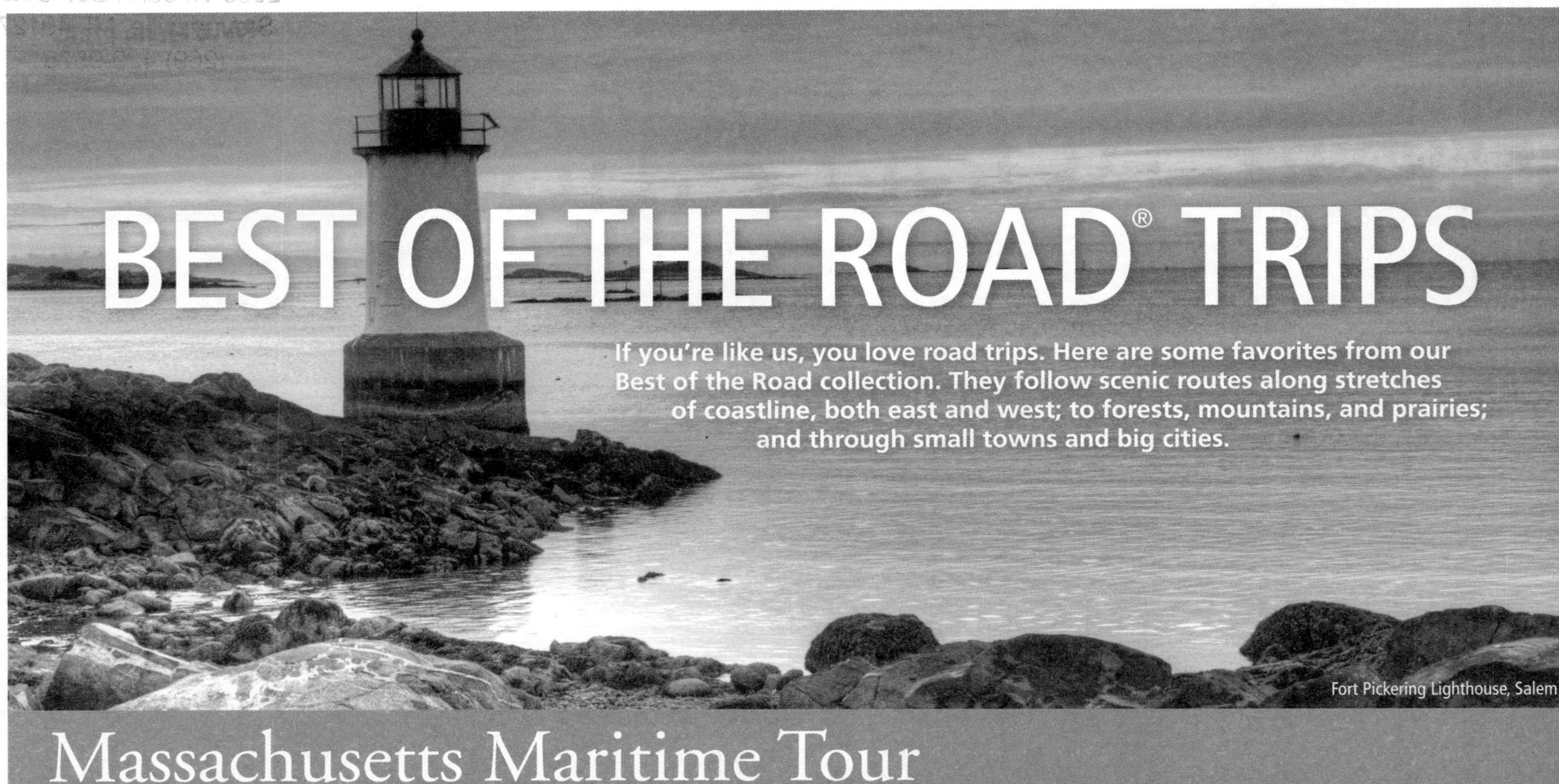

BEST OF THE ROAD® TRIPS

If you're like us, you love road trips. Here are some favorites from our Best of the Road collection. They follow scenic routes along stretches of coastline, both east and west; to forests, mountains, and prairies; and through small towns and big cities.

Fort Pickering Lighthouse, Salem

Massachusetts Maritime Tour

The close proximity to the Atlantic has long fostered a co-dependence between Massachusetts's coastal towns and the sea. To immerse yourself in the (aptly nicknamed) Bay State's rich maritime traditions, start at Newburyport's Custom House Maritime Museum on Boston's North Shore. Move from water to witches in Salem, home of the infamous trials.

A bit farther south, you'll hit the vibrant city of Boston, where history meets sports meets culture at every turn. Beyond, on the South Shore, you'll find Plymouth, famous landing place of the Pilgrims, and the Plimoth Plantation Living History Museum, where you can experience 17th-century life. Sights in the one-time whaling center of New Bedford highlight still more maritime history.

Newburyport

Custom House Maritime Museum. Settled in 1653 at the intersection of the Merrimack River and the Atlantic Ocean, Newburyport almost immediately solidified its importance as a commercial port. The museum, housed in a handsome Greek-revival building, contains objects that represent the town's maritime history. There are stunning models and paintings of the clipper ships that once plied their trade in this area as well as artifacts from actual ships that made it back to port and those salvaged from ships lost at sea. The museum's Coast Guard Room tells its history through art and photos and helps to explain exactly what the Coast Guard does. ***25 Water St., (978) 462-8681, www.customhousemaritimemuseum.org.***

Plimoth Plantation

Salem

The Salem Witch Museum. Salem is most known for, of course, the 1692 Witch Trials, one of the strangest episodes in Anglo-American colonial history. Fourteen women and five men were hanged after being convicted of sorcery, and one man died after being pressed to death over the course of two days. The museum has stage-sets that use figures and narration to bring this frightening era to life. The gift shop sells all sorts of one-of-a-kind witchy paraphernalia including Salem witch bottles (small glass vessels filled with sand, salt, a nail, and a charm that colonists used to use to ward off evil). *Washington Sq., (978) 744-1692, www.salemwitchmuseum.com.*

Boston

Faneuil Hall. Wealthy merchant Peter Faneuil built his namesake hall in 1741 to handle imported and exported goods (including, sadly, slaves). The building was used by Samuel Adams and other Sons of Liberty in the 1760s and '70s to denounce British Colonial rule. Still a popular venue for political speeches and public meetings, it now encompasses the original hall, as well as the North, South, and Quincy Market buildings. True to its commercial past, the whole complex is home to retail outlets, restaurants and bars, and small spaces that sell take-away food and souvenirs. *1 Faneuil Hall Sq., (617) 635-3105, www.cityofboston.gov/freedomtrail.*

New England Aquarium. Penguins, though not native to Boston, take pride of place here, but they're only a fraction of the aquarium's thousands of examples of marine life. Many different environments are recreated such as an Amazon rainforest, a coral reef, coastal Maine, and a harbor seal habitat. If you want to see whales—right whales, humpbacks, pilot whales—and dolphins, take the **Boston Harbor Cruises' New England Aquarium Whale Watch** (617/227-4321, www.bostonharborcruises.com/whale-watch), a three-hour tour offered in conjunction with the Aquarium. *1 Central Wharf, (617) 973-5200, www.neaq.org.*

Boston Tea Party Ships and Museum. On the evening of December 16, 1773, members of the underground group, Sons of Liberty, boarded three British trade ships anchored at Griffin's Wharf, and dumped their payload of tea chests into Boston Harbor. At this museum, you can board a replica of the *Beaver,* one of the ships at the wharf that night, and throw simulated bales of tea into the harbor. Abigail's Tea Room has tea (ahem), soft drinks, beer and wine, and assorted pastries and sandwiches. *Congress St. Bridge, (617) 338-1773, www.bostonteapartyship.com.*

Plymouth

Plimoth Plantation. This living-history museum recreates the daily life of Pilgrims and the native Wampanoags in 1627 through recreated homesteads, costumed re-enactors, and cooking demonstrations, lectures, and games. There's a crafts center, where workers use traditional tools and techniques to produce most of the items used on the grounds; a working grist mill; and the Nye Barn, where many of the animals are direct descendants of the cattle, sheep, goats, pigs, and birds the Pilgrims would have encountered or brought with them from England. The visitor center has a gift shop and a café. ***137 Warren Ave., (508) 746-1622, www.plimoth.org.***

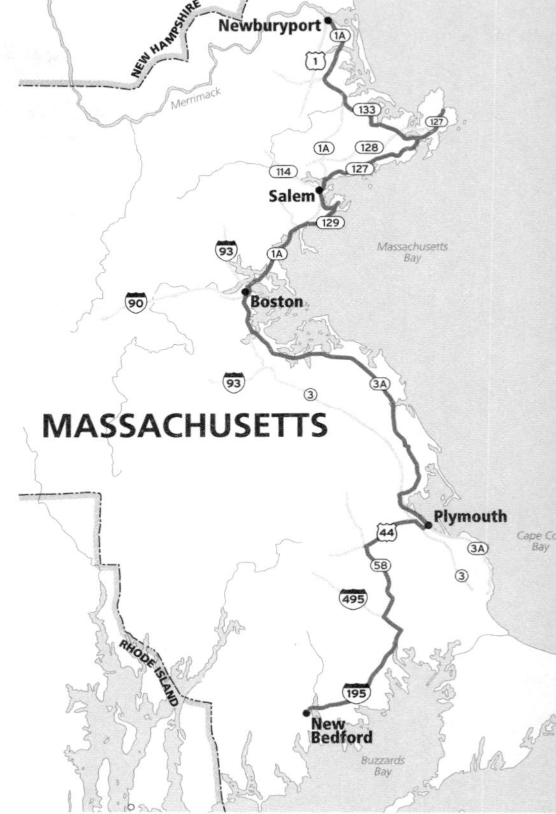

Atlas map B-15, p. 4

Distance: 135 miles point to poin

New Bedford

New Bedford Whaling National Historical Park. Whale-oil lamps were ubiquitous in the mid-19th century, and New Bedford was the world's premier whaling port and thus, the richest city. With a collection of museums, historic homes and buildings, and a working waterfront, the park invites you to explore the town in context of its golden past and its importance to the nation and the world. The visitors center has self-guided brochures and maps and a brief movie. Guided tours of New Bedford leave from the center daily and last about an hour. ***33 William St., (508) 996-4095, www.nps.gov/nebe.***

Marsh near Charleston

South Carolina: Highlights of Lowcountry

A road trip along coastal South Carolina means a relatively straight shot through seaside towns, many of which seem frozen in the elegance of a different era. From the 60-mile stretch of golden Grand Strand beaches to the mansions of historic Charleston to the plantations and seaside towns in between, Lowcountry charms you with its historical and natural beauty, great food, and Southern hospitality.

And, when you're not learning to dance the shag in North Myrtle Beach, you'll be touring centuries-old plantations and some of the country's oldest public gardens or following in the footsteps of movie stars in Beaufort, which served as the backdrop for classics like *Forrest Gump.*

harleston

North Myrtle Beach

at Harold's Beach Club. You can't blend in with the ocals until you can dance like them, and in Lowcountry hat means learning the shag. This is one of the best laces to get in step. The king of shag and founder of this lub, Harold Bessent, wouldn't have it any other way. The ociety of Stranders (SOS), a group devoted to the dance, olds events here, and the calendar is chockablock with essons—some of them free. *212 Main St., (843) 249-5779, www.fatharolds.com.*

Myrtle Beach

Myrtle Beach Boardwalk and Promenade. The eart of Myrtle Beach is its boardwalk, which runs from a ier at 14th Avenue North to another at 2nd Avenue North. ake a spin on the SkyWheel, or fly above things on a Myrtle Beach Zipline Adventures experience. **Broadway at the Beach** (www.broadwayatthebeach.com) has over two dozen restaurants; several theaters; myriad specialty shops; and attractions like WonderWorks, Ripley's Aquarium, and the Hollywood Wax Museum. The Pavilion Nostalgia and Carousel Park has tamer vintage offerings. *14th Ave. N. to 2nd Ave. N., myrtlebeachdowntown.com.*

Murrells Inlet

Brookgreen Gardens. In 1931, four rice fields were transformed into public gardens that, today, often make top-10 lists of the nation's best. Themed landscape areas include Live Oak Allee, with trees planted as far back as the 18th century; a medieval-style labyrinth; and the Palmetto Garden, which features the Sabal palmetto, South Carolina's state tree. Kids love the zoo filled with Lowcountry creatures, the Enchanted Storybook Forest, and the Children's Discovery Room and Sensory and Nature Trail. *1931 Brookgreen Dr., (843) 235-6000, www.brookgreen.org.*

Charleston

Fort Sumter National Monument. There's an eerie calmness at Fort Sumter, the same place that was shaken by explosions that set the American Civil War in motion. In the early hours of April 12, 1861, the fort came under Confederate attack and surrendered 34 hours later. It was left a smoldering heap of ruins in Charleston Harbor. Over time, it was rebuilt and is now listed on the National Register of Historic Places, a testament to the resiliency of the American South. Vessels operated by **Fort Sumter Tours** (843/722-2628, fortsumtertours.com) depart several times daily from Liberty Square, near the Fort Sumter Visitor Education Center. Trips last just over two hours. *Liberty Square, 340 Concord St., (843) 883-3123, www.nps.gov/fosu.*

Cannon at Fort Sumter

Middleton Place. The estate of Henry Middleton, President of the First Continental Congress, has decorative and fine arts from the mid-18th to the mid-19th centuries that document the history of this affluent South Carolina family. In addition to taking a 45-minute guided house tour, you can explore America's oldest formally designed garden, a vast landscape where there's something blooming just about year round: camellias in the winter; azaleas in the spring; magnolias, crepe myrtles, and roses in the summer. This National Historic Landmark site also has a restaurant serving plantation cuisine for lunch and dinner and an inn offering modern accommodations. *4300 Ashley River Rd., (843) 556-6020, www.middletonplace.org.*

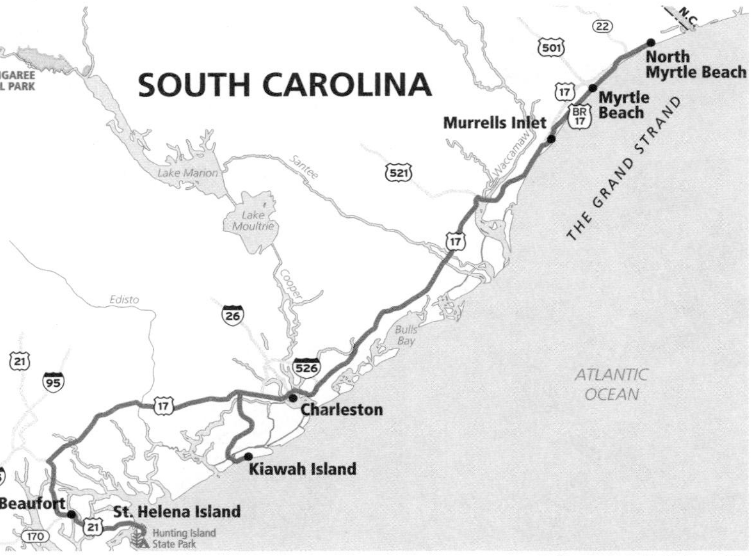

Atlas map E-13, p. 92

Distance: 230 miles point to point.

Kiawah Island

Beachwalker Park. Just 15 miles south of Charleston, the barrier island's only public park consistently makes the *Forbes* list of America's best beaches. There are dressing areas and bathrooms, picnic areas with grills, and seasonal beach chair and umbrella rentals as well as showers. The beach is just one reason to visit the island. Golf is another. The island, much of which is a gated resort community, has five championship courses. *8 Beachwalker Dr., (843) 768-2395, www.ccprc.com.*

Beaufort

Beaufort Tours. Beaufort was voted America's Happiest Seaside Town, and this tour operator aims to show you why. See locations used in films like *Forrest Gump* and *Something to Talk About*. Explore a haunted graveyard on a ghost tour, or visit a cotton plantation on the Plantation and Gullah Tour. A two-hour walking tour of Beaufort's historic district is also available. *1006 Bay St., (843) 838-2746, www.beauforttoursllc.com.*

St. Helena Island

Hunting Island State Park. Along with miles of sandy beaches and a working lighthouse, this island has more than 5,000 acres waiting to be explored. White egrets, great blue herons, osprey, bald eagles, pelicans, loggerhead turtles, and alligators are some of the creatures that make their homes here. The park also has nature trails and a nature center, a fishing pier, a boat ramp, and a store. *2555 Sea Island Pkwy., (843) 838-2011, www.huntingisland.com.*

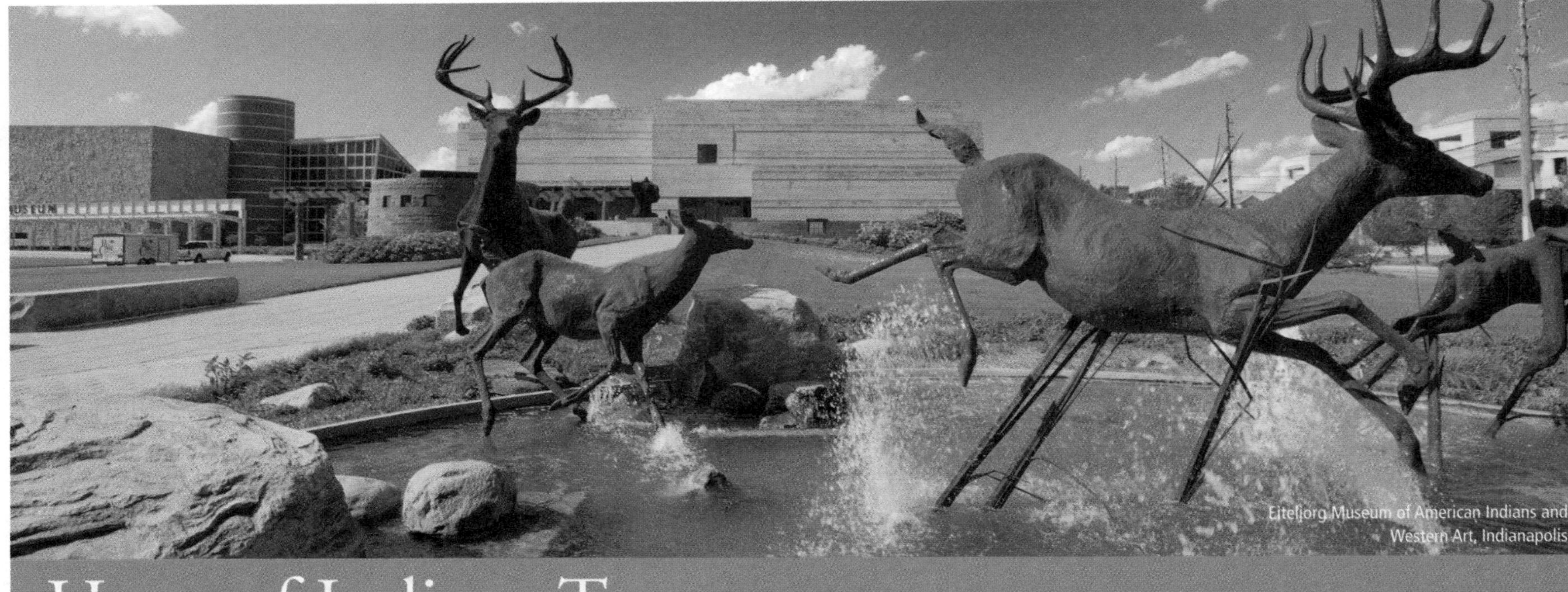
Eiteljorg Museum of American Indians and Western Art, Indianapolis

Heart of Indiana Tour

This tour samples the cultural vitality, scenic beauty, and increasingly sophisticated food scene in central Indiana. It begins in Indianapolis, the state capital, and then heads south to Columbus, one of the nation's top destinations for architecture lovers.

From Columbus, the road winds west into Brown County, a landscape of rolling ridges, mysterious hollows, and mist rising from forested valley floors. The American Impressionists of the Hoosier School migrated here to capture the countryside in watercolors and oils. Visit the T.C. Steele State Historic Site to hear their stories, or explore the wooded glens in Brown County State Park. A little farther west is Bloomington, a lively college town.

Indianapolis

Conner Prairie Interactive History Park. One of the nation's premier living-history museums brings 19th-century Indiana to life through costumed interpreters who go about their daily activities in five historic areas. Here you can be part of a Civil War raid, dance to a water drum and a gourd rattle in the Lenape Indian Camp, dip a candle at the William Conner Homestead, or learn about early aviation history at the 1859 Balloon Village. Note that the park is in the suburb of Fishers, about 25 miles northeast of downtown. *13400 Allisonville Rd., (317) 776-6006, www.connerprairie.org.*

Eiteljorg Museum of American Indians and Western Art. This museum celebrates the art, history, and cultures of North America's indigenous peoples and the American West. It has one of the nation's finest collections of contemporary Native American art as well as classic works by the likes of N.C. Wyeth, Frederic Remington, Charles Russell, and Kay WalkingStick. Its café serves Southwestern fare, and its store has many items produced by Native American artists. *500 W. Washington St., (317) 636-9378, www.eiteljorg.org.*

Brown County State Park

Edinburgh

Exit 76 Antique Mall. There's nothing fancy about this establishment, but treasures abound from more than 340 dealers displaying their wares in 600 booths and cases. Its 72,000 square feet make it one of the Midwest's largest antique malls. Those tired of shopping can relax in a lounge area with TV and vending machines. *12595 N. Executive Dr., (812) 526-7676, www.exit76antiques.com.*

Columbus

Columbus Architectural Tours. The Columbus Visitor Center offers a variety of tours of the city's internationally acclaimed architecture. Its signature two-hour guided bus excursion will introduce you to many of the nearly 70 eye-popping churches, commercial buildings, schools, and art installations. Along the way you'll learn about architects and artists that include I.M. Pei, Eliel Saarinen, Richard Meier, Harry Weese, Dale Chihuly, and Henry Moore. *506 5th St., (812) 378-2622, columbus.in.us.*

Columbus architecture

Gnaw Bone

Bear Wallow Distillery. This woman-owned business is continuing the long tradition of Hoosier moonshine, only with an upscale twist. Its copper stills create artisanal spirits from locally grown grains. Tours include samples of its signature liquors: Hidden Holler Corn Whisky Moonshine, Bear Trap Barrel Strength White Whiskey, and Liar's Bench Rye Whiskey. No need to worry about revenue agents—this moonshine is legal. *4484 E. Old State Rd. 46, (812) 657-4923, www.bearwallowdistillery.com.*

Nashville

Brown County State Park. Founded in 1929, this 16,000-acre oasis is nicknamed the Little Smokies because of its resemblance to the Great Smoky Mountains. Densely forested hills and valleys, rugged ridges, and deep ravines entice hikers and fall-foliage enthusiasts. *1450 State Rd. 46 E., (812) 988-6406, www.in.gov/dnr.*

T.C. Steele State Historic Site. Landscape painter Theodore C. Steele (1847–1926), the most highly respected of Indiana's painters, moved to Brown County in 1907 and helped introduce the area's beauty to an international audience. This state historic site preserves Steele's studio and home, which you can tour, as well

Atlas map J-9, p. 3

Distance: 97 miles point to point

as the gardens planted and tended by Selma Steele, the artist's wife. Five scenic hiking trails, from easy to steep, wind through the property, which also has a gift shop. *4220 T.C. Steele Rd., (812) 988-2785, www.tcsteele.org.*

Beanblossom

Bill Monroe Music Park & Campground. Known as the father of bluegrass music, Bill Monroe spent much of his life in tiny Beanblossom. His former home is now the site of the Bill Monroe Bluegrass Hall of Fame & Museum, featuring instruments, clothing, and memorabilia from the greats of bluegrass and country music collected during Monroe's 60 years as a performer. This is also where the world's oldest, continuous-running bluegrass festival is held: June's eight-day Bill Monroe Memorial Bluegrass Festival, which began in 1967 (make reservations well in advance). *5163 State Rd. 135 N., (812) 988-6422, www.billmonroemusicpark.com.*

Bloomington

Indiana University Art Museum. With a dramatically angled building designed by famed architect I.M. Pei and 40,000 objects dating from ancient Mesopotamia to the present, this is considered one of the country's top university art museums. There are paintings by Claude Monet, Jackson Pollack, and Pablo Picasso, and highly regarded collections of ancient jewelry and African masks and art. Angles Café—named after the building's unusual design—refreshes you with beverages and pastries. *1133 E. 7th St., (812) 855-5445, www.indiana.edu.*

The Alamo

Texas Hill Country

In this state, as the miles keep passing, you come to understand why Texans boast that everything is bigger here. A trip through Hill Country, though, is manageable, packing a lot of history and culture into a compact area that includes two great cities.

San Antonio seems to embody the full history of Texas, from its days under Spanish and Mexican rule to its struggle for independence ("Remember the Alamo," as the saying goes) and eventual statehood. Cutting-edge Austin, on the other hand, is the repository of all that history. Between them, you'll discover Wild West towns (some on the region's Wine Trail) that seem in no hurry to leave the 19th century.

San Antonio

The Alamo. In 1836, nearly 200 farmers, lawyers, surveyors, frontiersmen (including Jim Bowie and Davy Crockett), and others barricaded themselves inside the Alamo, determined to protect what they hoped would be the provisional capital of the Republic of Texas. Despite desperate requests for reinforcements, fewer than 100 men answered the call. Outside the walls, Mexico's Santa Anna marshaled his 1,800 men and waited. On March 6, the 13th day of the siege, Mexican soldiers breached the walls and killed all but a few women, children, and slaves, who were told to share what they had seen.

Hearing what happened on fact-filled ranger-led or self-guided-audio tours of the Alamo provides insight into one of the most unforgettable stories in American history. So does touring the museum within the Long Barrack, where the defenders made their final stand, and exploring the surrounding grounds, built as part of a WPA project. *300 Alamo Plaza, (210) 225-1391, www.thealamo.org.*

Field of Indian Paintbrush and Bluebonnets

River Walk. Designer Robert Hugman's vision of a lovely "scenescape" called Paseo del Rio, or River Walk, caught the imagination of San Antonio's citizens. It was completed as a WPA project, and to this day, its sinuous canals are enchanting, whether you walk along the promenade with its restaurants, cafés, bars, hotels, and boutiques, or embark with **San Antonio Cruises** (210/244-5700, www.riosanantonio.com) on a sail past scenes of old San Antonio. *110 Broadway, (210) 227-4262, www.thesanantonioriverwalk.com.*

Fredericksburg

National Museum of the Pacific War. Chester Nimitz grew up in land-locked Fredericksburg, but he went on to become one of the most respected of the U.S. Navy's admirals during WW II. This complex includes not only the Admiral Nimitz Museum but also the Center for Pacific War Studies, Plaza of Presidents, Memorial Courtyard, and Japanese Garden of Peace. Displays are packed with singular items like a PT boat, a Quonset hut, a mock field hospital, a midget Japanese sub that tried to reach Pearl Harbor, and the casing for a spare Fat Man atomic bomb. *340 E. Main St., (830) 997-8600, www.pacificwarmuseum.org.*

Dooley's 5-10-25. This place is a blast from the past, selling everything from broomstick toy ponies to Mexican jumping beans. What else can you stock up on? Things like Radio Flyer wagons, cast-iron cookware, kitchen gadgets, wind-up alarm clocks, plastic flowers, coonskin caps, Beemans gum, Blue Waltz perfume. . . the list goes on. *131 E. Main St., (830) 997-3458.*

Auslander. Combine a Bavarian biergarten with a Texas sports bar, and you get the Auslander. Drop into its bar or its German restaurant and select from roughly 70 beers, including those from Texas, Colorado, California, and Pennsylvania as well as those from Mexico, Holland, Belgium, Germany, and England. *323 E. Main St., (830) 997-7714, theauslander.com.*

Austin

Bullock Texas State History Museum. You can't miss this museum: Just look for the giant, bronze Lone Star sculpture. The first floor has Native American and Western artifacts, including an original wooden gate from the Alamo. Second-floor exhibits focus on the people and events that made Texas what it is—information you'll glean from diaries and letters dating from the days of early Mexican settlers, the Republic of Texas, the Civil War, and the Great Depression. The third level covers state geography, climate, infrastructure, and resources. *1800 N. Congress Ave., (512) 936-8746, www.thestoryoftexas.com.*

Waterloo Records. Music is the motor that moves Austin, and that motor is fueled by places like Waterloo Records. One of the city's finest record shops is packed with new and used CDs and LPs, including alternative/indie, rock/pop, folk/country, or blues/jazz. Texas artists are well represented, and the music-loving staffers will help you find new sounds. *600 N. Lamar Blvd., (512) 474-2500, www.waterloorecords.com.*

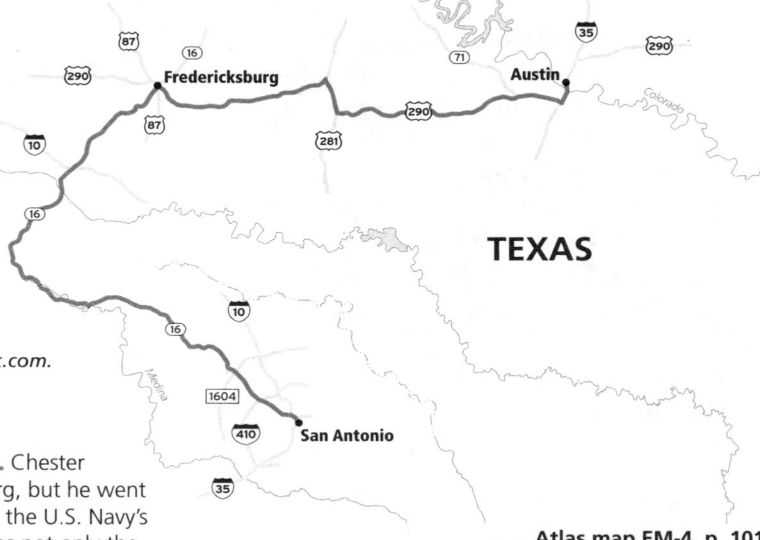

Atlas map EM-4, p. 101

Distance: 185 miles point to point.

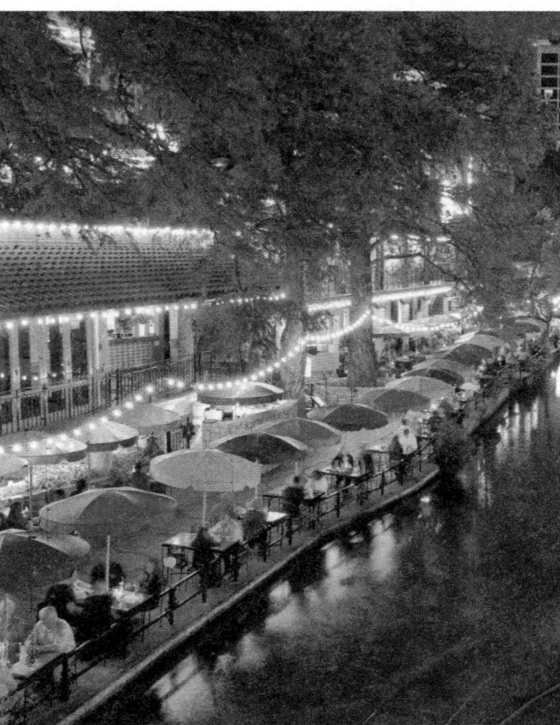

River Walk, San Antonio

Congress Avenue Bridge Bat Colony. More than a million Mexican free-tail bats, comprising North America's largest urban colony, hang out beneath the Ann W. Richards Congress Avenue Bridge. Just after sunset, you can stand on its span, and watch the entire colony emerge for its nightly food foray. The viewing "season" runs March through November; late July or early August sees lots of young pups starting to fly. Want viewing-time information? Call the Bat Hotline, which is really just the main number for a local branch of Bat Conservation International. *(512) 327-9721.*

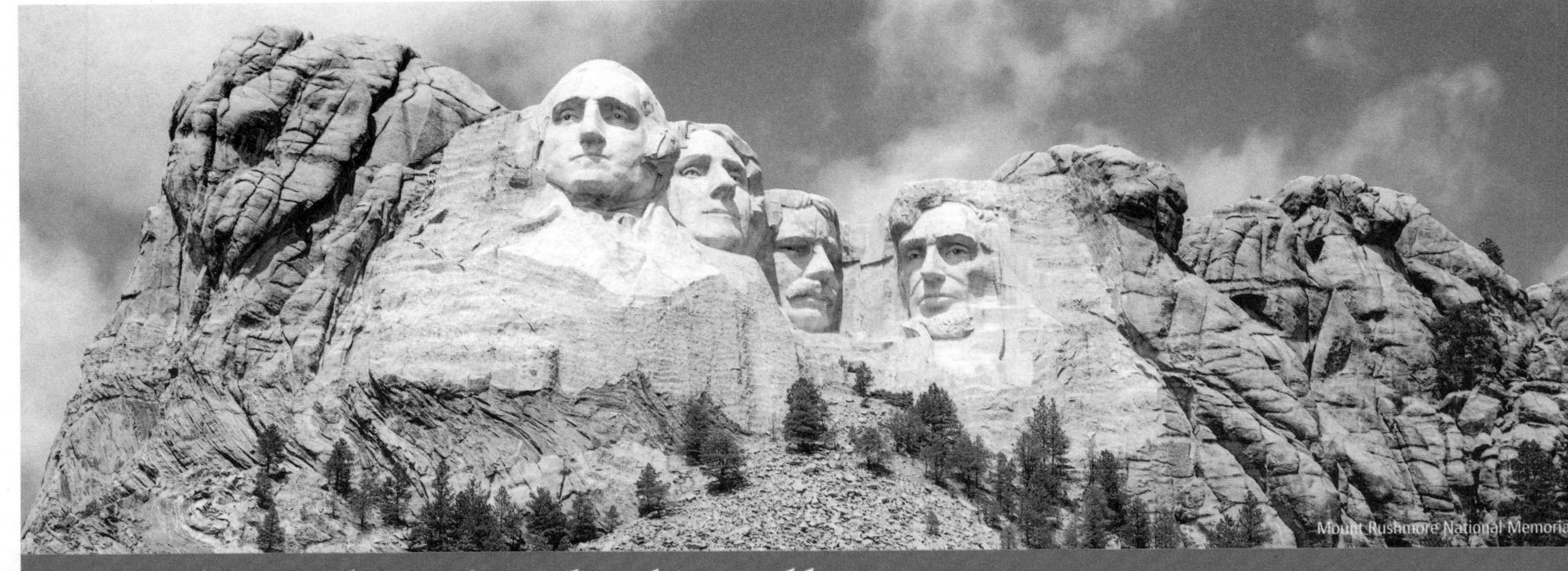

South Dakota's Black Hills

The Sioux called them Paha Sapa (Hills that are Black) for good reason: the pine forests are so dense that the landscape really does appear inky from a distance. And this drive through South Dakota's western edge affords plenty of chances to admire and experience all the storied, eerie beauty.

Curvaceous routes like US-385 cut swaths through Black Hills National Forest, amid sacred lands that have also safeguarded precious minerals and ores as well as prehistoric creatures. And the region is dotted with former pioneer and mining towns, where locals are on a first-name basis with long-dead gunslingers. If you have a bit more time, visit Badlands National Park to the east and Devils Tower National Monument to the west in Wyoming.

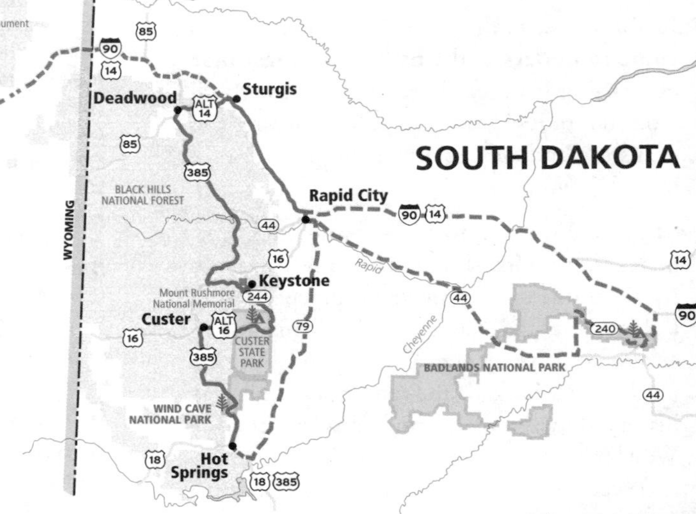

Atlas map E-3, p. 93

Distance: 130 miles point to point

Rapid City

The Journey Museum & Learning Center. This complex tells the story of the Northern Plains. The Sioux Indian Museum has ceremonial garments, containers, dolls, moccasins, and other everyday items highlighting Lakota culture and craftsmanship. The Minnilusa Pioneer Museum features mining, military, and settler artifacts and the stories of such historical figures as Wild Bill Hickok, George Armstrong Custer, Sitting Bull, and Crazy Horse. *222 New York St., (605) 394-6923, journeymuseum.org.*

Prairie Edge Trading Companies & Gallery. With a focus on Plains Indians culture, this gallery's exquisite paintings, traditional apparel, jewelry, and other items are created by local artists and artisans. Prices are on the high side, as befits the high quality and authenticity of the work. If you're planning to splurge on a cherished memento, this is the place. *606 Main St., (605) 342-3086, www.prairieedge.com.*

Sturgis

Sturgis Motorcycle Museum & Hall of Fame. For a week each August, the Black Hills rumble with the full-throttled roar of motorcycles thanks to the Sturgis Motorcycle Rally, held since 1938. It draws a half-million people—almost doubling the state's population—to its races, concerts, parties, and scenic tours. Year-round, you can get a taste of the rally spirit at this museum. Vintage bikes and memorabilia feature greatly in displays honoring the culture and community of motorcyclists. *999 Main St., (605) 347-2001, www.sturgismuseum.com.*

Deadwood

Original Deadwood Tours. A one-hour, narrated bus tour takes you through the storied streets of this Wild West mining town. Among the stops is Moriah (aka Boot Hill) Cemetery, where you can pay respects to Wild Bill Hickok, Calamity Jane Canary, Preacher Smith, Potato Creek Johnny, and local madam Dora DuFran—who was buried with her pet parrot. Departures are from the Midnight Star Casino, which like the tour company, is owned by the actor Kevin Costner. *677 Main St., (605) 578-2091, originaldeadwoodtour.com.*

Keystone

Mount Rushmore National Memorial. In 1927, Gutzon Borglum began carving the heads of Washington, Jefferson, Lincoln, and Theodore Roosevelt into a granite outcropping. The project took almost a million dollars, 400 workers, 14 years, and loads of dynamite. By the time Borglum's son Lincoln completed the work in 1941, roughly 450,000 tons of rock had been blasted away to create the 60-foot-high faces.

The paved, ½-mile Presidential Trail has an exhibit on area Native Americans and takes you beneath the sculpted heads. The Lincoln Borglum Museum, directly below the Grand View Terrace, has exhibits and a film. In warmer months, a 45-minute evening program concludes with the dramatic illumination of the faces to the sound of the National Anthem. *13000 SD Hwy. 244, (605) 574-2523, www.nps.gov/moru.*

Custer State Park

Custer

Custer State Park. The wildlife in Custer's 71,000 acres includes elk, deer, antelope, mountain goats and sheep, burros, and prairie dogs. But the main attraction is the 1,300-head bison herd, best seen from along the 18-mile Wildlife Loop Road. What's more, the park is a great area hub thanks to its many outstanding lodging and dining options. *Park Headquarters: 13329 U.S. 16A, (605) 255-4515, gfp.sd.gov/state-parks.*

Hot Springs

Wind Cave National Park. Sioux legend holds that a constant wind from the inner reaches of a Black Hills cave blew the buffalo herds from beneath the earth to feed the Lakota people. It might well have been this cave, the fourth-longest in the U.S. Size isn't its only unique quality. Rather than the usual stalactites or stalagmites, Wind Cave has unusual popcorn, flowstone, frostwork, and boxwork formations. Ranger-led tours depart from the visitors center. Above ground, 28,295 acres are home to elk and bison herds and prairie dog communities. *26611 US-385, (605) 745-4600, www.nps.gov/wica.*

The Mammoth Site. Ice Age mammoths and other creatures, in search of water fed by ancient hot springs, fell to their deaths in a sinkhole here. The sediment that later filled it preserved their remains, which were discovered in the 1970s. The museum offers exhibits and a 30-minute guided tour, during which you'll see fossilized skeletons still embedded in the ground. *1800 Hwy. 18 Bypass, (605) 745-6017, mammothsite.com.*

Black Hills

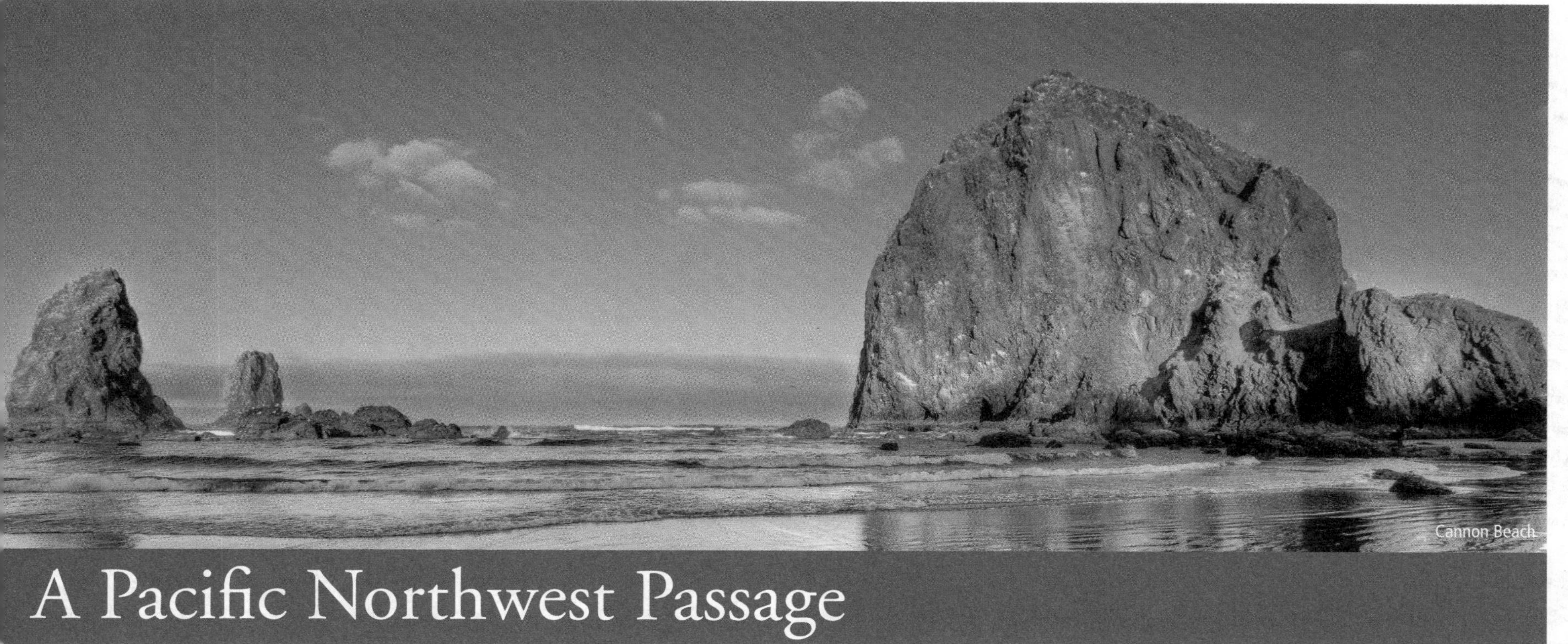

A Pacific Northwest Passage

Woods, water, and historic wonders await on this trip between two great metropolises of the Pacific Northwest. Few cities balance culture and commerce, nature and architecture, the past and the future as well as Seattle. The Emerald City makes a great jumping off point for a visit to the Olympic National Park and Forest.

The coastal route south from forested Washington to Oregon is as fun to drive as it is breathtaking. It also promises unique maritime experiences in towns like Astoria and Cannon Beach. Inland, you'll travel through one of Oregon's wine regions before reaching Portland, the so-called City of Roses, known for its gardens and its greenery. Here, as elsewhere along the route, expect great food, great views, and great stories—old and new.

oh Rain Forest, Olympic National Park

;eattle, WA

'ike Place Market. Founded in 1907, "the Market" is multilevel complex overlooking Elliott Bay and part of a -acre historic district. At street level on its western side re produce, fish, meat, flower, and craft stands. Across he narrow, cobblestoned Pike Place are more shops and estaurants. Watch fishmongers toss salmon, visit the first tarbucks outpost, and enjoy the antics of talented street erformers. *85 Pike St., (206) 682-7453, vww.pikeplacemarket.org.*

;pace Needle and Seattle Center. The 1962 Seattle Vorld's Fair left a legacy of icons, including the 605-foot pace Needle and its 360-degree views. Glass elevators ravel up to 10 mph to the observation deck, with its lisplays, shops, lounge, and revolving SkyCity restaurant.

elow the Space Needle are the Experience Music Project, vith rock-and-roll memorabilia; the Pacific Science Center; nd the Seattle Children's Museum. Arrive via the Monorail, vhich zips (in about 2 minutes!) between downtown's Vestlake Center Station and Seattle Center Station. *'00 Broad St., (206) 905-2100, www.spaceneedle.com.*

Pittock Mansion, Portland

Bill Speidel's Underground Tour. This 90-minute guided tour travels beneath historic Pioneer Square to 1890s walkways, where many storefronts and some interiors remain intact. You'll learn about Seattle's early timber days and famous Skid Row and get the back story of this three-block area, where the street level was raised from 8 to 35 feet after the 1889 Seattle Fire. *608 1st Ave., (206) 682-4646, www.undergroundtour.com.*

Port Angeles

Olympic National Park. Three ecosystems make up this 1,427-square-mile peninsular park: Pacific shoreline, subalpine forest and meadowland, and coastal-Northwest rain forest. You can readily combine a visit here with explorations of Olympic National Forest—which rings the park—and the coast.

The drive along U.S. 101 has many overlooks and short trails down to the beach. Near shore, in the park's southwestern reaches, is the Hoh Rain Forest. Learn about the mild climate and lush vegetation at its visitors center before exploring the mile-long Hall of Mosses or one of eight other trails. *3002 Mount Angeles Rd., (360) 565-3130, www.nps.gov/olym.*

Astoria, OR

Columbia River Maritime Museum. A massive window overlooks the Columbia River, and displays tell the stories of its vessels and the dangers they face on "the bar" at the river's mouth. Indeed, the collection of 30,000 maritime artifacts has many items salvaged from wrecks in the so-called Graveyard of the Pacific. Step into a simulator to see what it's like to pilot a tugboat before visiting the lightship *Columbia*. *1792 Marine Dr., (503) 325-2323, www.crmm.org.*

Cannon Beach

Ecola State Park. Kayakers and swimmers like the waters off this park's beautiful, half-mile Crescent and Indian beaches. You can also hike to a spot overlooking the 19th-century Tillamook Rock Lighthouse (in spring and fall, watch for gray whales). It's just off the 2.5-mile Clatsop Loop Trail, which travels through forests of giant Sitka spruce in the footsteps of Lewis and Clark. *Off Hwy. 101, (503) 436-2844, www.oregonstateparks.org.*

Forest Grove

David Hill Vineyards and Winery. Established by a German pioneer family in the late 1800s, David Hill has some of Willamette Valley's oldest Pinot Noir vines and also produces Gewürztraminer, Riesling, and other varieties. Stop by the tasting room any day of the week. *46350 N.W. David Hill Rd., (503) 992-8545, www.davidhillwinery.com.*

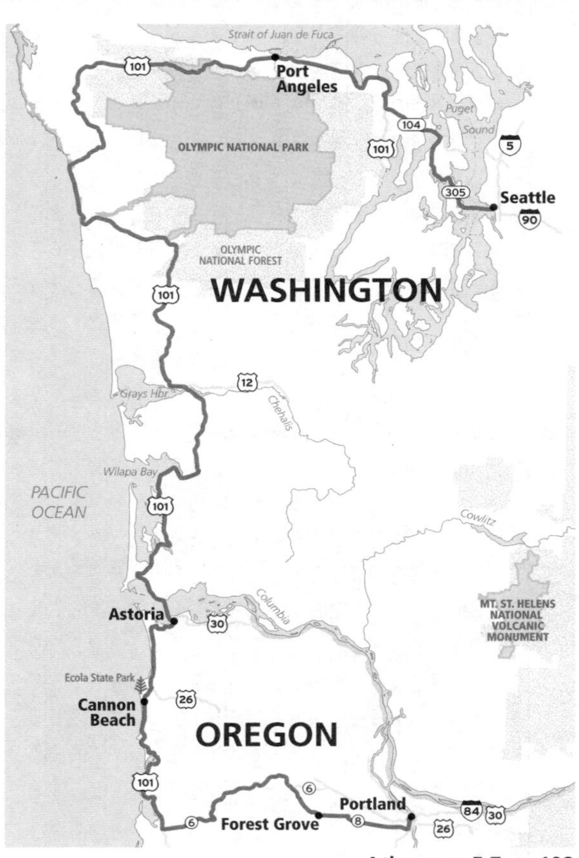

Atlas map F-7, p. 108

Distance: 442 miles point to point.

Portland

Pittock Mansion and Washington Park. Mansion is an understatement. It's more like a castle, or rather, a French Renaissance–style chateau. In the 1850s, Henry and Georgiana Pittock each traveled west along the Oregon Trail before meeting and marrying in Portland. Henry took over the *Daily Oregonian* newspaper and made a fortune in several endeavors.

Their 22-room sandstone residence was completed in 1914, and tours of it and the 46-acre estate highlight architecture, decorative arts, and the family. In nearby Washington Park, check out the Rose Test Garden, Japanese Garden, Discovery Museum, Portland Children's Museum, and Oregon Zoo. *3229 N.W. Pittock Dr., (508) 823-3623, pittockmansion.org.*

Powell's City of Books. It's been around for a while, is open 365 days a year, stocks new and used tomes, and has staffers and customers who truly love to read. Shop for books on local history or lore, scan the national best sellers, grab a cheap paperback, and have a cuppa at World Cup Coffee & Tea. *1005 W. Burnside, (503) 228-4651, www.powells.com.*

Mileage Chart

This handy chart offers more than 2,400 mileages covering 90 North American cities and U.S. national parks. Want more mileages? Visit **randmcnally.com/MC** and type in any two cities or addresses.

	Albuquerque, NM	Amarillo, TX	Atlanta, GA	Baltimore, MD	Billings, MT	Birmingham, AL	Boise, ID	Boston, MA	Branson, MO	Brownsville, TX	Buffalo, NY	Charleston, SC	Charleston, WV	Charlotte, NC	Cheyenne, WY	Chicago, IL	Cincinnati, OH	Cleveland, OH	Columbus, OH	Dallas, TX	Denver, CO	Des Moines, IA	Detroit, MI	El Paso, TX	Fargo, ND	Grand Junction, CO	Hartford, CT	Houston, TX	Indianapolis, IN	Jackson, MS	Jacksonville, FL	Kansas City, MO	Las Vegas, NV	Little Rock, AR	Los Angeles, CA	Louisville, KY	Memphis, TN	Miami, FL	Milwaukee, WI	Minneapolis, MN	Mobile, AL	Montpelier, VT	Nashville, TN	New Orleans, LA	New York, NY	Norfolk, VA	Oklahoma City, OK	Omaha, NE	Orlando, FL	Philadelphia, PA	Phoenix, AZ	Pittsburgh, PA	Portland, ME	Portland, OR	Raleigh, NC	Rapid City, SD	Reno, NV	Saint Louis, MO	Salt Lake City, UT	San Antonio, TX	San Diego, CA	San Francisco, CA	Savannah, GA	Seattle, WA	Spokane, WA	Tampa, FL	Washington, DC	Wichita, KS
Acadia N.P., ME	2490	2206	1366	671	2507	1448	2935	283	1704	2469	728	1241	1014	1112	2198	1254	1142	911	1034	2035	2242	1570	997	2626	1900	2484	372	2115	1208	1683	1417	1692	2988	1718	3256	1249	1583	1760	1348	1667	1698	293	1370	1791	478	840	1949	1707	1559	577	2952	841	172	3360	972	2171	3154	1453	2636	2310	3317	3371	1285	3325	3045	1613	710	1884
Albuquerque, NM		284	1386	1887	998	1241	938	2219	864	990	1782	1703	1543	1626	546	1333	1387	1598	1457	647	446	983	1570	260	1318	380	2118	884	1279	1047	1636	784	572	877	786	1300	1008	1952	1354	1225	1234	2203	1219	1165	2001	1910	542	863	1730	1924	462	1641	2315	1363	1761	843	1019	1037	599	712	810	1086	1634	1438	1320	1746	1885	591
Amarillo, TX	284		1102	1602	965	957	1243	1935	580	788	1498	1419	1259	1342	515	1049	1103	1314	1173	363	424	765	1286	407	1002	607	1834	589	995	762	1352	570	857	593	1072	1016	720	1668	1132	1009	949	1919	932	881	1716	1632	256	647	1446	1640	746	1357	2031	1669	1474	714	1304	752	883	510	1097	1370	1350	1743	1505	1462	1600	382
Anchorage, AK	3672	3641	4338	4321	2660	4284	2707	4495	3788	4430	4155	4532	4111	4389	3128	3617	3914	3965	3975	4097	3227	3450	3905	3940	2935	3288	4513	4339	3804	4302	4689	3572	3424	3959	3412	3919	4093	5004	3545	3165	4486	4318	4093	4485	4428	4506	3894	3391	4782	4380	3681	4082	4443	2448	4436	2995	3026	3825	3006	4152	3532	3084	4585	2276	2387	4798	4319	3736
Atlanta, GA	1386	1102		682	1831	146	2177	1095	652	1145	894	317	502	244	1439	715	461	714	567	780	1404	902	722	1418	1361	1643	996	794	533	380	346	800	1959	515	2174	420	379	661	809	1127	328	1165	248	468	882	558	844	992	440	780	1844	684	1192	2603	408	1508	2396	555	1878	986	2138	2472	247	2649	2369	451	637	955
Baltimore, MD	1887	1602	682		1952	780	2378	400	1079	1801	372	571	361	442	1644	699	513	369	409	1368	1673	1015	524	2003	1346	1916	300	1448	584	1017	744	1068	2420	1050	2670	604	914	1082	792	1112	1003	498	703	1124	192	228	1346	1153	889	98	2349	246	496	2804	302	1616	2599	829	2081	1642	2695	2816	605	2770	2491	942	39	1260
Big Bend N.P., TX	592	470	1344	1929	1393	1201	1530	2325	973	625	1939	1661	1610	1588	938	1442	1495	1755	1614	561	838	1182	1678	325	1525	949	2226	637	1388	964	1505	988	1043	880	1128	1400	1015	1820	1525	1427	1102	2395	1226	981	2128	1912	650	1102	1598	2028	757	1794	2422	1956	1753	1190	1491	1145	1191	404	1050	1507	1558	2021	1912	1614	1892	807
Billings, MT	998	965	1831	1952		1780	620	2236	1241	1758	1786	2132	1742	1990	453	1246	1546	1596	1606	1425	551	946	1535	1257	607	662	2143	1652	1435	1688	2182	1026	971	1407	1240	1539	1477	2497	1173	838	1874	2207	1586	1868	2041	2132	1203	845	2275	2011	1210	1713	2333	891	2067	323	956	1278	552	1480	1301	1173	2078	818	540	2291	1951	1064
Birmingham, AL	1241	957	146	780	1780		2126	1177	507	1020	908	463	564	390	1386	660	464	716	569	636	1329	848	724	1274	1307	1573	1078	668	478	237	434	749	1814	370	2029	366	234	746	754	1072	258	1247	192	343	960	715	699	939	534	880	1700	748	1274	2551	555	1456	2262	501	1826	861	1994	2327	393	2597	2318	537	744	810
Boise, ID	938	1243	2177	2378	620	2126		2660	1588	1928	2214	2473	2123	2336	736	1693	1943	2020	2013	1702	830	1360	1960	1205	1227	620	2566	1930	1835	2048	2528	1372	624	1786	842	1877	1825	2844	1732	1461	2236	2636	1925	2216	2465	2525	1497	1225	2622	2435	914	2137	2761	428	2444	942	422	1622	339	1651	958	639	2418	503	425	2638	2375	1338
Boston, MA	2219	1935	1095	400	2236	1177	2660		1433	2198	453	970	744	841	1927	983	870	638	763	1764	1970	1299	724	2373	1629	2210	101	1844	937	1412	1146	1421	2714	1447	2983	978	1312	1482	1074	1396	1427	179	1099	1520	207	569	1678	1436	1288	306	2681	570	110	3086	702	1900	2881	1182	2365	2039	3046	3098	1014	3054	2774	1342	439	1613
Branson, MO	864	580	652	1079	1241	507	1588	1433		1005	995	968	755	868	851	545	601	808	668	435	806	400	784	985	816	1049	1327	602	493	432	968	209	1437	172	1651	510	274	1284	630	643	620	1417	464	597	1201	1158	323	402	1062	1138	1326	851	1529	2013	1003	920	1806	249	1288	708	1675	1950	900	2059	1780	1078	1078	292
Brownsville, TX	990	788	1145	1801	1758	1020	1928	2198	1005		1853	1459	1525	1388	1303	1474	1409	1669	1528	547	1213	1230	1673	814	1614	1370	2099	354	1379	793	1225	1036	1550	794	1630	1314	929	1538	1557	1475	821	2268	1140	700	1981	1716	738	1192	1319	1900	1259	1708	2294	2354	1556	1515	1998	1177	1589	274	1552	2010	1320	2428	2296	1329	1765	896
Buffalo, NY	1782	1498	894	372	1786	908	2214	453	995	1853		866	435	656	1478	533	434	190	326	1378	1521	849	273	1908	1180	1762	397	1499	500	1125	1037	984	2266	1061	2535	540	922	1385	630	946	1166	428	712	1248	395	569	1242	987	1184	388	2245	216	553	2639	637	1450	2433	746	1915	1654	2596	2650	909	2604	2325	1235	382	1176
Calgary, AB	1542	1511	2357	2332	541	2305	747	2615	1783	2299	2165	2542	2122	2400	998	1627	1925	1976	1985	1967	1096	1461	1915	1809	956	1154	2524	2209	1814	2239	2703	1567	1284	1958	1557	1930	2028	3018	1555	1221	2481	2380	2116	2419	2438	2516	1763	1386	2797	2390	1524	2093	2505	787	2446	865	1276	1820	869	2021	1617	1500	2620	678	424	2833	2330	1606
Charleston, SC	1703	1419	317	571	2132	463	2473	970	968	1459	866		471	207	1740	908	620	721	636	1099	1706	1199	826	1734	1557	1946	871	1105	726	697	235	1103	2276	831	2491	613	696	583	1002	1323	602	1068	549	742	768	437	1160	1293	380	668	2165	654	1066	2904	278	1811	2698	856	2180	1300	2459	2789	106	2950	2671	433	530	1272
Charleston, WV	1543	1259	502	361	1742	564	2123	744	755	1525	435	471		264	1389	491	196	250	162	1049	1355	788	352	1684	1136	1595	644	1171	312	801	642	752	2099	732	2330	244	597	990	589	902	816	813	388	908	530	403	1002	943	792	466	2005	225	840	2554	322	1410	2342	506	1829	1324	2354	2564	514	2560	2281	840	362	945
Charlotte, NC	1626	1342	244	442	1990	390	2336	841	868	1388	656	207	264		1600	769	477	514	426	1023	1566	1057	616	1662	1414	1810	742	1038	583	624	379	961	2199	754	2414	470	619	728	867	1180	571	928	407	712	641	328	1084	1151	526	539	2088	446	938	2761	168	1670	2555	714	2037	1230	2381	2712	251	2808	2528	578	398	1092
Cheyenne, WY	546	515	1439	1644	453	1386	736	1927	851	1303	1478	1740	1389	1600		960	1210	1288	1281	971	100	628	1227	807	787	340	1834	1202	1104	1316	1792	634	829	1055	1102	1144	1091	2107	1000	865	1504	1899	1192	1488	1733	1792	720	492	1885	1703	1008	1405	2024	1161	1712	298	956	888	437	1025	1162	1172	1687	1225	993	1901	1642	608
Chicago, IL	1333	1049	715	699	1246	660	1693	983	545	1474	533	908	491	769	960		289	342	354	926	1002	332	280	1455	641	1242	888	1085	181	738	1068	526	1746	650	2015	296	531	1381	90	408	917	954	469	923	787	878	792	470	1153	757	1795	459	1079	2118	816	912	1913	296	1398	1202	2080	2130	951	2063	1785	1166	697	724
Cincinnati, OH	1387	1103	461	513	1546	464	1943	870	601	1409	434	620	196	477	1210	289		248	106	934	1187	580	259	1569	937	1427	767	1055	108	686	796	584	1932	617	2172	97	482	1127	381	703	721	855	273	804	637	605	846	722	905	571	1849	288	967	2369	521	1208	2163	348	1647	1210	2196	2380	664	2363	2084	916	512	779
Cleveland, OH	1598	1314	714	369	1596	716	2020	638	808	1669	190	721	250	514	1288	342	248		142	1194	1330	659	168	1721	990	1570	562	1315	315	937	892	799	2073	868	2342	347	729	1240	434	756	973	611	525	1057	460	551	1057	797	1043	428	2060	131	736	2446	572	1260	2240	560	1725	1457	2407	2458	764	2414	2135	1091	367	992
Columbus, OH	1457	1173	567	409	1606	569	2013	763	668	1528	326	636	162	426	1281	354	106	142		1039	1261	653	191	1578	1000	1501	661	1174	176	790	812	657	2004	724	2244	206	587	1164	445	766	826	747	378	910	533	570	917	792	954	468	1920	184	859	2439	486	1270	2234	421	1718	1314	2269	2451	680	2424	2144	1007	407	851
Crater Lake N.P., OR	1307	1595	2580	2772	1033	2528	422	3054	1990	2305	2609	2866	2515	2736	1129	2086	2336	2413	2406	1976	1223	1753	2353	1473	1640	972	2959	2212	2227	2375	2931	1775	754	2178	738	2270	2235	3246	2126	1874	2562	3038	2318	2494	2858	2917	1889	1618	3025	2828	1039	2530	3156	250	2837	1351	310	2015	691	2028	858	410	2810	422	493	3041	2768	1731
Dallas, TX	647	363	780	1368	1425	636	1702	1764	435	547	1378	1099	1049	1023	971	926	934	1194	1039		880	683	1163	635	1079	1124	1665	228	873	402	992	489	1220	319	1437	836	453	1307	1010	928	589	1824	664	519	1548	1350	204	656	1086	1467	1066	1221	1861	2128	1191	1061	1668	630	1403	276	1359	1734	996	2193	1964	1102	1332	361
Denver, CO	446	424	1404	1673	551	1329	830	1970	806	1213	1521	1706	1355	1566	100	1002	1187	1330	1261	880		670	1270	707	873	243	1876	1035	1083	1226	1756	603	747	965	1015	1109	1097	2069	1042	913	1414	1942	1158	1398	1775	1758	631	534	1851	1732	908	1447	2067	1256	1678	397	1051	854	533	935	1077	1268	1651	1320	1091	1860	1671	519
Des Moines, IA	983	765	902	1015	946	848	1360	1299	400	1230	849	1199	788	1057	628	332	580	659	653	683	670		599	1124	475	909	1206	938	474	828	1253	193	1413	573	1682	586	617	1567	371	242	998	1270	656	1008	1105	1196	545	137	1339	1074	1445	777	1395	1786	1107	626	1581	354	1065	960	1747	1798	1150	1764	1484	1354	1014	391
Detroit, MI	1570	1286	722	524	1535	724	1960	724	784	1673	273	826	352	616	1227	280	259	168	191	1163	1270	599		1702	930	1508	668	1319	288	945	1002	764	2013	885	2281	361	742	1354	374	696	978	718	534	1066	613	704	1029	736	1144	583	2032	285	825	2385	677	1200	2180	533	1664	1439	2346	2397	870	2353	2075	1178	522	964
El Paso, TX	260	407	1418	2003	1257	1274	1205	2373	985	814	1908	1734	1684	1662	807	1455	1569	1721	1578	635	707	1124	1702		1370	642	2300	744	1398	1038	1619	929	718	954	796	1474	1089	1934	1497	1377	1215	2347	1300	1095	2201	1986	660	1004	1712	2102	424	1774	2455	1630	1826	1110	1166	1157	866	554	718	1175	1632	1705	1587	1728	1966	730
Fargo, ND	1318	1002	1361	1346	607	1307	1227	1629	816	1614	1180	1557	1136	1414	787	641	937	990	1000	1079	873	475	930	1370		1115	1538	1321	825	1265	1708	600	1579	988	1848	944	1054	2025	569	235	1451	1601	1116	1445	1438	1529	875	420	1807	1405	1780	1107	1726	1497	1460	550	1564	841	1160	1343	1908	1781	1609	1424	1147	1813	1344	685
Grand Canyon N.P., AZ	400	684	1786	2294	1072	1641	861	2618	1264	1390	2182	2102	1943	2025	774	1729	1786	1997	1857	1047	676	1344	1969	600	1546	433	2518	1284	1679	1446	2036	1184	275	1277	490	1699	1408	2351	1716	1586	1634	2603	1619	1565	2406	2314	942	1208	2130	2324	218	2041	2715	1286	2160	1070	722	1436	522	1112	551	788	2033	1351	1243	2146	2285	990
Grand Junction, CO	380	607	1643	1916	662	1573	620	2210	1049	1370	1762	1946	1595	1810	340	1242	1427	1570	1501	1124	243	909	1508	642	1115		2115	1279	1324	1470	1994	844	506	1207	774	1349	1340	2308	1282	1152	1657	2184	1397	1638	2014	1997	870	774	2095	1975	571	1686	2309	1046	1917	639	799	1095	283	1092	835	968	1890	1121	1002	2099	1914	759
Grt. Smoky Mts. N.P., TN	1440	1151	189	536	1806	289	2142	940	684	1310	705	333	313	190	1408	585	293	548	406	882	1375	873	561	1522	1230	1614	843	962	399	528	510	771	2010	567	2224	286	430	862	682	996	520	1015	220	633	716	485	896	964	624	637	1903	496	1042	2577	326	1479	2371	527	1852	1151	2249	2528	378	2624	2344	640	502	908
Halifax, NS	2865	2581	1742	1046	2878	1823	3306	660	2079	2844	1103	1616	1390	1488	2569	1624	1517	1286	1409	2410	2612	1940	1335	3042	2271	2854	747	2490	1583	2059	1792	2067	3358	2093	3627	1624	1958	2145	1724	2037	2073	668	1745	2166	853	1216	2324	2078	1935	952	3328	1216	550	3731	1348	2541	3524	1828	3006	2685	3688	3741	1661	3695	3416	1988	1085	2259
Hartford, CT	2118	1834	996	300	2143	1078	2566	101	1327	2099	397	871	644	742	1834	888	767	562	661	1665	1876	1206	668	2300	1538	2115		1745	834	1313	1047	1318	2619	1348	2888	877	1213	1385	980	1304	1328	198	1000	1421	108	470	1577	1345	1189	207	2580	469	197	2992	602	1808	2786	1080	2271	1940	2930	3004	915	2960	2682	1242	340	1512
Houston, TX	884	589	794	1448	1652	668	1930	1844	602	354	1499	1105	1171	1038	1202	1085	1055	1315	1174	228	1035	938	1319	744	1321	1279	1745		1021	439	871	732	1457	439	1550	960	575	1186	1163	1171	468	1914	786	347	1632	1362	437	898	965	1547	1178	1354	1940	2356	1202	1291	1904	784	1634	197	1472	1929	971	2431	2192	980	1411	595
Indianapolis, IN	1279	995	533	584	1435	478	1835	937	493	1379	500	726	312	583	1104	181	108	315	176	873	1083	474	288	1398	825	1324	834	1021		671	874	482	1828	583	2068	113	464	1198	272	591	733	921	287	818	707	720	739	613	968	643	1742	359	1034	2260	628	1100	2056	243	1541	1149	2089	2273	770	2253	1973	984	582	674
Jackson, MS	1047	762	380	1017	1688	237	2048	1412	432	793	1125	697	801	624	1316	738	686	937	790	402	1226	828	945	1038	1265	1470	1313	439	671		590	664	1620	261	1838	586	209	905	830	1040	188	1482	414	183	1198	948	603	852	683	1115	1466	971	1509	2473	789	1371	2067	491	1749	635	1759	2133	580	2537	2229	699	980	707
Jacksonville, FL	1636	1352	346	744	2182	434	2528	1146	968	1225	1037	235	642	379	1792	1068	796	892	812	992	1756	1253	1002	1619	1708	1994	1047	871	874	590		1152	2210	832	2421	772	677	349	1163	1474	403	1245	596	547	939	613	1160	1343	141	844	2050	825	1243	2954	449	1860	2748	906	2229	1066	2343	2723	135	3000	2720	198	706	1272
Kansas City, MO	784	570	800	1068	1026	749	1372	1421	209	1036	984	1103	752	961	634	526	584	799	657	489	603	193	764	929	600	844	1318	732	482	664	1152		1349	381	1616	507	451	1466	565	436	850	1405	555	844	1196	1155	348	187	1246	1127	1246	840	1518	1797	1074	704	1591	250	1073	766	1597	1808	1048	1844	1564	1252	1066	193
Key West, FL	2099	1815	809	1251	2646	905	2992	1659	1431	1688	1544	742	1149	886	2256	1534	1275	1399	1325	1455	2222	1726	1515	2082	2178	2466	1560	1334	1348	1053	507	1617	2673	1294	2884	1238	1159	162	1632	1944	866	1758	1063	1010	1446	1120	1623	1807	387	1357	2514	1332	1756	3417	956	2326	3211	1370	2693	1529	2806	3186	642	3464	3185	402	1213	1735
Las Vegas, NV	572	857	1959	2420	971	1814	624	2714	1437	1550	2266	2276	2099	2199	829	1746	1932	2073	2004	1220	747	1413	2013	718	1579	506	2619	1457	1828	1620	2210	1349		1450	270	1854	1581	2525	1786	1656	1808	2688	1792	1739	2518	2486	1112	1278	2303	2480	285	2190	2813	1022	2334	1039	447	1600	419	1272	331	569	2206	1128	1138	2319	2428	1164
Little Rock, AR	877	593	515	1050	1407	370	1786	1447	172	794	1061	831	732	754	1055	650	617	868	724	319	965	573	885	954	988	1207	1348	439	583	261	832	381	1450		1665	520	137	1147	724	815	449	1506	348	425	1230	1035	335	574	925	1150	1340	905	1543	2211	889	1093	1898	345	1488	594	1676	1963	763	2275	1948	941	1014	446
Los Angeles, CA	786	1072	2174	2670	1240	2029	842	2983	1651	1630	2535	2491	2330	2414	1102	2015	2172	2342	2244	1437	1015	1682	2281	796	1848	774	2888	1550	2068	1838	2421	1616	270	1665		2085	1794	2735	2055	1925	2014	2957	2006	1894	2787	2707	1326	1546	2515	2713	370	2428	3082	963	2548	1312	470	1821	688	1357	120	380	2422	1134	1215	2525	2670	1377
Louisville, KY	1300	1016	420	604	1539	366	1877	978	510	1314	540	613	244	470	1144	296	97	347	206	836	1109	586	361	1474	944	1349	877	960	113	586	772	507	1854	520	2085		384	1085	390	710	620	962	174	705	740	649	759	699	858	676	1762	388	1074	2310	568	1214	2104	263	1586	1111	2109	2321	658	2357	2077	872	606	701
Memphis, TN	1008	720	379	914	1477	234	1825	1312	274	929	922	696	597	619	1091	531	482	729	587	453	1097	617	742	1089	1054	1340	1213	575	464	209	677	451	1581	137	1794	384		1012	622	831	382	1369	212	394	1094	898	466	641	778	1014	1471	768	1408	2245	753	1160	2029	283	1524	727	1819	2095	626	2299	2018	779	879	577
Mexico City, DF	1392	1332	1718	2372	2301	1592	2330	2768	1548	570	2424	2029	2095	1962	1846	2017	1979	2239	2098	1090	1756	1790	2254	1124	2158	1772	2669	924	1963	1364	1796	1598	1755	1364	1839	1884	1500	2111	2100	2032	1392	2838	1710	1272	2571	2286	1282	1735	1889	2471	1469	2279	2865	2756	2126	2139	2202	1721	1991	821	1700	2218	1906	2830	2711	1905	2335	1440
Miami, FL	1952	1668	661	1082	2497	746	2844	1482	1284	1538	1385	583	990	728	2107	1381	1127	1240	1164	1307	2069	1567	1354	1934	2025	2308	1385	1186	1198	905	349	1466	2525	1147	2735	1085	1012		1475	1791	719	1587	913	861	1288	950	1476	1658	229	1180	2362	1173	1585	3260	797	2173	3063	1221	2544	1379	2656	3038	483	3315	3035	255	1044	1587
Milwaukee, WI	1354	1132	809	792	1173	754	1732	1074	630	1557	630	1002	589	867	1000	90	381	434	445	1010	1042	371	374	1497	569	1282	980	1163	272	830	1163	565	1786	724	2055	390	622	1475		336	1011	1054	564	1015	879	969	875	509	1258	849	1817	551	1176	2062	914	840	1953	379	1437	1285	2118	2170	1045	1990	1712	1260	788	763
Minneapolis, MN	1225	1009	1127	1112	838	1072	1461	1396	643	1475	946	1323	902	1180	865	408	703	756	766	928	913	242	696	1377	235	1152	1304	1171	591	1040	1474	436	1656	815	1925	710	831	1791	336		1224	1367	881	1223	1204	1295	788	372	1573	1171	1687	874	1492	1727	1227	575	1818	563	1308	1205	1986	2040	1374	1655	1377	1578	1110	634
Mobile, AL	1234	949	328	1003	1874	258	2236	1427	620	821	1166	602	816	571	1504	917	721	973	826	589	1414	998	978	1215	1451	1657	1328	468	733	188	403	850	1808	449	2014	620	382	719	1011	1224		1497	447	144	1202	887	791	1038	497	1101	1643	1000	1523	2661	737	1557	2255	645	1936	662	1936	2320	502	2727	2478	509	965	894
Montpelier, VT	2203	1919	1165	498	2207	1247	2636	179	1417	2268	428	1068	813	928	1899	954	855	611	747	1824	1942	1270	718	2347	1601	2184	198	1914	921	1482	1245	1405	2688	1506	2957	962	1369	1587	1054	1367	1497		1160	1589	306	668	1662	1408	1387	405	2666	612	220	3061	800	1871	2854	1166	2336	2096	3018	3071	1113	3025	2746	1440	538	1597
Montréal, QC	2129	1845	1218	548	2099	1299	2523	310	1342	2311	393	1118	822	980	1790	847	824	578	714	1722	1832	1163	560	2261	1496	2072	328	1884	847	1517	1294	1330	2576	1451	2845	931	1314	1646	938	1262	1549	133	1105	1640	381	717	1588	1302	1436	454	2591	603	258	2948	850	1766	2743	1092	2228	1998	2912	2960	1162	2916	2638	1490	587	1529
Nashville, TN	1219	932	248	703	1586	192	1925	1099	464	1140	712	549	388	407	1192	469	273	525	378	664	1158	656	534	1300	1116	1397	1000	786	287	414	596	555	1792	348	2006	174	212	913	564	881	447	1160		532	884	688	677	747	683	802	1682	560	1196	2357	542	1262	2151	310	1633	939	2030	2306	495	2404	2124	700	666	688
New Orleans, LA	1165	881	468	1124	1868	343	2216	1520	597	700	1248	742	908	712	1488	923	804	1057	910	519	1398	1008	1066	1095	1445	1638	1421	347	818	183	547	844	1739	425	1894	705	394	861	1015	1223	144	1589	532		1304	1026	722	1032	641	1222	1523	1090	1616	2642	878	1551	2186	675	1920	541	1816	2252	642	2716	2409	651	1087	880
New York, NY	2001	1716	882	192	2041	960	2465	207	1201	1981	395	768	530	641	1733	787	637	460	533	1548	1775	1105	613	2201	1438	2014	108	1632	707	1198	939	1196	2518	1230	2787	740	1094	1288	879	1204	1202	306	884	1304		370	1460	1245	1089	97	2463	369	304	2891	502	1708	2685	954	2170	1822	2809	2902	811	2858	2580	1138	228	1391
Norfolk, VA	1910	1632	558	228	2132	715	2525	569	1158	1716	569	437	403	328	1792	878	605	551	570	1350	1758	1196	704	1986	1529	1997	470	1362	720	948	613	1155	2486	1035	2707	649	898	950	969	1295	887	668	688	1026	370		1366	1335	755	270	2373	425	666	2962	183	1799	2744	911	2238	1557	2730	2973	481	2949	2671	808	189	1349
Oklahoma City, OK	542	256	844	1346	1203	699	1497	1678	323	738	1242	1160	1002	1084	720	792	846	1057	917	204	631	545	1029	660	875	870	1577	437	739	603	1160	348	1112	335	1326	759	466	1476	875	788	791	1662	677	722	1460	1366		452	1254	1384	1005	1100	1775	1922	1218	857	1563	496	1200	468	1351	1627	1092	1948	1710	1270	1343	158
Omaha, NE	863	647	992	1153	845	939	1225	1436	402	1192	987	1293	943	1151	492	470	722	797	792	656	534	137	736	1004	420	774	1345	898	613	852	1343	187	1278	574	1546	699	641	1658	509	372	1038	1408	747	1032	1245	1335	452		1436	1212	1325	914	1533	1650	1266	525	1445	439	930	920	1613	1662	1239	1663	1383	1445	1151	298
Orlando, FL	1730	1446	440	889	2275	534	2622	1288	1062	1319	1184	380	792	526	1885	1153	905	1043	954	1086	1851	1339	1144	1712	1807	2095	1189	965	968	683	141	1246	2303	925	2515	858	778	229	1258	1573	497	1387	683	641	1089	755	1254	1436		986	2145	975	1385	3048	597	1956	2841	999	2323	1160	2436	2816	280	3093	2814	84	849	1365
Philadelphia, PA	1924	1640	780	98	2011	880	2435	306	1138	1900	388	668	466	539	1703	757	571	428	468	1467	1732	1074	583	2102	1405	1975	207	1547	643	1115	844	1127	2480	1150	2713	676	1014	1180	849	1171	1101	405	802	1222	97	270	1384	1212	986		2387	304	402	2861	399	1675	2656	888	2140	1742	2738	2873	703	2828	2550	1040	137	1319
Phoenix, AZ	462	746	1844	2349	1210	1700	914	2681	1326	1259	2245	2165	2005	2088	1008	1795	1849	2060	1920	1066	908	1445	2032	424	1780	571	2580	1178	1742	1466	2050	1246	285	1340	370	1762	1471	2362	1817	1687	1643	2666	1682	1523	2463	2373	1005	1325	2145	2387		2104	2778	1332	2224	1305	733	1499	653	985	352	749	2091	1414	1381	2153	2348	1053
Pittsburgh, PA	1641	1357	684	246	1713	748	2137	570	851	1708	216	654	225	446	1405	459	288	131	184	1221	1447	777	285	1774	1107	1686	469	1354	359	971	825	840	2190	905	2428	388	768	1173	551	874	1000	612	560	1090	369	425	1100	914	975	304	2104		666	2563	499	1378	2357	604	1842	1495	2452	2574	697	2530	2252	1023	244	1035
Portland, ME	2315	2031	1192	496	2333	1274	2761	110	1529	2294	553	1066	840	938	2024	1079	967	736	859	1861	2067	1395	825	2455	1726	2309	197	1940	1034	1509	1243	1518	2813	1543	3082	1074	1408	1585	1176	1492	1523	220	1196	1616	304	666	1775	1533	1385	402	2778	666		3186	798	1996	2979	1279	2461	2136	3143	3196	1111	3150	2871	1438	535	1710
Portland, OR	1363	1669	2603	2804	891	2551	428	3086	2013	2354	2639	2904	2554	2761	1161	2118	2369	2446	2439	2128	1256	1786	2385	1630	1497	1046	2992	2356	2260	2473	2954	1797	1022	2211	963	2310	2245	3260	2062	1727	2661	3061	2357	2642	2891	2962	1922	1650	3048	2861	1332	2563	3186		2897	1214	578	2050	765	2076	1083	635	2844	172	351	3064	2800	1764
Québec, QC	2283	1999	1372	694	2257	1455	2681	396	1497	2472	552	1264	979	1134	1948	1004	979	735	870	1876	1991	1320	715	2416	1650	2230	427	2123	1001	1676	1440	1484	2734	1606	3003	1086	1470	1792	1096	1417	1703	259	1262	1795	524	863	1742	1457	1582	600	2745	760	275	3107	996	1921	2901	1246	2386	2152	3067	3119	1308	3074	2795	1636	733	1683
Raleigh, NC	1761	1474	408	302	2067	555	2444	702	1003	1556	637	278	322	168	1712	816	521	572	486	1191	1678	1107	677	1826	1460	1917	602	1202	628	789	449	1074	2334	889	2548	568	753	797	914	1227	737	800	542	878	502	183	1218	1266	597	399	2224	499	798	2897		1735	2690	830	2172	1397	2551	2847	322	2885	2605	648	262	1227
Rapid City, SD	843	714	1508	1616	323	1456	942	1900	920	1515	1450	1811	1410	1670	298	912	1208	1260	1270	1061	397	626	1200	1110	550	639	1808	1291	1100	1371	1860	704	1039	1093	1312	1214	1160	2173	840	575	1557	1871	1262	1551	1708	1799	857	525	1956	1675	1305	1378	1996	1214	1735		1167	959	649	1242	1372	1384	1756	1141	862	1960	1615	699
Regina, SK	1284	1253	1904	1882	472	1850	1092	2090	1321	2046	1721	2066	1674	1937	740	1151	1445	1503	1510	1510	838	1016	1441	1551	513	1080	2080	1753	1337	1805	2220	1104	1443	1525	1712	1454	1594	2570	1078	743	2009	1914	1659	1985	1994	2037	1307	927	2348	1946	1682	1619	2039	1120	2002	532	1428	1360	1024	1774	1773	1645	2117	1046	767	2360	1878	1149
Reno, NV	1019	1304	2396	2599	956	2262	422	2881	1806	1998	2433	2698	2342	2555	956	1913	2163	2240	2234	1668	1051	1581	2180	1166	1564	799	2786	1904	2056	2067	2748	1591	447	1898	470	2104	2029	3063	1953	1818	2255	2854	2151	2186	2685	2744	1563	1445	2841	2656	733	2357	2979	578	2690	1167		1844	518	1720	558	217	2644	720	793	2857	2595	1558
Saint Louis, MO	1037	752	555	829	1278	501	1622	1182	249	1177	746	856	506	714	888	296	348	560	421	630	854	354	533	1157	841	1095	1080	784	243	491	906	250	1600	345	1821	263	283	1221	379	563	645	1166	310	675	954	911	496	439	999	888	1499	604	1279	2050	830	959	1844		1326	906	1845	2061	802	2096	1817	1008	827	442
Salt Lake City, UT	599	883	1878	2081	552	1826	339	2365	1288	1589	1915	2180	1829	2037	437	1398	1647	1725	1718	1403	533	1065	1664	866	1160	283	2271	1634	1541	1749	2229	1073	419	1488	688	1586	1524	2544	1437	1308	1936	2336	1633	1920	2170	2238	1200	930	2323	2140	653	1842	2461	765	2172	649	518	1326		1311	750	735	2125	839	720	2339	2079	1042
San Antonio, TX	712	510	986	1642	1480	861	1651	2039	708	274	1654	1300	1324	1230	1025	1202	1210	1457	1314	276	935	960	1439	554	1343	1092	1940	197	1149	635	1066	766	1272	594	1357	1111	727	1379	1285	1205	662	2096	939	541	1822	1557	468	920	1160	1742	985	1495	2136	2076	1397	1242	1720	906	1311		1278	1736	1161	2150	2018	1170	1606	625
San Diego, CA	810	1097	2138	2695	1301	1994	958	3046	1675	1552	2596	2459	2354	2381	1162	2080	2196	2407	2269	1359	1077	1747	2346	718	1908	835	2930	1472	2089	1759	2343	1597	331	1676	120	2109	1819	2656	2118	1986	1936	3018	2030	1816	2809	2730	1351	1613	2436	2738	352	2452	3143	1083	2551	1372	558	1845	750	1278		501	2356	1256	1468	2447	2693	1401
San Francisco, CA	1086	1370	2472	2816	1173	2327	639	3098	1950	2010	2650	2789	2564	2712	1172	2130	2380	2458	2451	1734	1268	1798	2397	1175	1781	968	3004	1929	2273	2133	2723	1808	569	1963	380	2321	2095	3038	2170	2040	2320	3071	2306	2252	2902	2973	1627	1662	2816	2873	749	2574	3196	635	2847	1384	217	2061	735	1736	501		2720	807	874	2832	2812	1775
Sault Ste. Marie, ON	1777	1493	1040	852	1273	1014	1893	923	991	1918	514	1156	683	947	1411	471	577	496	521	1370	1428	710	347	1910	665	1692	904	1527	540	1180	1333	951	2196	1089	2465	649	972	1685	398	538	1268	740	823	1355	921	1037	1236	850	1475	911	2240	614	871	2165	1007	1118	2364	740	1848	1646	2502	2581	1201	2090	1812	1492	851	1150
Savannah, GA	1634	1350	247	605	2078	393	2418	1014	900	1320	909	106	514	251	1687	951	664	764	680	996	1651	1150	870	1632	1609	1890	915	971	770	580	135	1048	2206	763	2422	658	626	483	1045	1374	502	1113	495	642	811	481	1092	1239	280	703	2091	697	1111	2844	322	1756	2644	802	2125	1161	2356	2720		2896	2616	333	575	1202
Seattle, WA	1438	1743	2649	2770	818	2597	503	3054	2059	2428	2604	2950	2560	2808	1225	2063	2363	2414	2424	2193	1320	1764	2353	1705	1424	1121	2960	2431	2253	2537	3000	1844	1128	2275	1134	2357	2299	3315	1990	1655	2727	3025	2404	2716	2858	2949	1948	1663	3093	2828	1414	2530	3150	172	2885	1141	720	2096	839	2150	1256	807	2896		278	3109	2768	1828
Shenandoah N.P., VA	1794	1488	556	119	1951	634	2399	519	1016	1655	382	516	260	317	1650	698	474	368	389	1223	1614	1014	523	1863	1345	1855	420	1306	563	872	687	1012	2359	904	2582	506	768	1035	798	1111	886	618	558	978	320	181	1233	1155	847	217	2238	245	616	2824	263	1615	2604	768	2107	1496	2586	2842	567	2769	2490	885	82	1207
Spokane, WA	1320	1505	2369	2491	540	2318	425	2774	1780	2296	2325	2671	2281	2528	993	1785	2084	2135	2144	1964	1091	1484	2075	1587	1147	1002	2682	2192	1973	2229	2720	1564	1138	1948	1215	2077	2018	3035	1712	1377	2478	2746	2124	2409	2580	2671	1710	1383	2814	2550	1381	2252	2871	351	2605	862	793	1817	720	2018	1468	874	2616	278		2830	2490	1600
Tampa, FL	1746	1462	451	942	2291	537	2638	1342	1078	1329	1235	433	840	578	1901	1166	916	1091	1007	1102	1860	1354	1178	1728	1813	2099	1242	980	984	699	198	1252	2319	941	2525	872	779	255	1260	1578	509	1440	700	651	1138	808	1270	1445	84	1040	2153	1023	1438	3064	648	1960	2857	1008	2339	1170	2447	2832	333	3109	2830		902	1381
Thunder Bay, ON	1566	1348	1376	1288	1049	1322	1670	1298	983	1830	942	1570	1118	1382	1210	656	949	932	957	1270	1253	583	784	1718	441	1492	1305	1522	840	1361	1728	776	1996	1156	2265	957	1153	2041	585	341	1547	1121	1130	1545	1349	1473	1127	720	1822	1339	2028	1049	1246	1938	1443	913	2006	870	1648	1547	2326	2224	1613	1866	1588	1828	1286	974
Toronto, ON	1800	1516	963	472	1771	968	2194	548	1014	1919	98	964	535	756	1462	519	493	290	426	1393	1504	834	232	1932	1167	1744	490	1551	518	1186	1135	1001	2247	1120	2517	601	983	1483	609	933	1222	465	774	1306	489	669	1259	974	1284	497	2262	316	592	2620	737	1438	2414	763	1899	1669	2583	2632	1007	2588	2310	1333	482	1188
Tucson, AZ	449	735	1732	2320	1326	1588	1030	2669	1314	1145	2233	2052	1994	1975	995	1784	1836	2048	1908	952	895	1433	2020	312	1769	687	2569	1066	1728	1353	1936	1234	401	1271	485	1749	1406	2250	1805	1675	1530	2654	1617	1410	2448	2303	990	1313	2029	2383	116	2092	2766	1447	2142	1293	848	1485	776	871	407	864	1949	1529	1496	2040	2283	1040
Vancouver, BC	1574	1878	2785	2906	953	2733	638	3188	2195	2564	2740	3086	2696	2944	1372	2198	2499	2548	2560	2338	1465	1900	2487	1841	1559	1256	3094	2565	2389	2675	3136	1980	1264	2421	1275	2493	2437	3451	2125	1790	2894	2982	2540	2851	2993	3084	2083	1799	3229	2963	1550	2665	3286	313	3021	1277	890	2232	973	2286	1398	947	3032	141	413	3245	2903	1973
Washington, DC	1885	1600	637	39	1951	744	2375	439	1078	1765	382	530	362	398	1642	697	512	367	407	1332	1671	1014	522	1966	1344	1914	340	1411	582	980	706	1066	2428	1014	2670	606	879	1044	788	1110	965	538	666	1087	228	189	1343	1151	849	137	2348	244	535	2800	262	1615	2595	827	2079	1606	2693	2812	575	2768	2490	902		1258
Wichita, KS	591	382	955	1260	1064	810	1338	1613	292	896	1176	1272	945	1092	608	724	779	992	851	361	519	391	964	730	685	759	1512	595	674	707	1272	193	1164	446	1377	701	577	1587	763	634	894	1597	688	880	1391	1349	158	298	1365	1319	1053	1035	1710	1764	1227	699	1558	442	1042	625	1401	1775	1202	1828	1600	1381	1258	

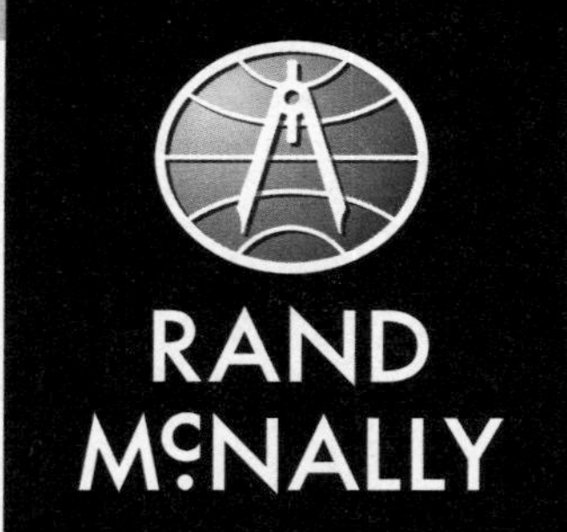

Road Atlas 2016

MAPS

MAPS

INDEXES

Quick Map References

State & Province Maps

Selected City Maps

This list contains only 70 of more than 350 detailed city maps in the Road Atlas. To find more city maps, consult the state & province map list above and turn to the pages indicated.

National Park Maps

Photo credits: Table of contents: (t to b) ©Juli Scalzi Photography/istockphoto, ©Rand McNally (3); p. ii (t to b), ©Juli Scalzi Photography/istockphoto, ©2G1R/istockphoto, p. iii (t to b) ©Daniela Duncan/Getty, ©jctdesign/istockphoto, ©visionsofmaine/istockphoto; p. iv (t to b) ©Cathy Melloan/Alamy, ©Brent Waltermire/Alamy, ©Danita Delimont/Alamy; p. v (t to b) ©laddio1234/istockphoto, ©Natalia Bratslovsky/istockphoto, ©Daniel Dempster Photography/Alamy; p.vi (t to b) ©Andrey Krav/istockphoto, ©tonda/istockphoto, ©CraftyLenz/istockphoto; p. vii (t to b) ©Thye Gn/Alamy, ©Design Pics Inc./Alamy, ©KingWu/istockphoto. p. 5 ©Mobile Bay CVB; p. 7 & 9 ©Greater Phoenix CVB; p. 11 ©CJRW/Bernie Jungkind; p. 13, 16, 18, 33 & 123 ©Rand McNally; p. 15, 49, 63 71, 73, 83, 85, 97, 101, 103, 109 & 110 ©Getty Images; p. 17 ©Santa Barbara Conference & Visitors Bureau and Film Commission/J. Sinclair; p. 19 ©Huntington Beach CVB; p. 21 ©Denver Metro CVB/Ron Ruhoff; p. 22 ©Denver Metro CVB/Randy Brown; p. 25 ©St. Petersburg/Clearwater Area CVB; p. 27 ©Visit Florida; p. 29 ©GA Dept. of C&CA; p. 34 ©City of Chicago/Hedrich Blessing; p. 35 ©The Children's Museum of Indianapolis; p. 37 ©Brown County State Park; p. 39 ©IA DED Div. of Tourism; p. 41 ©Kansas Dept. of Commerce & Housing/Charlie Riedel; p. 43 ©Kentucky Tourism; p. 47 ©MD Office of Tourism Dev.; p. 51 ©Michigan DNR; p. 52 ©Robert J. Eovaldi; p.53 ©Walker Art Center; p. 55 ©MN Office of Tourism; p. 57 & 59 ©MO Div. of Tourism; p. 61 ©Travel Montana/Donnie Sexton; p. 67 ©NJ C&EGC, OT&T; p. 72 ©Photodisc; p. 75 & 76 ©NC Div of Tourism Film & Sports Dev.; p. 79 ©Ohio Tourism; p. 81 ©Warren County CVB; p. 87 ©Commonwealth Media Services; p. 89 ©GPTMC; p. 90 ©Greater Pittsburgh CVB; p. 95 ©TN Dept. Tourist Dev.; p. 96 ©Kingsport CVB; p. 99 ©State of Texas Travel CVB; p. 105 ©Virginia Tourism Corp.; p.107 ©National Park Service; p. 113 ©Kenosha Area CVB; p. 115 ©Wisconsin Dept. of Tourism; p. 125 ©J-F Bergeron/Enviro Foto/Quebec City Tourism.

If you have a comment, suggestion, or even a compliment, please visit us at randmcnally.com/contact or write to:
Rand McNally Consumer Affairs
P.O. Box 7600
Chicago, Illinois 60680-9915

Published and printed in U.S.A.

1 2 3 VE 16 15

United States

Capital: Washington, G-17
Land area: 3,537,438 sq. mi.
Population: 308,745,538
Largest city: New York, 8,175,133, E-18

Index of cities Pg. 129

Selected places of interest

- Acadia National Park, C-20
- Arches National Park, G-6
- Badlands National Park, E-9
- Big Bend National Park, L-8
- Biscayne National Park, M-18
- Bryce Canyon National Park, G-5
- Canyonlands National Park, G-6
- Capitol Reef National Park, G-5
- Carlsbad Caverns National Park, J-7
- Channel Islands National Park, H-1
- Congaree National Park, I-17
- Crater Lake National Park, D-2
- Cuyahoga Valley National Park, F-16
- Death Valley National Park, G-3
- Denali National Park, L-4
- Dry Tortugas National Park, M-17
- Everglades National Park, M-17
- Glacier Bay National Park, M-6
- Glen Canyon National Recreation
- Grand Canyon National Park, H-4
- Grand Teton National Park, E-6
- Great Sand Dunes Nat'l Park & P
- Great Smoky Mountains Nat'l Par
- Guadalupe Mountains National P

One inch represents approximately 155 miles

© Rand McNally

- lā National Park, L-2
- Volcanoes National Park, L-2
- ngs National Park, I-12
- le National Park, C-13
- nyon National Park, G-2
- ad National Recreation Area, H-4
- Lassen Volcanic National Park, E-2
- Mammoth Cave National Park, H-14
- Mesa Verde National Park, H-6
- Mount Rainier National Park, B-3
- North Cascades National Park, B-4
- Olympic National Park, B-3
- Petrified Forest National Park, I-5
- Redwood National Park, D-1
- Rocky Mountain National Park, F-7
- Sequoia National Park, G-2
- Shenandoah National Park, G-17
- Theodore Roosevelt National Park, D-8
- Voyageurs National Park, C-12
- Waterton-Glacier Int'l Peace Park, B-5
- Wind Cave National Park, E-8
- Yellowstone National Park, D-6
- Yosemite National Park, F-2
- Zion National Park, G-5

Alabama

Nickname: The Heart of Dixie
Capital: Montgomery, J-8
Land area: 50,744 sq. mi. (rank: 28th)
Population: 4,779,736 (rank: 23rd)
Largest city: Birmingham, 212,237, F-7

Index of cities Pg. 129

Get more Alabama info at www.randmcnally.com/AL

Tourism Information
Alabama Bureau of Tourism & Travel: (800) 252-2262, (334) 242-4169; www.alabama.travel

Road Conditions & Construction
(888) 588-2848; www.dot.state.al.us, alitsweb2.dot.state.al.us/RoadConditions

Toll Road Information
Foley Beach Expressway (Baldwin Co.): (251) 968-3415; www.beachexpress.com

Determining distances along roads

Highway distances (segments of one mile or less not shown):
Cumulative miles (red): the distance between red arrows
Intermediate miles (black): the distance between intersections &

Interchanges and exit numbers
For most states, the mileage between interchanges may be deter
by subtracting one number from the other.

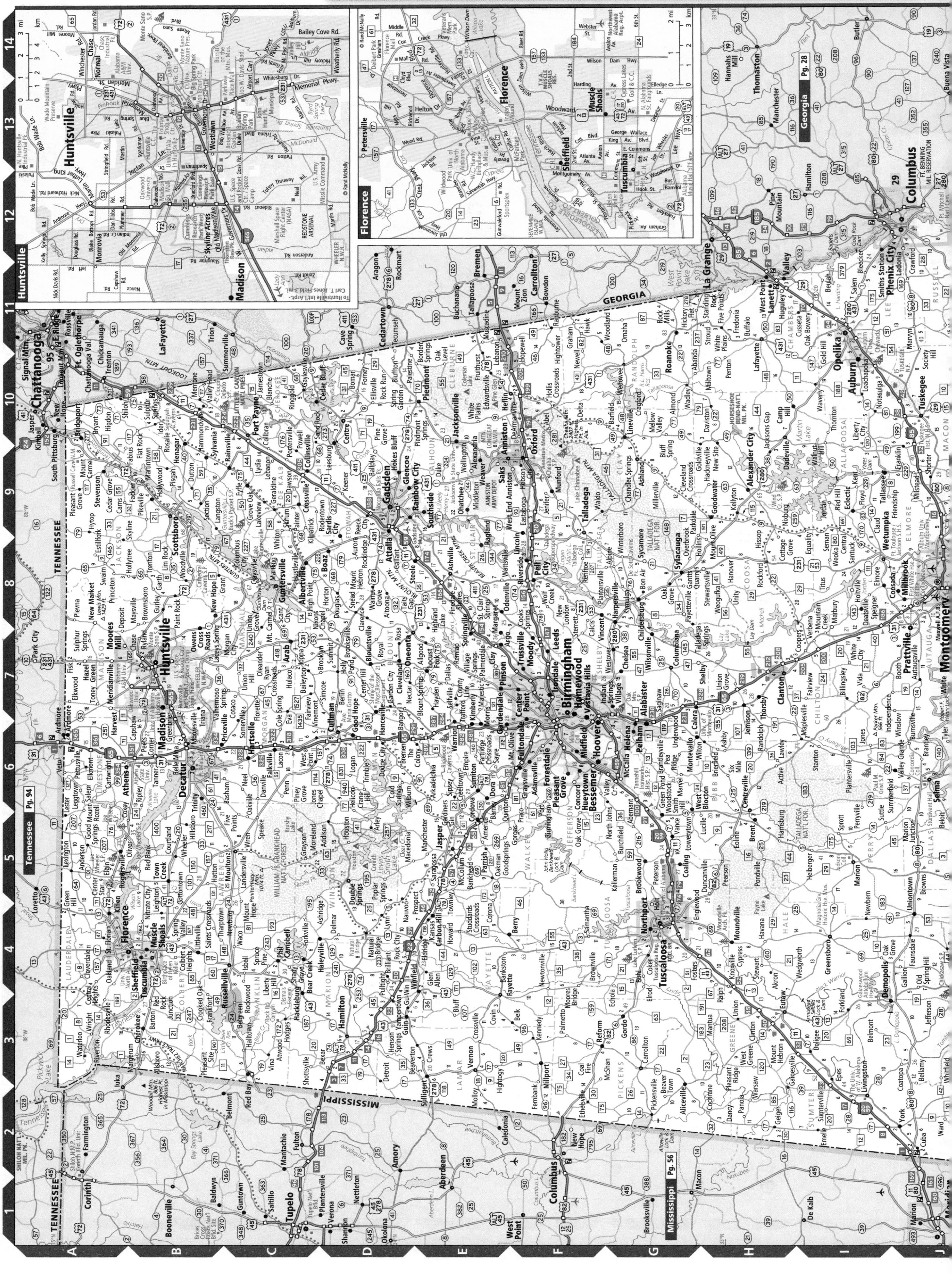
Huntsville
Florence
TENNESSEE
GEORGIA
MISSISSIPPI
Tennessee Pg. 94
Georgia Pg. 28
Mississippi Pg. 56
Birmingham
Montgomery
Chattanooga
Columbus
Tuscaloosa
Gadsden
Anniston

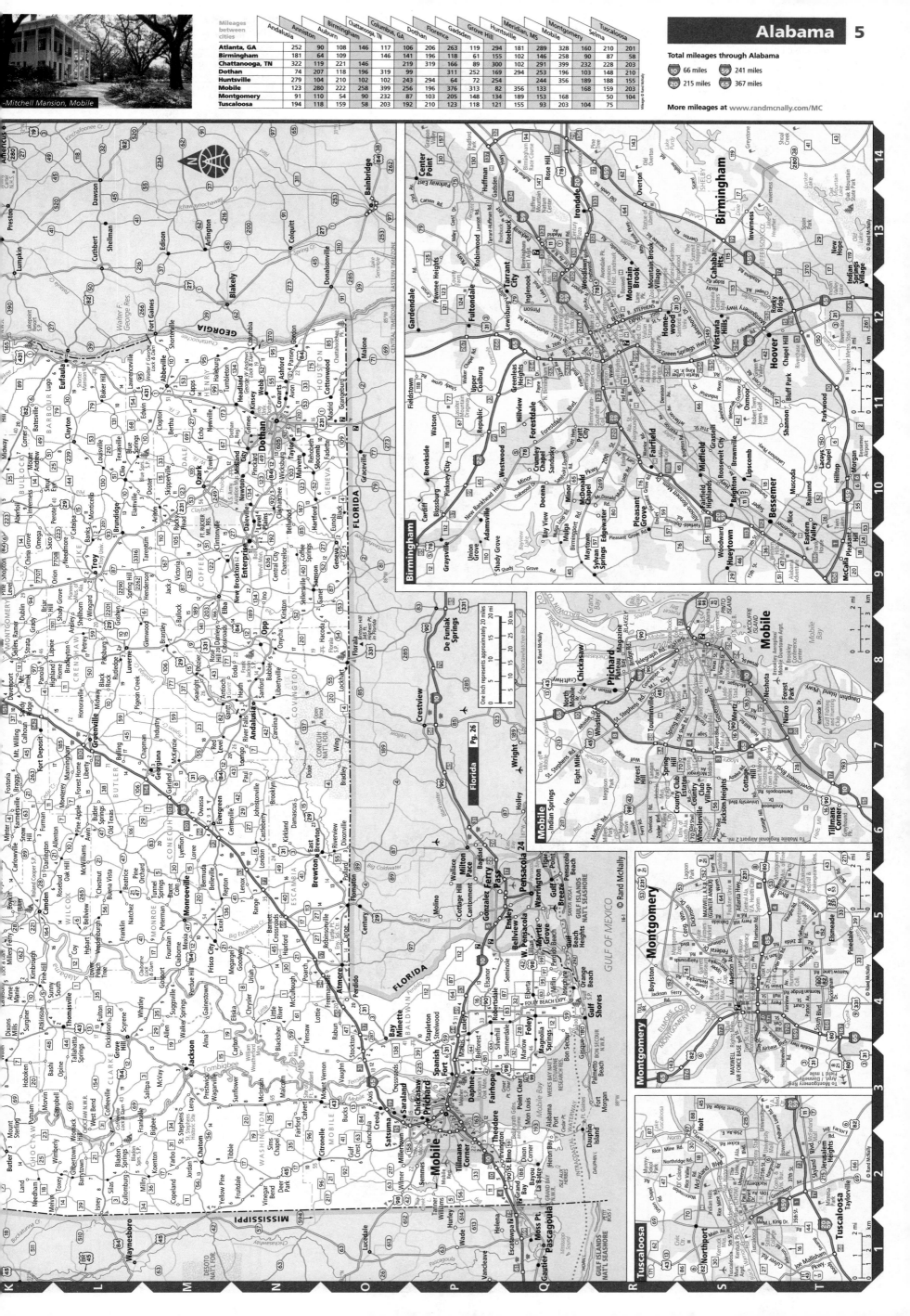

-Mitchell Mansion, Mobile

Mileages between cities	Andalusia	Anniston	Auburn	Birmingham	Chattanooga, TN	Columbus, GA	Dothan	Florence	Gadsden	Grove Hill	Huntsville	Meridian, MS	Mobile	Montgomery	Selma	Tuscaloosa
Atlanta, GA	252	90	108	146	117	106	206	263	119	294	181	289	328	160	210	201
Birmingham	181	64	109		146	141	196	118	61	155	102	146	258	90	87	58
Chattanooga, TN	322	119	221	146		219	319	166	89	300	102	291	399	232	228	203
Dothan	74	207	118	196	319	99		311	252	169	294	253	196	103	148	210
Huntsville	279	104	210	102	102	243	294	64	72	254		244	356	189	188	155
Mobile	123	280	222	258	399	256	196	376	313	82	356	133		168	159	203
Montgomery	91	110	54	90	232	87	103	205	148	134	189	153	168		50	104
Tuscaloosa	194	118	159	58	203	192	210	123	118	121	155	93	203	104	75	

Total mileages through Alabama

- I-10: 66 miles
- I-20: 215 miles
- I-59: 241 miles
- I-65: 367 miles

More mileages at www.randmcnally.com/MC

Alaska

Nickname: The Last Frontier
Capital: Juneau, H-12
Land area: 571,951 sq. mi. (rank: 1st)
Population: 710,231 (rank: 47th)
Largest city: Anchorage, 291,826, G-7

Index of cities Pg. 129

Mileages between cities	Anchorage	Denali N.P.	Fairbanks	Haines	Homer	Prince Rupert, BC	Tok	Valdez
Anchorage		236	358	756	221	1557	317	297
Fairbanks	358	122		640	578	1441	202	362
Haines	756	762	640		975	919	438	691
Homer	221	457	578	975		1776	537	277
Kenai	157	393	514	911	83	1713	473	213
Seward	126	362	483	880	168	1682	442	182
Tok	317	324	202	438	537	1240		252
Valdez	297	346	362	691	277	1493	252	

Total mileages through Alaska

① 408 miles ③ 325 miles
② 202 miles

More mileages at www.randmcnally.com/MC

Plan a trip at www.randmcnally.com/AK

Tourism Information
State of Alaska Tourism Office:
(800) 862-5275; www.travelalaska.com

Road Conditions & Construction 511
511; www.511.alaska.gov,
www.dot.state.ak.us

Toll Rd. Info
No toll roads

Determining Distance
(segmen one mil not sho
Cumulative miles (red): the distance between red a
Intermediate miles (black): the distance between intersections & places

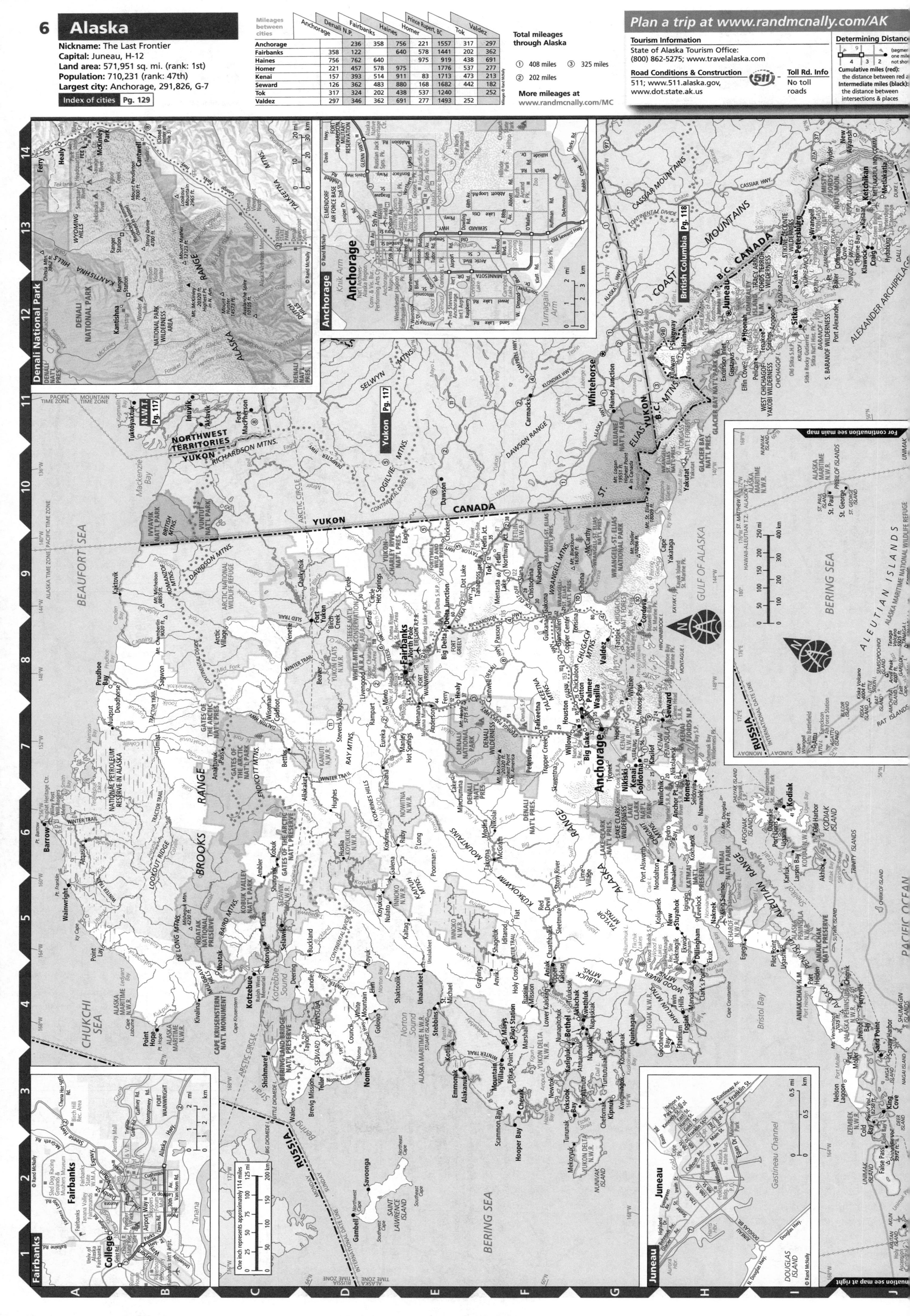

rica dancers

City sights to see

- Arizona Historical Society Sanguinetti House Museum, Yuma, L-6
- Arizona Museum of Natural History, Mesa, J-7
- Arizona Science Center, Phoenix, M-3
- Arizona State Capitol, Phoenix, M-1
- Heard Museum, Phoenix, L-2
- Painted Desert Inn Museum, Petrified Forest N.P., L-10
- Phoenix Art Museum, Phoenix, L-2
- Taliesin West, Scottsdale, H-7
- Tusayan Ruin and Museum, Grand Canyon N.P., D-9
- Yavapai Observation Station, Grand Canyon N.P., D-8
- Yuma Territorial Prison State Historic Park, Yuma, L-6

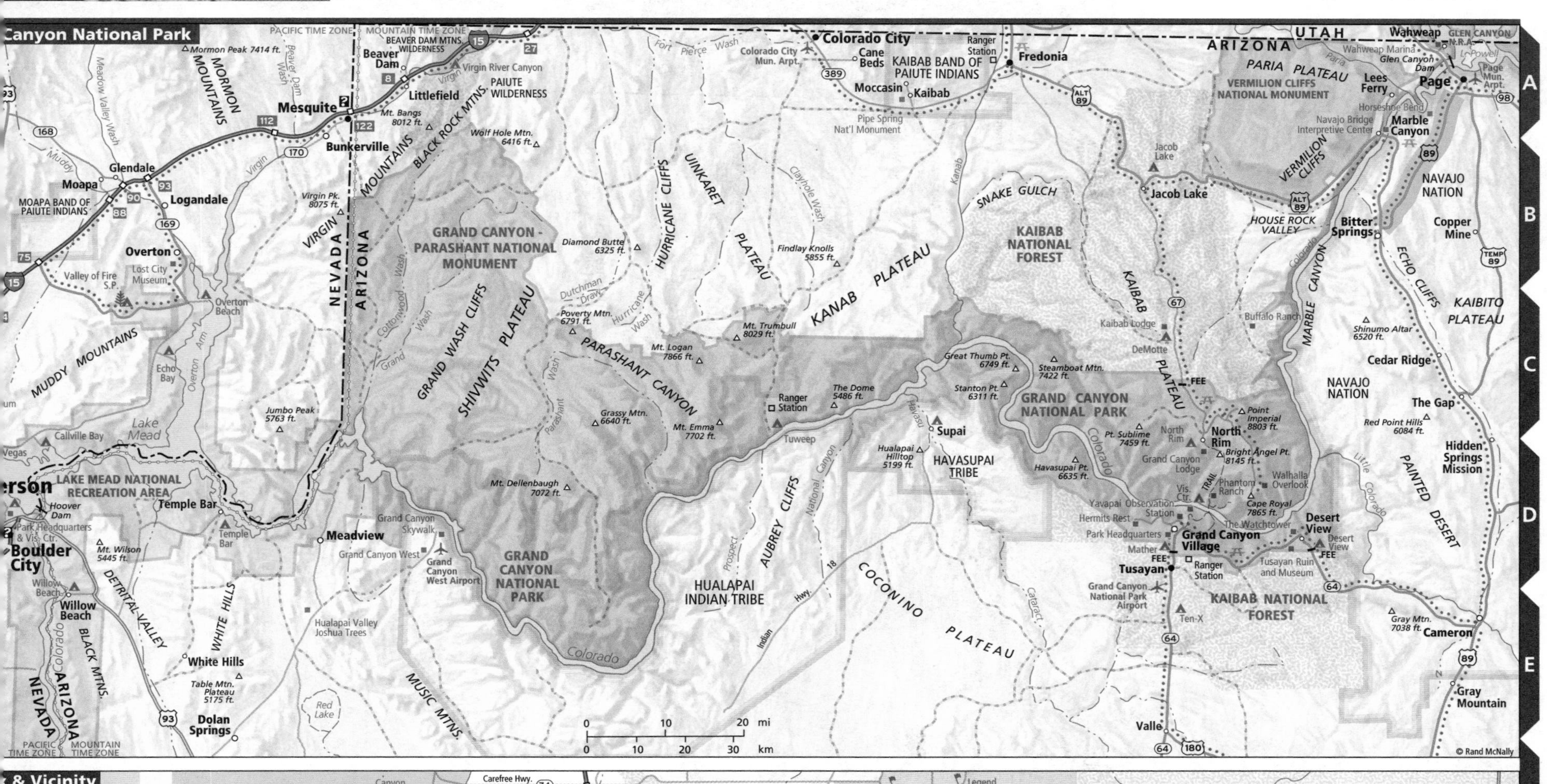

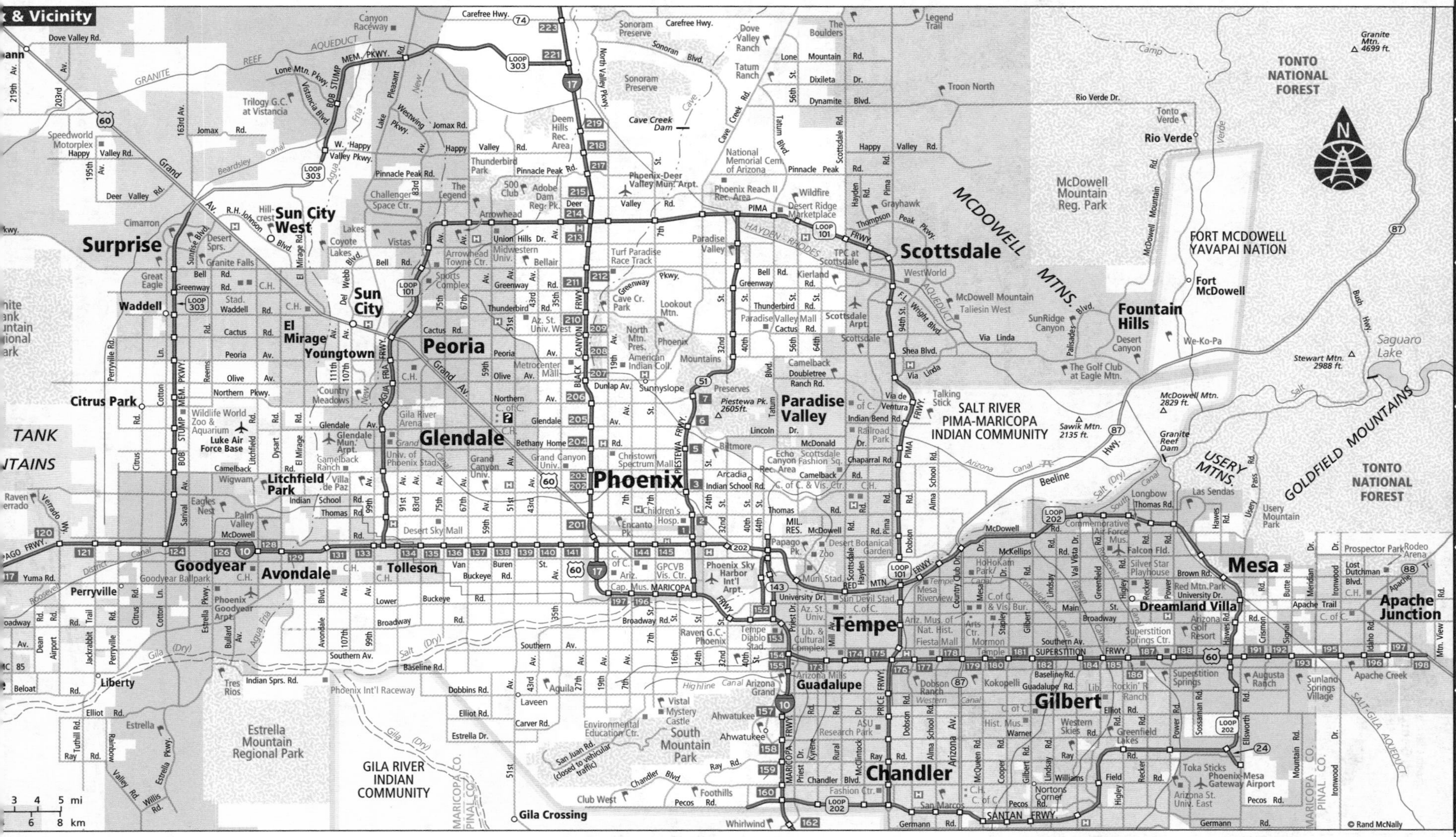

& Vicinity

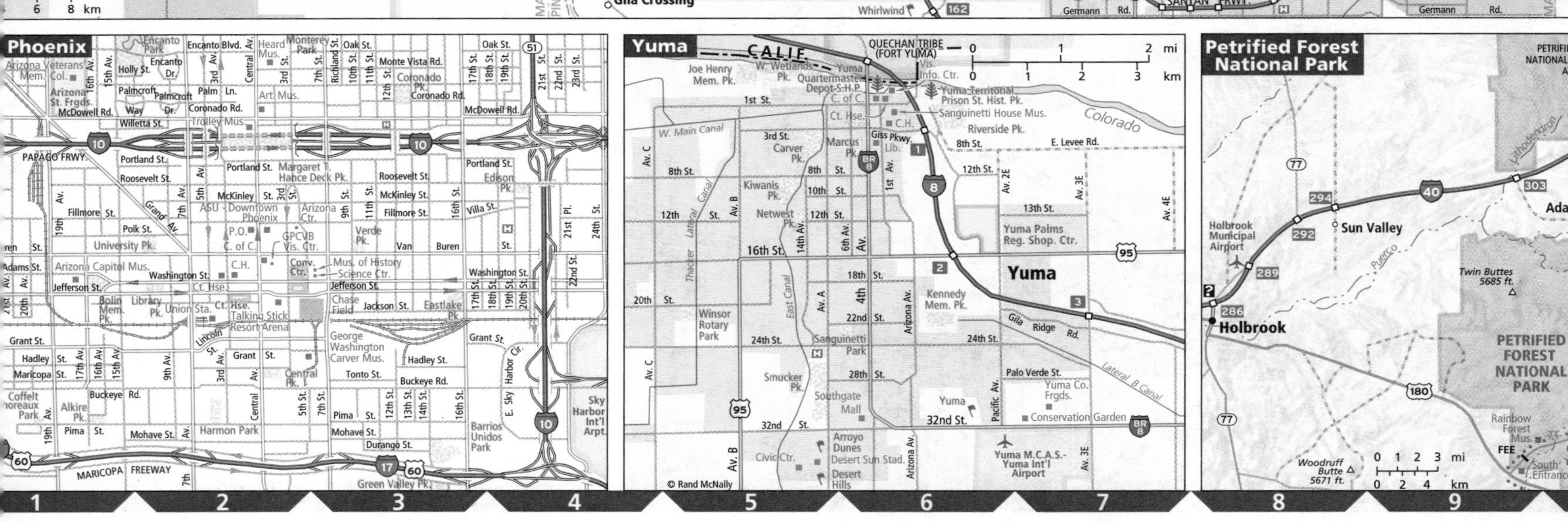

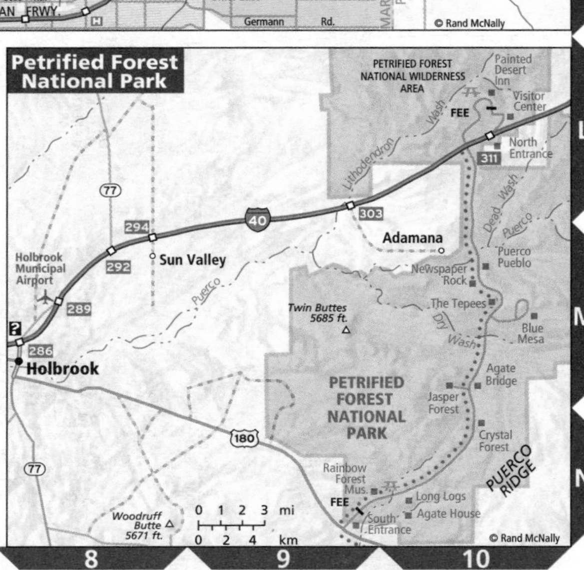

Nickname: The Grand Canyon State
Capital: Phoenix, J-7
Land area: 113,635 sq. mi. (rank: 6th)
Population: 6,392,017 (rank: 16th)
Largest city: Phoenix, 1,445,632, J-7

Index of cities Pg. 129

Plan an Arizona trip at www.randmcnally.com/AZ

Tourism Information
Arizona Office of Tourism: (866) 275-5816, (602) 364-3700; www.arizonaguide.com

Road Conditions & Construction
511, (888) 411-7623; www.az511.com, www.azdot.gov

Toll Road Information
No toll roads

Determining distances along roads

Highway distances (segments of one mile or less not shown):
Cumulative miles (red): the distance between red arrows
Intermediate miles (black): the distance between intersections &

Interchanges and exit numbers
For most states, the mileage between interchanges may be dete
by subtracting one number from the other.

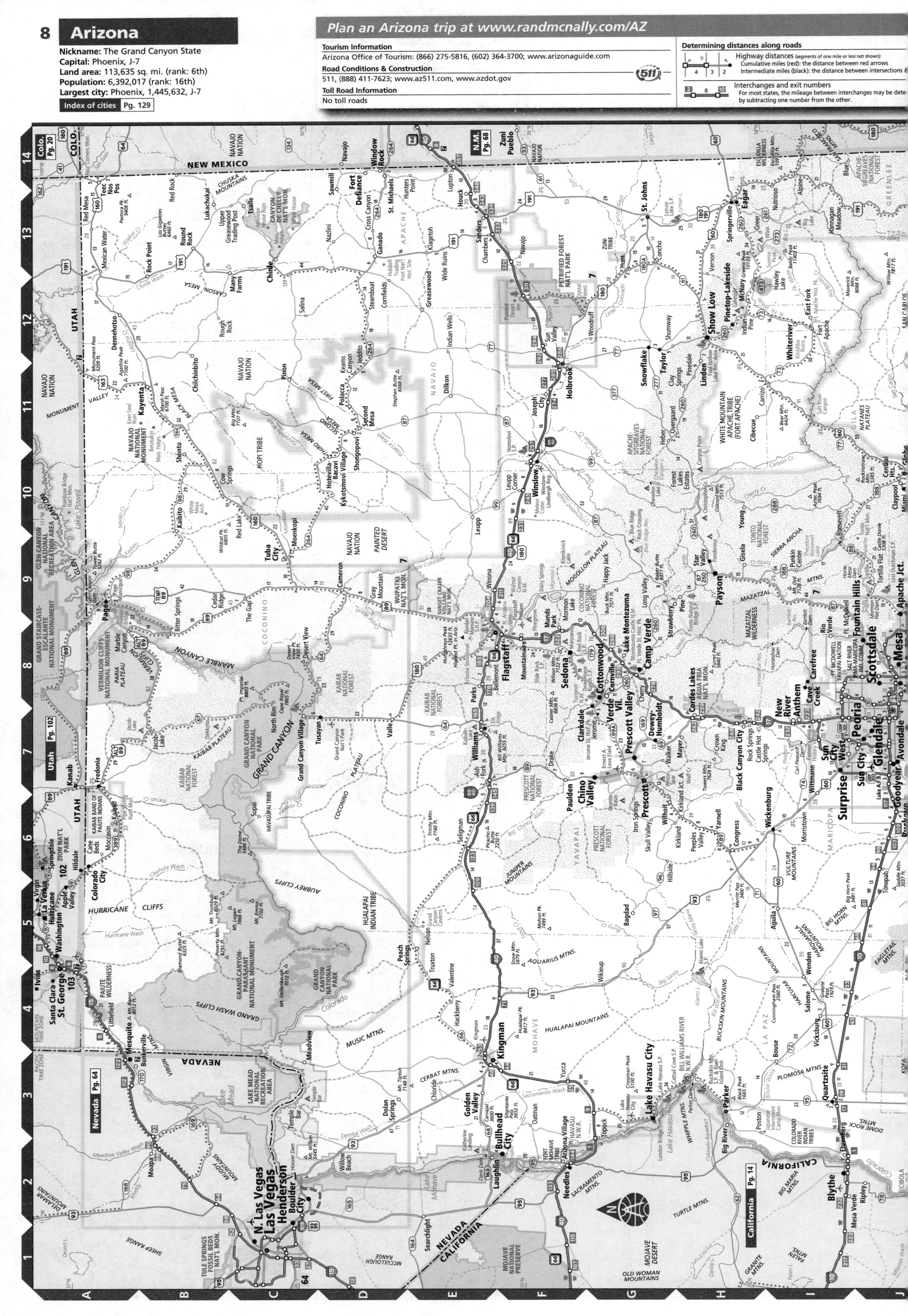

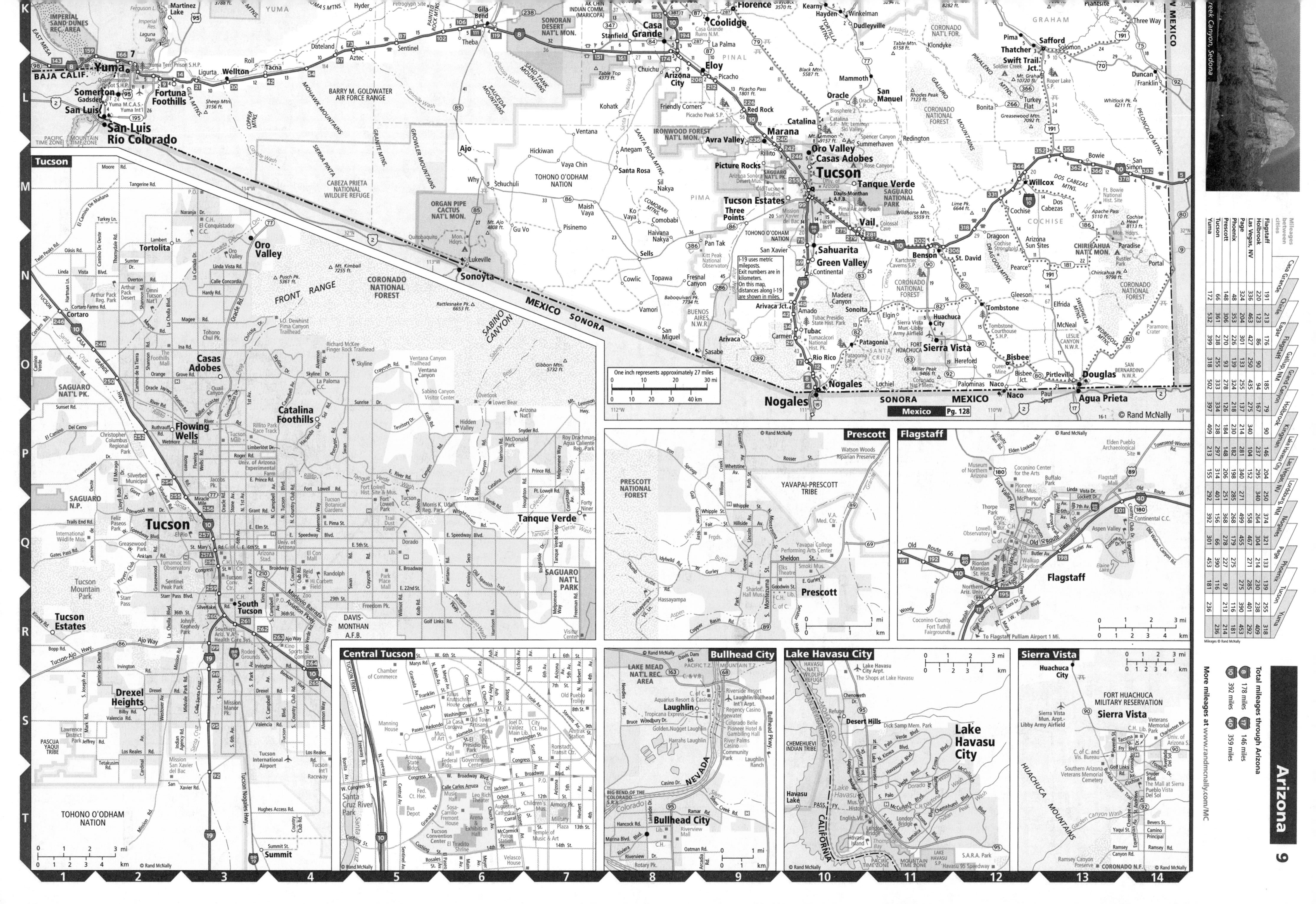

Mileages between cities

	Casa Grande	Chinle	Eagar	Flagstaff	Gallup, NM	Grand Canyon	Holbrook	Kingman	Lake Havasu City	Las Vegas, NV	Lordsburg, NM	Nogales	Page	Phoenix	Tucson	Yuma
Flagstaff	191	213	176		185	79	90	146	204	250	374	321	133	139	255	318
Holbrook	220	123	86	90	94	167		237	295	340	264	304	214	230	238	409
Las Vegas, NV	336	463	427	250	435	275	340	104	152		558	467	271	285	401	292
Page	324	204	301	133	255	137	214	281	340	271	499	455		275	390	453
Phoenix	48	353	226	139	324	218	230	182	198	285	268	179	275		116	181
Prescott	148	306	270	93	278	126	184	148	206	251	368	278	227	97	213	214
Tucson	66	361	238	255	333	334	238	297	314	401	156	66	390	116		236
Yuma	172	532	399	318	502	397	409	213	155	292	392	301	453	181	236	

Total mileages through Arizona

- 8: 178 miles
- 17: 146 miles
- 10: 392 miles
- 40: 359 miles

More mileages at www.randmcnally.com/MC

Nickname: The Natural State
Capital: Little Rock, G-7
Land area: 52,068 sq. mi. (rank: 27th)
Population: 2,915,918 (rank: 32nd)
Largest city: Little Rock, 193,524, G-7

Index of cities Pg. 129

Get more Arkansas info at www.randmcnally.com/AR

Tourism Information
Arkansas Department of Parks & Tourism; (800) 628-8725, (501) 682-7777; www.arkansas.com

Road Conditions & Construction
(800) 245-1672, (501) 569-2000, (501) 569-2374; www.arkansashighways.com

Toll Road Information
No toll roads

Determining distances along roads

Highway distances (segments of one mile or less not shown):
Cumulative miles (red): the distance between red arrows
Intermediate miles (black): the distance between intersections &

Interchanges and exit numbers
For most states, the mileage between interchanges may be deter
by subtracting one number from the other.

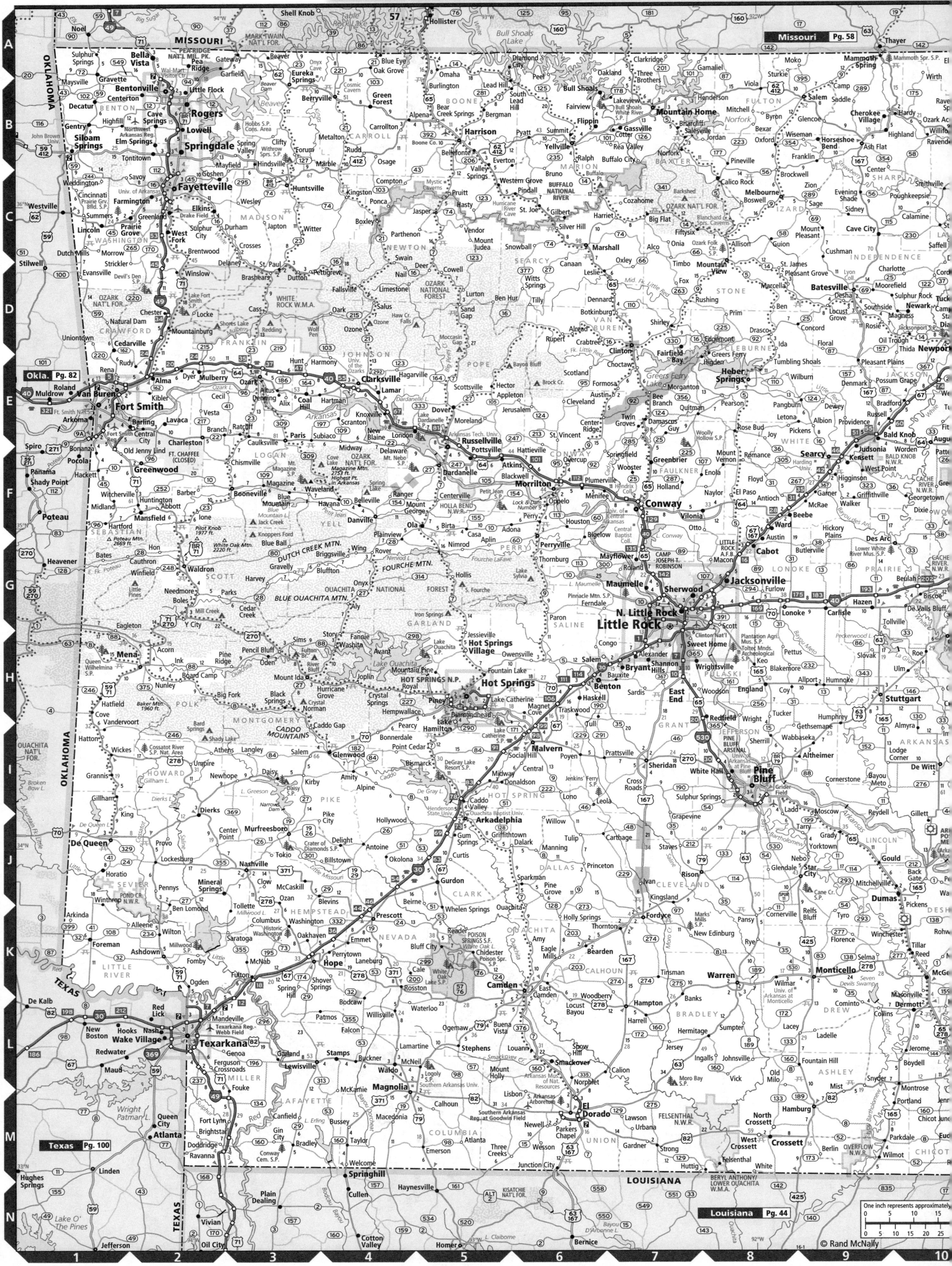

Missouri Pg. 58

Okla. Pg. 82

Texas Pg. 100

Louisiana Pg. 44

One inch represents approximately

Mileages between cities

	Batesville	Branson, MO	DeQueen	El Dorado	Fayetteville	Fort Smith	Greenville, MS	Hot Springs	Jonesboro	Little Rock	Memphis, TN	Mountain Home	Pine Bluff	Rogers	Russellville	Texarkana
El Dorado	209	287	141		304	227	109	121	245	118	250	268	91	325	190	88
Fayetteville	251	98	184	304		58	335	184	250	188	318	123	231	24	115	236
Fort Smith	219	158	130	227	58		304	130	261	158	286	187	199	81	84	182
Jonesboro	68	203	272	245	250	261	219	182		130	70	126	171	253	173	270
Little Rock	94	172	143	118	188	158	147	54	130		137	151	43	208	74	142
Memphis, TN	119	274	278	250	318	286	152	188	70	137		195	152	339	204	276
Mountain Home	78	83	287	268	123	187	298	198	126	151	195		194	126	125	287
Texarkana	234	306	54	88	236	182	198	110	270	142	276	287	152	258	209	

Total mileages through Arkansas

- I-30: 143 miles
- I-55: 72 miles
- I-40: 284 miles
- US 65: 309 miles

More mileages at www.randmcnally.com/MC

Nickname: The Golden State
Capital: Sacramento, NK-7
Land area: 155,959 sq. mi. (rank: 3rd)
Population: 37,253,956 (rank: 1st)
Largest city: Los Angeles, 3,792,621, SJ-11

Index of cities Pg. 129

Explore California at www.randmcnally.com/CA

Tourism Information
California Tourism: (877) 225-4367, (916) 444-4429; www.visitcalifornia.com

Road Conditions & Construction
(800) 427-7623; www.dot.ca.gov;
Sacramento region: 511; www.sacregion511.org
San Francisco Bay area: 511; www.511.org

Toll Bridge Informaton *(all use FasTrak)*
Golden Gate Bridge (San Francisco Bay area): (415) 921-5858; www.goldengatebridge.org
Bay Area Toll Authority (all other San Francisco Bay area bridges): (510) 817-5700; bata.mtc.ca.gov

Determining distances along roads
Highway distances (segments of one mile or less not shown):
Cumulative miles (red): the distance between red arrows
Intermediate miles (black): the distance between intersections

Interchanges and exit numbers
For most states, the mileage between interchanges may be determined by subtracting one number from the other.

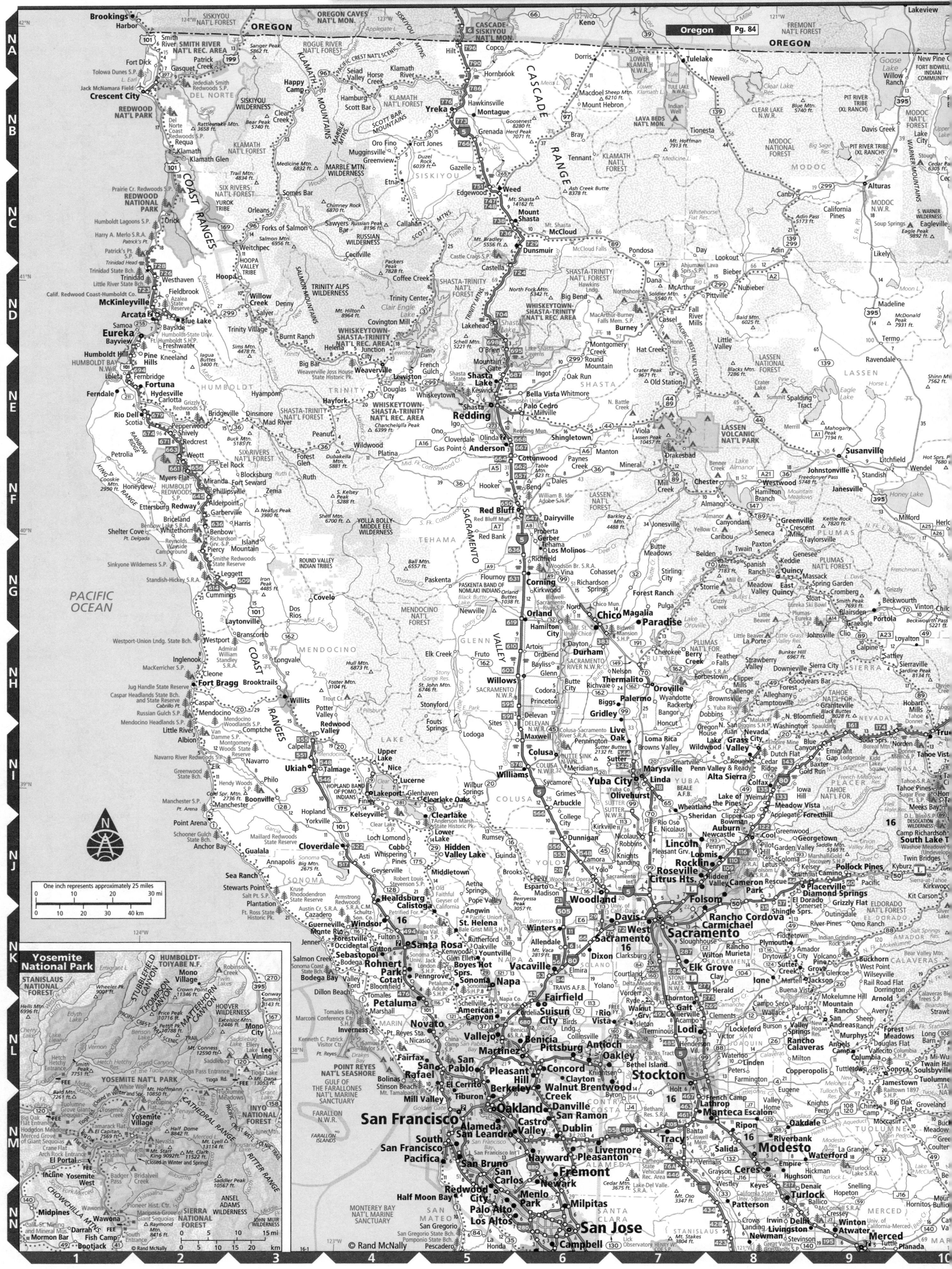

Oregon Pg. 84

PACIFIC OCEAN

One inch represents approximately 25 miles

Yosemite National Park

Mileages between cities	Bishop	Crescent City	Los Angeles	Oroville	Redding	Sacramento	San Francisco	San Jose	Santa Rosa	S. Lake Tahoe	Stockton	Susanville	Ukiah	Vallejo	Yosemite N.P.	Yreka
Alturas	371	280	648	225	144	302	357	385	365	228	349	103	330	329	392	176
Bishop		614	265	326	400	269	295	290	364	176	224	286	418	328	138	454
Eureka	546	81	644	222	146	289	272	315	217	392	325	259	158	262	454	198
Redding	400	208	544	94		161	216	244	198	264	209	112	188	187	332	98
Sacramento	269	372	383	68	161		87	115	95	100	47	217	145	58	160	257
San Francisco	295	355	380	150	216	87		45	55	187	82	303	115	30	189	312
San Jose	290	396	340	178	244	115	45		96	215	74	330	156	64	182	340
S. Lake Tahoe	176	472	445	157	264	100	187	215	195		147	143	248	159	189	311

Total mileages through California

5: 797 miles
101: 791 miles
80: 199 miles

More mileages at www.randmcnally.com/MC

Nickname: The Golden State
Capital: Sacramento, NK-7
Land area: 155,959 sq. mi. (rank: 3rd)
Population: 37,253,956 (rank: 1st)
Largest city: Los Angeles, 3,792,621, SJ-11

Index of cities Pg. 129

Get more California info at www.randmcnally.com/CA

Tourism Information
California Tourism: (877) 225-4367, (916) 444-4429; www.visitcalifornia.com

Road Conditions & Construction (511)
(800) 427-7623; www.dot.ca.gov
Los Angeles metro area: 511; www.go511.com
San Diego area: 511; www.511sd.com

Toll Road Information *(all use FasTrak)*
The Toll Roads (Orange Co.): (949) 727-4800; www.thetollroads.com
South Bay Expressway (San Diego Co.): (619) 661-7070; www.southbayexpressway.com

Determining distances along roads

Highway distances (segments of one mile or less not shown):
Cumulative miles (red): the distance between red arrows
Intermediate miles (black): the distance between intersections & p

Interchanges and exit numbers
For most states, the mileage between interchanges may be determ by subtracting one number from the other.

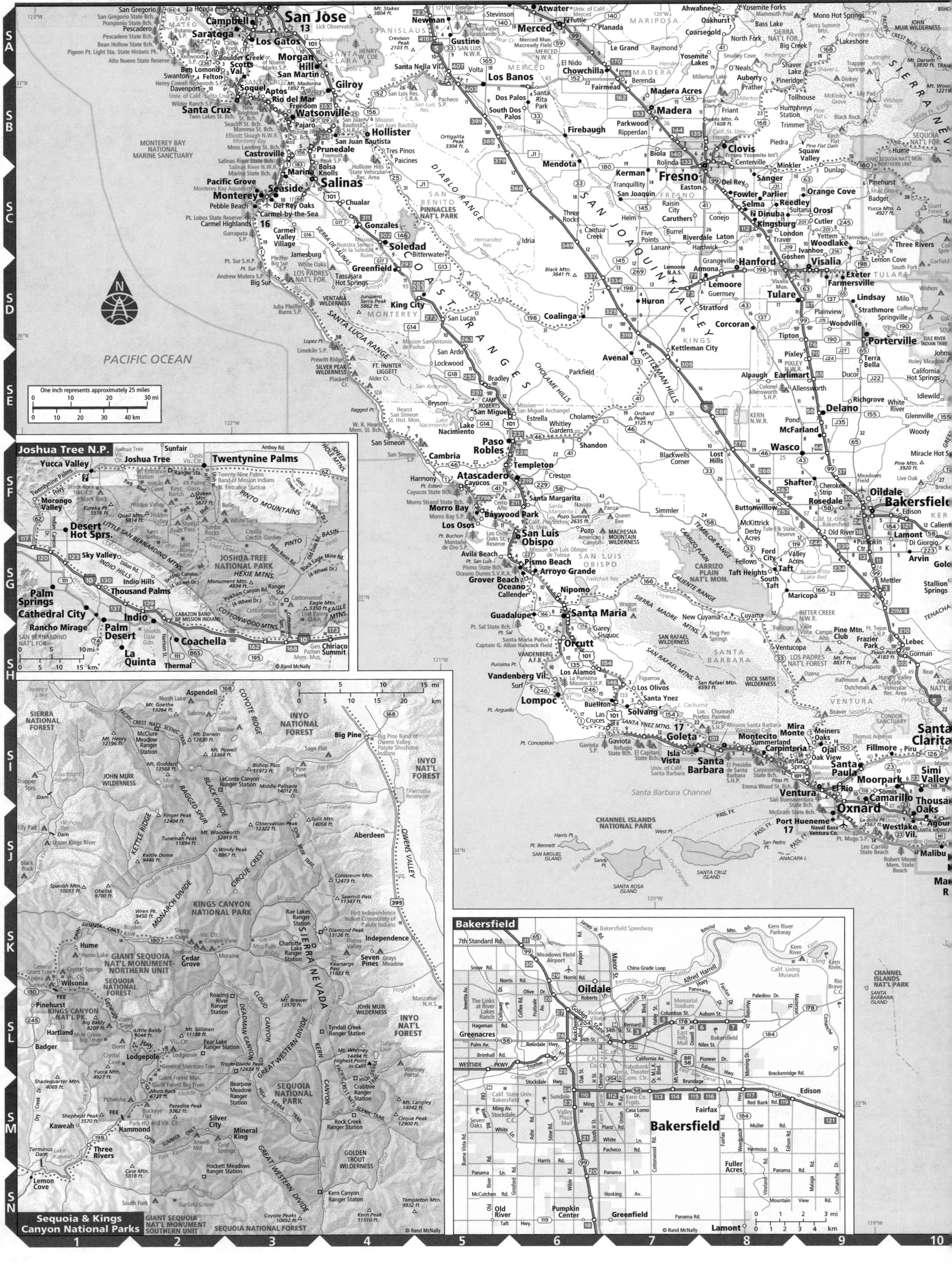

PACIFIC OCEAN

One inch represents approximately 25 miles

Joshua Tree N.P.

Bakersfield

Sequoia & Kings Canyon National Parks

© Rand McNally

Mileages between cities	Bakersfield	Barstow	El Centro	Fresno	Las Vegas, NV	Los Angeles	Monterey	Needles	Palm Springs	Riverside	San Bernardino	San Diego	San Francisco	San Luis Obispo	Santa Barbara	Sequoia N.P.
Bakersfield		129	322	109	286	112	222	272	216	166	166	232	284	130	147	122
Fresno	109	239	429		395	218	150	381	323	271	273	339	183	130	254	77
Las Vegas, NV	286	156	312	395		270	507	110	278	234	225	331	569	415	358	410
Los Angeles	112	114	212	218	270		319	256	107	54	60	120	380	189	94	232
Monterey	222	350	530	150	507	319		494	424	372	373	439	112	142	237	226
Palm Springs	216	123	108	323	278	107	424	188		52	54	139	486	296	201	338
San Diego	232	176	113	339	331	120	439	317	139	97	106		501	313	214	352
Santa Barbara	147	203	306	254	358	94	237	345	201	148	150	214	325	94		268

Total mileages through California

- I-5: 797 miles
- I-10: 243 miles
- I-15: 287 miles
- I-40: 155 miles

More mileages at www.randmcnally.com/MC

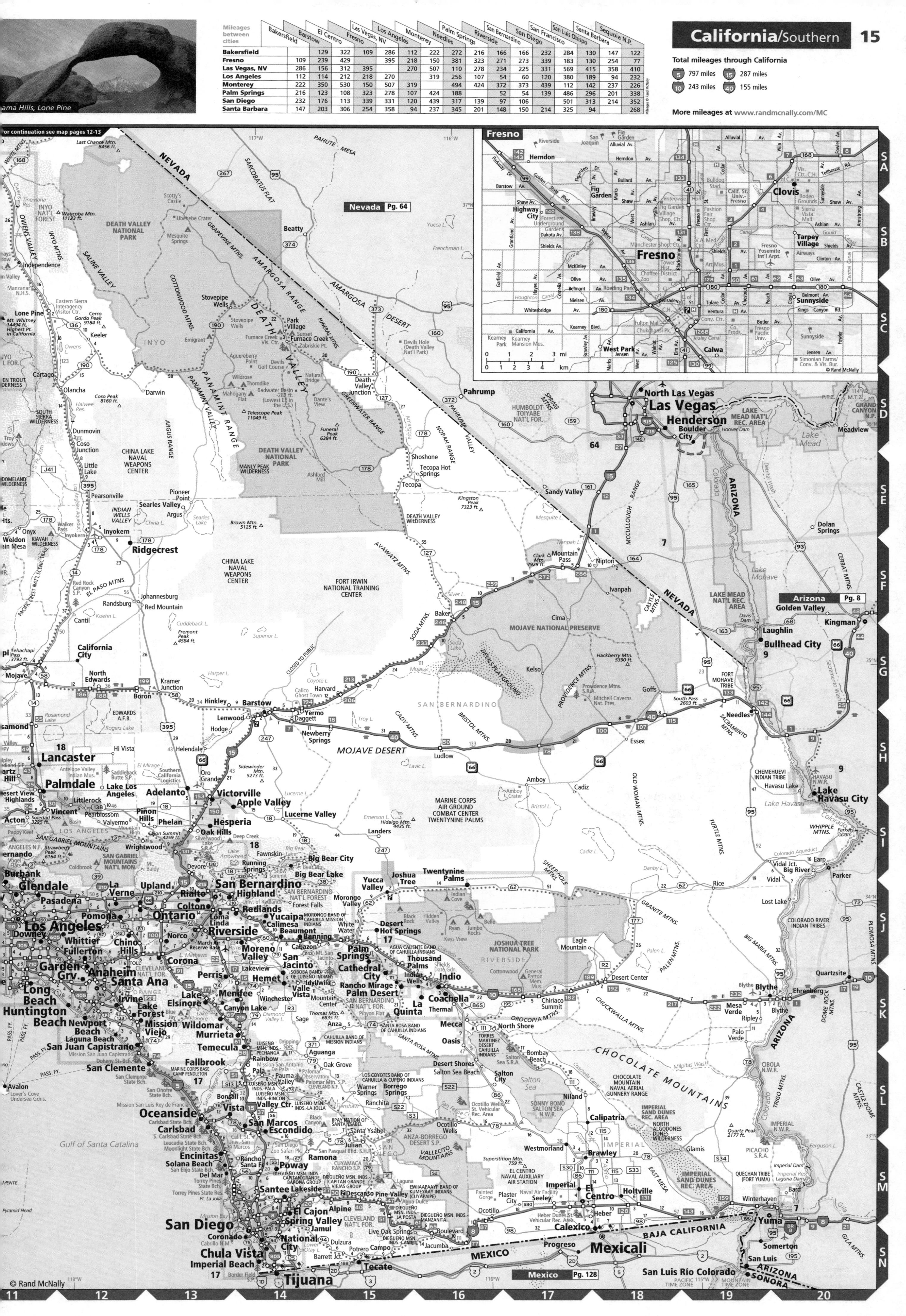

City sights to see

- California State Capitol, Sacramento, I-6
- California State Railroad Museum, Sacramento, H-6
- Chinatown, San Francisco, C-8
- Coit Memorial Tower, San Francisco, B-8
- Crocker Art Museum, Sacramento, I-5
- Fisherman's Wharf, San Francisco, A-7
- Ghirardelli Square, San Francisco, B-7
- Golden Gate Bridge, San Francisco, A-2
- Monterey Bay Aquarium, Monterey, M-1
- Pier 39, San Francisco, A-8
- San Francisco Cable Car Museum, San Francisco, C-8
- Squaw Valley U.S.A., Olympic Valley, F-8

San Francisco Fort Mason Center

ta Barbara harbor and coastline

City sights to see

- Balboa Park, San Diego, K-10
- Birch Aquarium at Scripps Institute, San Diego, G-1
- Cabrillo National Monument, San Diego, K-1
- Gaslamp Quarter Historic District, San Diego, M-9
- Legoland California, Carlsbad, J-8
- The Living Desert Nature Preserve, Palm Desert, G-10
- Museum of Contemporary Art, San Diego, L-8
- Palm Springs Art Museum, Palm Springs, E-7
- San Diego Zoo, San Diego, J-3
- SeaWorld, San Diego, I-1
- Stearns Wharf, Santa Barbara, B-5

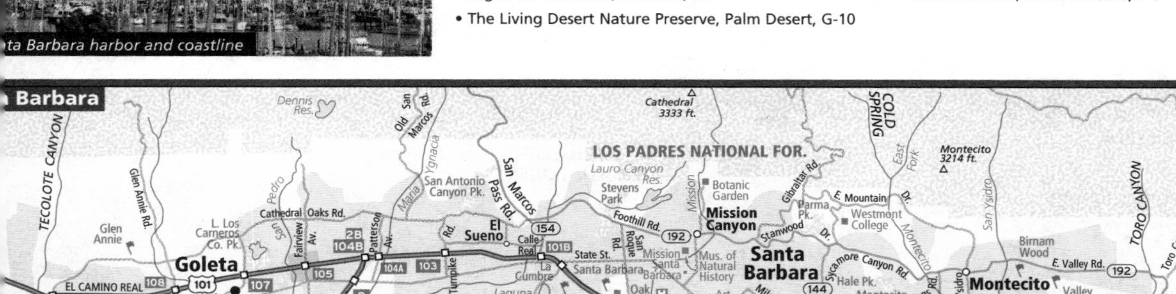

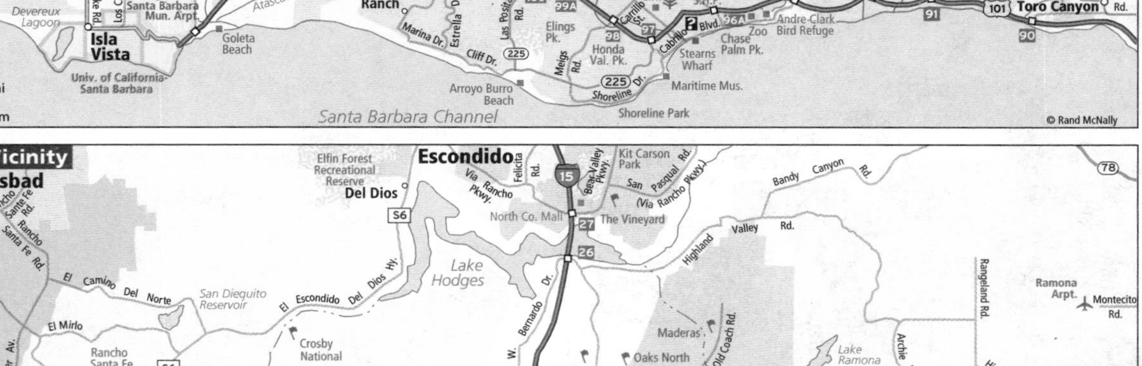

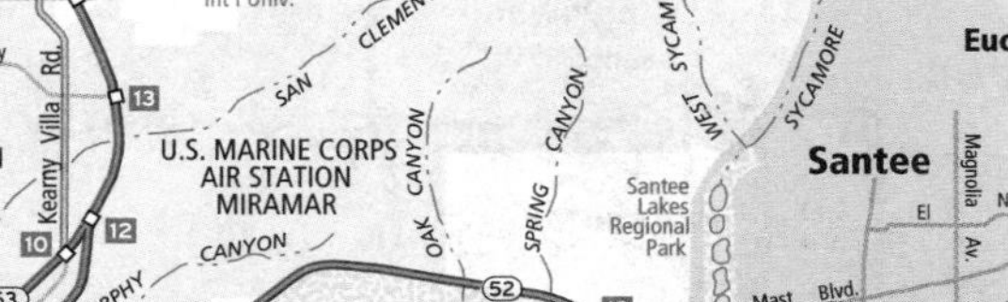

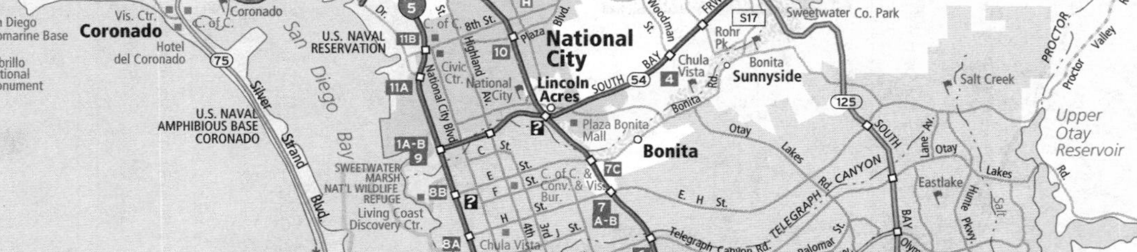

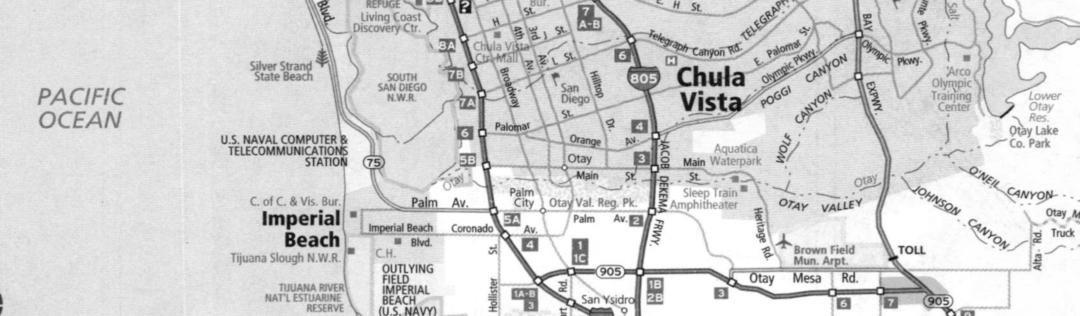

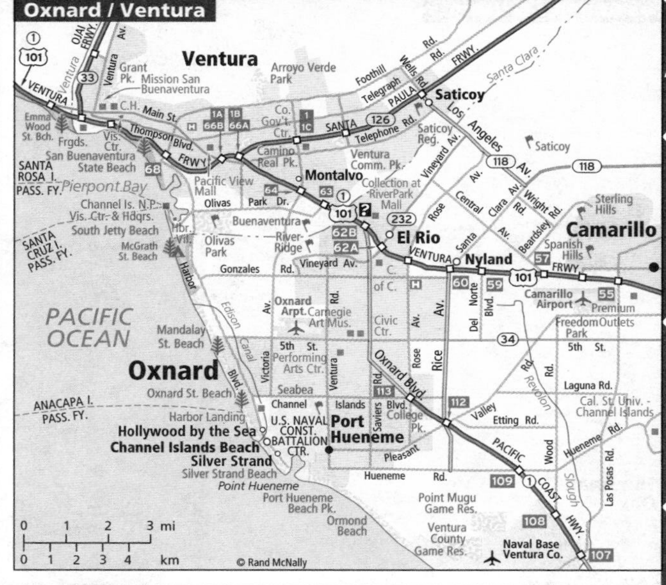

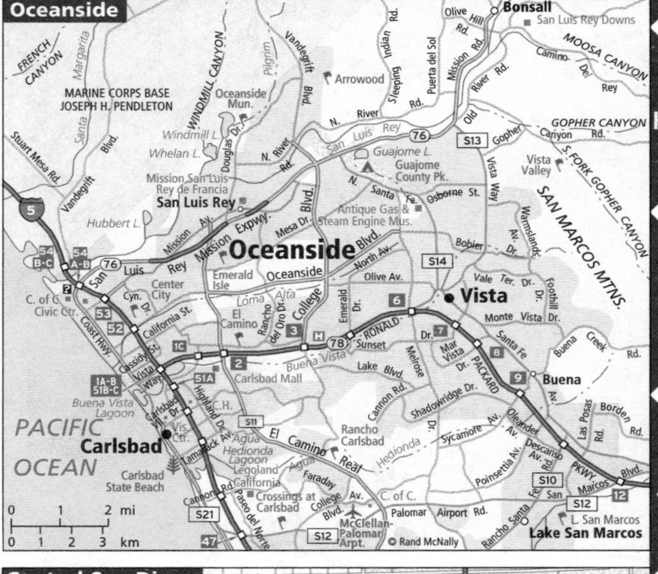

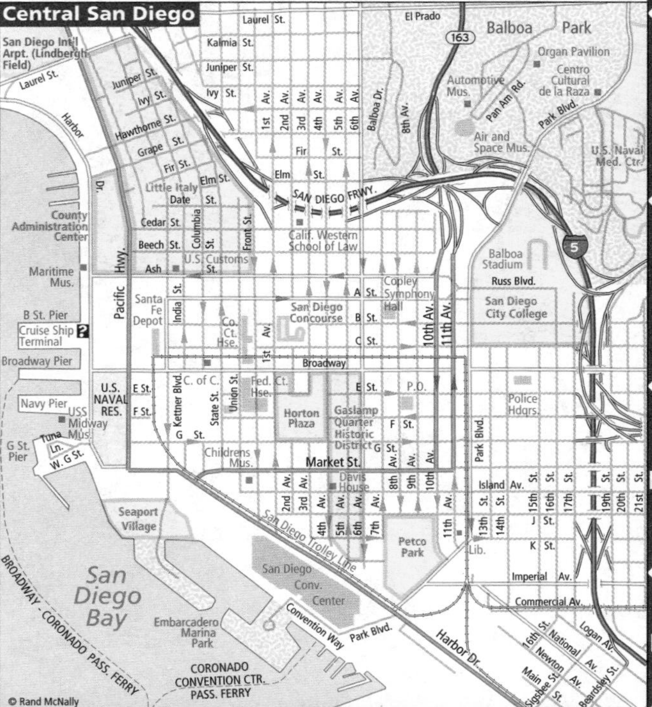

City sights to see

- Aquarium of the Pacific, Long Beach, J-8
- Disneyland, Anaheim, I-11
- Dodger Stadium, E-7
- El Pueblo de Los Angeles, K-2
- Getty Center, E-4
- Hollywood Bowl, D-6
- Huntington Library, San Marino, D-8
- Japanese American National Museum, K-3
- Knott's Berry Farm, Buena Park, H-10
- Los Angeles County Art Museum, E-5
- Los Angeles Maritime Museum, J-7

Walt Disney Concert Hall

Los Angeles & Vicinity

Central Los Angeles

Lancaster / Palmdale

© Rand McNally

Huntington Beach Pier, Huntington Beach

City sights to see

- Los Angeles Zoo and Botanical Gardens, D-6
- Old Pasadena, Pasadena, D-8
- Oldest Winery in California, Rancho Cucamonga, D-14
- The Queen Mary, Long Beach, J-8
- Richard M. Nixon Library & Birthplace, Yorba Linda, H-12
- Santa Monica Pier, Santa Monica, F-4
- Universal City, D-5
- Venice Boardwalk, F-4
- Walt Disney Concert Hall, K-1
- Warner Bros. Studio, Burbank, D-6
- Will Rogers State Historic Park, Pacific Palisades, E-4

Nickname: The Centennial State
Capital: Denver, E-13
Land area: 103,718 sq. mi. (rank: 8th)
Population: 5,029,196 (rank: 22nd)
Largest city: Denver, 600,158, E-13

Index of cities Pg. 129

Explore Colorado at www.randmcnally.com/CO

Tourism Information
Colorado Tourism Office:
(800) 265-6723; www.colorado.com

Road Conditions & Construction
511, (303) 573-7623, (303) 639-1111
www.cotrip.org

Toll Road Information
E-470 (Denver metro) *(ExpressToll)*: (303) 537-3470, (888) 946-3470; www.expresstoll.com
Northwest Parkway (Denver metro) *(GoPass)*: (303) 533-1200; www.northwestparkway.org

Determining distances along roads
Highway distances (segments of one mile or less not shown):
Cumulative miles (red): the distance between red arrows
Intermediate miles (black): the distance between intersections & pl
Interchanges and exit numbers
For most states, the mileage between interchanges may be determi by subtracting one number from the other.

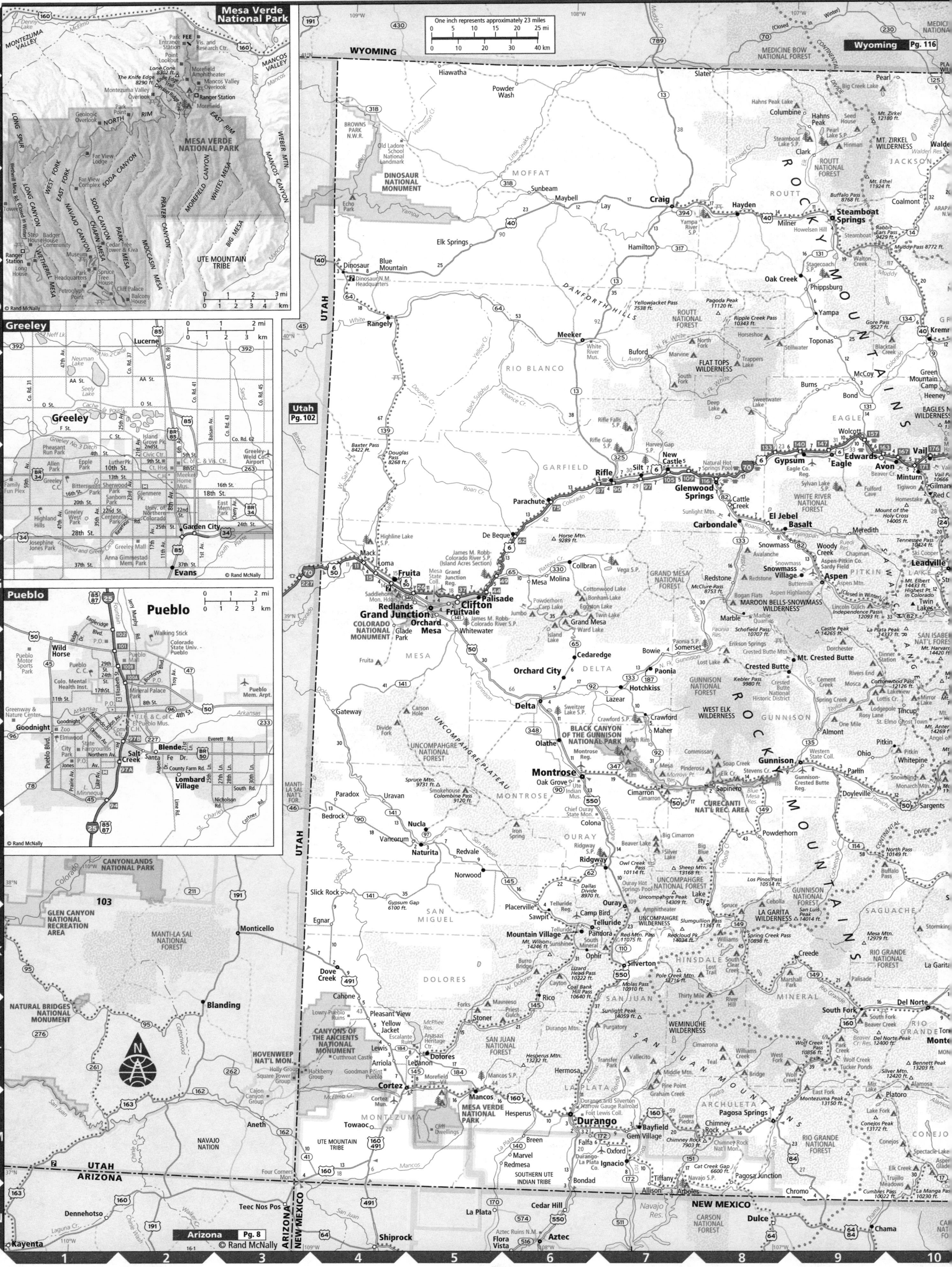

Wyoming Pg. 116
Utah Pg. 102
Arizona Pg. 8

Mileages between cities

	Alamosa	Aspen	Burlington	Colorado Springs	Craig	Denver	Durango	Estes Park	Fort Collins	Grand Junction	Gunnison	Lamar	Leadville	Pueblo	Sterling	Trinidad
Burlington	311	363		151	363	166	460	222	220	408	324	108	265	189	142	230
Colorado Springs	163	155	151		264	69	313	133	133	309	166	158	121	42	194	128
Denver	234	197	166	69	197		336	64	63	243	200	208	99	112	125	198
Durango	149	246	460	313	312	336		402	396	168	142	351	253	269	458	258
Fort Collins	296	258	220	133	201	63	396	42		303	260	261	160	175	102	261
Grand Junction	247	128	408	309	151	243	168	258	303		126	448	174	287	364	370
Leadville	135	58	265	121	145	99	253	143	160	174	102	276		154	222	204
Trinidad	109	232	230	128	392	198	258	262	261	370	209	136	204	85	322	

Total mileages through Colorado

- I-25: 300 miles
- I-70: 451 miles
- I-76: 185 miles
- US-50: 467 miles

More mileages at www.randmcnally.com/MC

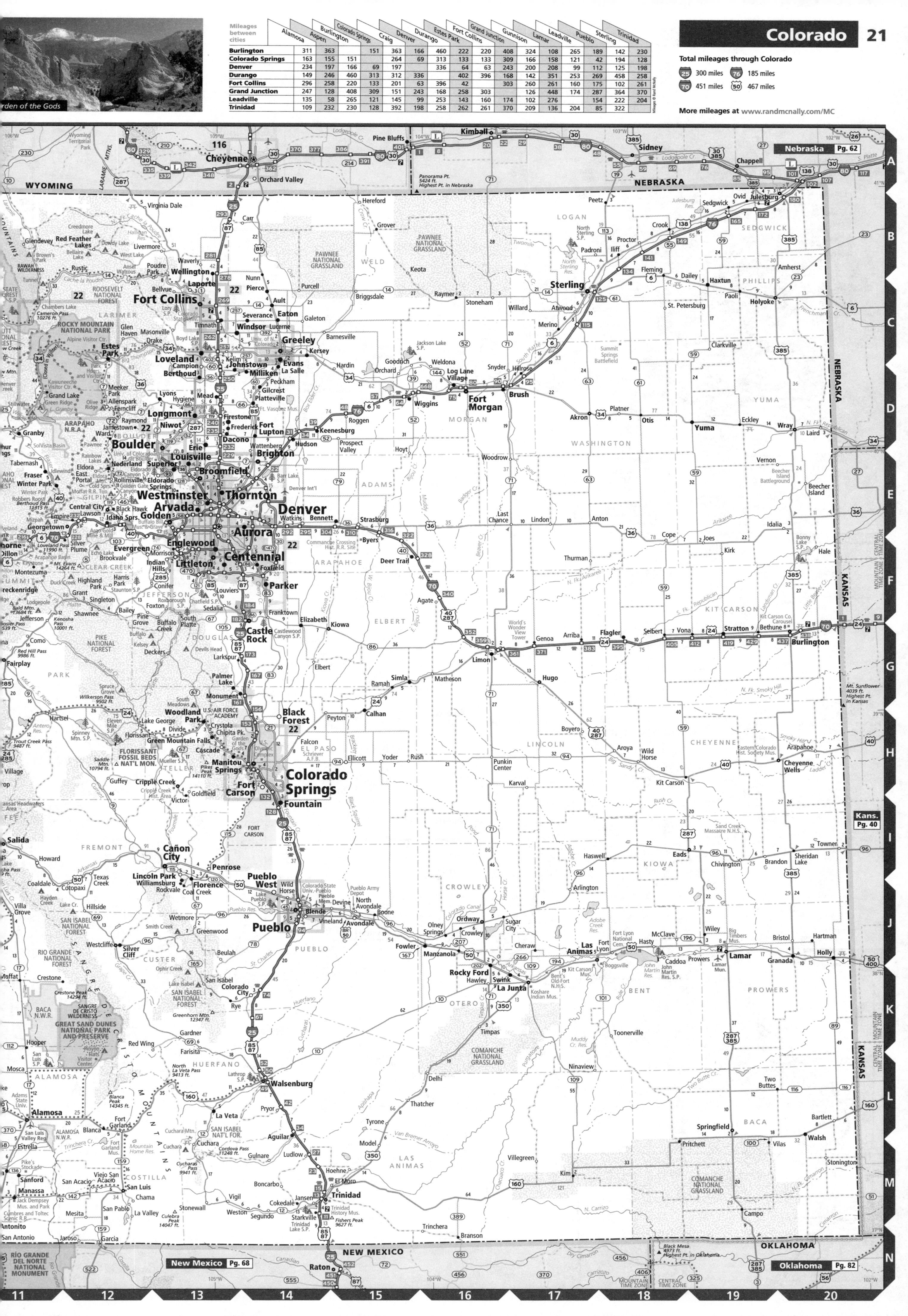

City sights to see

- Black American West Museum & Heritage Center, Denver, L-3
- Cave of the Winds, Colorado Springs, G-1
- Colorado History Museum, Denver, M-2
- Colorado State Capitol, Denver, M-2
- Denver Art Museum, Denver, M-2
- Denver Museum of Nature & Science, Denver, I-7
- Garden of the Gods, Colorado Springs, G-1
- National Center for Atmospheric Research, Boulder, D-4
- Old Town National Historic District, Fort Collins, B-9
- ProRodeo Hall of Fame, Colorado Springs, F-2
- United States Mint, Denver, M-2
- World Figure Skating Hall of Fame, Colorado Springs, I-2

The Pepsi Center, Denver

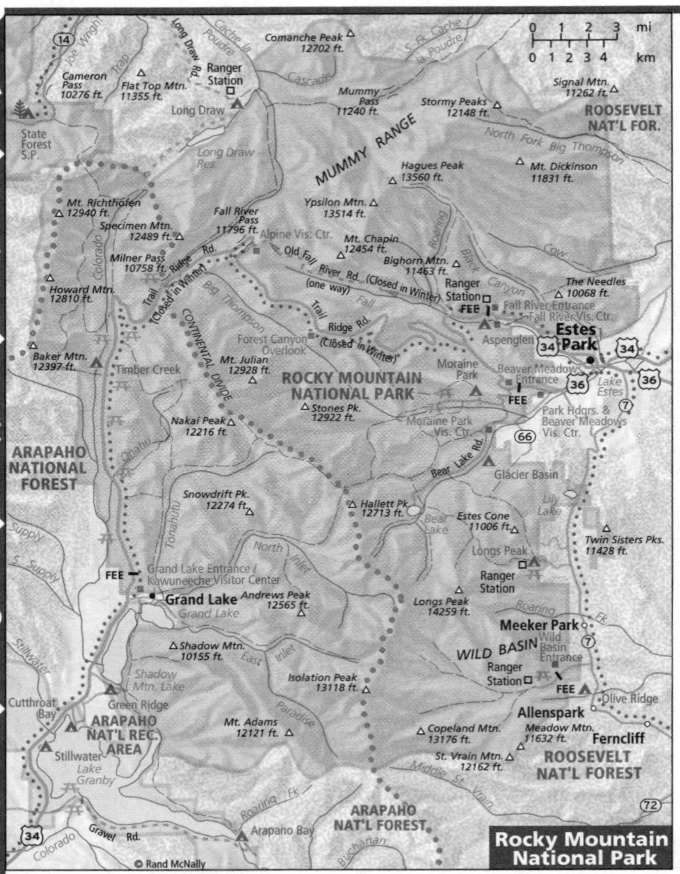

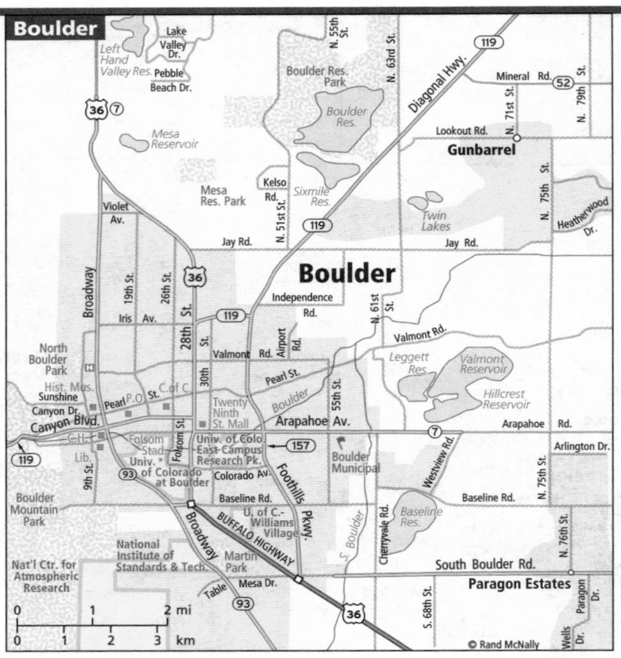

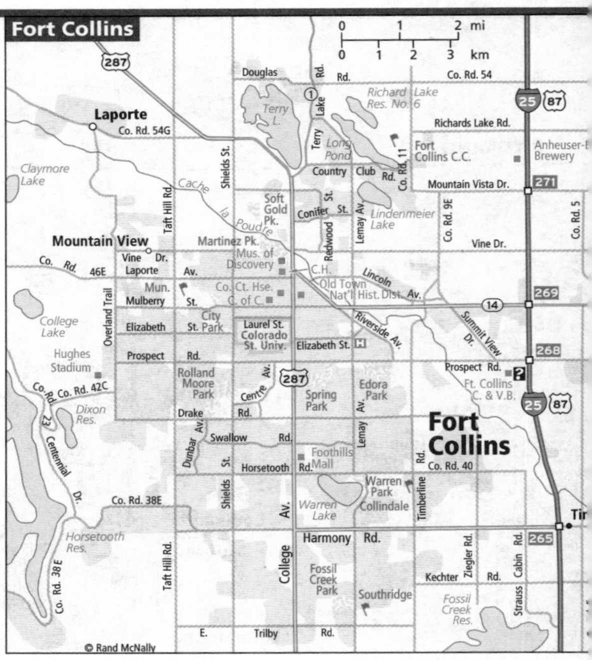

Rocky Mountain National Park

Boulder

Fort Collins

Denver & Vicinity

Colorado Springs

Central Denver

© Rand McNally

…et travel info at www.randmcnally.com/CT

…rism Information
…n. Office of Tourism: (860) 256-2800; www.ctvisit.com

…d Conditions & Construction
…) 594-2000, (860) 594-2650; www.ct.gov/dot

…Road Information
…toll roads

Determining Distances
(segments of one mile or less not shown)
Cumulative miles (red): the distance between red arrows
Intermediate miles (black): the distance between intersections & places

Total mileages through Connecticut
84: 98 miles
91: 58 miles
95: 112 miles
395: 55 miles

More mileages at www.randmcnally.com/MC

Mileages between cities	Bridgeport	Hartford	New Haven	New London	New York, NY	Putnam	Torrington	Waterbury
Bridgeport		55	18	64	54	107	50	30
Danbury	29	57	35	81	62	104	47	27
Hartford	55		38	45	108	47	26	30
New Haven	18	38		46	72	89	43	22
New London	64	45	46		118	47	79	63
Putnam	107	47	89	47	162		73	78
Torrington	50	26	43	79	109	73		20
Waterbury	30	30	22	63	89	78	20	

Connecticut

Nickname: The Constitution State
Capital: Hartford, C-9
Land area: 4,845 sq. mi. (rank: 48th)
Population: 3,574,097 (rank: 29th)
Largest city: Bridgeport, 144,229, H-5

Index of cities Pg. 129

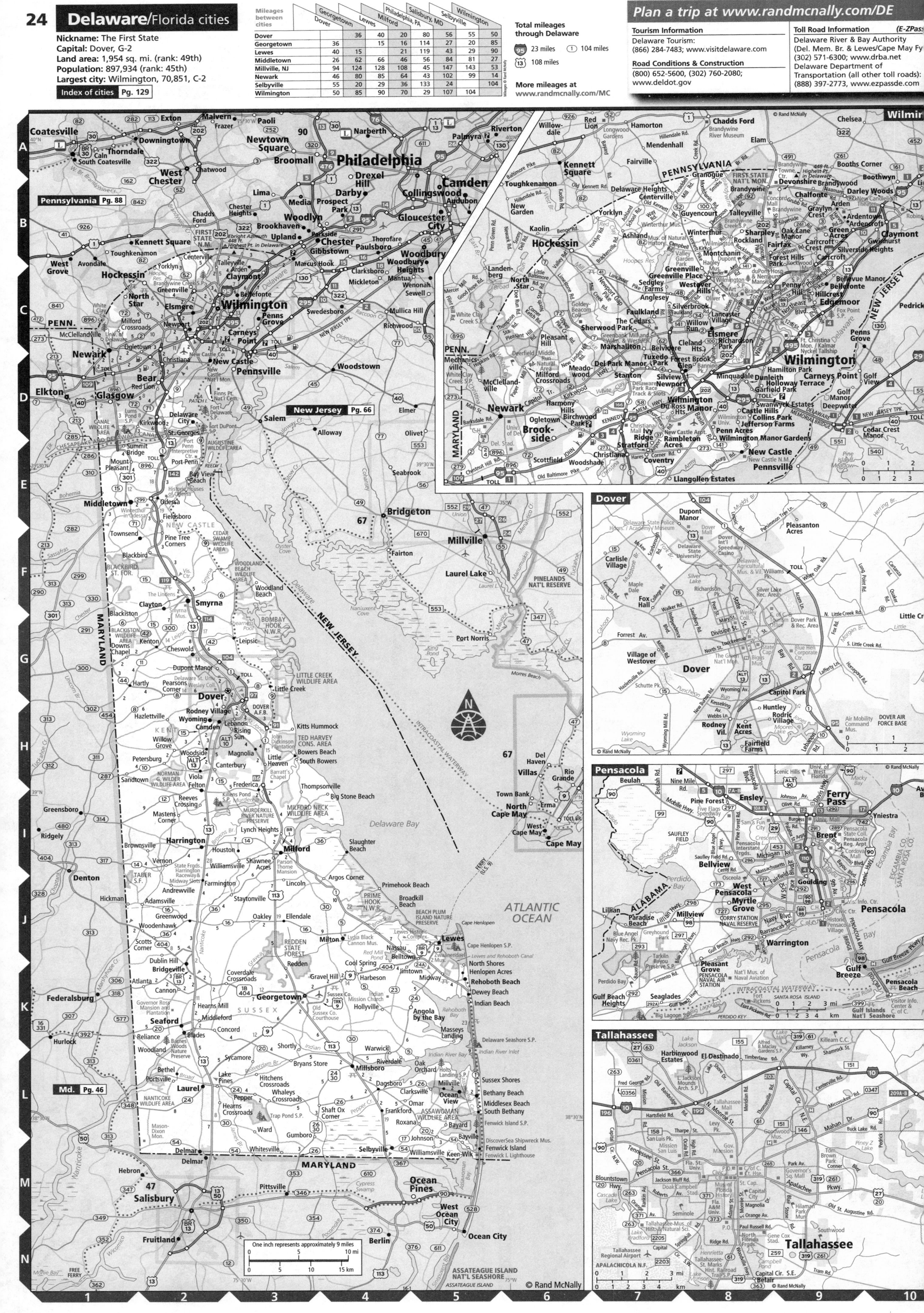

Mileages between cities	Dover	Georgetown	Lewes	Milford	Philadelphia, PA	Salisbury, MD	Selbyville	Wilmington
Dover		36	40	20	80	56	55	50
Georgetown	36		15	16	114	27	20	85
Lewes	40	15		21	119	43	29	90
Middletown	26	62	66	46	56	84	81	27
Millville, NJ	94	124	128	108	45	147	143	53
Newark	46	80	85	64	43	102	99	14
Selbyville	55	20	29	36	133	24		104
Wilmington	50	85	90	70	29	107	104	

...e beach at St. Petersburg/Clearwater

City sights to see

- Art Deco National Historic District, Miami Beach, L-9
- Busch Gardens, Tampa, B-4
- Hugh Taylor Birch State Park, Fort Lauderdale, H-9
- Marie Selby Botanical Gardens, Sarasota, H-3
- Miami Seaquarium, Miami, M-9
- Norton Museum of Art, Palm Beach, B-10
- Ringling Center for the Cultural Arts, Sarasota, G-3
- Salvador Dali Museum, St. Petersburg, D-2
- St. Petersburg Museum of History, St. Petersburg, D-2
- Thomas A. Edison & Henry Ford Winter Estates, Fort Myers, M-2
- Vizcaya Museum and Gardens, Miami, M-8

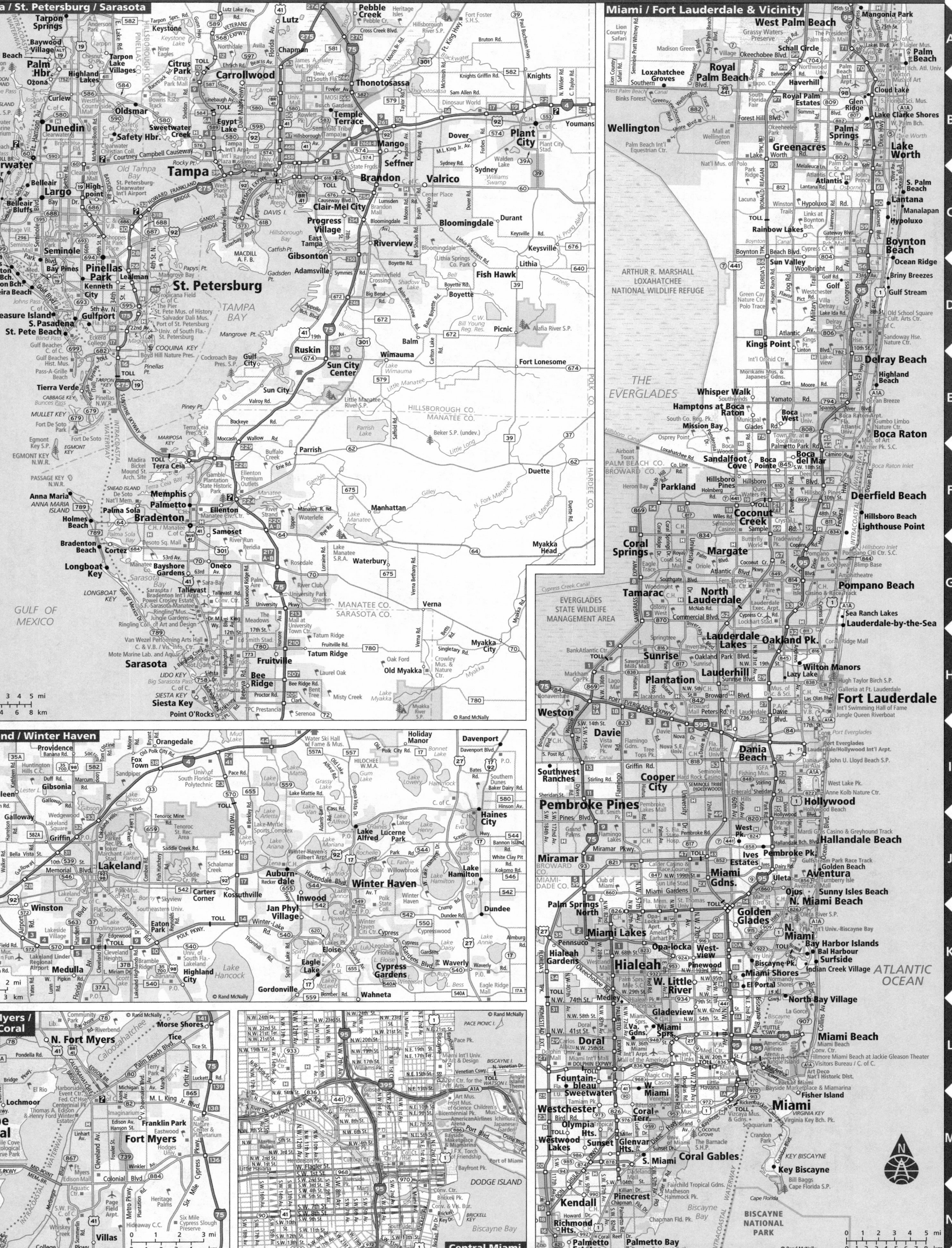

Nickname: The Sunshine State
Capital: Tallahassee, B-2
Land area: 53,927 sq. mi. (rank: 26th)
Population: 18,801,310 (rank: 4th)
Largest city: Jacksonville, 821,784, C-9

Index of cities Pg. 129

Plan a Florida trip at www.randmcnally.com/FL

Tourism Information
Visit Florida: (888) 735-2872, (850) 488-5607; www.visitflorida.com

Road Conditions & Construction
511, (866) 374-3368; www.fl511.com, www.dot.state.fl.us

Toll Road Information
Florida's Turnpike *(SunPass)*: (800) 749-7453; floridasturnpike.com

Determining distances along roads

Highway distances (segments of one mile or less not shown):
Cumulative miles (red): the distance between red arrows
Intermediate miles (black): the distance between intersections & pla

Interchanges and exit numbers
For most states, the mileage between interchanges may be determin
by subtracting one number from the other.

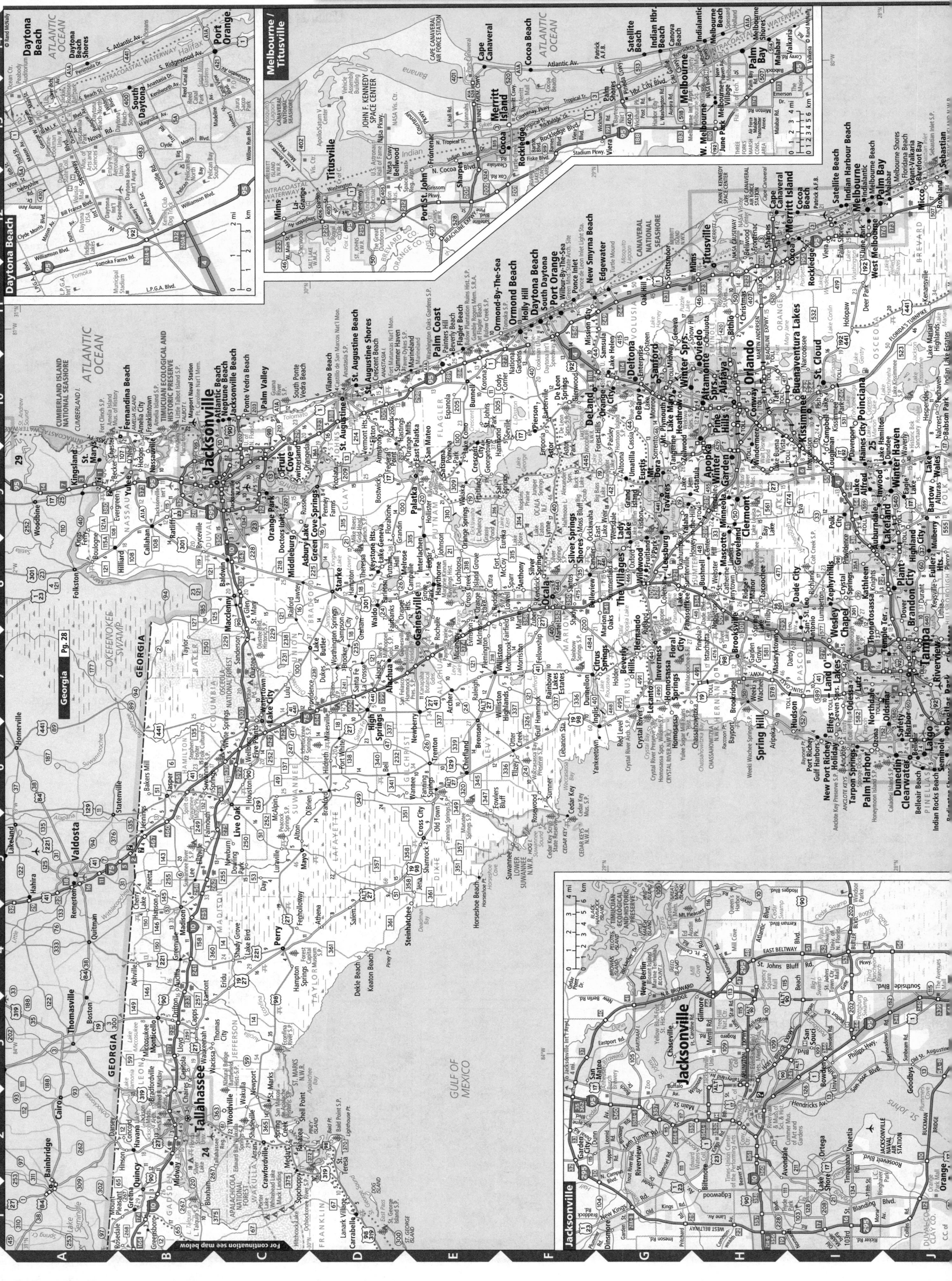

Georgia Pg. 28

For continuation see map below

Mileages between cities	Daytona Beach	Fort Myers	Fort Pierce	Gainesville	Jacksonville	Key West	Miami	Orlando	Panama City	Pensacola	St. Petersburg	Sarasota	Tallahassee	Tampa	Titusville	West Palm Beach
Fort Myers	225		128	254	312	279	152	171	497	589	117	80	397	130	209	124
Jacksonville	92	312	227	72		507	349	141	264	355	222	253	164	198	136	284
Key West	414	279	284	483	507		162	387	727	821	390	352	627	402	371	231
Miami	256	152	123	336	349	162		229	579	663	262	225	479	255	213	68
Orlando	54	171	110	114	141	387	229		357	451	106	132	257	84	39	159
Pensacola	442	589	549	338	355	821	663	451	102		458	511	193	459	487	594
Tallahassee	253	397	364	148	164	627	479	257	96	193	257	328		273	295	413
Tampa	137	130	151	127	198	402	255	84	373	459	23	60	273		124	202

Total mileages through Florida

- 4: 132 miles
- 75: 471 miles
- 10: 362 miles
- 95: 382 miles

More mileages at www.randmcnally.com/MC

Georgia

Nickname: The Peach State
Capital: Atlanta, E-4
Land area: 57,906 sq. mi. (rank: 21st)
Population: 9,687,653 (rank: 9th)
Largest city: Atlanta, 420,003, E-4

Index of cities Pg. 130

Explore Georgia at www.randmcnally.com/GA

Tourism Information
Georgia Department of Economic Development: (800) 847-4842; www.exploregeorgia.org

Road Conditions & Construction
511, (888) 635-8287, (877) 694-2511, (404) 635-8000; www.511ga.org

Toll Road Information
No toll roads

Determining distances along roads

Highway distances (segments of one mile or less not shown):
Cumulative miles (red): the distance between red arrows
Intermediate miles (black): the distance between intersections & pl

Interchanges and exit numbers
For most states, the mileage between interchanges may be determi
by subtracting one number from the other.

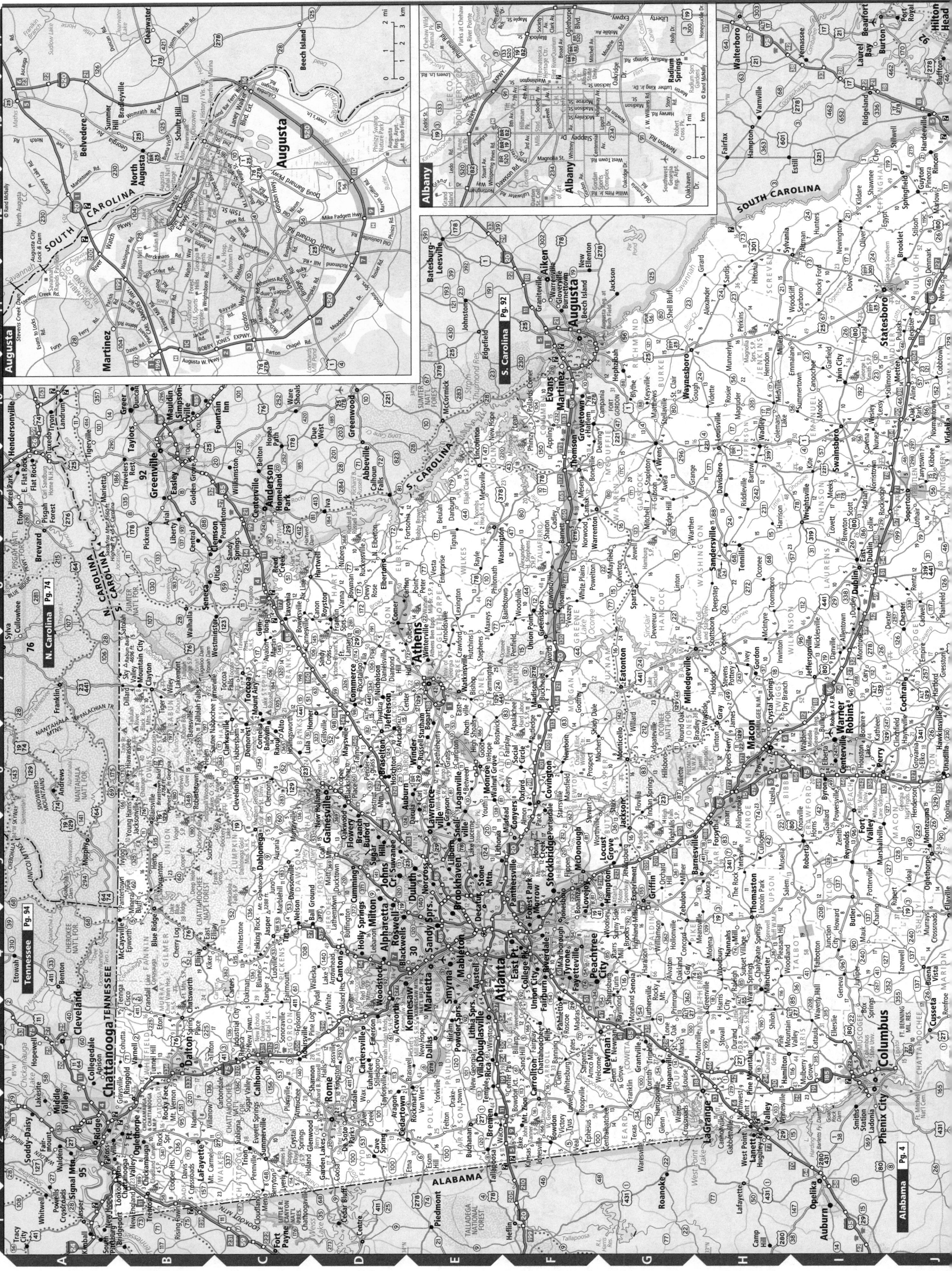

Augusta

Albany

South Carolina

Atlanta

Athens

Macon

Columbus

Augusta

maha River

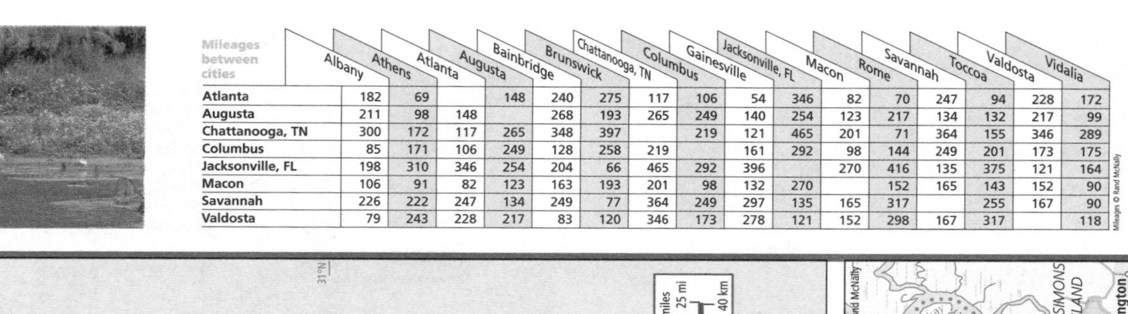

Mileages between cities	Albany	Athens	Atlanta	Augusta	Bainbridge	Brunswick	Chattanooga, TN	Columbus	Gainesville	Jacksonville, FL	Macon	Rome	Savannah	Toccoa	Valdosta	Vidalia
Atlanta	182	69		148	240	275	117	106	54	346	82	70	247	94	228	172
Augusta	211	98	148		268	193	265	249	140	254	123	217	134	132	217	99
Chattanooga, TN	300	172	117	265	348	397		219	121	465	201	71	364	155	346	289
Columbus	85	171	106	249	128	258	219		161	292	98	144	249	201	173	175
Jacksonville, FL	198	310	346	254	204	66	465	292	396		270	416	135	375	121	164
Macon	106	91	82	123	163	193	201	98	132	270		152	165	143	152	90
Savannah	226	222	247	134	249	77	364	249	297	135	165	317		255	167	90
Valdosta	79	243	228	217	83	120	346	173	278	121	152	298	167	317		118

Total mileages through Georgia

- 20: 203 miles
- 85: 180 miles
- 75: 355 miles
- 95: 112 miles

More mileages at www.randmcnally.com/MC

Nickname: The Aloha State
Capital: Honolulu, N-4
Land area: 6,423 sq. mi. (rank: 47th)
Population: 1,360,301 (rank: 40th)
Largest city: Honolulu, 337,256, N-4

Index of cities Pg. 130

Mileages between cities

	Hilo	Honolulu	Kahului	Kailua	Kailua Kona	Kapa'a	Lahaina	Wahiawā
Hilo		225*	127*	237*	74	337*	149*	236*
Honolulu	225*		108*	11	177*	116*	130*	20
Kahului	127*	108*		22*	93*	214*	22	119*
Kailua Kona	74	177*	93*	188*		283*	116*	188*
Kapa'a	337*	116*	214*	128*	283*		236*	128*
Kaunakakai	177*	68*	55*	79*	144*	174*	77*	79*
Lahaina	149*	130*	22	43*	116*	236*		141*
Wahiawā	236*	20	119*	26	188*	128*	141*	

*Via plane

Total mileages through Hawaii
H1 27 miles
H2 8 miles
H3 15 miles

More mileages at www.randmcnally.com/MC

Plan a trip at www.randmcnally.com/HI

Tourism Information
Hawaii Visitors & Convention Bureau:
(800) 464-2924, (808) 923-1811; www.gohawaii.com

Road Conditions & Construction
(808) 597-2220; hidot.hawaii.gov

Toll Road Information
No toll roads

Determining Distances
(segments one mile or less not shown)
Cumulative miles (red): the distance between red arrows
Intermediate miles (black): the distance between intersections & places

t travel info at www.randmcnally.com/ID

sm Information
Tourism: (800) 847-4843, (208) 334-2470;
.visitidaho.org

Conditions & Construction 511 –
(888) 432-7623;
.511.idaho.gov, www.itd.idaho.gov

Toll Rd. Info
No toll roads

Determining Distances
(segments of one mile or less not shown)
Cumulative miles (red): the distance between red arrows
Intermediate miles (black): the distance between intersections & places

Total mileages through Idaho
15 196 miles
84 276 miles
86 63 miles
90 74 miles

More mileages at www.randmcnally.com/MC

Mileages between cities	Boise	Coeur d'Alene	Lewiston	Missoula, MT	Mountain Home	Pocatello	Salmon	Twin Falls
Boise		383	268	367	44	234	247	128
Bonners Ferry	459	76	191	212	504	573	351	589
Coeur d'Alene	383		115	166	428	525	303	513
Idaho Falls	279	478	526	312	237	49	160	159
Lewiston	268	115		214	313	504	332	398
Pocatello	234	525	504	361	191		209	114
Salmon	247	303	332	138	287	209		247
Twin Falls	128	513	398	384	85	114	247	

Nickname: The Gem State
Capital: Boise, K-2
Land area: 82,747 sq. mi. (rank: 11th)
Population: 1,567,582 (rank: 39th)
Largest city: Boise, 205,671, K-2

Index of cities Pg. 130

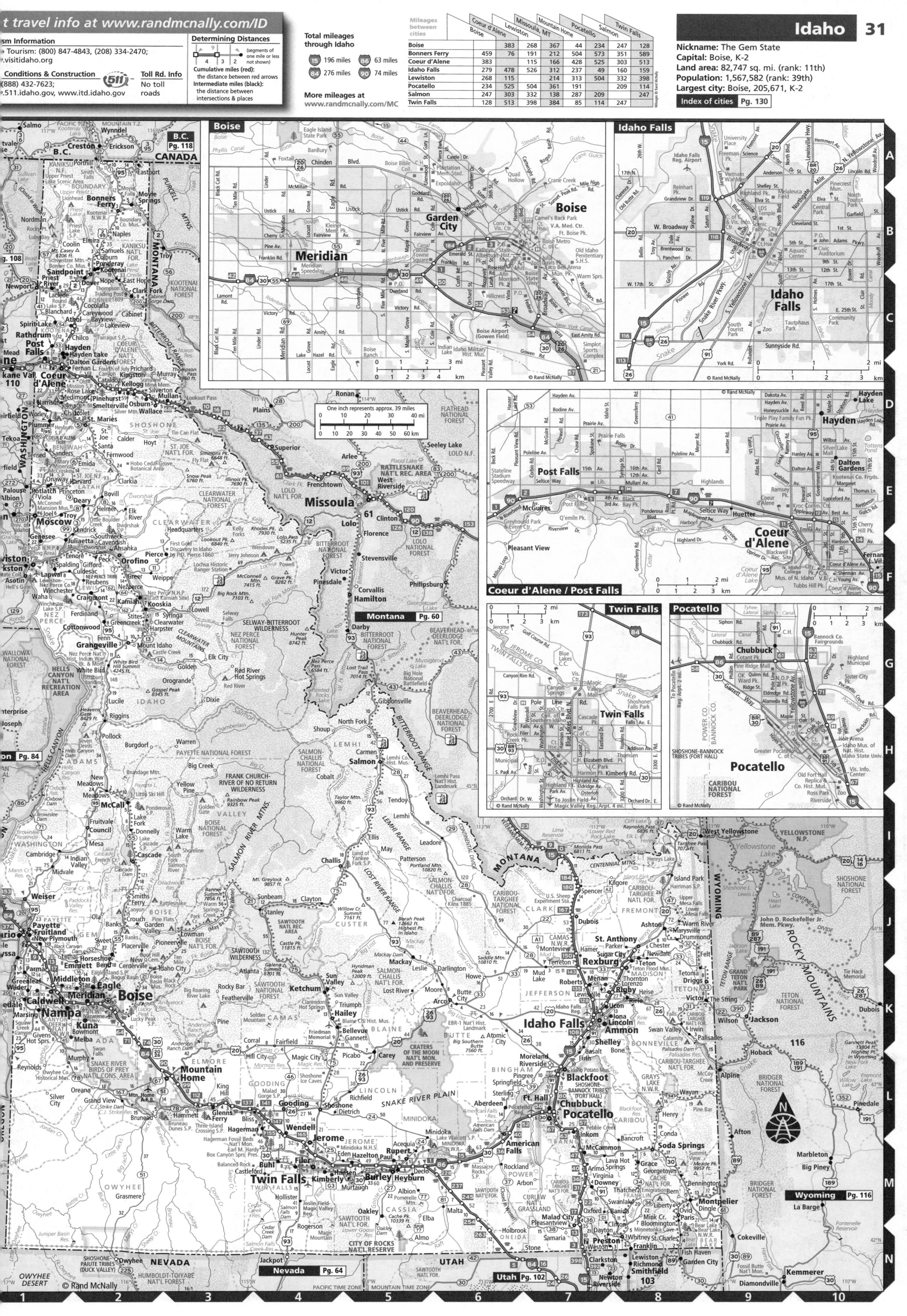

Nickname: Land of Lincoln
Capital: Springfield, J-8
Land area: 55,584 sq. mi. (rank: 24th)
Population: 12,830,632 (rank: 5th)
Largest city: Chicago, 2,695,598, C-13

Index of cities Pg. 130

Plan an Illinois trip at www.randmcnally.com/IL

Tourism Information
Illinois Office of Tourism: (800) 226-6632; www.enjoyillinois.com

Road Conditions & Construction
(800) 452-4368, (312) 368-4636; www.gettingaroundillinois.com, www.dot.il.gov

Toll Road/Bridge Information *(all use I-Pass)*
Chicago Skyway: (312) 552-7100; www.chicagoskyway.org
Illinois Tollway (all other toll roads): (800) 824-7277; www.illinoistollway.com

Determining distances along roads
Highway distances (segments of one mile or less not shown):
Cumulative miles (red): the distance between red arrows
Intermediate miles (black): the distance between intersections & p

Interchanges and exit numbers
For most states, the mileage between interchanges may be determ by subtracting one number from the other.

Mileages between cities	Bloomington	Carbondale	Champaign	Chicago	Decatur	Dubuque, IA	Kankakee	Lawrenceville	Moline	Mt. Vernon	Peoria	Quincy	Rockford	St. Louis, MO	Springfield	Waukegan
Carbondale	245		200	330	176	406	272	146	332	57	240	240	379	104	170	374
Champaign	51	200		135	48	256	78	130	182	147	89	194	185	180	85	180
Chicago	132	330	135		179	177	58	247	166	277	154	309	84	296	198	38
Moline	131	332	182	166	171	75	158	307		308	93	148	120	261	164	190
Peoria	38	240	89	154	78	167	108	214	93	215		130	138	168	71	184
Rockford	132	379	185	84	180	93	139	309	120	326	138	268		294	197	73
St. Louis, MO	162	104	180	296	135	335	252	144	261	79	168	139	294		98	326
Springfield	66	170	85	198	38	238	157	153	164	138	71	112	197	98		229

Total mileages through Illinois

55 313 miles
80 164 miles
70 156 miles
90 124 miles

More mileages at www.randmcnally.com/MC

City sights to see

- Adler Planetarium, G-15
- Art Institute of Chicago, E-13
- Chicago Botanic Garden, Glencoe, D-8
- Field Museum, G-14
- Frank Lloyd Wright Home & Studio, Oak Park, H-8
- John G. Shedd Aquarium, G-14
- John Hancock Center, C-13
- Lincoln Park Zoo, H-9
- Millennium Park, E-13
- Museum of Science & Industry, J-10
- Navy Pier, D-14
- Willis Tower, E-12
- Wrigley Field, G-9

Chicago Cultural Center

Chicago & Vicinity

LAKE MICHIGAN
El. 579 ft. above sea level

Chicago

ildren's Museum of Indianapolis

City sights to see

- Abraham Lincoln Presidential Library & Museum, Springfield, M-16
- Children's Museum of Indianapolis, Indianapolis, D-18
- Eiteljorg Museum, Indianapolis, E-17
- Fort Wayne Children's Zoo, Fort Wayne, L-19
- Illinois State Capitol Complex, Springfield, M-16
- Indiana State Capitol, Indianapolis, H-19
- Indiana State Museum, Indianapolis, H-19
- Indianapolis Motor Speedway and Hall of Fame Museum, Indianapolis, D-16
- NCAA Hall of Champions, Indianapolis, H-18
- President Benjamin Harrison Home, Indianapolis, F-20

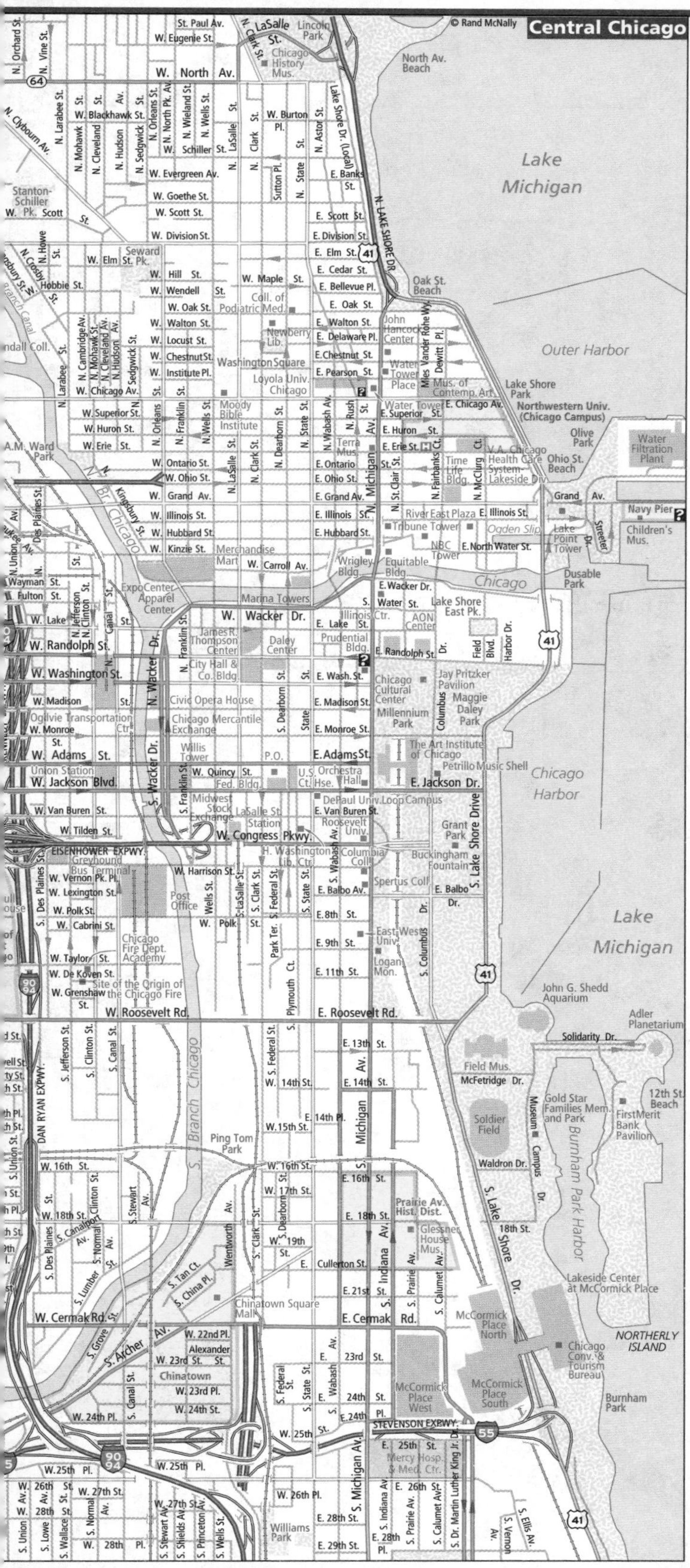

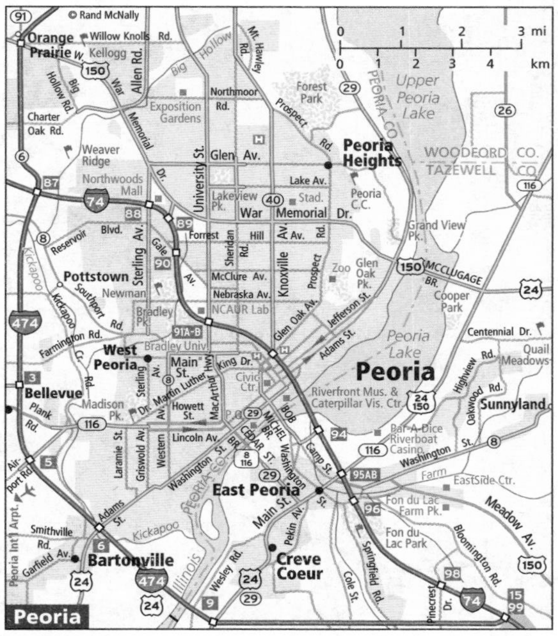

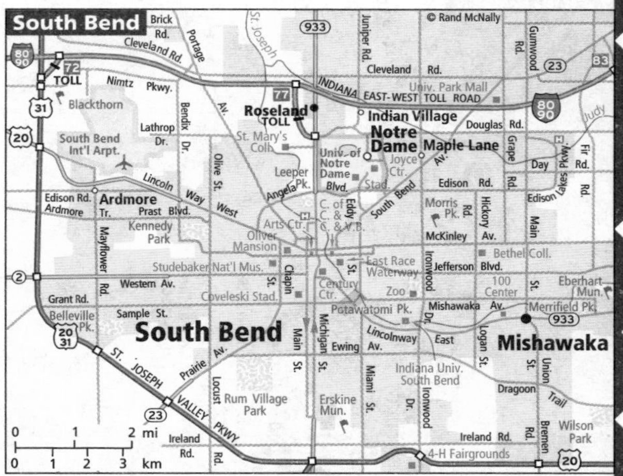

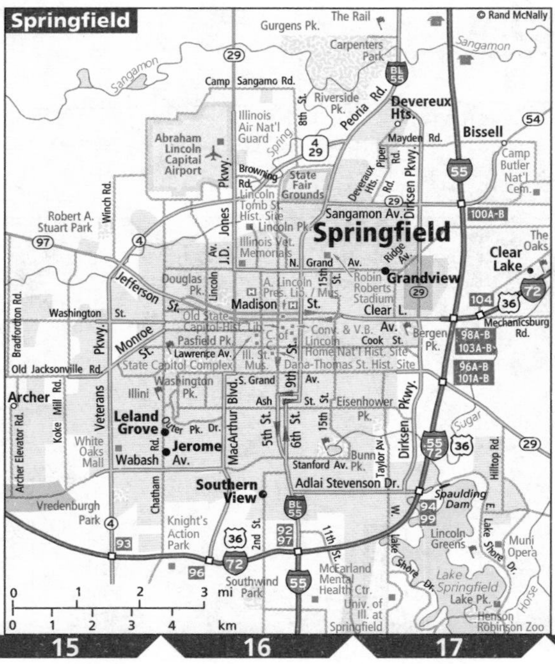

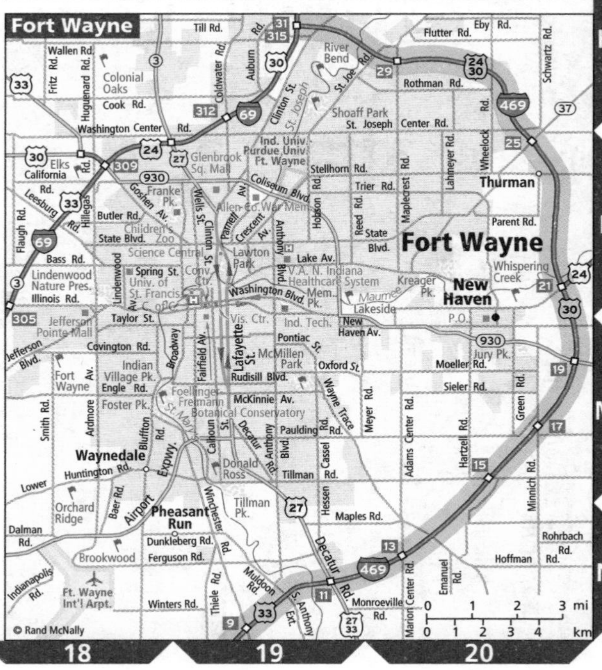

Central Chicago

Indianapolis

Central Indianapolis

Peoria

South Bend

Springfield

Fort Wayne

© Rand McNally

Nickname: The Hoosier State
Capital: Indianapolis, J-9
Land area: 35,867 sq. mi. (rank: 38th)
Population: 6,483,802 (rank: 15th)
Largest city: Indianapolis, 820,445, J-9

Index of cities Pg. 130

Explore Indiana at www.randmcnally.com/IN

Tourism Information
Indiana Office of Tourism Development: (800) 677-9800; www.visitindiana.com

Road Conditions & Construction
(866) 849-1368, (317) 232-5533; www.in.gov/dot

Toll Road Information
Indiana Toll Road (*E-ZPass*): (888) 496-6690; www.ezpassin.com

Determining distances along roads

Highway distances (segments of one mile or less not shown):
Cumulative miles (red): the distance between red arrows
Intermediate miles (black): the distance between intersections & pla

Interchanges and exit numbers
For most states, the mileage between interchanges may be determir by subtracting one number from the other.

Michigan Pg. 50

Ohio Pg. 78

Elkhart

Lafayette

Anderson

Muncie

Mileages between cities	Angola	Bloomington	Chicago, IL	Crawfordsville	Evansville	Fort Wayne	Gary	Greensburg	Indianapolis	Kokomo	Lafayette	Muncie	New Albany	Richmond	South Bend	Terre Haute
Evansville	347	120	289	178		309	273	202	180	234	198	244	112	255	320	109
Fort Wayne	39	178	160	162	309		132	147	129	86	117	72	238	92	89	205
Gary	135	200	30	118	273	132		203	151	127	91	196	266	222	64	164
Indianapolis	166	52	181	49	180	129	151	50		51	63	61	114	73	145	76
New Albany	276	88	296	163	112	238	266	94	114	168	178	172		184	256	146
Richmond	139	123	252	119	255	92	222	62	73	115	134	43	184		202	150
South Bend	77	195	93	135	320	89	64	183	145	87	106	143	256	202		216
Terre Haute	242	58	180	58	109	205	164	123	76	129	89	139	146	150	216	

Total mileages through Indiana

- 65: 261 miles
- 74: 172 miles
- 70: 157 miles
- 90: 156 miles

More mileages at www.randmcnally.com/MC

Iowa

Nickname: The Hawkeye State
Capital: Des Moines, I-10
Land area: 55,869 sq. mi. (rank: 23rd)
Population: 3,046,355 (rank: 30th)
Largest city: Des Moines, 203,433, I-10

Index of cities Pg. 131

Get more Iowa info at www.randmcnally.com/IA

Tourism Information
Iowa Tourism Office: (888) 472-6035; www.traveliowa.com

Road Conditions & Construction
511, (800) 288-1047; www.511ia.org, www.iowadot.gov

Toll Road Information
No toll roads

Determining distances along roads

Highway distances (segments of one mile or less not shown):
Cumulative miles (red): the distance between red arrows
Intermediate miles (black): the distance between intersections & places

Interchanges and exit numbers
For most states, the mileage between interchanges may be determined by subtracting one number from the other.

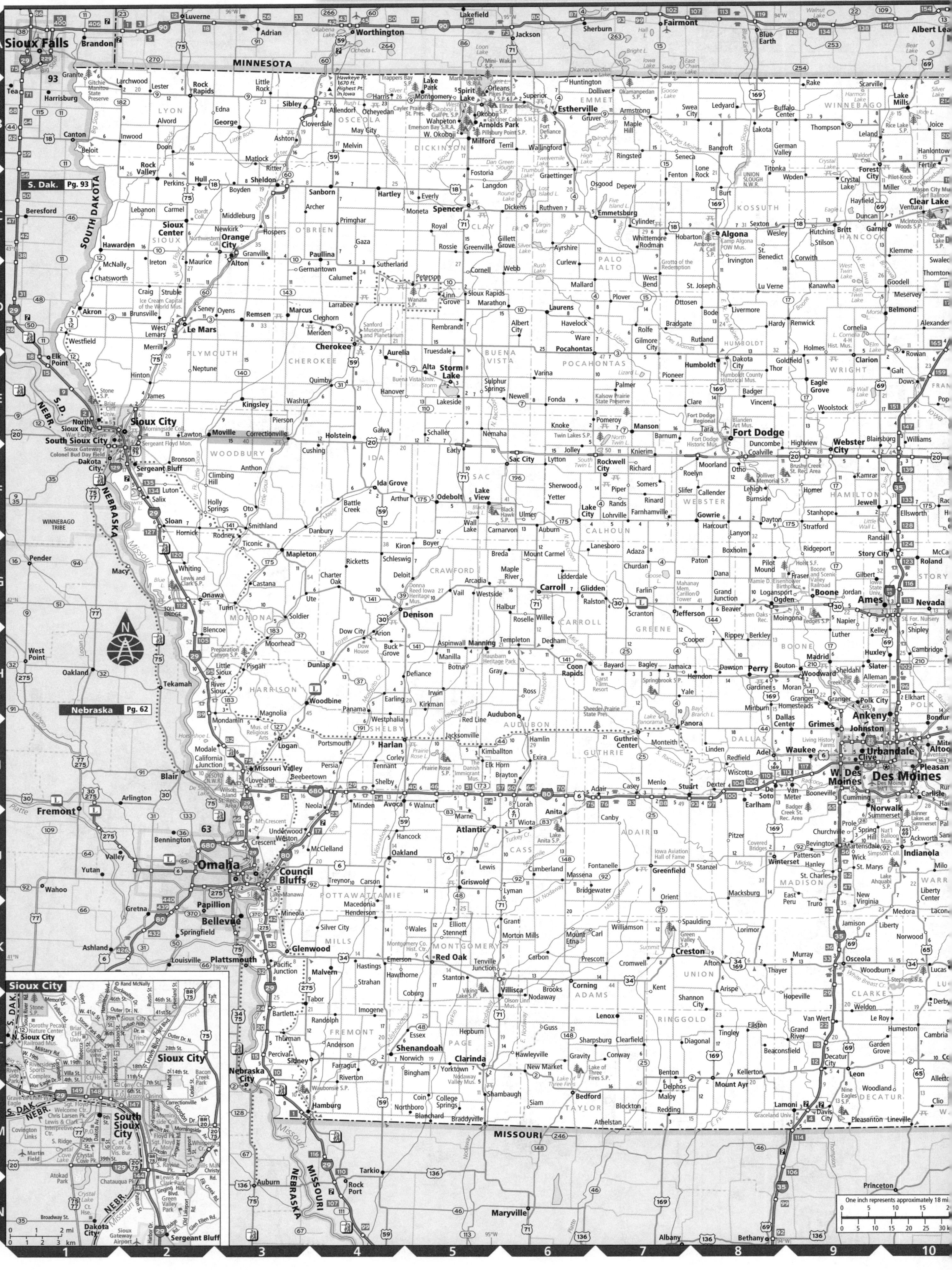

S. Dak. Pg. 93

Nebraska Pg. 62

Sioux City

One inch represents approximately 18 miles.

adison County bridge

Mileages between cities	Ames	Burlington	Cedar Rapids	Council Bluffs	Davenport	Decorah	Des Moines	Dubuque	Iowa City	Mason City	Ottumwa	Sioux City	Sioux Falls, SD	Spirit Lake	Storm Lake	Waterloo
Burlington	209		100	294	77	206	167	150	77	238	78	366	451	355	312	155
Cedar Rapids	108	100		253	82	105	126	70	28	136	110	268	357	252	212	53
Council Bluffs	160	294	253		295	328	127	327	241	246	213	94	180	176	122	253
Davenport	191	77	82	295		167	167	71	57	220	133	366	441	336	294	136
Des Moines	33	167	126	127	167	201		199	114	119	86	198	283	200	154	126
Dubuque	185	150	70	327	71	96	199		84	174	184	305	395	290	249	91
Mason City	91	238	136	246	220	88	119	174	165		203	200	222	118	135	83
Sioux City	175	366	268	94	366	304	198	305	312	200	285		85	109	78	218

Mileages © Rand McNally

Total mileages through Iowa

29 155 miles
80 303 miles
35 218 miles
218 257 miles

More mileages at www.randmcnally.com/MC

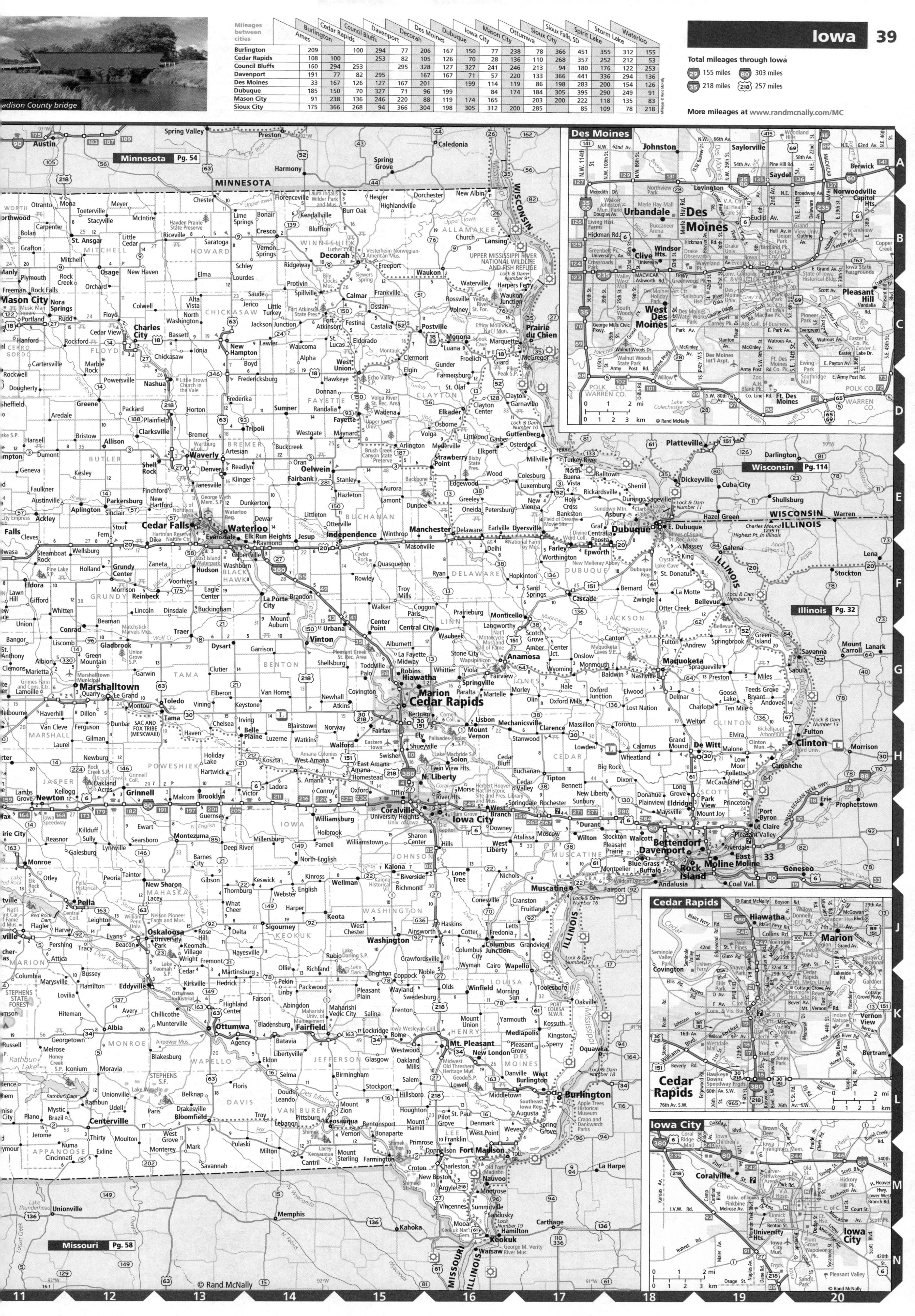

Nickname: The Sunflower State
Capital: Topeka, D-16
Land area: 81,815 sq. mi. (rank: 13th)
Population: 2,853,118 (rank: 33rd)
Largest city: Wichita, 382,368, H-13

Index of cities Pg. 131

Plan a Kansas trip at www.randmcnally.com/KS

Tourism Information
Kansas Dept. of Wildlife, Parks & Tourism: (800) 252-6727, (785) 296-2009; www.travelks.com

Road Conditions & Construction
511, (866) 511-5368, (785) 296-3566; 511.ksdot.org, www.ksdot.org

Toll Road Information
Kansas Turnpike Authority *(K-TAG)*: (316) 682-4537; www.ksturnpike.com

Determining distances along roads

Highway distances (segments of one mile or less not shown):
Cumulative miles (red): the distance between red arrows
Intermediate miles (black): the distance between intersections & places

Interchanges and exit numbers
For most states, the mileage between interchanges may be determined by subtracting one number from the other.

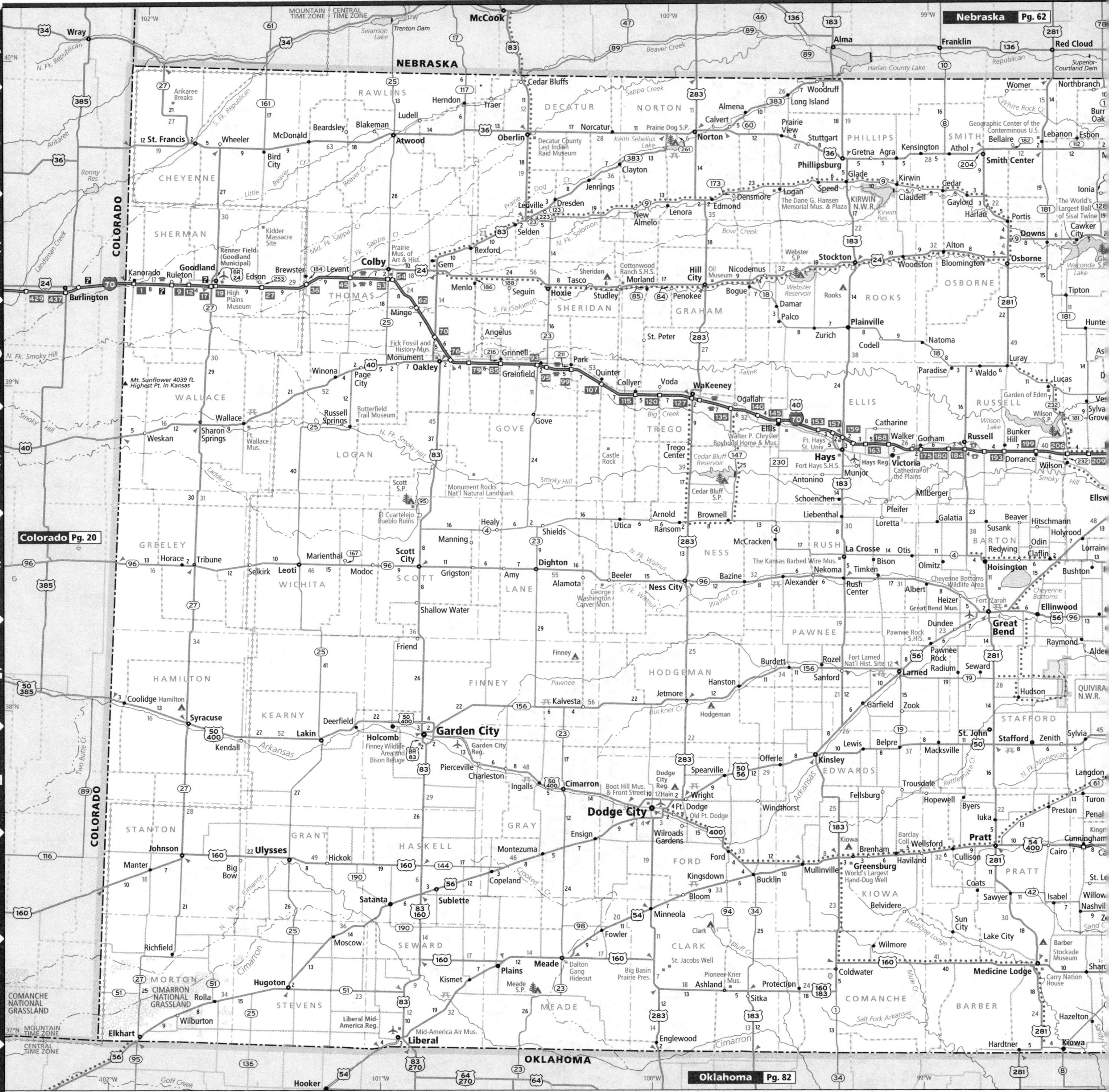

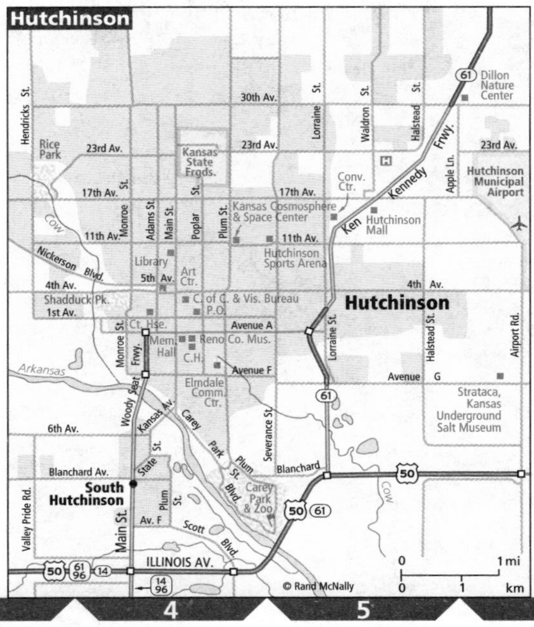

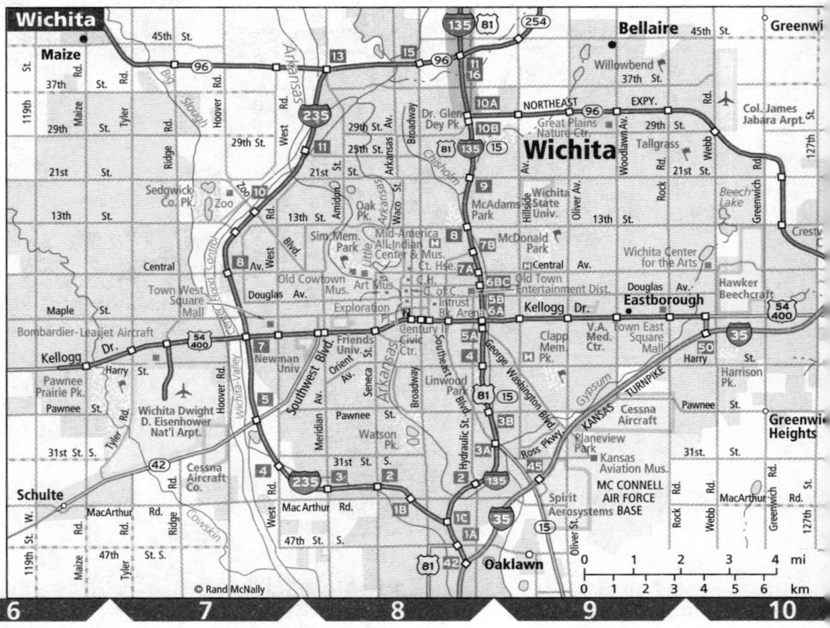

Nebraska Pg. 62

Colorado Pg. 20

Oklahoma Pg. 82

Salina

Hutchinson

Wichita

© Rand McNally

Mileages between cities

	Arkansas City	Atchison	Coffeyville	Dodge City	Emporia	Fort Scott	Goodland	Hays	Hutchinson	Joplin, MO	Kansas City	Liberal	Manhattan	Salina	Topeka	Wichita
Dodge City	212	323	288		240	304	192	104	122	337	333	82	227	164	273	154
Goodland	384	395	455	192	349	472		144	268	505	406	209	299	235	344	323
Joplin, MO	150	196	65	337	177	60	505	366	233		154	395	252	274	196	183
Kansas City	228	58	172	333	109	94	406	266	220	154		406	117	173	62	196
Salina	151	160	224	164	117	238	235	96	65	274	173	246	65		109	90
Smith Center	266	213	338	195	231	342	175	91	155	387	263	277	150	117	206	205
Topeka	170	55	155	273	58	136	344	204	162	196	62	349	56	109		137
Wichita	61	188	134	154	85	149	323	183	51	183	196	212	130	90	137	

Total mileages through Kansas

- 35: 235 miles
- 70: 424 miles
- 56: 464 miles
- 81: 220 miles

More mileages at www.randmcnally.com/MC

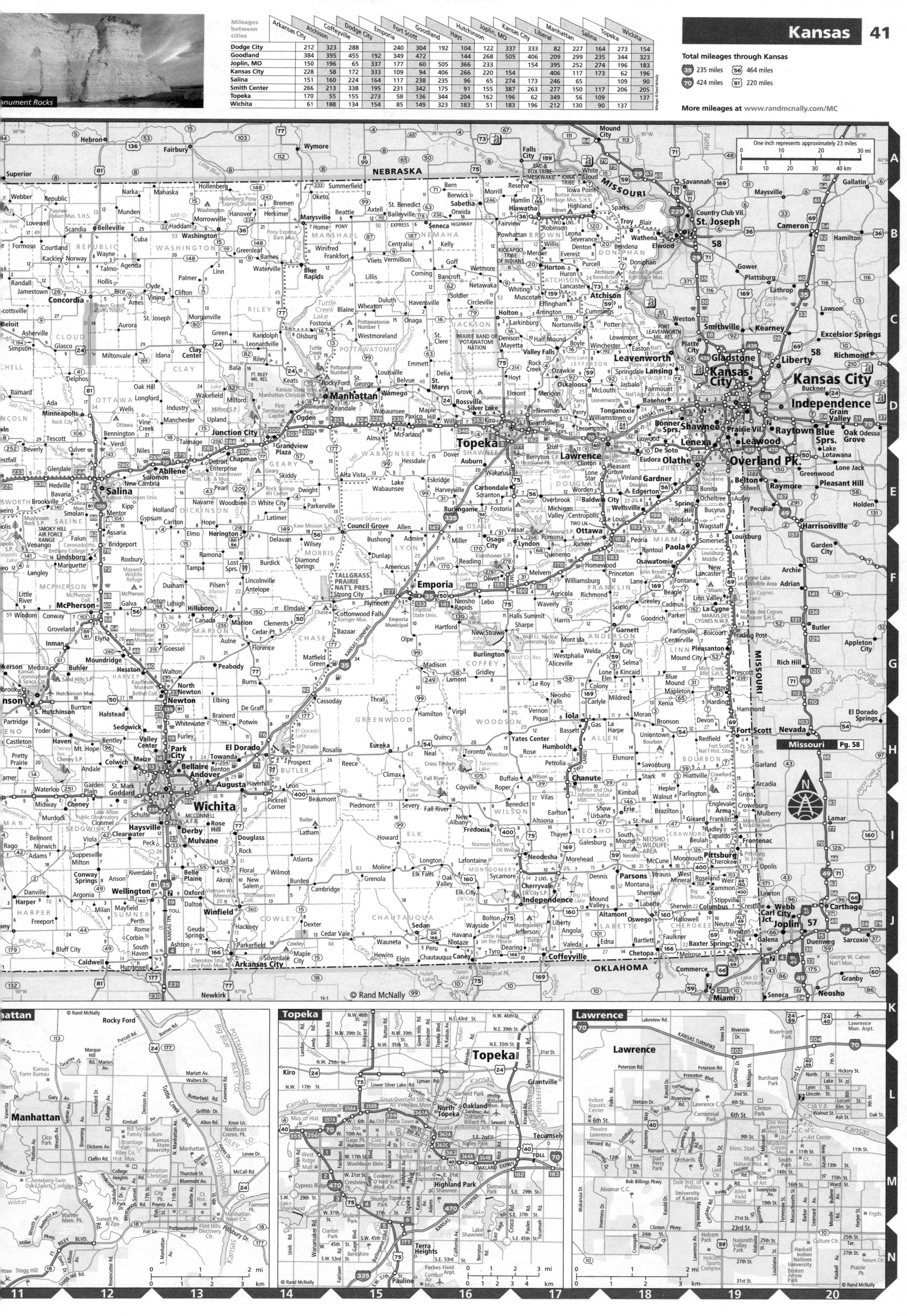

Kentucky

Nickname: The Bluegrass State
Capital: Frankfort, G-11
Land area: 39,728 sq. mi. (rank: 36th)
Population: 4,339,367 (rank: 26th)
Largest city: Louisville, 597,337, G-8

Index of cities Pg. 131

Explore Kentucky at www.randmcnally.com/KY

Tourism Information
Kentucky Department of Travel: (800) 225-8747; www.kentuckytourism.com

Road Conditions & Construction
511

Toll Road Information
No toll roads

Determining distances along roads
Highway distances (segments of one mile or less not shown):
Cumulative miles (red): the distance between red arrows
Intermediate miles (black): the distance between intersections & places

Interchanges and exit numbers
For most states, the mileage between interchanges may be determined by subtracting one number from the other.

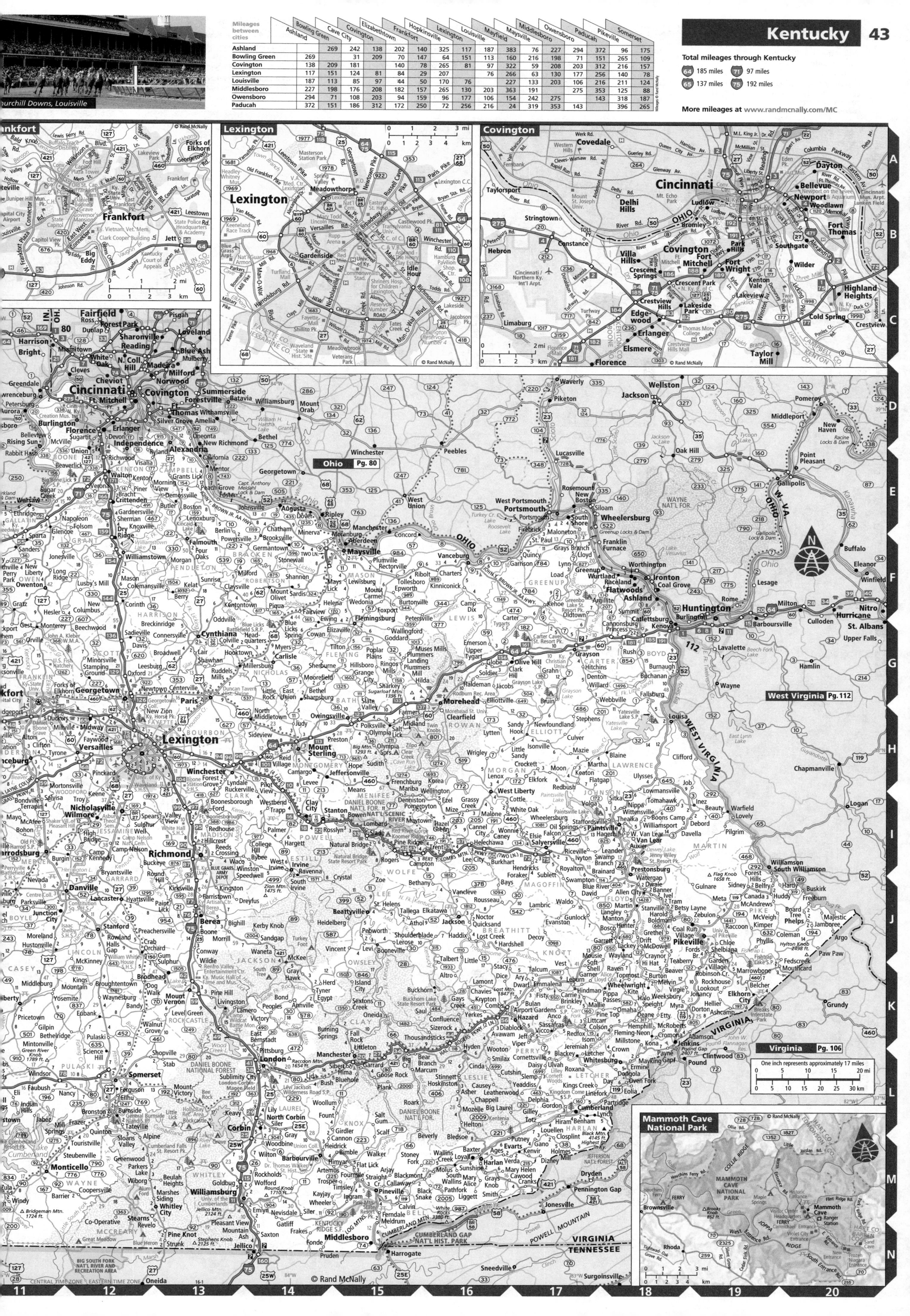

Mileages between cities

	Ashland	Bowling Green	Cave City	Covington	Elizabethtown	Frankfort	Hopkinsville	Lexington	Louisville	Mayfield	Maysville	Middlesboro	Owensboro	Paducah	Pikeville	Somerset
Ashland		269	242	138	202	140	325	117	187	383	76	227	294	372	96	175
Bowling Green	269		31	209	70	147	64	151	113	160	216	198	71	151	265	109
Covington	138	209	181		140	78	265	81	97	322	59	208	203	312	216	157
Lexington	117	151	124	81	84	29	207		76	266	63	130	177	256	140	78
Louisville	187	113	85	97	44	50	170	76		227	133	203	106	216	211	124
Middlesboro	227	198	176	208	182	157	265	130	203	363	191		275	353	125	88
Owensboro	294	71	108	203	94	159	96	177	106	154	242	275		143	318	187
Paducah	372	151	186	312	172	250	72	256	216	24	319	353	143		396	265

Total mileages through Kentucky

64: 185 miles; 71: 97 miles; 65: 137 miles; 75: 192 miles

More mileages at www.randmcnally.com/MC

Louisiana

Nickname: The Pelican State
Capital: Baton Rouge, G-7
Land area: 43,562 sq. mi. (rank: 33rd)
Population: 4,533,372 (rank: 25th)
Largest city: New Orleans, 343,829, H-9

Index of cities Pg. 131

Mileages between cities

	Baton Rouge	Beaumont, TX	Houma	Lake Charles	Monroe	New Orleans	Shreveport	Vicksburg, MS
Alexandria	125	155	190	97	95	218	123	147
Baton Rouge		183	85	124	186	79	250	157
Gulfport, MS	134	318	131	258	276	78	375	201
Lafayette	55	133	102	73	182	134	211	212
Lake Charles	124	60	177		190	203	184	243
New Orleans	79	262	56	203	281		340	207
Shreveport	250	206	314	184	98	340		171
Vicksburg, MS	157	301	234	243	74	207	171	

Total mileages through Louisiana

10: 274 miles
20: 190 miles
49: 208 miles
55: 66 miles

More mileages at www.randmcnally.com/MC

Get travel info at www.randmcnally.com/LA

Tourism Information
Office of Tourism:
(800) 994-8626; www.louisianatravel.com

Toll Bridge (Lake Ponchartrain Causeway)
(504) 835-3118, (985) 674-3641;
www.thecauseway.us

Road Conditions & Construction
511, (877) 452-3683
www.511la.org
www.dotd.la.gov

Arkansas Pg. 10
Mississippi Pg. 56
Texas Pg. 100

One inch represents approximately 29 miles

Plan a trip at www.randmcnally.com/ME

ourism Information
laine Office of Tourism: (888) 624-6345; www.visitmaine.com

oad Conditions & Construction
11, (866) 282-7578,
07) 624-3595;
ww.511maine.gov
ww.maine.gov/mdot

Toll Road Information
Maine Turnpike Authority *(E-ZPass)*:
(888) 682-7277
www.maineturnpike.com

Determining Distances
(segments of one mile or less not shown)
Cumulative miles (red): the distance between red arrows
Intermediate miles (black): the distance between intersections & places

Total mileages through Maine
95: 299 miles — 2: 273 miles
1: 315 miles — 201: 164 miles

More mileages at
www.randmcnally.com/MC

Mileages between cities	Auburn	Bangor	Bar Harbor	Eastport	Houlton	Millinocket	Portland	Rangeley
Bangor	107		47	120	118	72	128	120
Eastport	226	120	118		115	125	247	242
Houlton	225	118	167	115		69	246	238
Madawaska	326	219	267	218	102	170	347	339
Portland	35	128	174	247	246	181		118
Portsmouth, NH	81	180	225	301	298	231	51	165
Rangeley	84	120	165	242	238	153	118	
Waterville	53	55	101	174	173	107	75	77

Nickname: The Pine Tree State
Capital: Augusta, F-4
Land area: 30,862 sq. mi. (rank: 39th)
Population: 1,328,361 (rank: 41st)
Largest city: Portland, 66,194, H-3

Index of cities Pg. 131

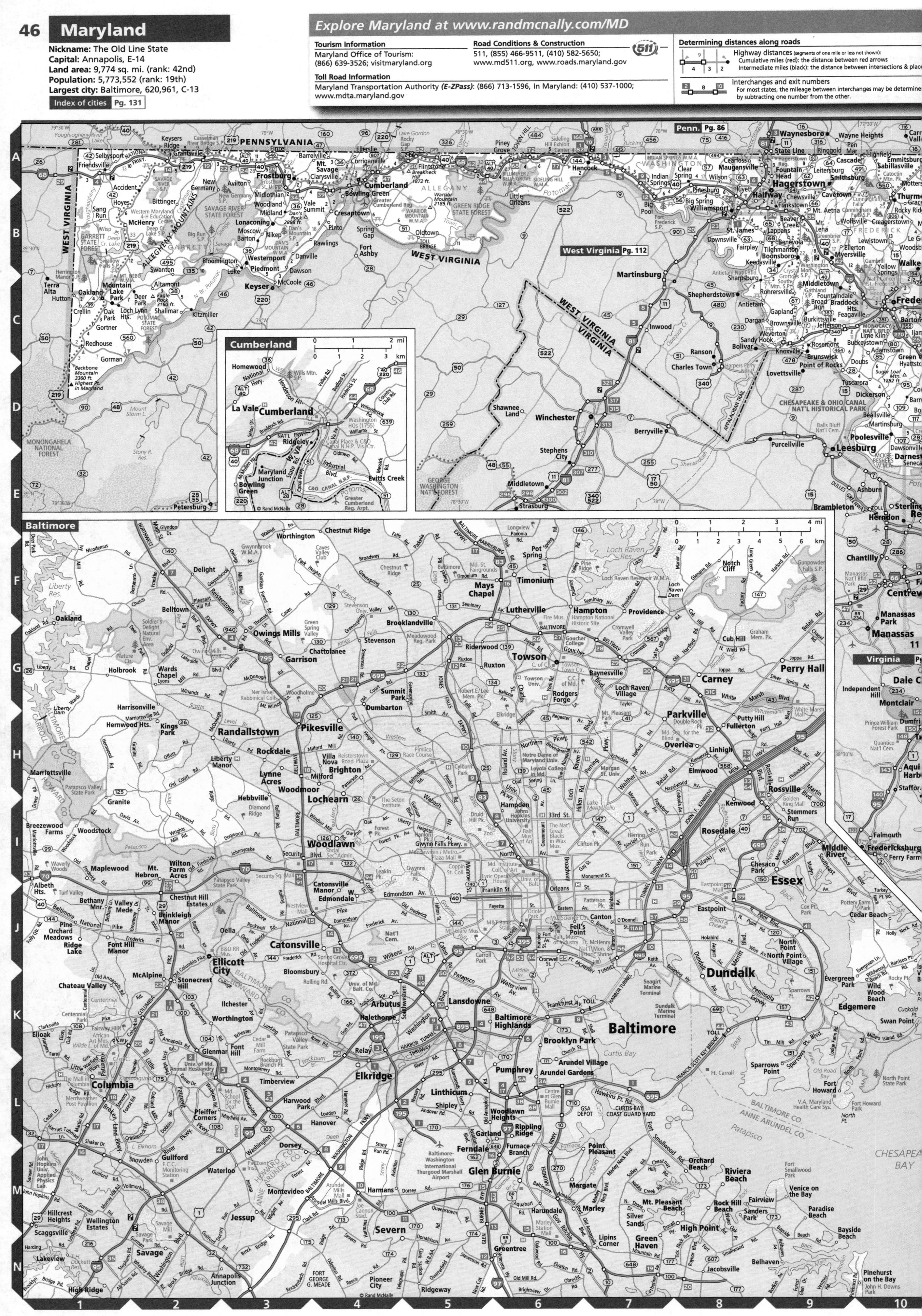
Maryland
Nickname: The Old Line State
Capital: Annapolis, E-14
Land area: 9,774 sq. mi. (rank: 42nd)
Population: 5,773,552 (rank: 19th)
Largest city: Baltimore, 620,961, C-13
Index of cities Pg. 131
Explore Maryland at www.randmcnally.com/MD
Tourism Information
Maryland Office of Tourism:
(866) 639-3526; visitmaryland.org
Road Conditions & Construction
511, (855) 466-9511, (410) 582-5650;
www.md511.org, www.roads.maryland.gov
Toll Road Information
Maryland Transportation Authority (E-ZPass): (866) 713-1596, In Maryland: (410) 537-1000;
www.mdta.maryland.gov
Determining distances along roads
Highway distances (segments of one mile or less not shown):
Cumulative miles (red): the distance between red arrows
Intermediate miles (black): the distance between intersections & places
Interchanges and exit numbers
For most states, the mileage between interchanges may be determined by subtracting one number from the other.
Penn. Pg. 86
West Virginia Pg. 112
Cumberland
Baltimore
Virginia
PENNSYLVANIA
WEST VIRGINIA
VIRGINIA
Baltimore
© Rand McNally

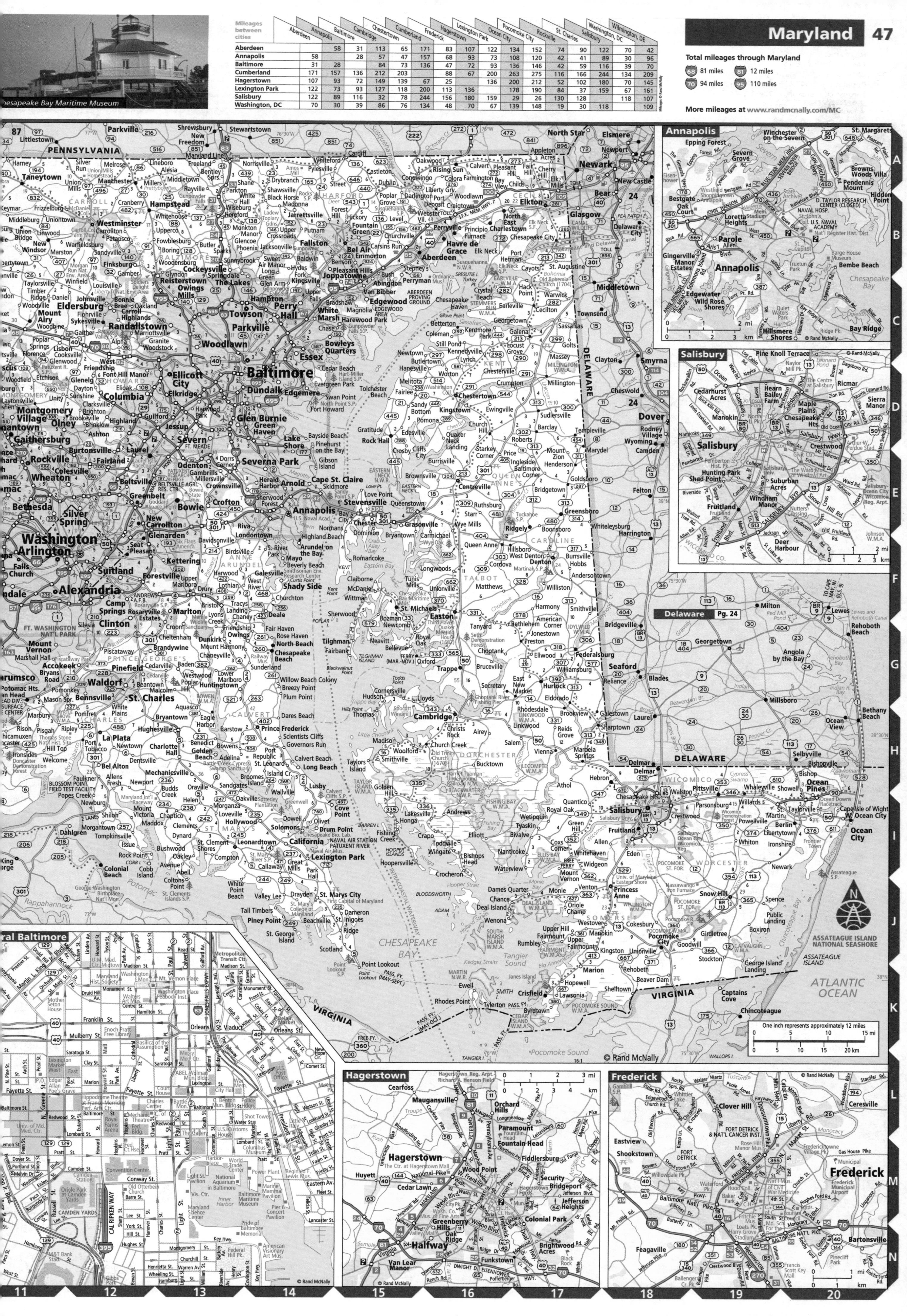

Mileages between cities	Aberdeen	Annapolis	Baltimore	Cambridge	Chestertown	Cumberland	Frederick	Hagerstown	Lexington Park	Ocean City	Pocomoke City	Rockville	St. Charles	Salisbury	Washington, DC	Wilmington, DE
Aberdeen		58	31	113	65	171	83	107	122	134	152	74	90	122	70	42
Annapolis	58		28	57	47	157	68	93	73	108	120	42	41	89	30	96
Baltimore	31	28		84	73	136	47	72	93	136	146	42	59	116	39	70
Cumberland	171	157	136	212	203		88	67	200	263	275	116	166	244	134	209
Hagerstown	107	93	72	149	139	67	25		136	200	212	52	102	180	70	145
Lexington Park	122	73	93	127	118	200	113	136		178	190	84	37	159	67	161
Salisbury	122	89	116	32	78	244	156	180	159	29	26	130	128		118	107
Washington, DC	70	30	39	86	76	134	48	70	67	139	148	19	30	118		109

Nickname: The Bay State
Capital: Boston, E-14
Land area: 7,840 sq. mi. (rank: 45th)
Population: 6,547,629 (rank: 14th)
Largest city: Boston, 617,594, E-14

Index of cities Pg. 131

Plan a Massachusetts trip at www.randmcnally.com/MA

Tourism Information
Massachusetts Office of Travel & Tourism: (800) 227-6277, (617) 973-8500; www.massvacation.com

Road Conditions & Construction
511, Metro Boston: (617) 986-5511
Central: (508) 499-5511, Western: (413) 754-5511
www.mass511.com, www.mhd.state.ma.us

Toll Road Information
Mass. Dept. of Transportation (E-ZPass):
(877) 627-7745;
www.massdot.state.ma.us/highway

Determining distances along roads
Highway distances (segments of one mile or less not shown):
Cumulative miles (red): the distance between red arrows
Intermediate miles (black): the distance between intersections & places

Interchanges and exit numbers
For most states, the mileage between interchanges may be determined by subtracting one number from the other.

Mileages between cities	Boston	Brockton	Falmouth	Fitchburg	Gloucester	Greenfield	Lowell	Nantucket	New Bedford	North Adams	Pittsfield	Plymouth	Providence, RI	Provincetown	Springfield	Worcester
Boston		24	76	47	39	94	29	101*	58	157	136	40	50	116	90	43
Gloucester	39	63	114	74		120	47	140*	97	157	169	78	90	154	122	75
Lowell	29	50	102	32	47	78		130*	84	115	139	69	69	145	92	41
New Bedford	58	37	40	94	97	148	84	77*		182	161	37	31	91	114	71
Pittsfield	136	150	189	124	169	79	139	226*	161	22		167	130	240	51	98
Provincetown	116	106	69	162	154	208	145	78*	91	262	240	77	119		194	146
Springfield	90	103	143	77	122	38	92	180*	114	73	51	121	83	194		51
Worcester	43	56	96	26	75	72	41	133*	71	120	98	74	40	146	51	

*Via ferry

Mileages © Rand McNally

Total mileages through Massachusetts

90 136 miles · 93 47 miles
91 55 miles · 95 92 miles

More mileages at www.randmcnally.com/MC

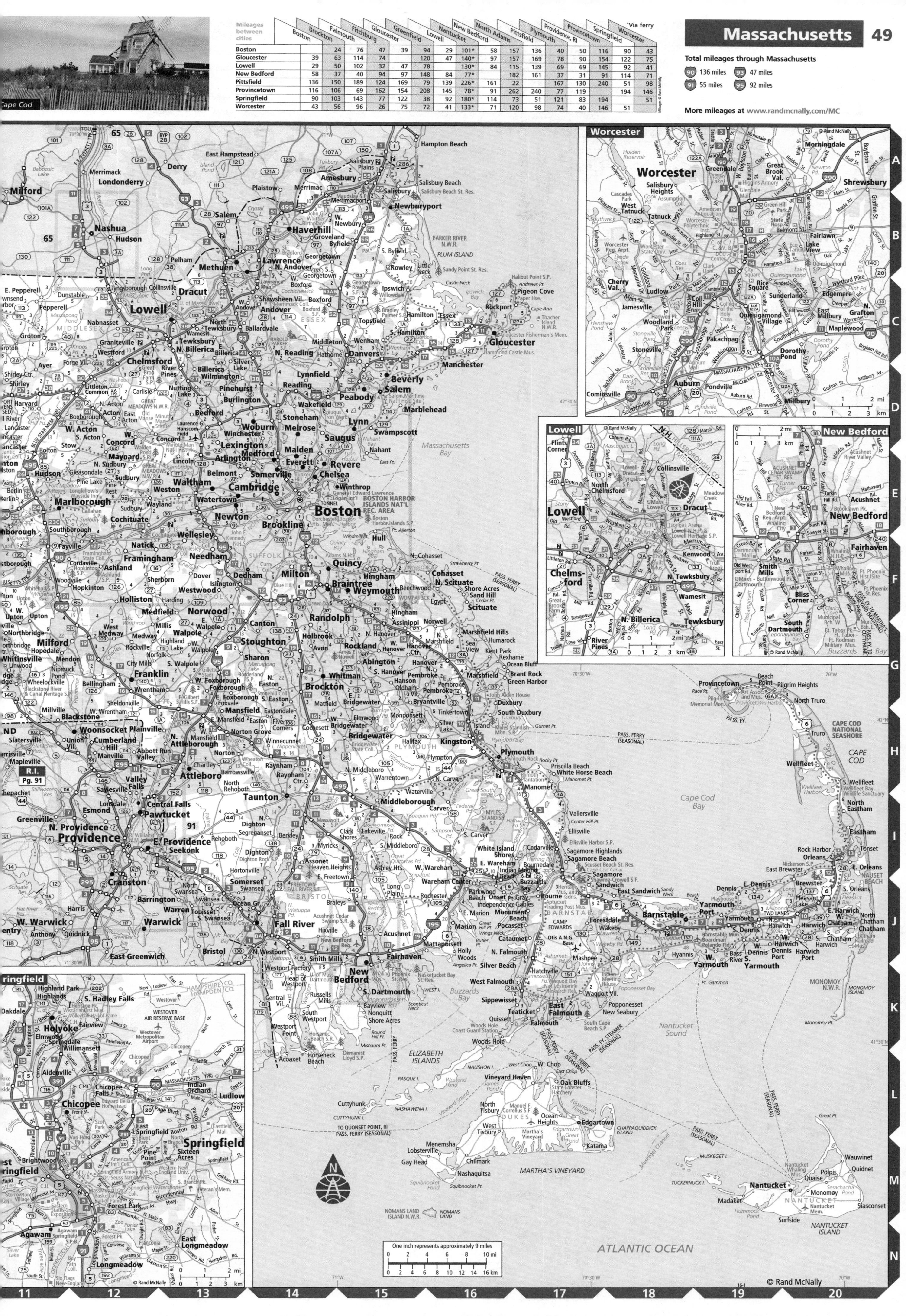

Nickname: The Great Lake State
Capital: Lansing, Q-9
Land area: 56,804 sq. mi. (rank: 22nd)
Population: 9,883,640 (rank: 8th)
Largest city: Detroit, 713,777, R-12

Index of cities Pg. 131

Get more Michigan info at www.randmcnally.com/MI

Tourism Information
Travel Michigan: (888) 784-7328, (800) 644-2489; www.michigan.org

Road Conditions & Construction
(800) 381-8477, (517) 335-3084; www.michigan.gov/drive

Toll Bridge/Tunnel Information
Ambassador Bridge (Detroit): (800) 462-7434; www.ambassadorbridge.com
Detroit-Windsor Tunnel ***(NEXPRESS or NEXUS)***: (313) 567-4422 ext. 200, (519) 258-7424 ext. 200; www.dwtunnel.com
Michigan Department of Transportation (all other toll bridges): (517) 373-2090; www.michigan.gov/mdot, www.mackinacbridge.org

Determining distances along roads
Highway distances (segments of one mile or less not shown):
Cumulative miles (red): the distance between red arrows
Intermediate miles (black): the distance between intersections & place

Interchanges and exit numbers
For most states, the mileage between interchanges may be determined by subtracting one number from the other.

Lansing

Isle Royale National Park

Saginaw

For continuation see map at left

For continuation see map at right

For continuation see main map

Porcupine Mountains

Mileages between cities	Alpena	Chicago, IL	Detroit	Grand Rapids	Houghton	Ironwood	Kalamazoo	Ludington	Mackinaw City	Menominee	Muskegon	Port Huron	Saginaw	Sault Ste. Marie	Toledo, OH	Traverse City
Ann Arbor	227	240	43	132	538	584	98	228	272	473	172	102	86	329	51	238
Detroit	244	280		157	553	599	140	252	290	488	197	62	102	345	59	255
Flint	178	271	68	113	489	534	130	186	224	423	152	66	37	280	107	188
Grand Rapids	249	177	157		502	552	50	97	236	438	41	180	115	292	185	140
Ironwood	405	403	599	552	109		544	319	311	195	586	600	499	307	636	413
Kalamazoo	298	145	140	50	556	544		146	287	408	91	197	161	344	150	190
Lansing	228	216	90	68	494	539	75	162	228	429	107	122	88	284	118	180
Mackinaw City	94	412	290	236	266	311	287	218		200	251	290	188	56	327	102

Total mileages through Michigan

69 199 miles
94 275 miles
75 396 miles
96 192 miles

More mileages at www.randmcnally.com/MC

City sights to see

- Cranbrook Art Museum, Bloomfield Hills, G-5
- Detroit Zoo, Royal Oak, H-6
- Edsel & Eleanor Ford House, Grosse Pointe Shores, I-9
- Frederik Meijer Gardens, Grand Rapids, A-3
- Gerald R. Ford Museum, Grand Rapids, B-2
- Gerald R. Ford Presidential Library, Ann Arbor, B-10
- Henry Ford Museum, Dearborn, K-5
- Motown Historical Museum, Detroit, J-7
- New Detroit Science Center, Detroit, J-7
- Renaissance Center, Detroit, N-10
- University of Michigan, Ann Arbor, B-9

Detroit Institute of Art

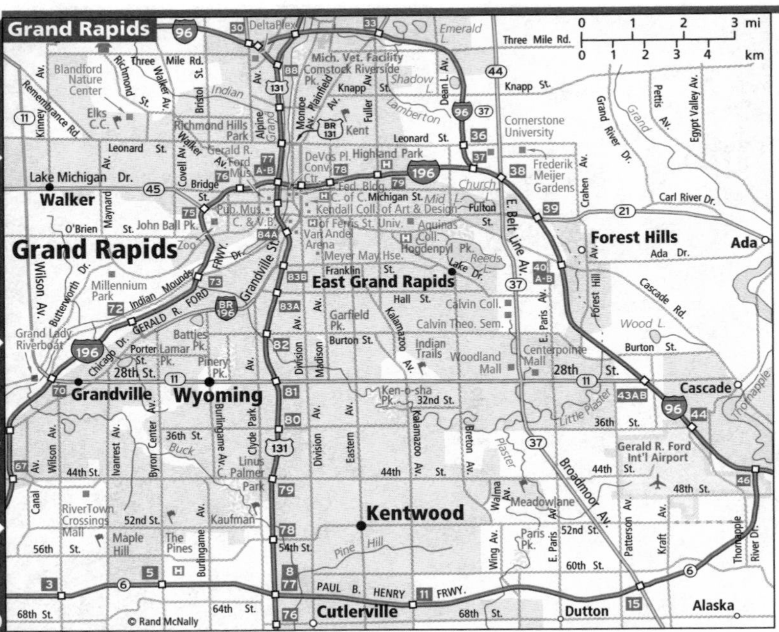

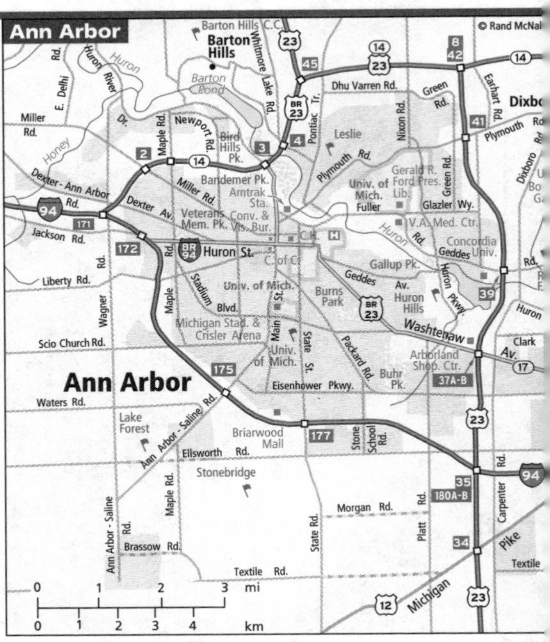

Grand Rapids

Flint

Ann Arbor

Detroit & Vicinity

Central Detroit

City sights to see

- Bell Museum of Natural History, Minneapolis, L-4
- Cathedral of St. Paul, St. Paul, M-7
- Frederick R. Weisman Art Museum, Minneapolis, M-4
- Mall of America, Bloomington, I-5
- Mill City Museum, Minneapolis, L-3
- Minneapolis Institute of the Arts, Minneapolis, N-2
- Minneapolis Sculpture Garden, Minneapolis, M-1
- Minnesota History Center, Minneapolis, M-7
- Minnesota State Capitol, St. Paul, L-7
- Ordway Center for the Performing Arts, St. Paul, M-7
- Science Museum of Minnesota, St. Paul, M-7
- Walker Art Center, Minneapolis, M-1

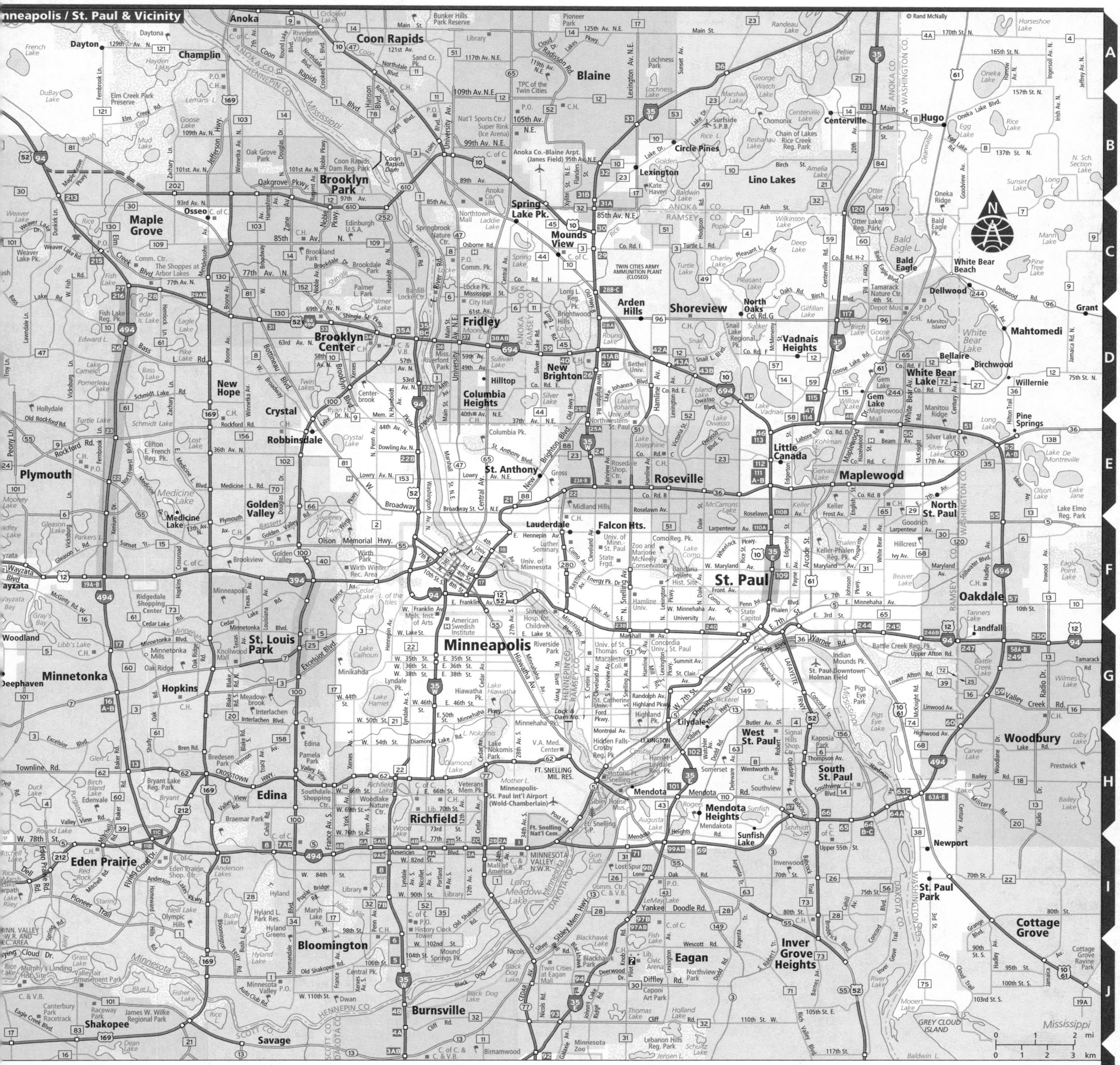

Minneapolis / St. Paul & Vicinity

Anoka, Dayton, Champlin, Coon Rapids, Blaine, Lino Lakes, Centerville, Hugo, Circle Pines, Lexington, Maple Grove, Osseo, Brooklyn Park, Spring Lake Pk., Mounds View, Arden Hills, Shoreview, North Oaks, Vadnais Heights, White Bear Lake, Dellwood, Grant, Mahtomedi, Birchwood, Willernie, Brooklyn Center, Fridley, New Brighton, Hilltop, Columbia Heights, New Hope, Crystal, Robbinsdale, Plymouth, St. Anthony, Roseville, Little Canada, Maplewood, North St. Paul, Golden Valley, Lauderdale, Falcon Hts., St. Paul, Oakdale, Wayzata, Minneapolis, St. Louis Park, Minnetonka, Hopkins, Deephaven, Woodland, Landfall, Lilydale, West St. Paul, South St. Paul, Woodbury, Edina, Richfield, Mendota, Mendota Heights, Sunfish Lake, Newport, St. Paul Park, Eden Prairie, Bloomington, Inver Grove Heights, Eagan, Cottage Grove, Burnsville, Shakopee, Savage

0 1 2 mi
0 1 2 3 km

© Rand McNally

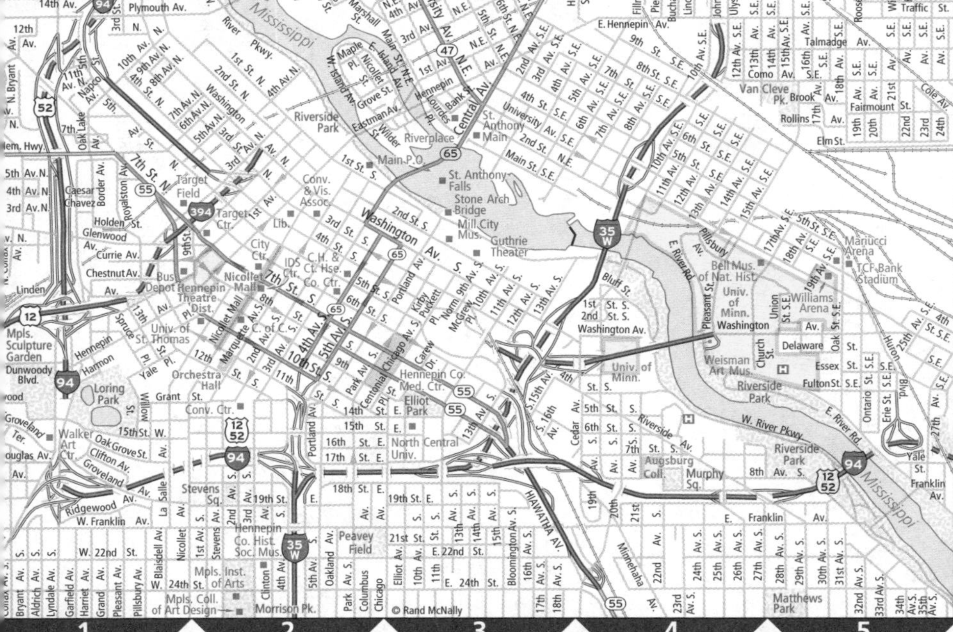

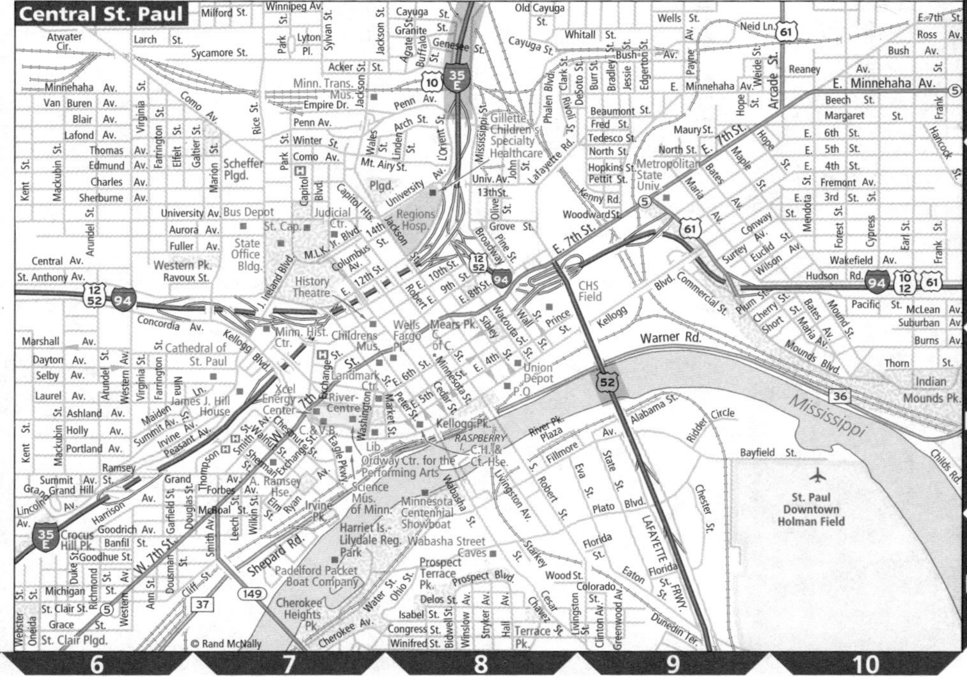

Minnesota

Nickname: The North Star State
Capital: St. Paul, O-10
Land area: 79,610 sq. mi. (rank: 14th)
Population: 5,303,925 (rank: 21st)
Largest city: Minneapolis, 382,578, O-9

Index of cities Pg. 132

Explore Minnesota at www.randmcnally.com/MN

Tourism Information
Explore Minnesota Tourism: (888) 868-7476, (651) 296-5029, (651) 757-1845; www.exploreminnesota.com

Road Conditions & Construction
511, (651) 296-3000, In MN: (800) 657-3774; www.511mn.org, www.dot.state.mn.us

Toll Road Information
No toll roads

Determining distances along roads

Highway distances (segments of one mile or less not shown):
Cumulative miles (red): the distance between red arrows
Intermediate miles (black): the distance between intersections & places

Interchanges and exit numbers
For most states, the mileage between interchanges may be determined by subtracting one number from the other.

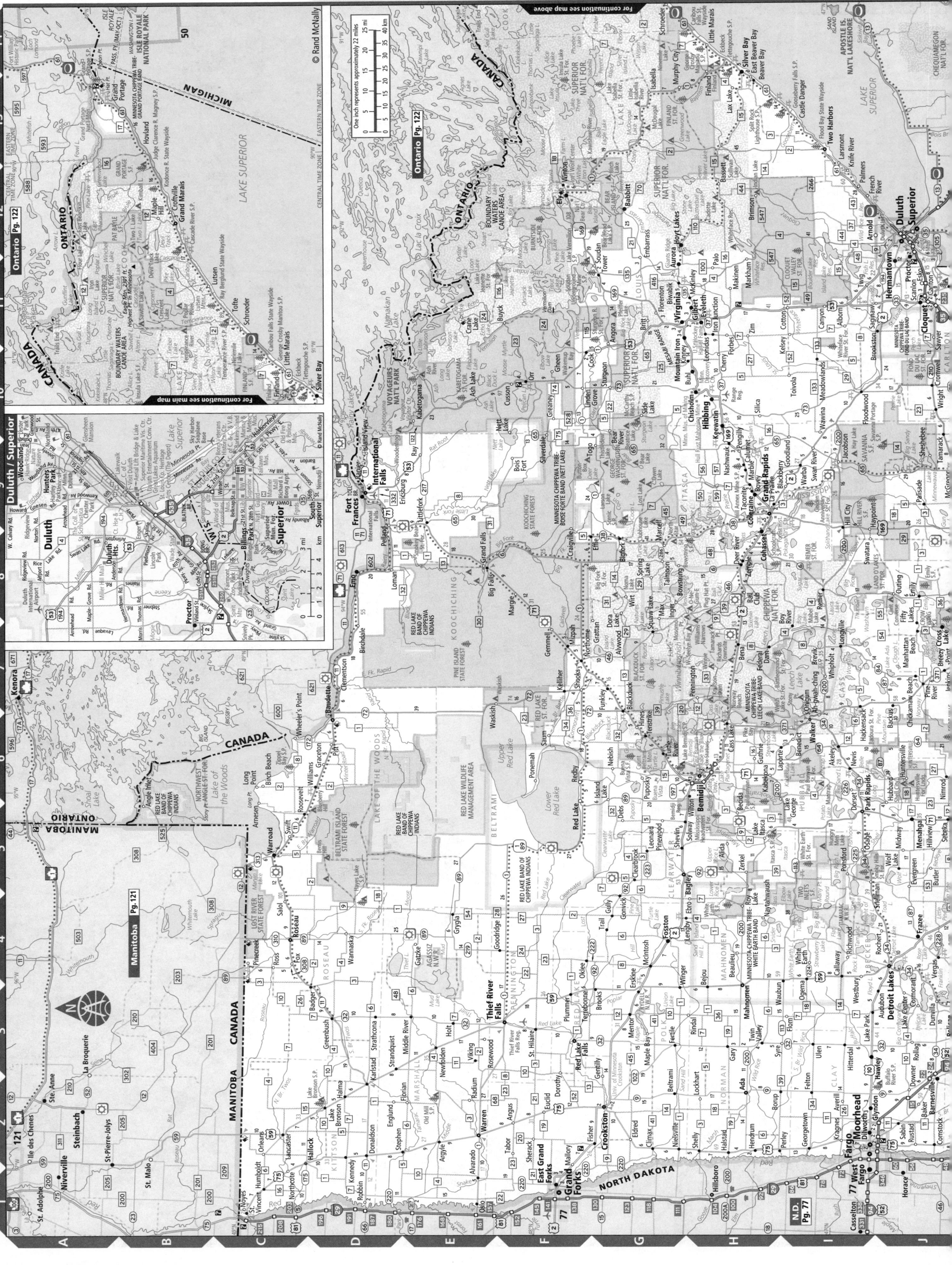

Mileages between cities

	Albert Lea	Bemidji	Brainerd	Duluth	Grand Forks, ND	Grand Marais	Hibbing	International Falls	Mankato	Marshall	Minneapolis	Moorhead	Rochester	St. Cloud	Sioux Falls, SD	Willmar
Bemidji	316		97	151	114	259	105	112	290	258	222	135	306	151	380	188
Duluth	247	151	113		266	110	76	162	233	273	152	250	226	141	390	204
Minneapolis	96	222	130	152	314	262	208	293	80	153		233	86	65	236	93
Moorhead	328	135	136	250	82	361	212	249	303	206	233		321	170	244	172
Rochester	62	306	213	226	401	338	280	366	86	194	86	321		153	236	178
St. Cloud	160	151	63	141	251	253	173	251	135	130	65	170	153		220	62
St. Paul	98	230	137	149	325	260	204	290	87	159	9	243	78	75	241	102
Sioux Falls, SD	176	380	281	390	319	500	456	494	155	91	236	244	236	220		158

Total mileages through Minnesota

35 260 miles
94 260 miles
90 276 miles
2 255 miles

More mileages at www.randmcnally.com/MC

Nickname: The Magnolia State
Capital: Jackson, H-6
Land area: 46,907 sq. mi. (rank: 31st)
Population: 2,967,297 (rank: 31st)
Largest city: Jackson, 173,514, H-6

Index of cities Pg. 132

Mileages between cities	Batesville	Biloxi	Hattiesburg	Jackson	Memphis, TN	Natchez	Tupelo	Vicksburg
Biloxi	320		80	172	379	228	315	214
Greenville	112	293	210	121	152	152	177	91
Jackson	149	172	89		209	103	190	44
Memphis, TN	61	379	297	209		304	105	245
Meridian	176	172	89	91	234	194	142	134
New Orleans, LA	335	90	109	183	394	171	340	207
Tupelo	74	315	232	190	105	283		225
Vicksburg	188	214	131	44	245	70	225	

Total mileages through Mississippi

10: 77 miles
20: 169 miles
55: 290 miles
59: 172 miles

More mileages at www.randmcnally.com/MC

Plan a trip at www.randmcnally.com/MS

Tourism Information
Visit Mississippi:
(866) 733-6477, (601) 359-3297; www.visitmississippi.org

Road Conditions & Construction
511, (601) 987-1211, (601) 359-7001;
www.mdot.ms.gov, www.mdottraffic.com

Toll Rd. Info
No toll roads

Determining Distances
(segments of one mile or less not shown)
Cumulative miles (red): the distance between red arrows
Intermediate miles (black): the distance between intersections & places

ateway Arch, St. Louis

City sights to see

- Andy Williams Moon River Theatre, Branson, M-8
- Anheuser-Busch Brewery, St. Louis, I-7
- Bass Pro Shops® Outdoor World®, Springfield, C-3
- Dolly Parton's Dixie Stampede, Branson, M-9
- Gateway Arch, St. Louis, L-4
- Laumeier Sculpture Park, St. Louis, J-4
- Magic House, Kirkwood, I-4
- Missouri Botanical Garden, St. Louis, I-6
- Shoji Tabuchi Theatre, Branson, L-7
- St. Louis Art Museum, St. Louis, H-6
- St. Louis Science Center, St. Louis, H-6
- St. Louis Zoo, St. Louis, H-6
- Shepherd of the Hills, Branson, K-6
- White Water, Branson, M-7

ngfield

Joplin

Cape Girardeau

ouis & Vicinity

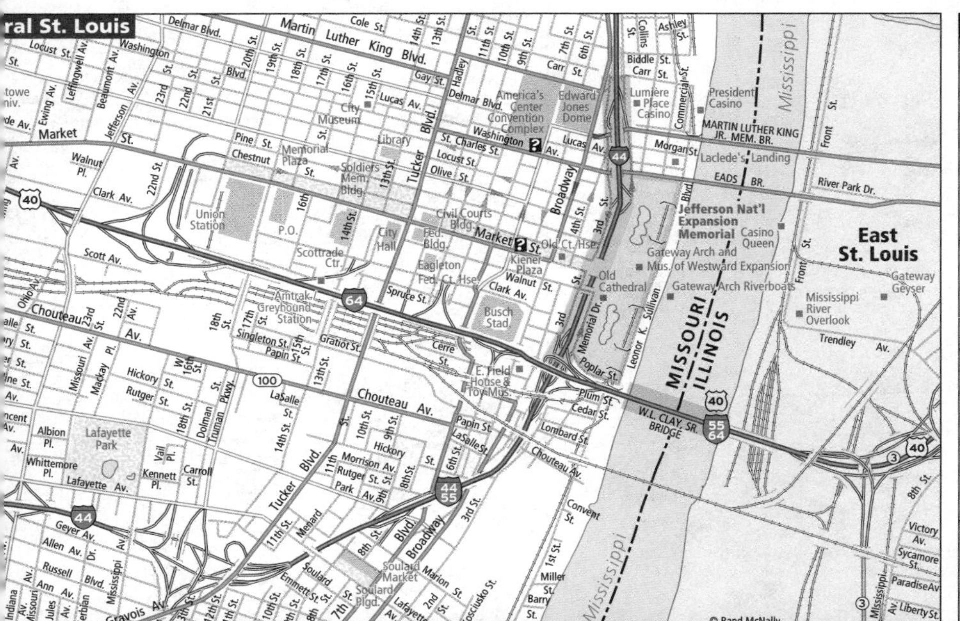

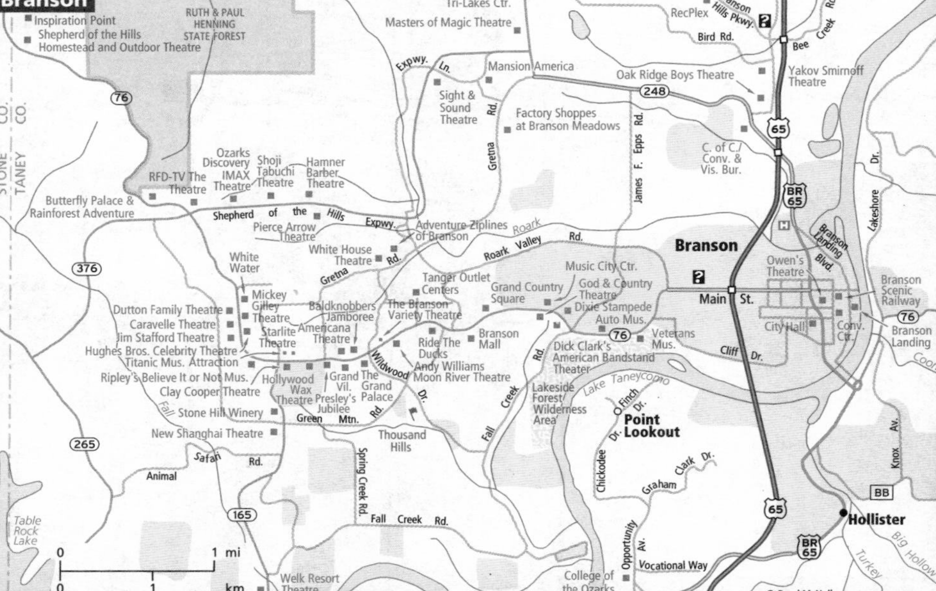

Nickname: The Show Me State
Capital: Jefferson City, G-14
Land area: 68,886 sq. mi. (rank: 18th)
Population: 5,988,927 (rank: 18th)
Largest city: Kansas City, 459,787, F-9

Index of cities Pg. 132

Explore Missouri at www.randmcnally.com/MO

Tourism Information
Missouri Division of Tourism: (573) 751-4133; www.visitmo.com

Road Conditions & Construction
(888) 275-6636, (573) 751-2551; www.modot.org

Toll Road Information
No toll roads

Determining distances along roads

Highway distances (segments of one mile or less not shown):
Cumulative miles (red): the distance between red arrows
Intermediate miles (black): the distance between intersections & places

Interchanges and exit numbers
For most states, the mileage between interchanges may be determined by subtracting one number from the other.

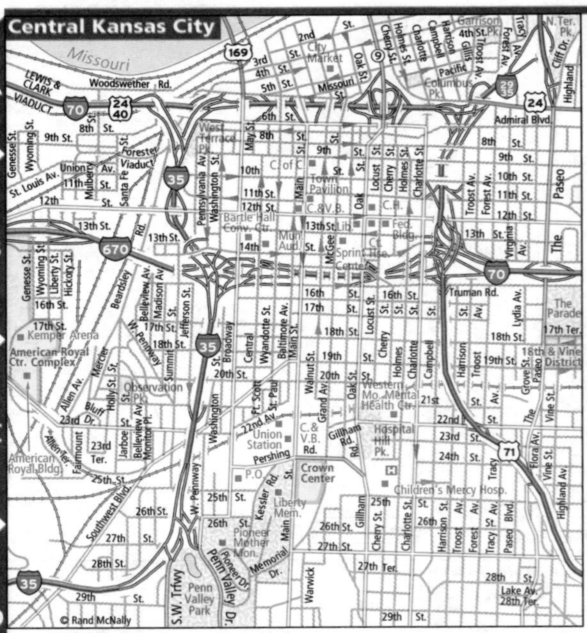

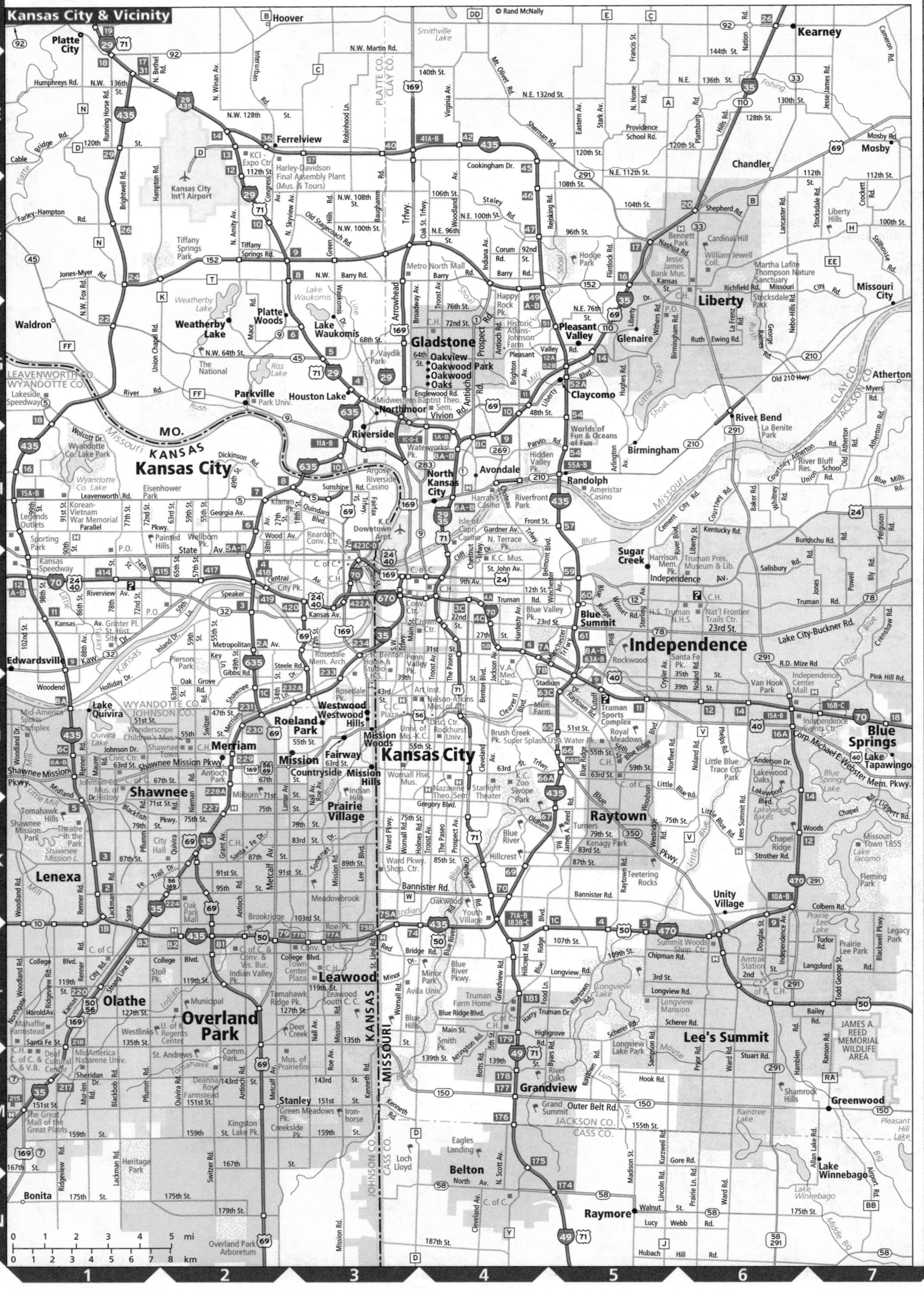

Central Kansas City

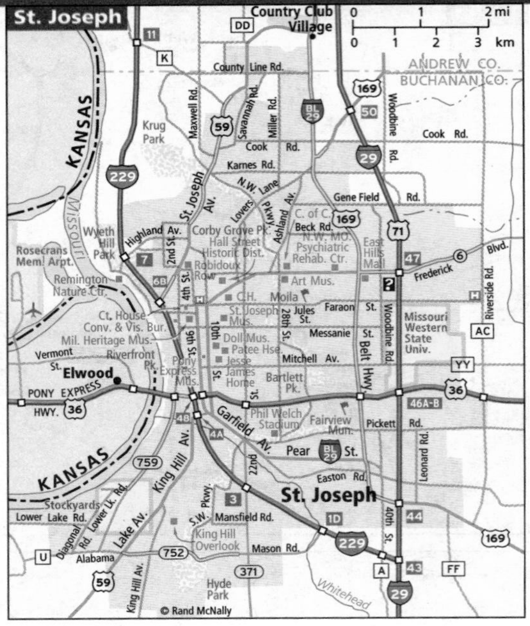

St. Joseph

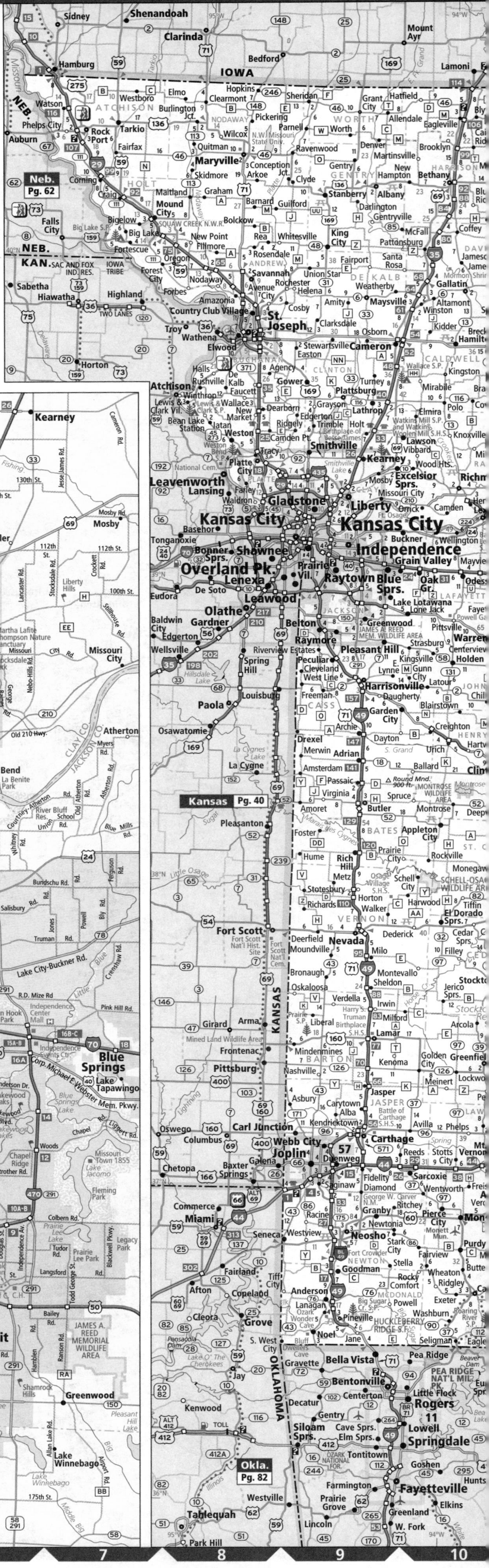

Kansas City & Vicinity

© Rand McNally

Neb. Pg. 62

Kansas Pg. 40

Okla. Pg. 82

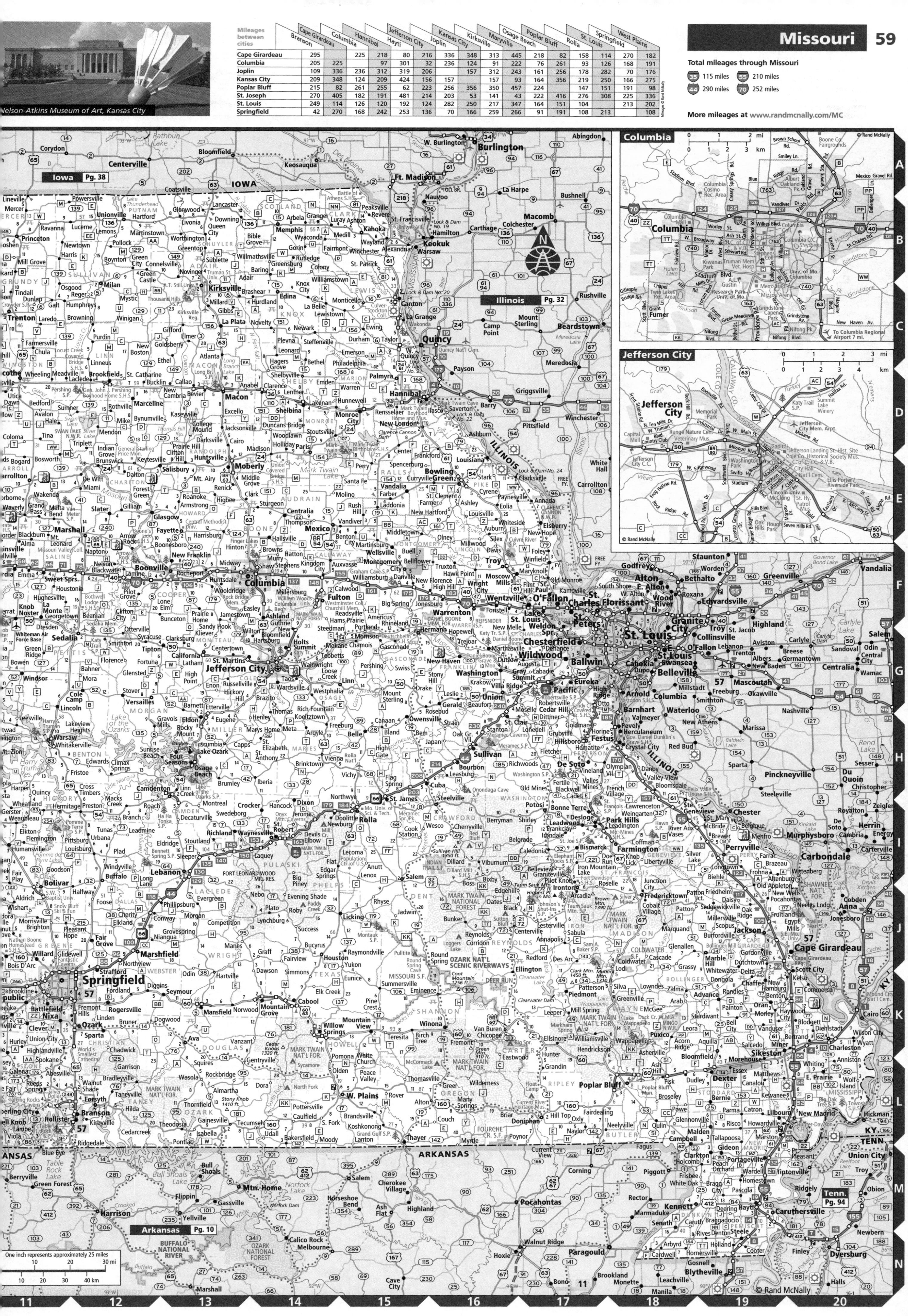

Mileages between cities

	Branson	Cape Girardeau	Columbia	Hannibal	Hayti	Jefferson City	Joplin	Kansas City	Kirksville	Maryville	Osage Beach	Poplar Bluff	Rolla	St. Louis	Springfield	West Plains
Cape Girardeau	295		225	218	80	216	336	348	313	445	218	82	158	114	270	182
Columbia	205	225		97	301	32	236	124	91	222	76	261	93	126	168	191
Joplin	109	336	236	312	319	206		157	312	243	161	256	178	282	70	176
Kansas City	209	348	124	209	424	156	157		157	93	164	356	219	250	166	275
Poplar Bluff	215	82	261	255	62	223	256	356	350	457	224		147	151	191	98
St. Joseph	270	405	182	191	481	214	203	53	141	43	222	416	276	308	225	336
St. Louis	249	114	126	120	192	124	282	250	217	347	164	151	104		213	202
Springfield	42	270	168	242	253	136	70	166	259	266	91	191	108	213		108

Mileages © Rand McNally

Total mileages through Missouri

- 35: 115 miles
- 55: 210 miles
- 44: 290 miles
- 70: 252 miles

More mileages at www.randmcnally.com/MC

Montana

Nickname: The Treasure State
Capital: Helena, G-7
Land area: 145,552 sq. mi. (rank: 4th)
Population: 989,415 (rank: 44th)
Largest city: Billings, 104,170, I-13

Index of cities Pg. 132

Get more Montana info at www.randmcnally.com/MT

Tourism Information
Montana Office of Tourism: (800) 847-4868; www.visitmt.com

Road Conditions & Construction
511, (800) 226-7623, (406) 444-6200; www.mdt511.com, www.mdt.mt.gov

Toll Road Information
No toll roads

Determining distances along roads
Highway distances (segments of one mile or less not shown):
Cumulative miles (red): the distance between red arrows
Intermediate miles (black): the distance between intersections & places

Interchanges and exit numbers
For most states, the mileage between interchanges may be determined by subtracting one number from the other.

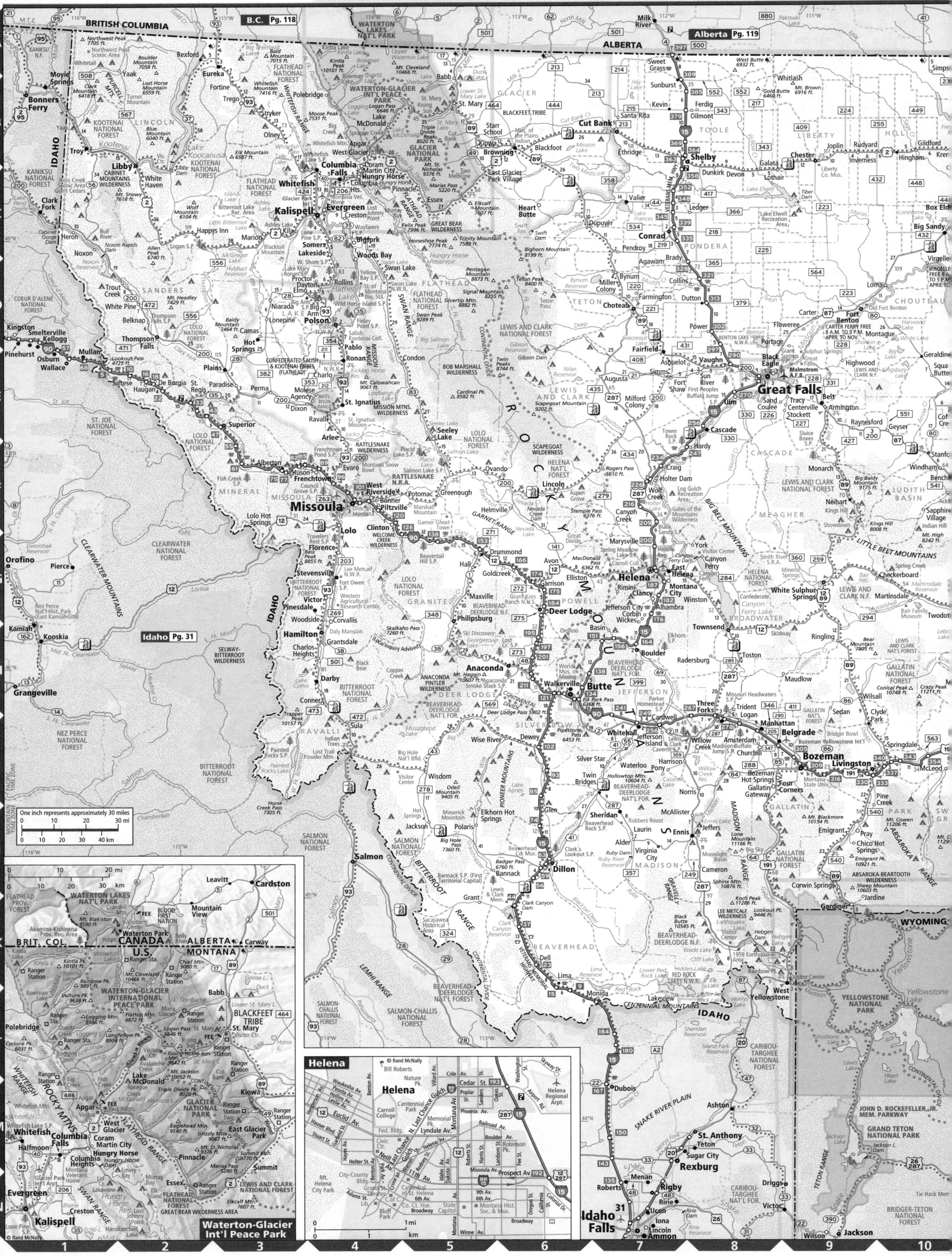

B.C. Pg. 118
Alberta Pg. 119
Idaho Pg. 31

One inch represents approximately 30 miles

Helena

Waterton-Glacier Int'l Peace Park

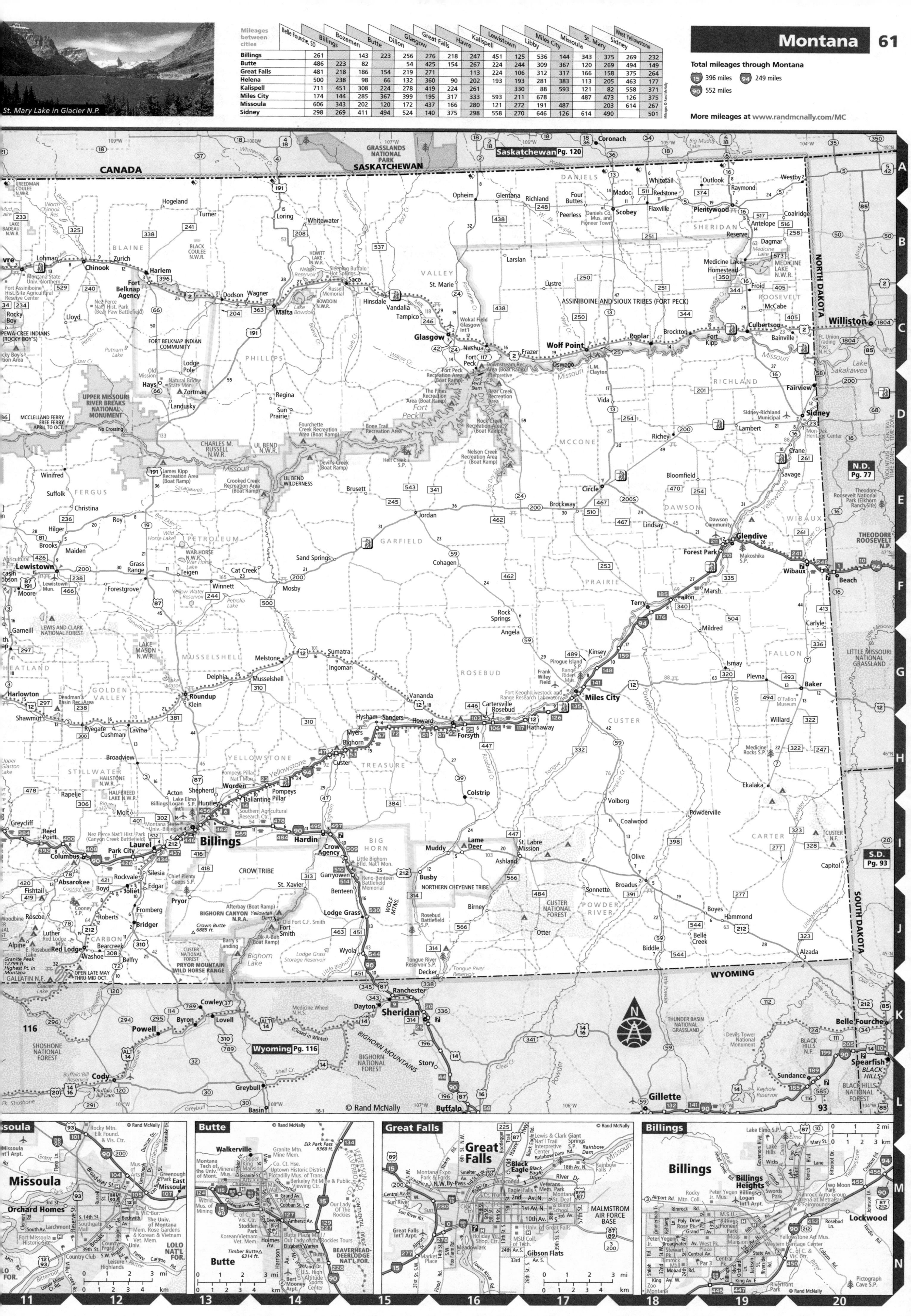

St. Mary Lake in Glacier N.P.

Mileages between cities	Belle Fourche, SD	Billings	Bozeman	Butte	Dillon	Glasgow	Great Falls	Havre	Kalispell	Lewistown	Libby	Miles City	Missoula	St. Mary	Sidney	West Yellowstone
Billings	261		143	223	256	276	218	247	451	125	536	144	343	375	269	232
Butte	486	223	82		54	425	154	267	224	244	309	367	120	269	494	149
Great Falls	481	218	186	154	219	271		113	224	106	312	317	166	158	375	264
Helena	500	238	98	66	132	360	90	202	193	193	281	383	113	205	463	177
Kalispell	711	451	308	224	278	419	224	261		330	88	593	121	82	558	371
Miles City	174	144	285	367	399	195	317	333	593	211	678		487	473	126	375
Missoula	606	343	202	120	172	437	166	280	121	272	191	487		203	614	267
Sidney	298	269	411	494	524	140	375	298	558	270	646	126	614	490		501

Total mileages through Montana

15: 396 miles
94: 249 miles
90: 552 miles

More mileages at www.randmcnally.com/MC

Nebraska

Nickname: The Cornhusker State
Capital: Lincoln, K-17
Land area: 76,872 sq. mi. (rank: 15th)
Population: 1,826,341 (rank: 38th)
Largest city: Omaha, 408,958, J-19

Index of cities Pg. 132

Plan a Nebraska trip at www.randmcnally.com/NE

Tourism Information
Nebraska Tourism Commision: (888) 444-1867; www.visitnebraska.com

Road Conditions & Construction
511, (800) 906-9069, (402) 471-4533; www.511.nebraska.gov, www.dor.state.ne.us

Toll Road Information
No toll roads

Determining distances along roads

Highway distances (segments of one mile or less not shown):
Cumulative miles (red): the distance between red arrows
Intermediate miles (black): the distance between intersections & places

Interchanges and exit numbers
For most states, the mileage between interchanges may be determined by subtracting one number from the other.

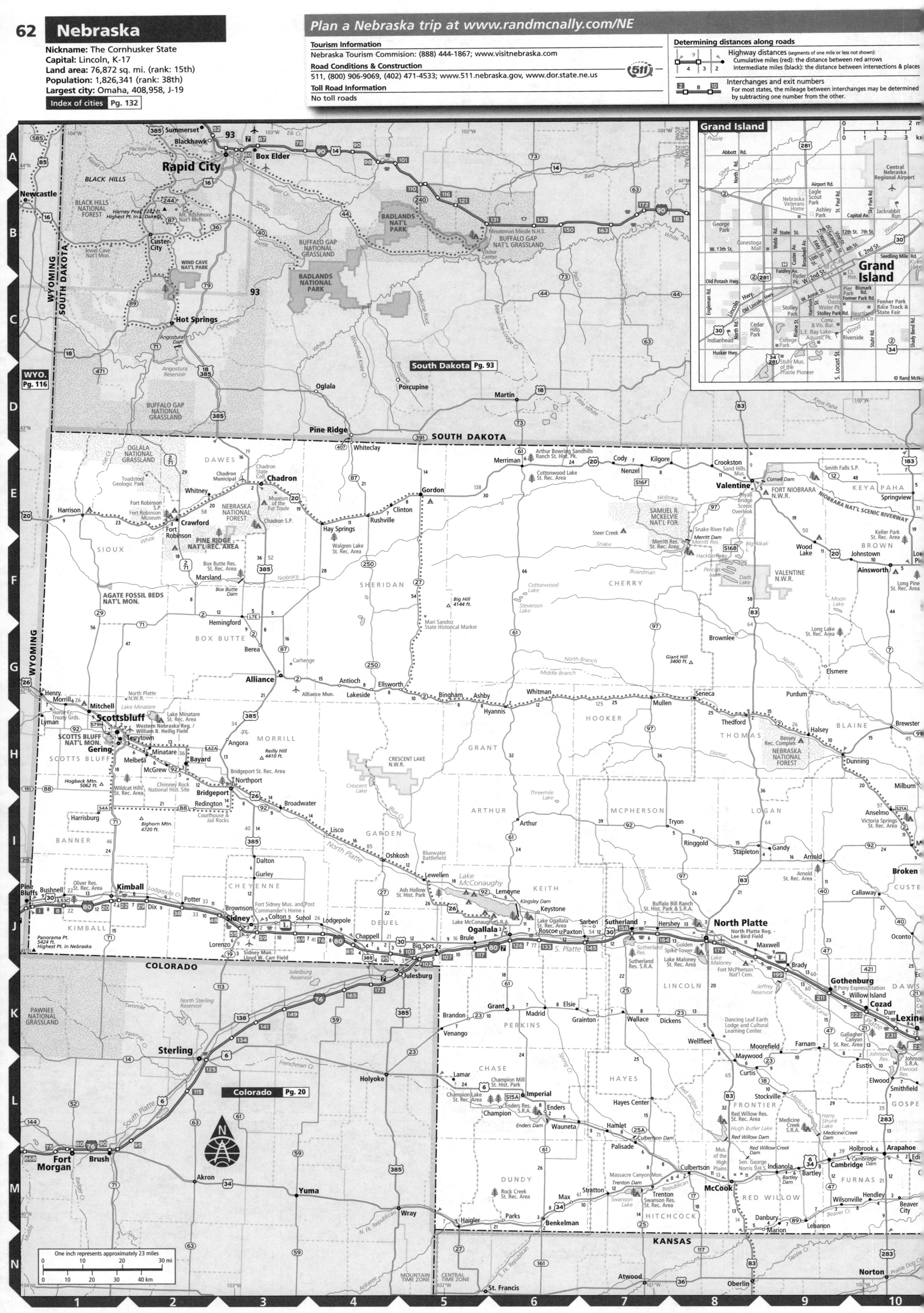

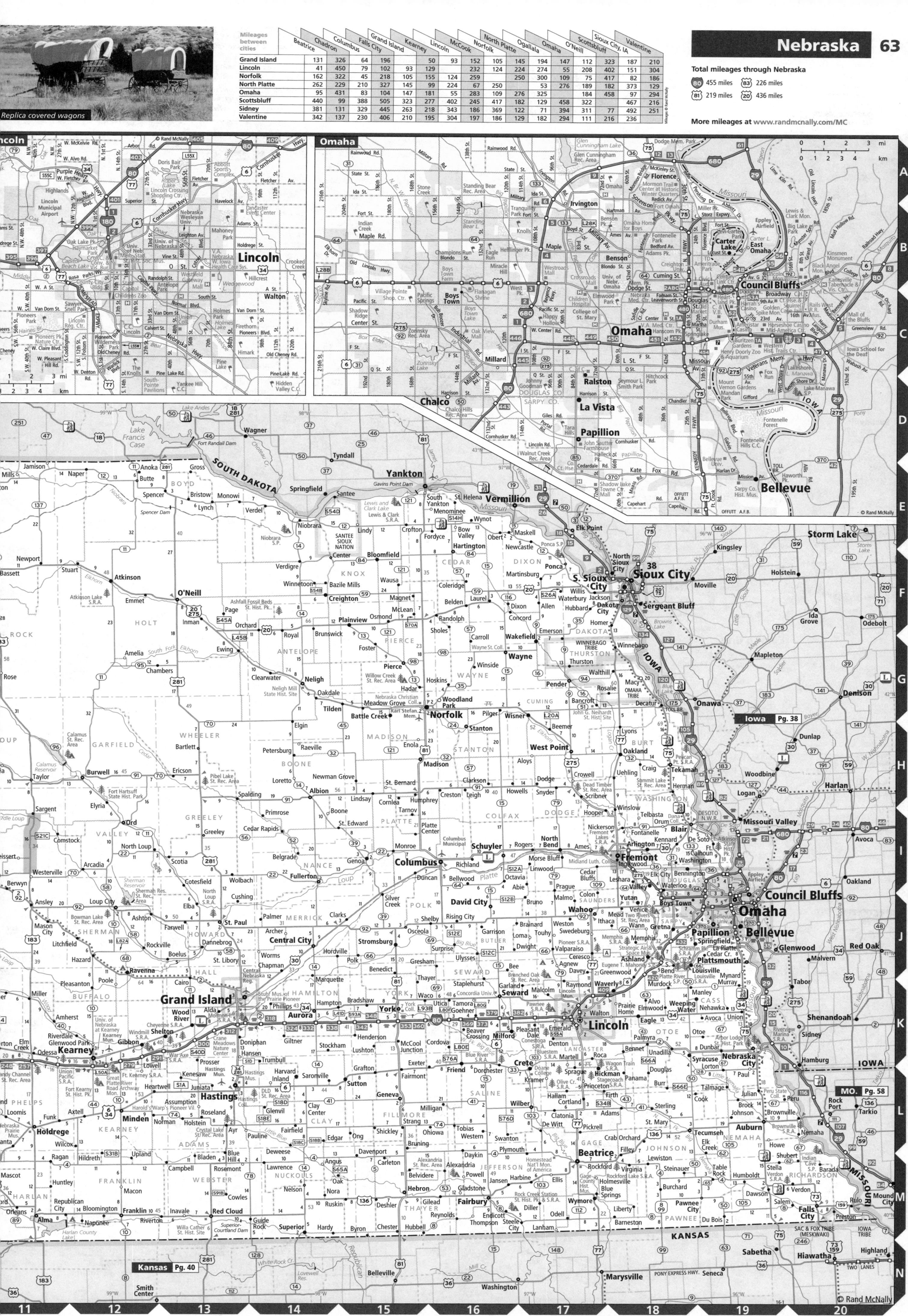

Mileages between cities

	Beatrice	Chadron	Columbus	Falls City	Grand Island	Kearney	Lincoln	McCook	Norfolk	North Platte	Ogallala	Omaha	O'Neill	Scottsbluff	Sioux City, IA	Valentine
Grand Island	131	326	64	196		50	93	152	105	145	194	147	112	323	187	210
Lincoln	41	450	79	102	93	129		232	124	224	274	55	208	402	151	304
Norfolk	162	322	45	218	105	155	124	259		250	300	109	75	417	82	186
North Platte	262	229	210	327	145	99	224	67	250		53	276	189	182	373	129
Omaha	95	431	83	104	147	181	55	283	109	276	325		184	458	97	294
Scottsbluff	440	99	388	505	323	277	402	245	417	182	129	458	322		467	216
Sidney	381	131	329	445	263	218	343	186	369	122	71	394	311	77	492	251
Valentine	342	137	230	406	210	195	304	197	186	129	182	294	111	216	236	

Mileages © Rand McNally

Total mileages through Nebraska

80 455 miles · 83 226 miles
81 219 miles · 20 436 miles

More mileages at www.randmcnally.com/MC

Nevada

Nickname: The Silver State
Capital: Carson City, F-2
Land area: 109,826 sq. mi. (rank: 7th)
Population: 2,700,551 (rank: 35th)
Largest city: Las Vegas, 583,756, L-8

Index of cities Pg. 132

Mileages between cities	Carson City	Elko	Ely	Jackpot	Las Vegas	Reno	Tonopah	Winnemucca
Elko	304		188	117	429	288	252	125
Ely	319	188		205	241	319	167	271
Las Vegas	435	429	241	446		447	210	472
Reno	32	288	319	405	447		237	163
S. Lake Tahoe, CA	27	332	347	450	451	60	237	208
Tonopah	225	252	167	373	210	237		261
West Wendover	414	109	120	125	361	397	288	232
Winnemucca	179	125	271	240	472	163	261	

Mileages © Rand McNally

Total mileages through Nevada

15 124 miles 6 307 miles
80 411 miles 95 652 miles

More mileages at
www.randmcnally.com/MC

Get travel info at www.randmcnally.com/NV

Tourism Information
Nevada Commission on Tourism;
(800) 638-2328, (775) 687-4322; www.travelnevada.com

Road Conditions & Construction
511; (877) 687-6237, (775) 888-7000
www.nevadadot.com, www.nvroads.com

Toll Rd. Info
No toll roads

Determining Distances
9 / 4 3 2 (segments of one mile or less not shown)
Cumulative miles (red): the distance between red arrows
Intermediate miles (black): the distance between intersections & places

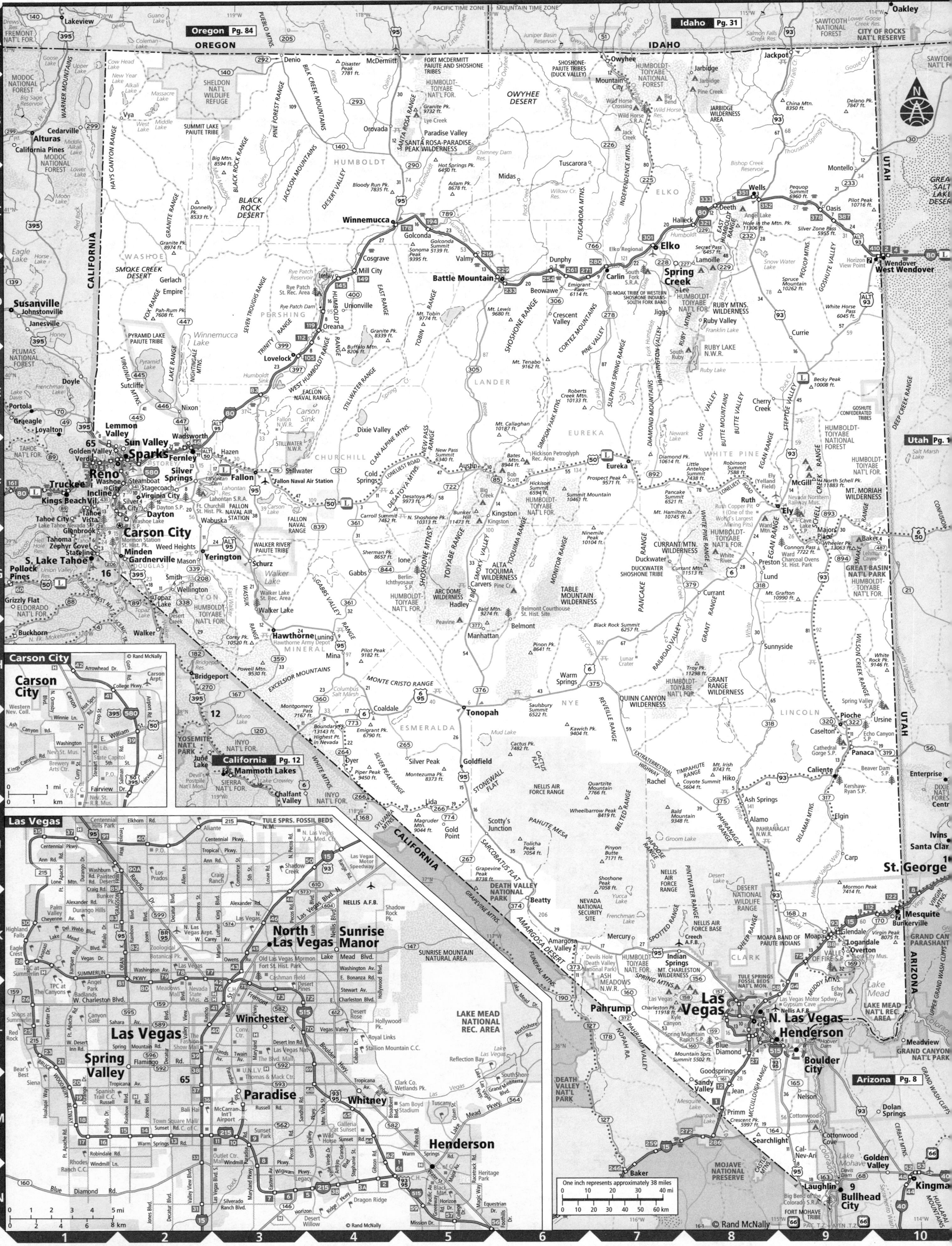

Oregon Pg. 84
Idaho Pg. 31
Utah Pg. 1
California Pg. 12
Arizona Pg. 8

Carson City

Las Vegas

One inch represents approximately 38 miles

Plan a trip at www.randmcnally.com/NH

Tourism Information
New Hampshire Division of Travel & Tourism Development: (603) 271-2665; www.visitnh.com

Road Conditions & Construction
511, (603) 271-6862; www.nhtmc.com, www.nh.gov/dot

Toll Road Information
N.H. Department of Transportation (*E-ZPass*): (877) 643-9727; www.nh.gov/dot

Total mileages through New Hampshire
89: 61 miles; 95: 16 miles; 93: 132 miles; 2: 36 miles

More mileages at www.randmcnally.com/MC

Mileages between cities	Colebrook	Concord	Conway	Keene	Laconia	Littleton	Nashua	Portsmouth
Berlin	49	115	40	168	97	42	151	117
Concord	137		77	51	27	87	36	44
Keene	181	51	130		80	136	50	99
Lebanon	128	57	88	64	58	82	89	111
Littleton	56	87	54	136	66		121	129
Manchester	155	18	95	55	45	105	18	43
Nashua	172	36	113	50	63	121		54
Portsmouth	180	44	77	99	57	129	54	

New Hampshire

Nickname: The Granite State
Capital: Concord, K-7
Land area: 8,968 sq. mi. (rank: 44th)
Population: 1,316,470 (rank: 42nd)
Largest city: Manchester, 109,565, L-7

Index of cities Pg. 132

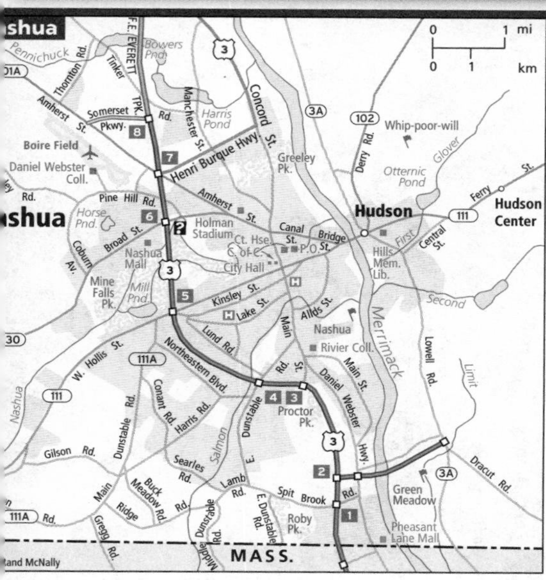

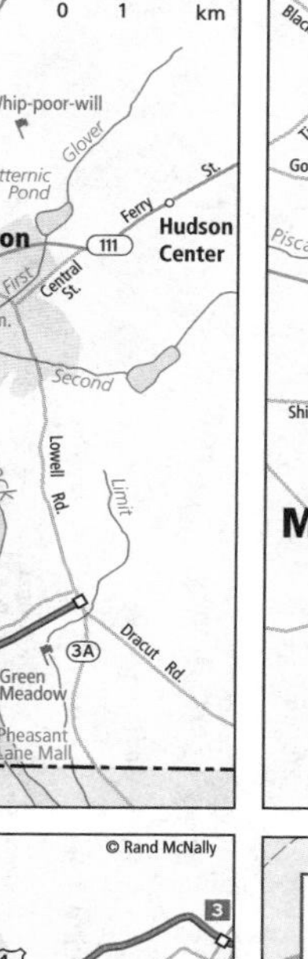

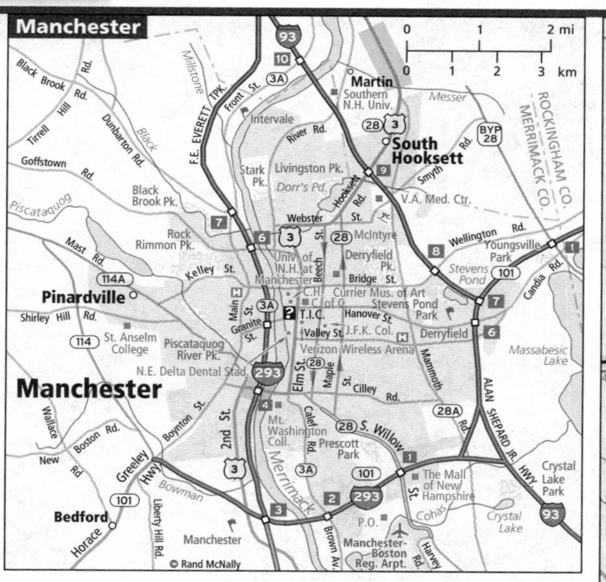

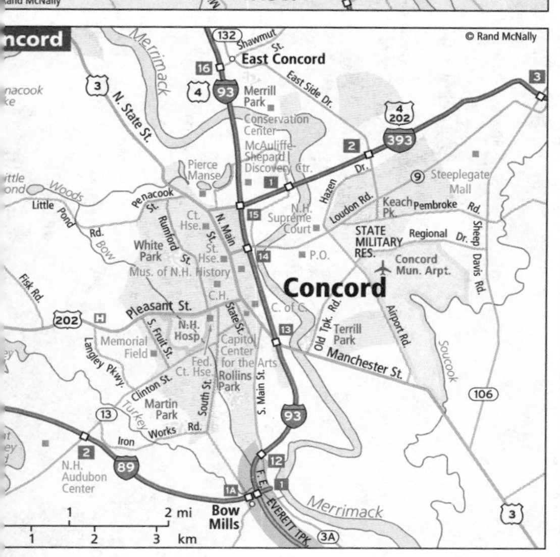

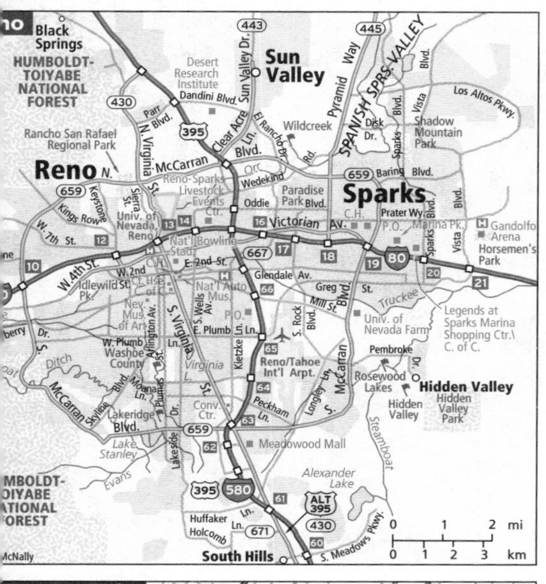

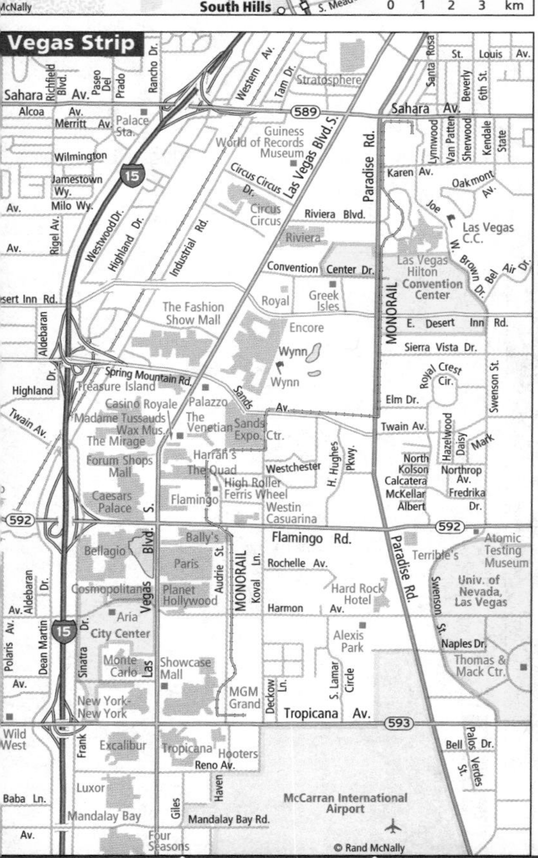

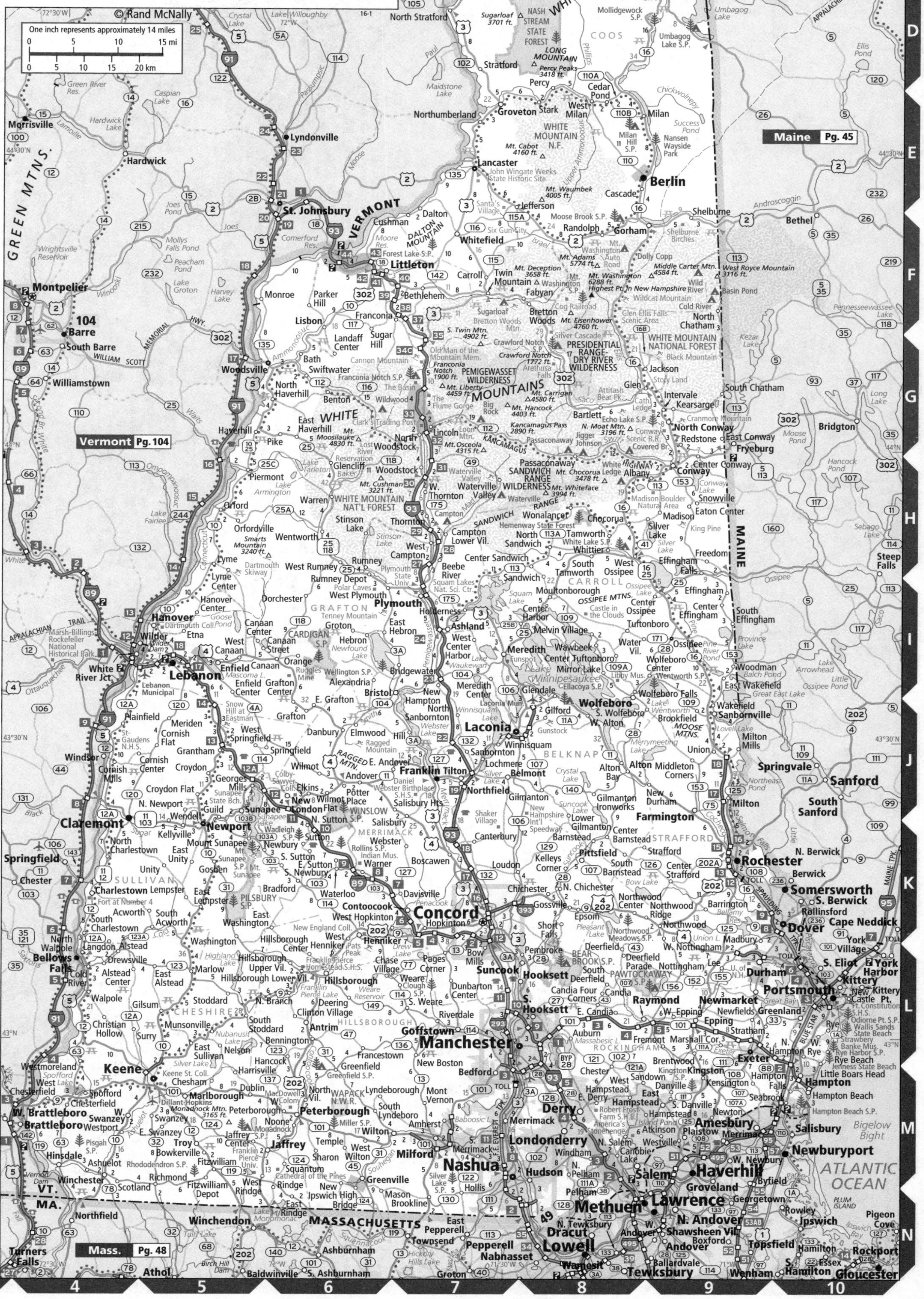

Québec Pg. 124
Maine Pg. 45
Vermont Pg. 104
Mass. Pg. 48

Nickname: The Garden State
Capital: Trenton, J-8
Land area: 7,417 sq. mi. (rank: 46th)
Population: 8,791,894 (rank: 11th)
Largest city: Newark, 277,140, F-12

Index of cities Pg. 132

Explore New Jersey at www.randmcnally.com/NJ

Tourism Information
New Jersey Division of Travel & Tourism:
(609) 599-6540; www.visitnj.org

Road Conditions & Construction
511, (866) 511-6538
www.511nj.org, www.state.nj.us/transportation

Toll Road Information: *(all use E-ZPass)*
Burlington County Bridge Commission: (856) 829-1900, (609) 387-1480; www.bcbridges.org
Delaware River & Bay Authority (Del. Mem. Br., Cape May/Lewes Fy.): (302) 571-6300; www.drba.net
Delaware River Port Authority (Phila. area bridges): (877) 567-3772; www.drpa.org
N.J. Turnpike Authority (N.J. Turnpike, Gdn. St. Pkwy.): (732) 750-5300; www.state.nj.us
Port Authority of N.Y. & N.J. (N.Y. City area bridges & tunnels): (800) 221-9903; www.panynj.gov
South Jersey Transportation Authority (Atlantic City Expressway): (609) 965-6060; www.sjta.com

Boardwalk at Atlantic City

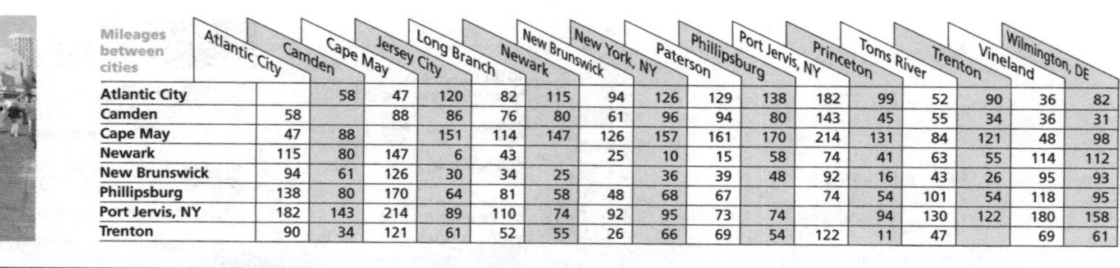

Mileages between cities

	Atlantic City	Camden	Cape May	Jersey City	Long Branch	Newark	New Brunswick	New York, NY	Paterson	Phillipsburg	Port Jervis, NY	Princeton	Toms River	Trenton	Vineland	Wilmington, DE
Atlantic City		58	47	120	82	115	94	126	129	138	182	99	52	90	36	82
Camden	58		88	86	76	80	61	96	94	80	143	45	55	34	36	31
Cape May	47	88		151	114	147	126	157	161	170	214	131	84	121	48	98
Newark	115	80	147	6	43		25	10	15	58	74	41	63	55	114	112
New Brunswick	94	61	126	30	34	25		36	39	48	92	16	43	26	95	93
Phillipsburg	138	80	170	64	81	58	48	68	67		74	54	101	54	118	95
Port Jervis, NY	182	143	214	89	110	74	92	95	73	74		94	130	122	180	158
Trenton	90	34	121	61	52	55	26	66	69	54	122	11	47		69	61

Total mileages through New Jersey

78 68 miles
95 98 miles
80 68 miles

More mileages at www.randmcnally.com/MC

Trenton

Cape May

New Mexico

Nickname: Land of Enchantment
Capital: Santa Fe, D-6
Land area: 121,356 sq. mi. (rank: 5th)
Population: 2,059,179 (rank: 36th)
Largest city: Albuquerque, 545,852, E-4

Index of cities Pg. 133

Mileages between cities	Albuquerque	Carlsbad	Clayton	Gallup	Las Cruces	Socorro	Taos	Tucumcari
Albuquerque		277	270	137	222	78	128	173
Carlsbad	277		374	412	206	241	336	263
Clayton	270	374		407	415	347	163	111
Clovis	219	180	168	356	292	248	246	83
Farmington	180	455	418	121	404	258	202	354
Las Cruces	222	206	415	338		146	351	303
Roswell	199	76	293	336	184	165	260	182
Santa Fe	58	268	215	197	282	136	68	166

Mileages © Rand McNally

Total mileages through New Mexico

10: 164 miles
25: 462 miles
40: 374 miles

More mileages at www.randmcnally.com/MC

Get travel info at www.randmcnally.com/NM

Tourism Information
New Mexico Tourism Department
(505) 827-7400; www.newmexico.org

Road Conditions & Construction
511, (800) 432-4269, (505) 827-5100
www.nmroads.com, www.dot.state.nm.us

Toll Rd. Info
No toll roads

Determining Distances
(segments of one mile or less not shown)
Cumulative miles (red): the distance between red arrows
Intermediate miles (black): the distance between intersections & places

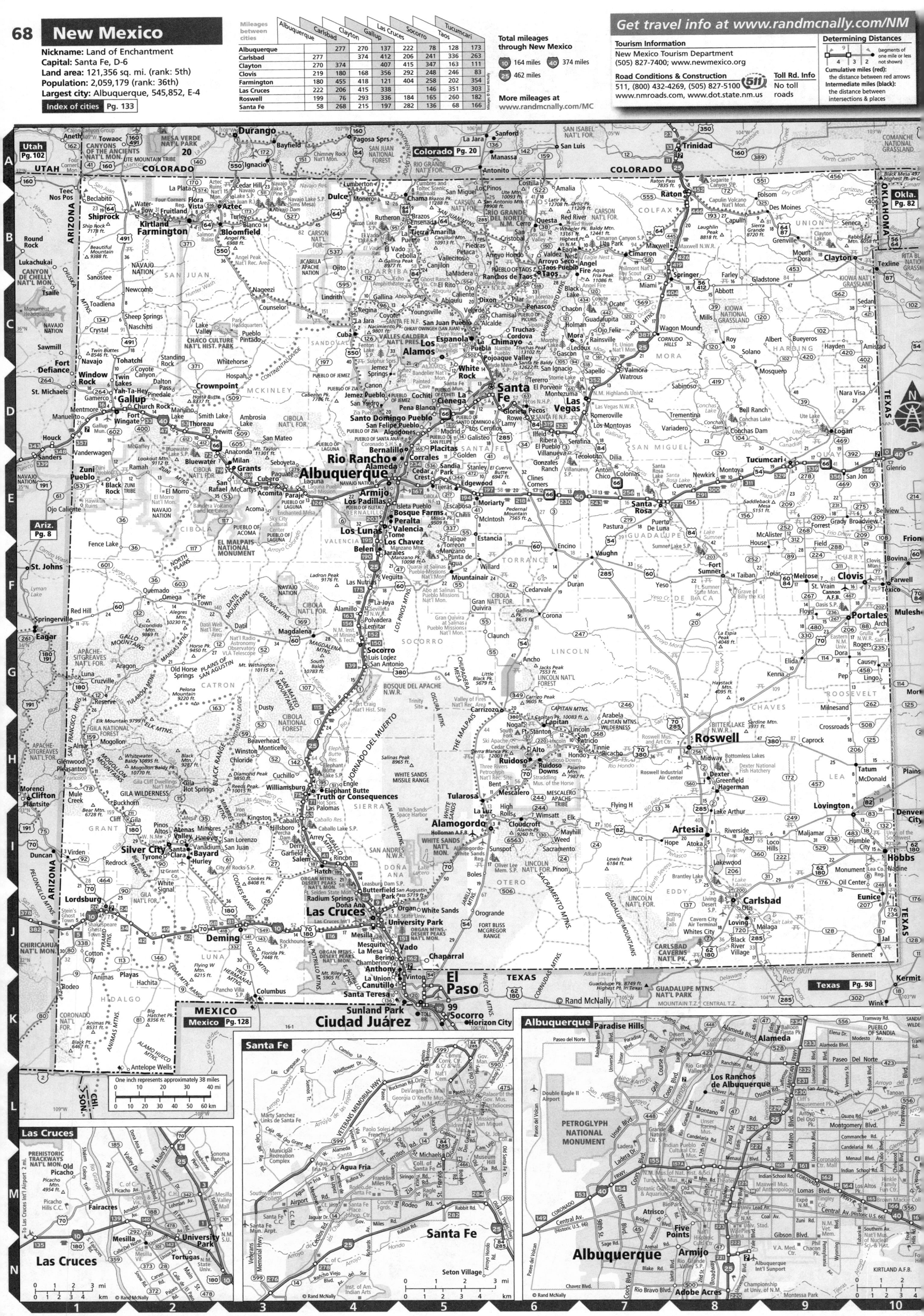

Plan a trip at www.randmcnally.com/NY

Tourism Information
N.Y. State Division of Tourism: (800) 225-5697; www.iloveny.com

Toll Road Info
see next page for listings

Road Conditions & Construction
511, (888) 465-1169, (518) 457-6195
www.511ny.org, www.dot.ny.gov
Thruway: (800) 847-8929; www.thruway.ny.gov

Determining Distances
(segments of one mile or less not shown)
Cumulative miles (red): the distance between red arrows
Intermediate miles (black): the distance between intersections & places

Total mileages through New York

84 72 miles
95 24 miles
87 334 miles
495 66 miles

More mileages at
www.randmcnally.com/MC

Mileages between cities	Albany	Buffalo	Hempstead	Newburgh	New York	Poughkeepsie	Riverhead	White Plains
Albany		289	167	87	156	75	219	138
Buffalo	289		423	361	395	362	471	394
Hempstead	167	423		78	12	92	59	34
Kingston	55	339	116	37	106	19	168	87
Montauk	260	513	97	172	107	184	42	126
Newburgh	87	361	78		72	19	130	49
New York	156	395	12	72		84	66	26
Poughkeepsie	75	362	92	19	84		143	60

Nickname: The Empire State
Capital: Albany, NK-19
Land area: 47,214 sq. mi. (rank: 30th)
Population: 19,378,102 (rank: 3rd)
Largest city: New York, 8,175,133, SF-6

Index of cities Pg. 133

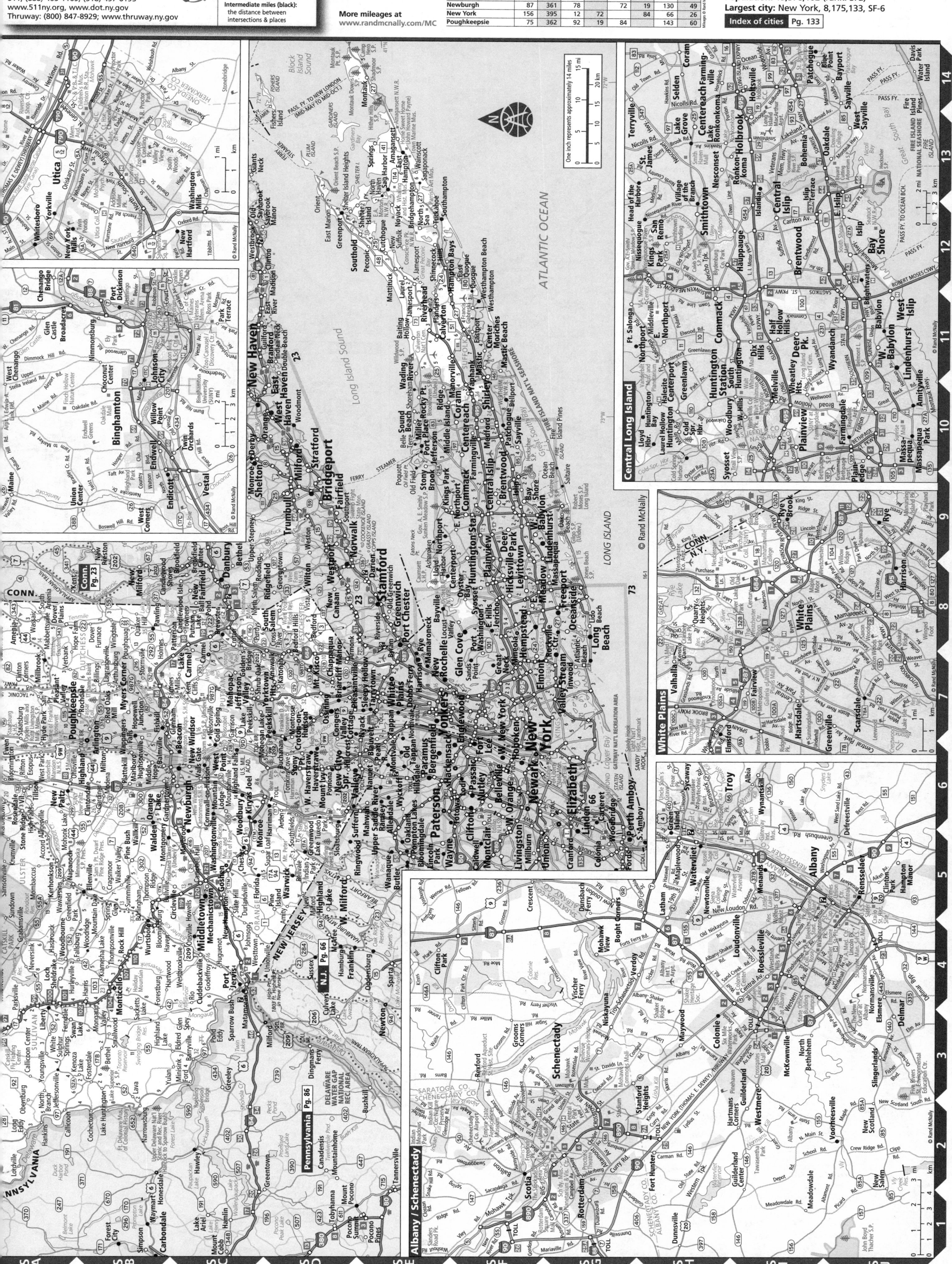

Nickname: The Empire State
Capital: Albany, NK-19
Land area: 47,214 sq. mi. (rank: 30th)
Population: 19,378,102 (rank: 3rd)
Largest city: New York, 8,175,133, SF-6

Index of cities Pg. 133

Explore New York at www.randmcnally.com/NY

Tourism Information
New York State Division of Tourism: (800) 225-5697; www.iloveny.com

Road Conditions & Construction
511, (888) 465-1169, (518) 457-6195; www.511ny.org, www.dot.ny.gov
Thruway: (800) 847-8929; www.thruway.ny.gov

Toll Road Information: *(all use E-ZPass)*
MTA (N.Y. City in-state bridges & tunnels): 511, say "Bridges & Tunnels"; web.mta.info
New York State Bridge Authority (Hudson River bridges): (845) 691-7245; www.nysba.state.ny.us
New York State Thruway: (800) 333-8655; www.thruway.ny.gov
Port Authority of N.Y. & N.J. (N.Y. City inter-state bridges & tunnels): (800) 221-9903; www.panynj.gov

International Toll Bridge Information:
Buffalo & Ft. Erie Public Br. Auth. (Peace Br.) *(E-ZPass)*: (716) 884-6744, (905) 871-1608; www.peacebridge.com
Niagara Falls Bridge Comm. *(ExpressPass or NEXUS)*: (716) 285-6322, (905) 354-5641; www.niagarafallsbridges.com
Ogdensburg Bridge & Port Auth.: (315) 393-4080; www.ogdensport.com
Seaway Int'l Bridge Corp. (near Massena): (613) 932-6601; www.sibc.ca
Thousand Islands Br. Auth. (Alexandria Bay): (315) 482-2501; www.tibridge.com

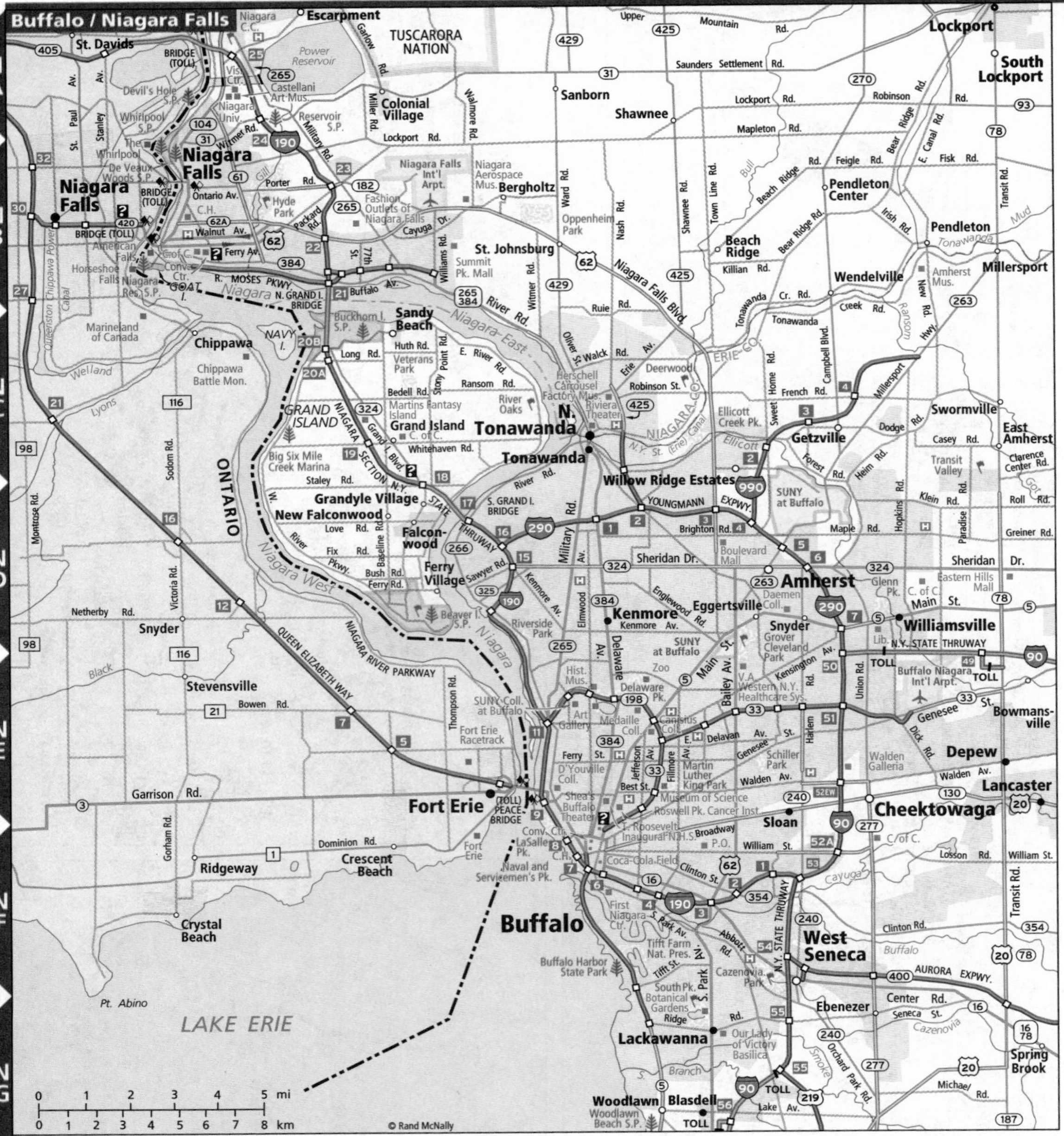

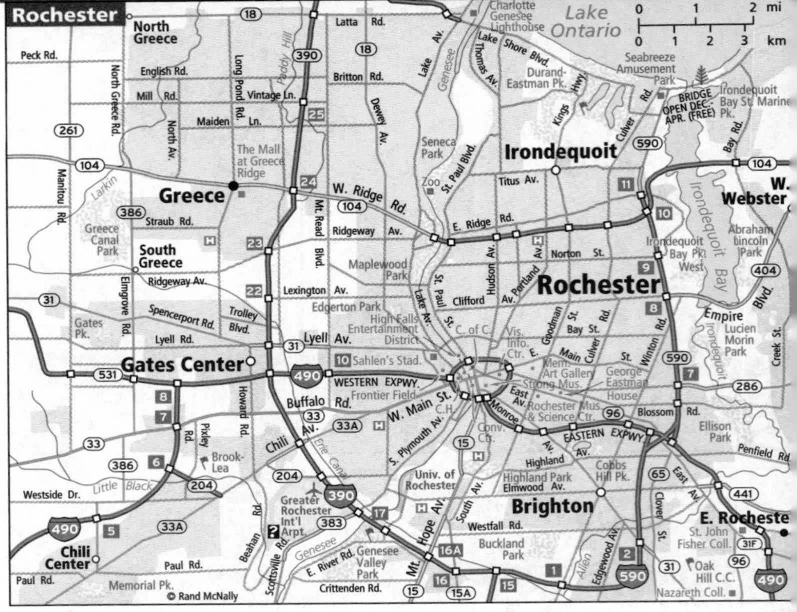

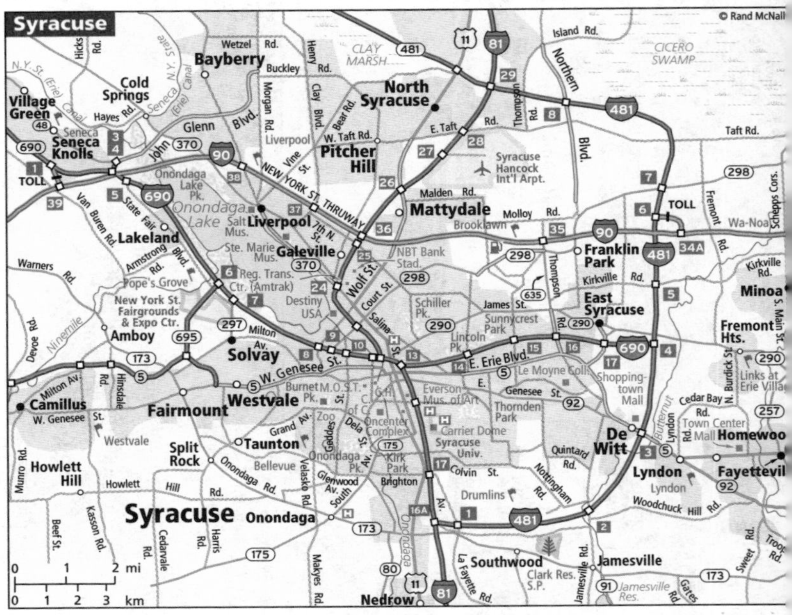

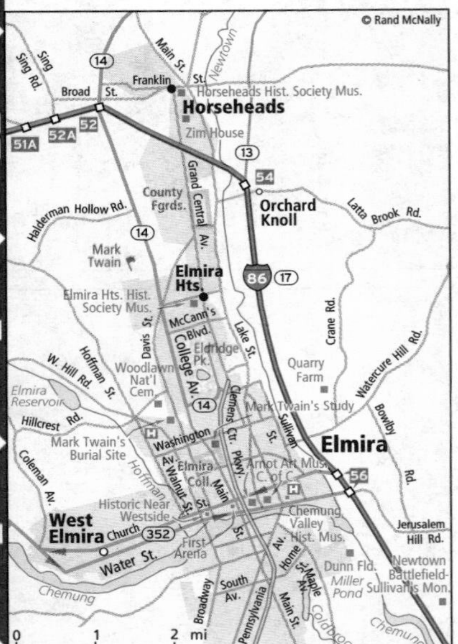

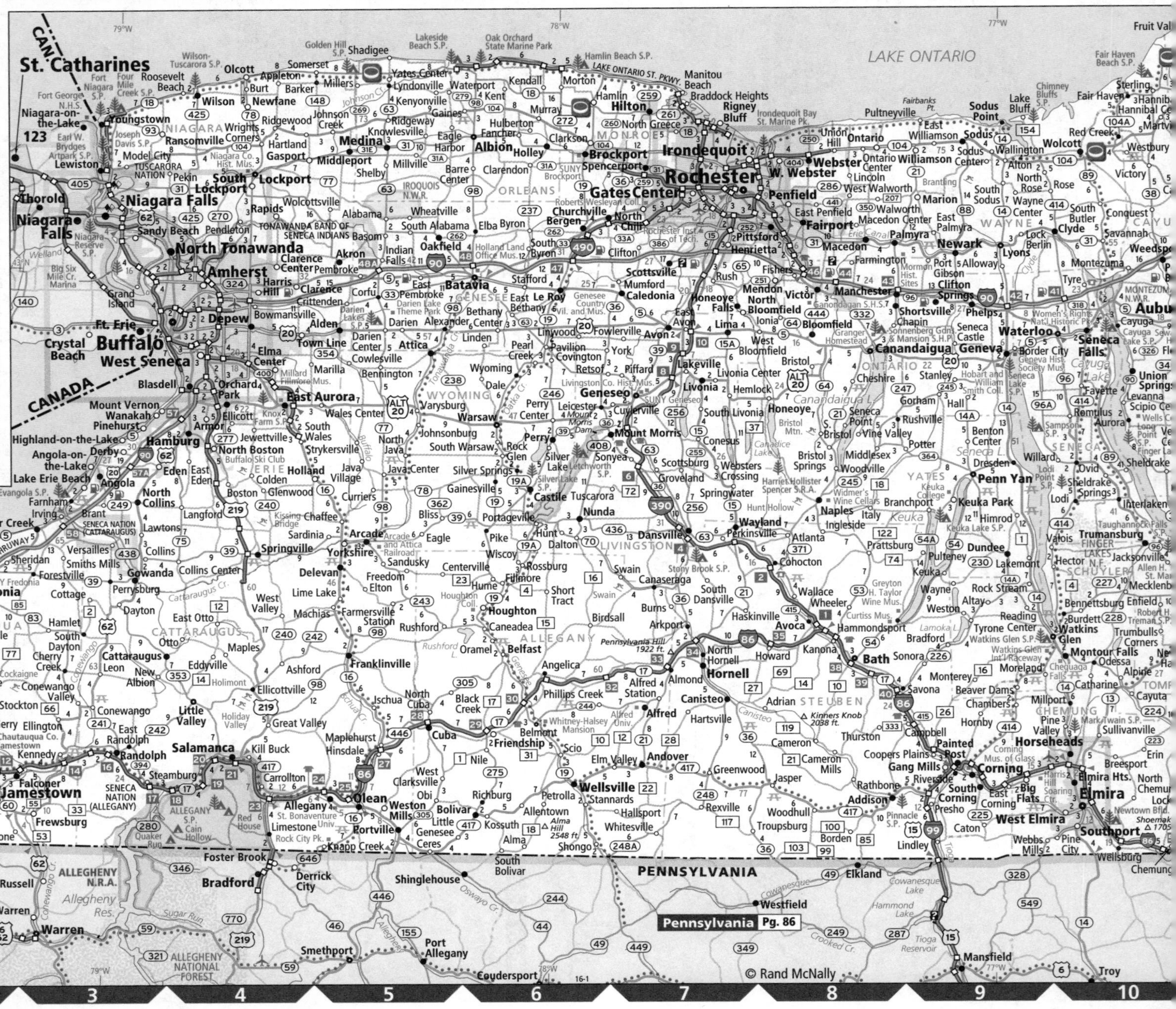

Buffalo / Niagara Falls

0 1 2 3 4 5 mi
0 1 2 3 4 5 6 7 8 km

© Rand McNally

Rochester

0 1 2 mi
0 1 2 3 km

© Rand McNally

Syracuse

0 1 2 mi
0 1 2 3 km

© Rand McNally

Elmira

0 1 2 mi
0 1 2 3 km

© Rand McNally

LAKE ONTARIO

LAKE ERIE

PENNSYLVANIA

CANADA

Pennsylvania Pg. 86

© Rand McNally

Niagara Falls

Mileages between cities	Albany	Binghamton	Buffalo	Elmira	Glens Falls	Jamestown	Kingston	Lake Placid	Massena	New York	Niagara Falls	Plattsburgh	Rochester	Syracuse	Utica	Watertown
Albany		140	289	195	53	356	55	140	217	156	302	160	226	145	94	175
Binghamton	140		222	56	179	218	130	266	231	176	235	287	159	73	89	143
Buffalo	289	222		148	313	71	339	337	305	395	21	373	73	150	198	212
Jamestown	356	218	71	163	395		349	404	370	392	92	436	139	214	263	278
Plattsburgh	160	287	373	342	110	436	214	50	82	317	384		308	227	183	165
Rochester	226	159	73	120	248	139	277	275	242	332	87	308		86	135	149
Syracuse	145	73	150	90	160	214	195	195	159	246	162	227	86		53	70
Watertown	175	143	212	160	179	278	226	125	89	316	225	165	149	70	80	

Total mileages through New York

- 81: 184 miles
- 86: 176 miles
- 87: 334 miles
- 90: 385 miles

More mileages at www.randmcnally.com/MC

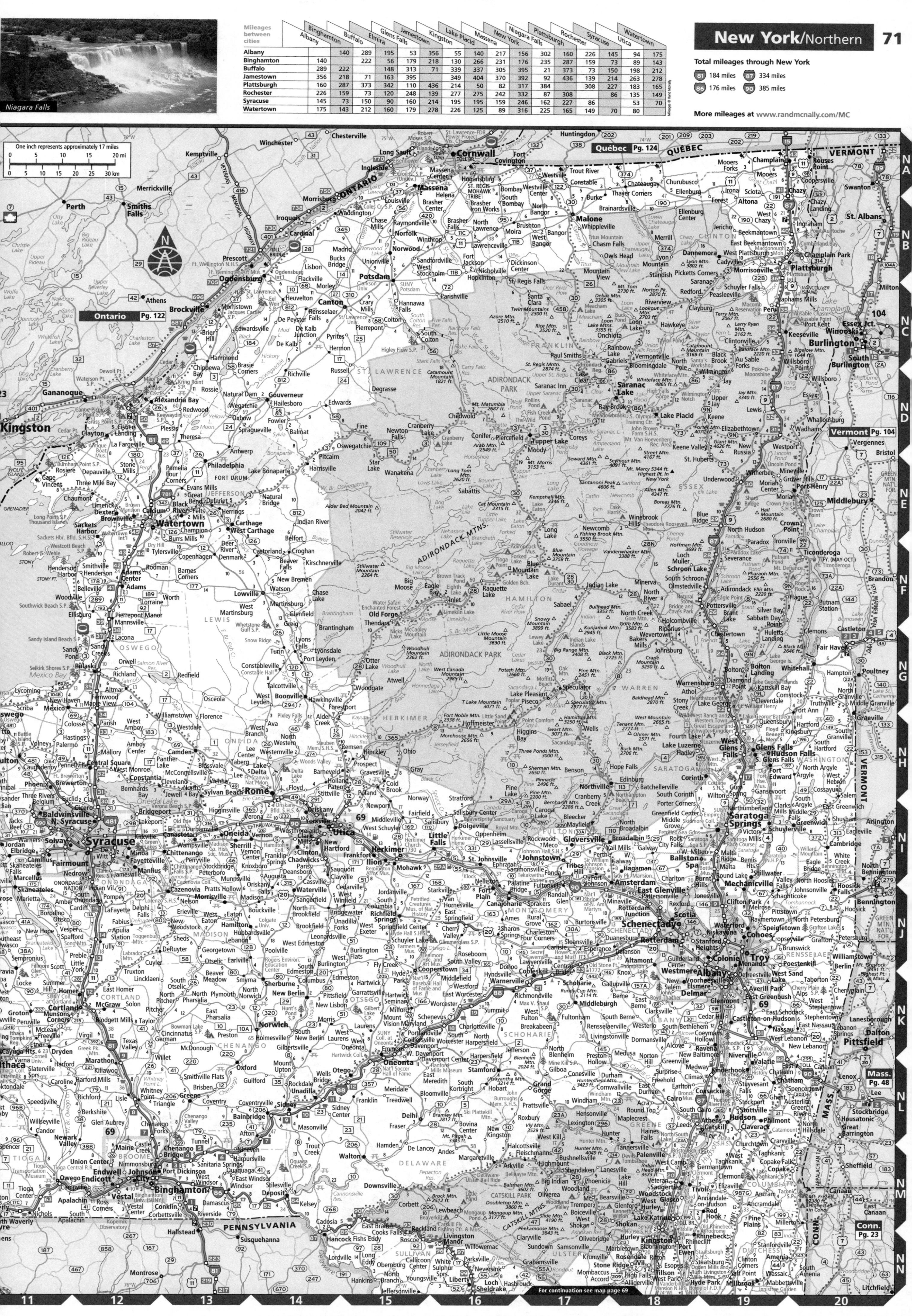

City sights to see

- American Museum of Natural History, A-4
- Battery Park, I-1
- Bronx Zoo, E-12
- Brooklyn Bridge, H-2
- Carnegie Hall, C-4
- Central Park, B-4
- Chrysler Building, D-4
- Coney Island, L-10
- Ellis Island, I-9
- Empire State Building, D-3
- Greenwich Village, H-10
- Grand Central Terminal, D-4

Ellis Island Museum

Manhattan

New York City & Vicinity

Brooklyn Bridge, New York City

City sights to see

- Guggenheim Museum, A-5
- Intrepid Sea-Air Space Museum, C-2
- Lincoln Center, B-3
- Madison Square Garden, D-2
- Metropolitan Museum of Art, B-5
- National Sept. 11 Memorial, H-1
- New York Stock Exchange and Wall Street, H-1
- Rockefeller Center, C-4
- Staten Island Ferry, I-2 and J-8
- Statue of Liberty, I-9
- Times Square, D-3
- Yankee Stadium, E-11

North Carolina

Nickname: The Tar Heel State
Capital: Raleigh, E-12
Land area: 48,711 sq. mi. (rank: 29th)
Population: 9,535,483 (rank: 10th)
Largest city: Charlotte, 731,424, F-5

Index of cities Pg. 133

Plan a North Carolina trip at www.randmcnally.com/NC

Tourism Information
North Carolina Division of Tourism: (800) 847-4862, (919) 733-4171; www.visitnc.com

Road Conditions & Construction
511, (877) 511-4662; www.ncdot.gov/travel/511, www.ncdot.gov

Toll Road Information NC Quick Pass
North Carolina Turnpike Authority: (877) 769-7277; www.ncdot.gov/turnpike

Determining distances along roads

Highway distances (segments of one mile or less not shown):
Cumulative miles (red): the distance between red arrows
Intermediate miles (black): the distance between intersections & places

Interchanges and exit numbers
For most states, the mileage between interchanges may be determined by subtracting one number from the other.

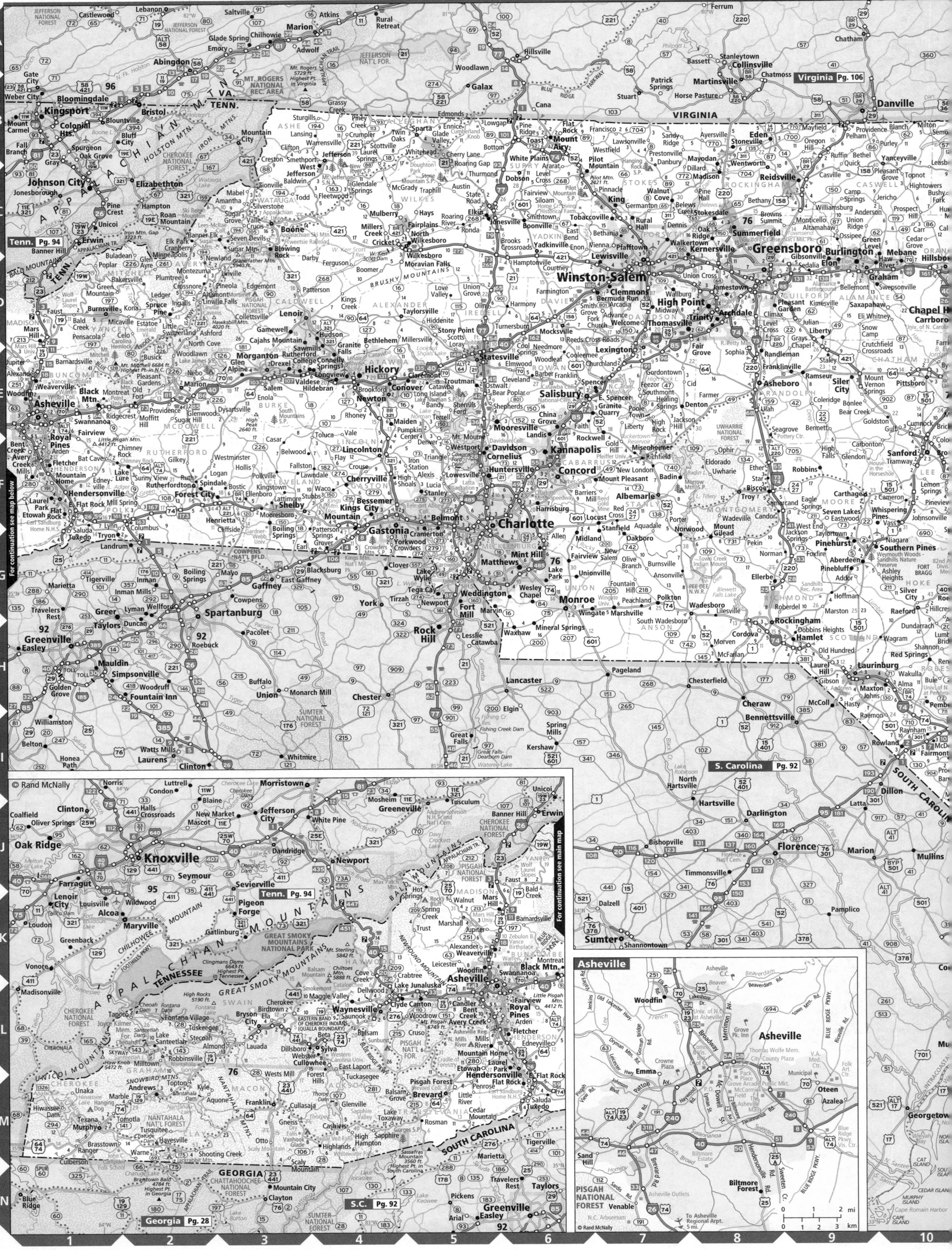
Virginia Pg. 106
Tenn. Pg. 94
S. Carolina Pg. 92
For continuation see map below
For continuation see main map
Tenn. Pg. 94
S.C. Pg. 92
Georgia Pg. 28
Asheville
© Rand McNally
Charlotte
Winston-Salem
Greensboro
High Point
Asheville
Hickory
Gastonia
Spartanburg
Greenville
Knoxville
Florence

inn Cove Viaduct

Mileages between cities	Asheville	Boone	Charlotte	Durham	Elizabeth City	Greensboro	Hickory	Morehead City	Murphy	Nags Head	New Bern	Raleigh	Roanoke Rapids	Rockingham	Wilmington	Winston-Salem
Asheville		94	128	224	412	172	77	393	110	444	358	251	308	200	327	145
Charlotte	128	100		144	332	93	57	313	223	364	278	168	231	71	197	77
Elizabeth City	412	354	332	185		241	338	152	520	56	119	164	97	259	208	269
Fayetteville	261	202	137	89	203	94	189	138	369	234	130	63	127	64	89	119
Greensboro	172	113	93	53	241		98	223	279	271	188	80	138	83	207	29
Greenville	332	273	250	101	97	156	258	79	440	129	44	82	86	176	116	188
Raleigh	251	192	168	22	164	80	177	146	358	195	111		89	98	130	107
Wilmington	327	319	197	156	208	207	259	91	428	230	90	130	178	127		236

Total mileages through North Carolina

- 40: 419 miles
- 85: 233 miles
- 77: 102 miles
- 95: 182 miles

More mileages at www.randmcnally.com/MC

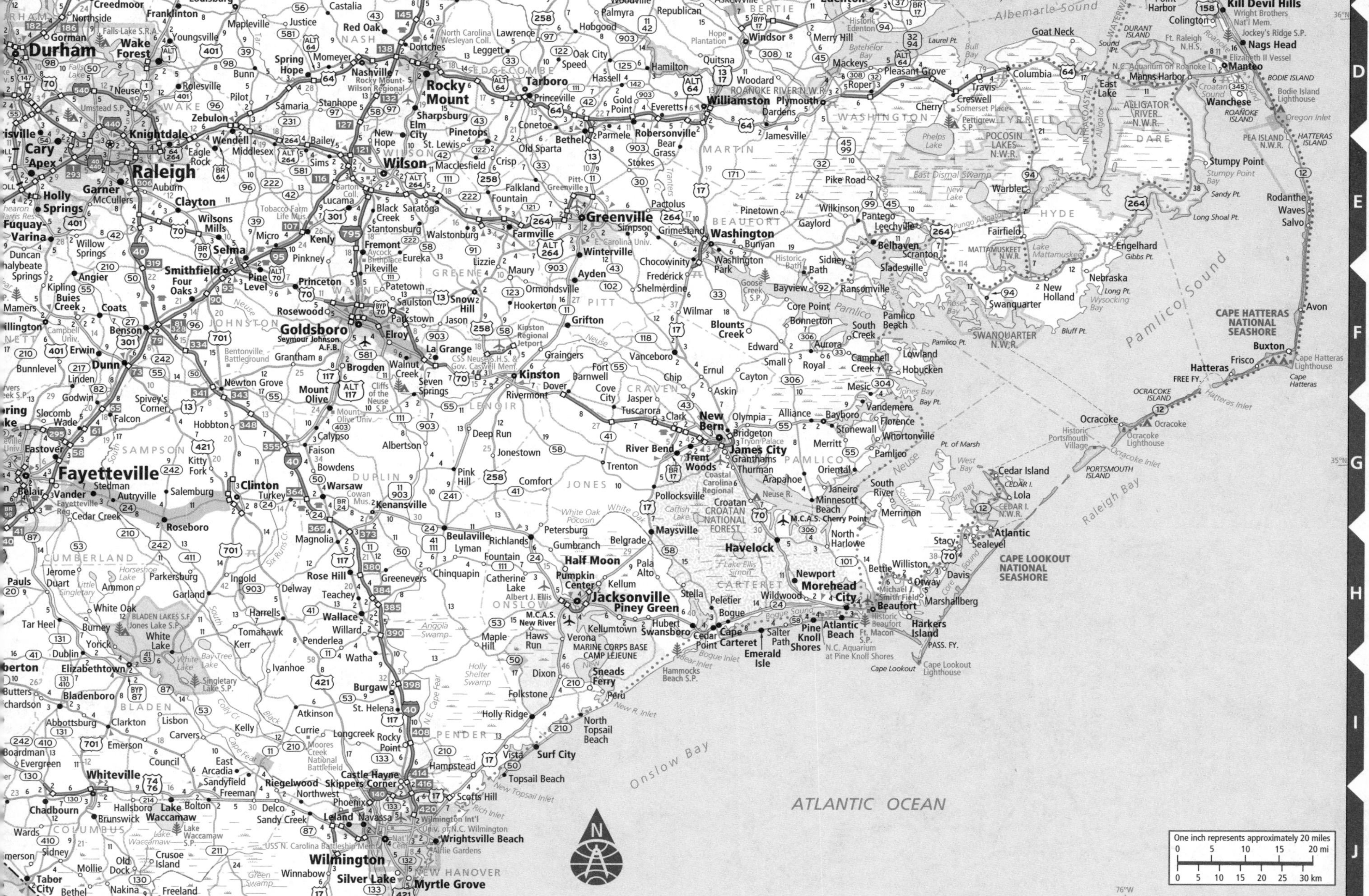

Wilmington

Fayetteville

Gastonia

One inch represents approximately 20 miles

City sights to see

- Discovery Place, Charlotte, H-4
- Duke Homestead State Historic Site and Tobacco Museum, Durham, F-9
- Historic Bethabara Park, Winston-Salem, A-1
- Mint Museum of Art, Charlotte, H-5
- Morehead Planetarium and Science Center, Chapel Hill, H-8
- North Carolina Museum of History, Raleigh, I-12
- North Carolina Museum of Life and Science, Durham, F-10
- North Carolina State Capitol, Raleigh, I-13
- North Carolina State University, Raleigh, I-13
- Old Salem, Winston-Salem, B-2
- Reynolda House, Winston-Salem, B-1

Old Salem, Winston-Salem

Great Smoky Mountains National Park

Raleigh / Durham / Chapel Hill

Greensboro / Winston-Salem / High Point

Charlotte & Vicinity

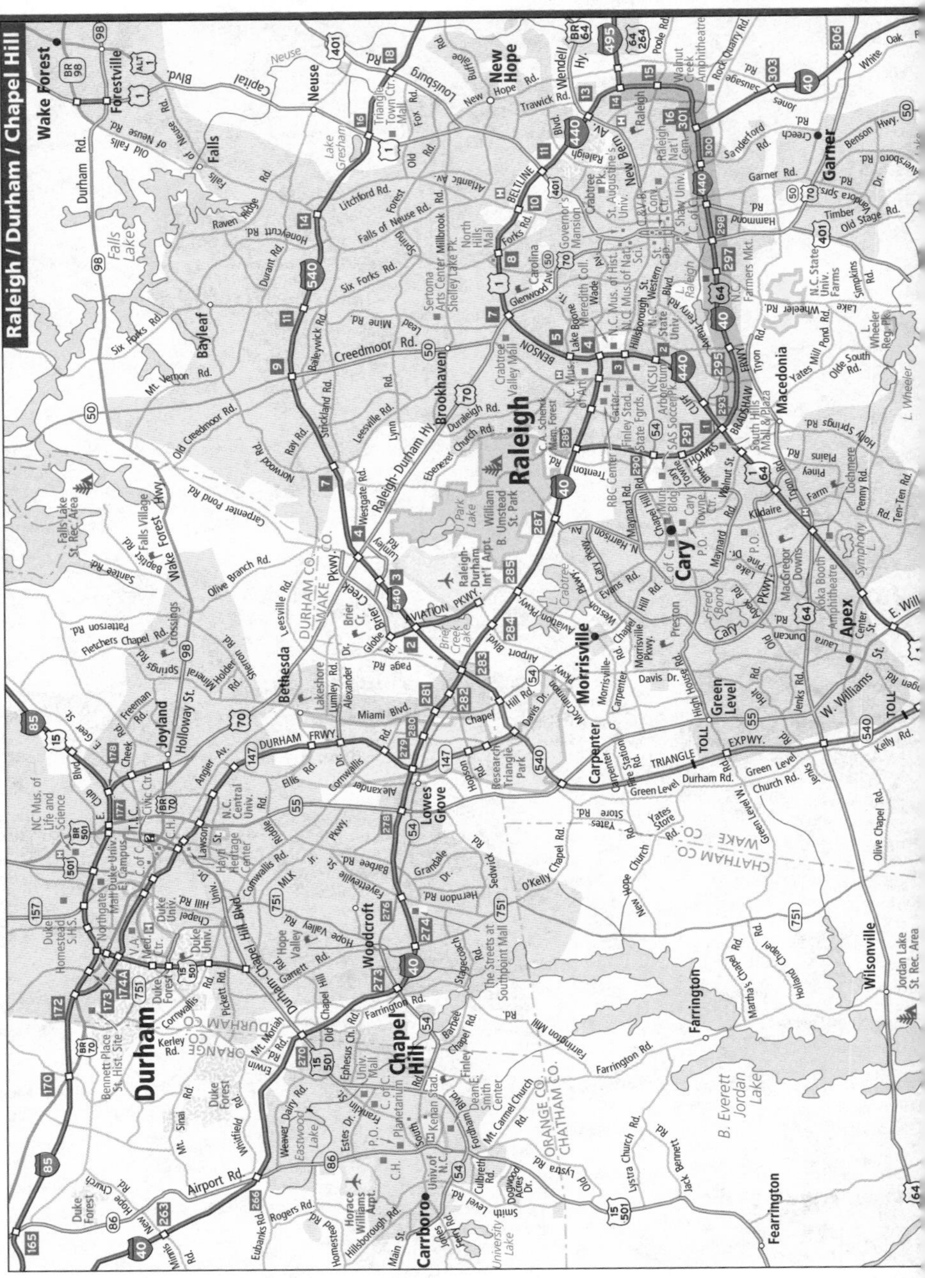

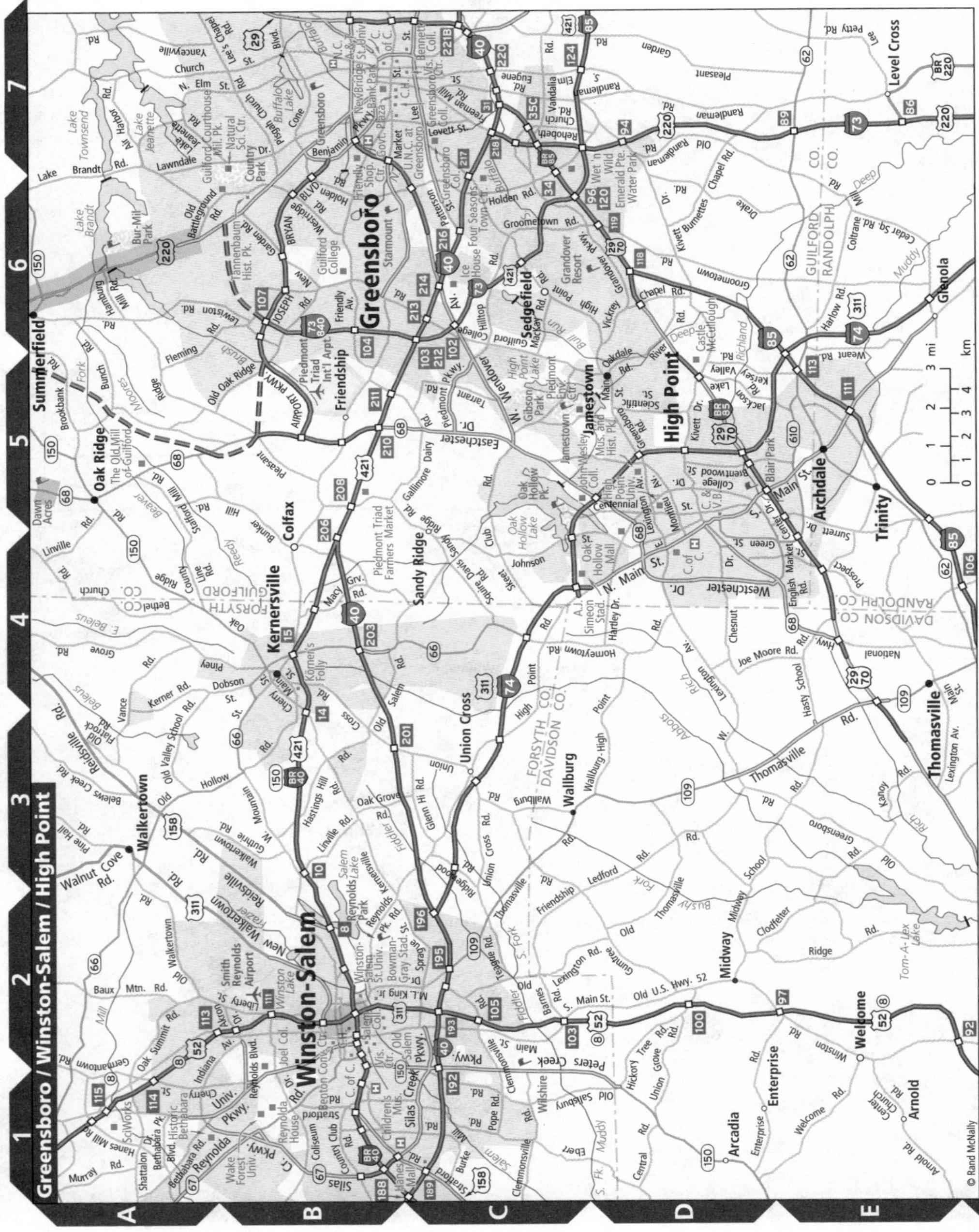

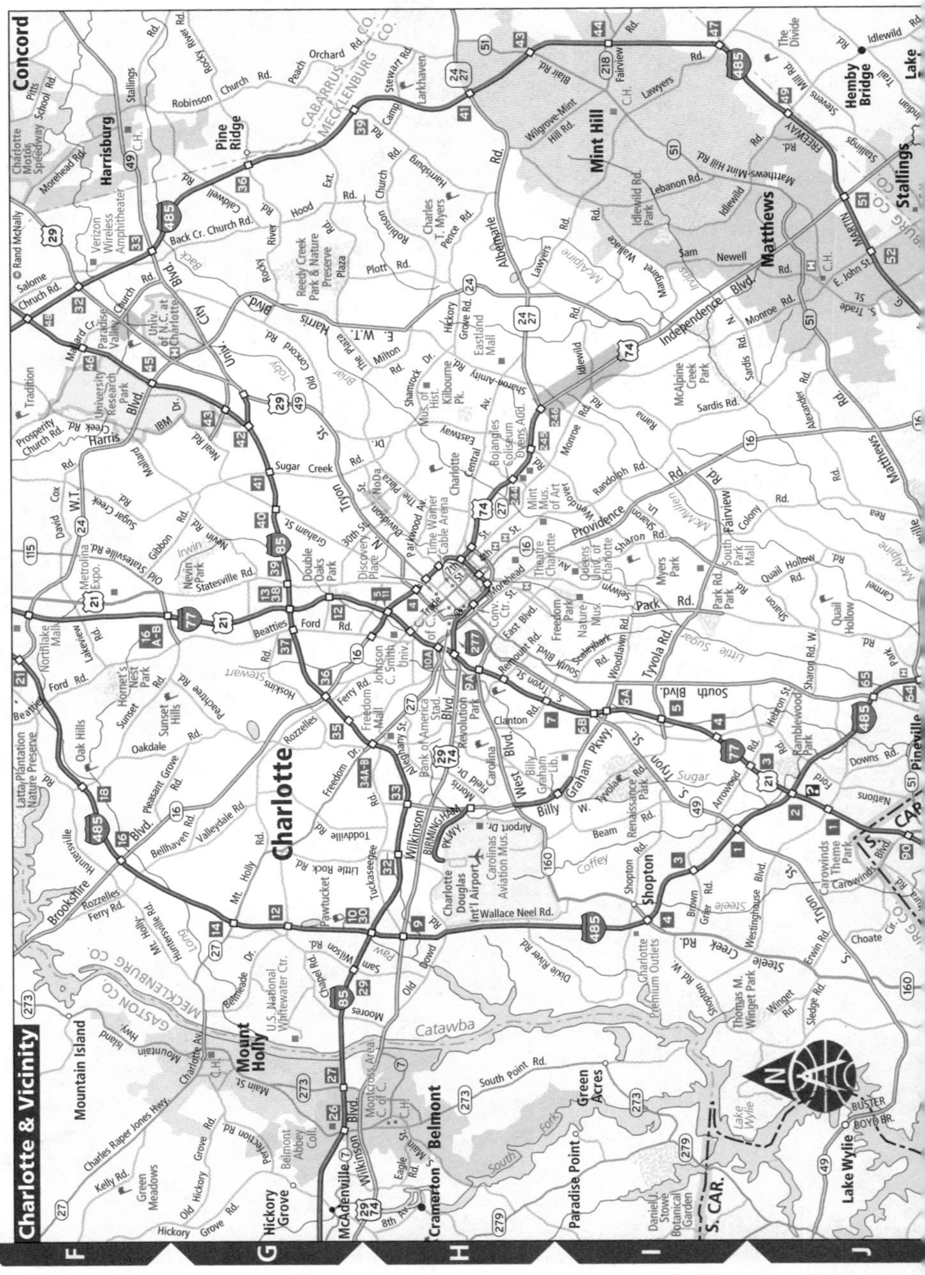

Get travel info at www.randmcnally.com/ND

ourism Information
.D. Tourism Division: (800) 435-5663,
701) 328-2525; www.ndtourism.com

oad Conditions & Construction
11, (855) 637-6237, (866) 696-3511
www.dot.nd.gov, www.dot.nd.gov/travel-info-v2

Toll Rd. Info
No toll roads

511

Determining Distances
9 · 4 · 3 · 2 (segments of one mile or less not shown)
Cumulative miles (red): the distance between red arrows
Intermediate miles (black): the distance between intersections & places

Total mileages through North Dakota
- 29: 218 miles
- 94: 352 miles
- 2: 359 miles
- 83: 265 miles

More mileages at www.randmcnally.com/MC

Mileages between cities	Bismarck	Bowman	Fargo	Garrison	Grand Forks	Jamestown	Williston	Winnipeg, MB
Bismarck		174	195	75	272	102	228	413
Devils Lake	180	354	165	167	89	99	245	230
Dickinson	97	78	292	149	368	198	132	509
Fargo	195	368		266	80	94	422	222
Grand Forks	272	444	80	256		171	334	146
Minot	110	260	268	47	210	170	124	299
Wahpeton	243	416	54	315	131	142	470	273
Williston	228	170	422	144	334	293		424

Mileages © Rand McNally

North Dakota

Nickname: The Peace Garden State
Capital: Bismarck, H-7
Land area: 68,976 sq. mi. (rank: 17th)
Population: 672,591 (rank: 48th)
Largest city: Fargo, 105,549, H-13

Index of cities Pg. 133

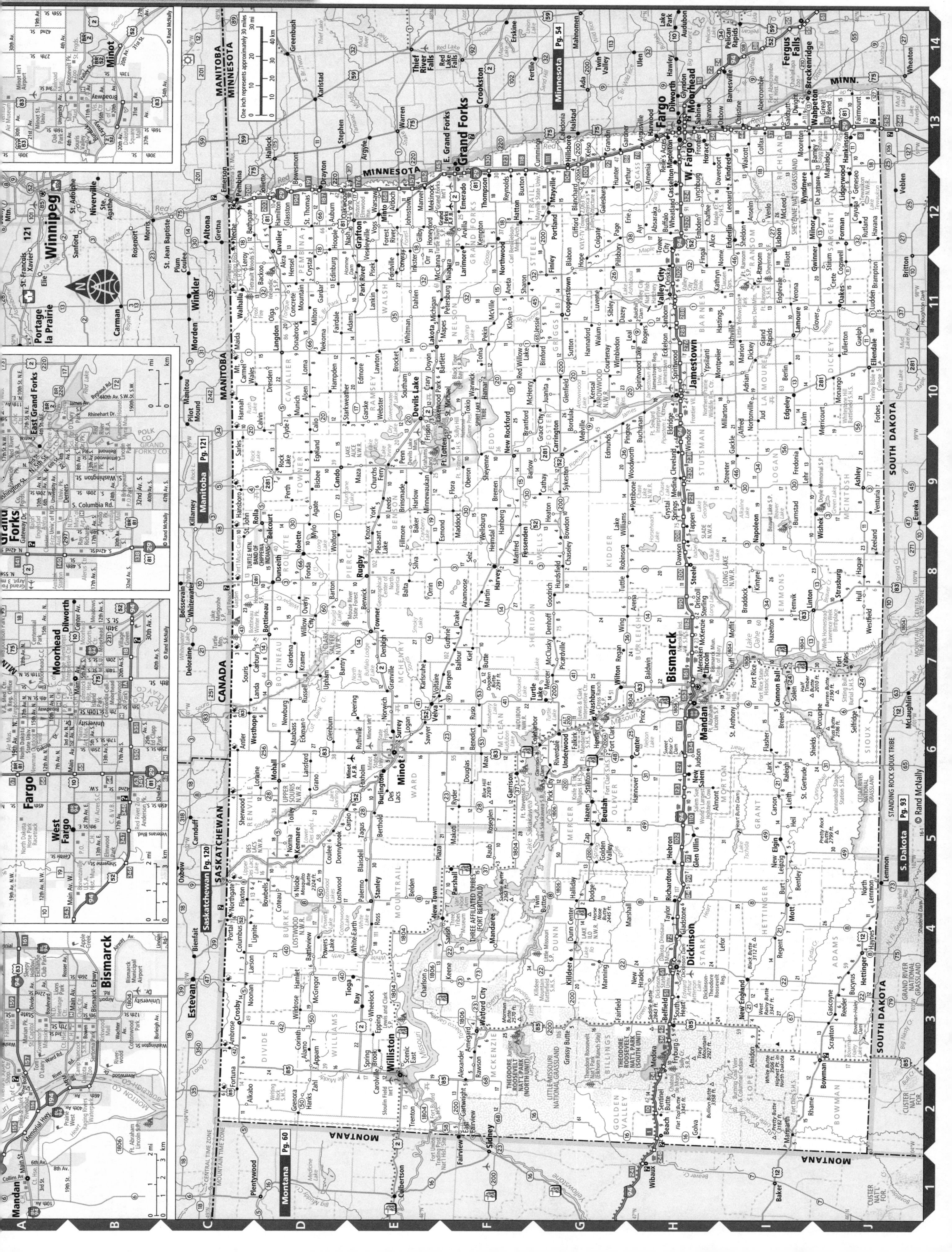

Nickname: The Buckeye State
Capital: Columbus, SB-9
Land area: 40,948 sq. mi. (rank: 35th)
Population: 11,536,504 (rank: 7th)
Largest city: Columbus, 787,033, SB-9

Index of cities Pg. 133

Explore Ohio at www.randmcnally.com/OH

Tourism Information
TourismOhio:
(800) 282-5393; www.discoverohio.com

Road Conditions & Construction
(614) 466-7170; www.dot.state.oh.us, www.buckeyetraffic.org
Ohio Turnpike: (440) 234-2030, (440) 234-2081, www.ohioturnpike.org

Toll Road Information
J.W. Shocknessy Ohio Turnpike (*E-ZPass*):
(888) 876-7453; www.ohioturnpike.org

Determining distances along roads

Highway distances (segments of one mile or less not shown):
Cumulative miles (red): the distance between red arrows
Intermediate miles (black): the distance between intersections & places

Interchanges and exit numbers
For most states, the mileage between interchanges may be determined by subtracting one number from the other.

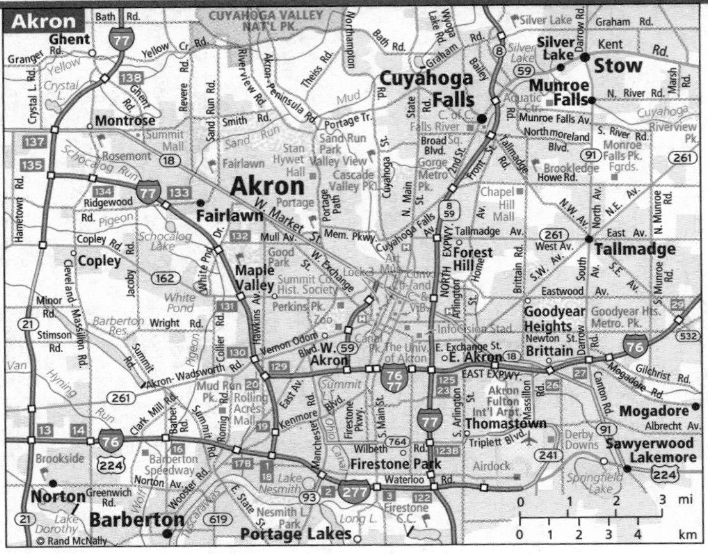

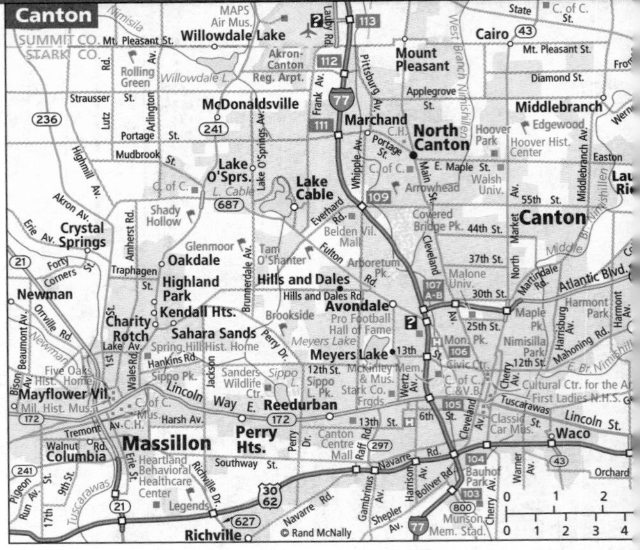

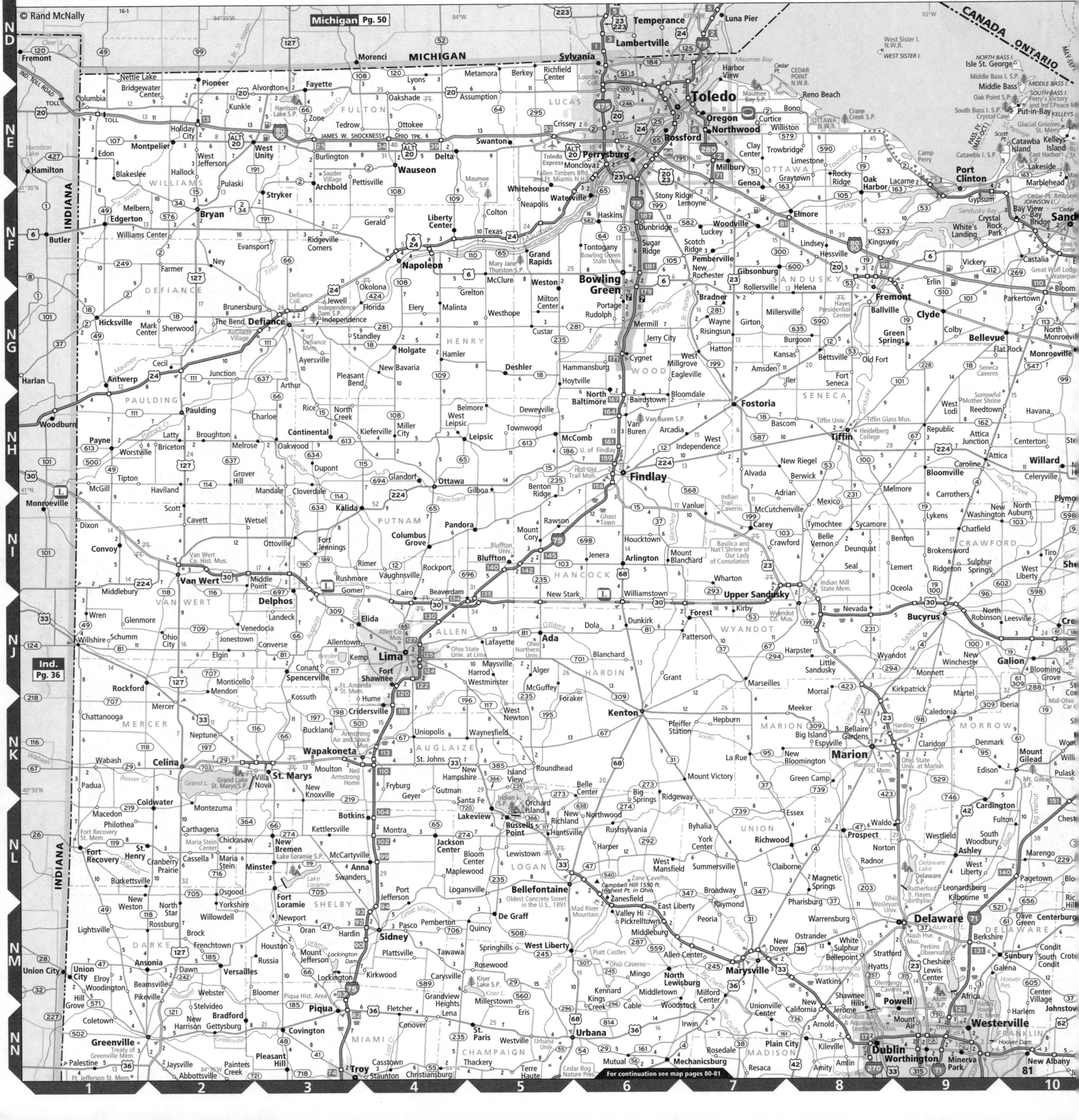

Toledo

Akron

Canton

Michigan Pg. 50

Ind. Pg. 36

For continuation see map pages 80-81

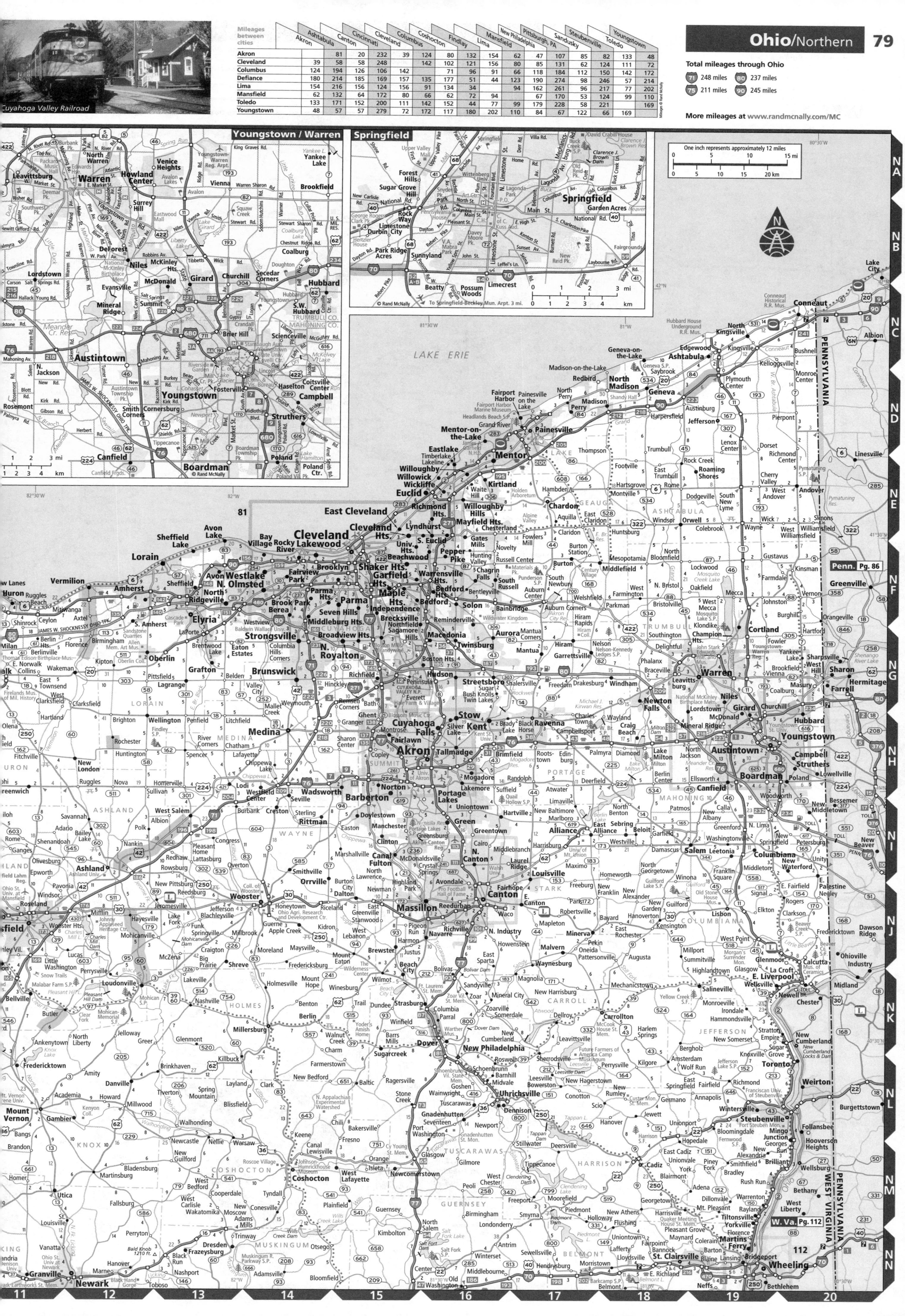

Mileages between cities

	Akron	Ashtabula	Canton	Cincinnati	Cleveland	Columbus	Coshocton	Findlay	Lima	Mansfield	New Philadelphia	Pittsburgh, PA	Sandusky	Steubenville	Toledo	Youngstown
Akron		81	20	232	39	124	80	132	154	62	47	107	85	82	133	48
Cleveland	39	58	58	248		142	102	121	156	80	85	131	62	124	111	72
Columbus	124	194	126	106	142		71	96	91	66	118	184	112	150	142	172
Defiance	180	214	185	169	157	135	177	51	44	123	190	274	98	246	57	214
Lima	154	216	156	124	156	91	134	34		94	162	261	96	217	77	202
Mansfield	62	132	64	172	80	66	62	72	94		67	170	53	124	99	110
Toledo	133	171	152	200	111	142	152	44	77	99	179	228	58	221		169
Youngstown	48	57	57	279	72	172	117	180	202	110	84	67	122	66	169	

Nickname: The Buckeye State
Capital: Columbus, SB-9
Land area: 40,948 sq. mi. (rank: 35th)
Population: 11,536,504 (rank: 7th)
Largest city: Columbus, 787,033, SB-9

Index of cities Pg. 133

Explore Ohio at www.randmcnally.com/OH

Tourism Information
TourismOhio:
(800) 282-5393; www.discoverohio.com

Road Conditions & Construction
(614) 466-7170; www.dot.state.oh.us, www.buckeyetraffic.org
Cincinnati metro area: 511

Toll Road Information
J.W. Shocknessy Ohio Turnpike (*E-ZPass*):
(888) 876-7453; www.ohioturnpike.org

Determining distances along roads

Highway distances (segments of one mile or less not shown):
Cumulative miles (red): the distance between red arrows
Intermediate miles (black): the distance between intersections & places

Interchanges and exit numbers
For most states, the mileage between interchanges may be determined by subtracting one number from the other.

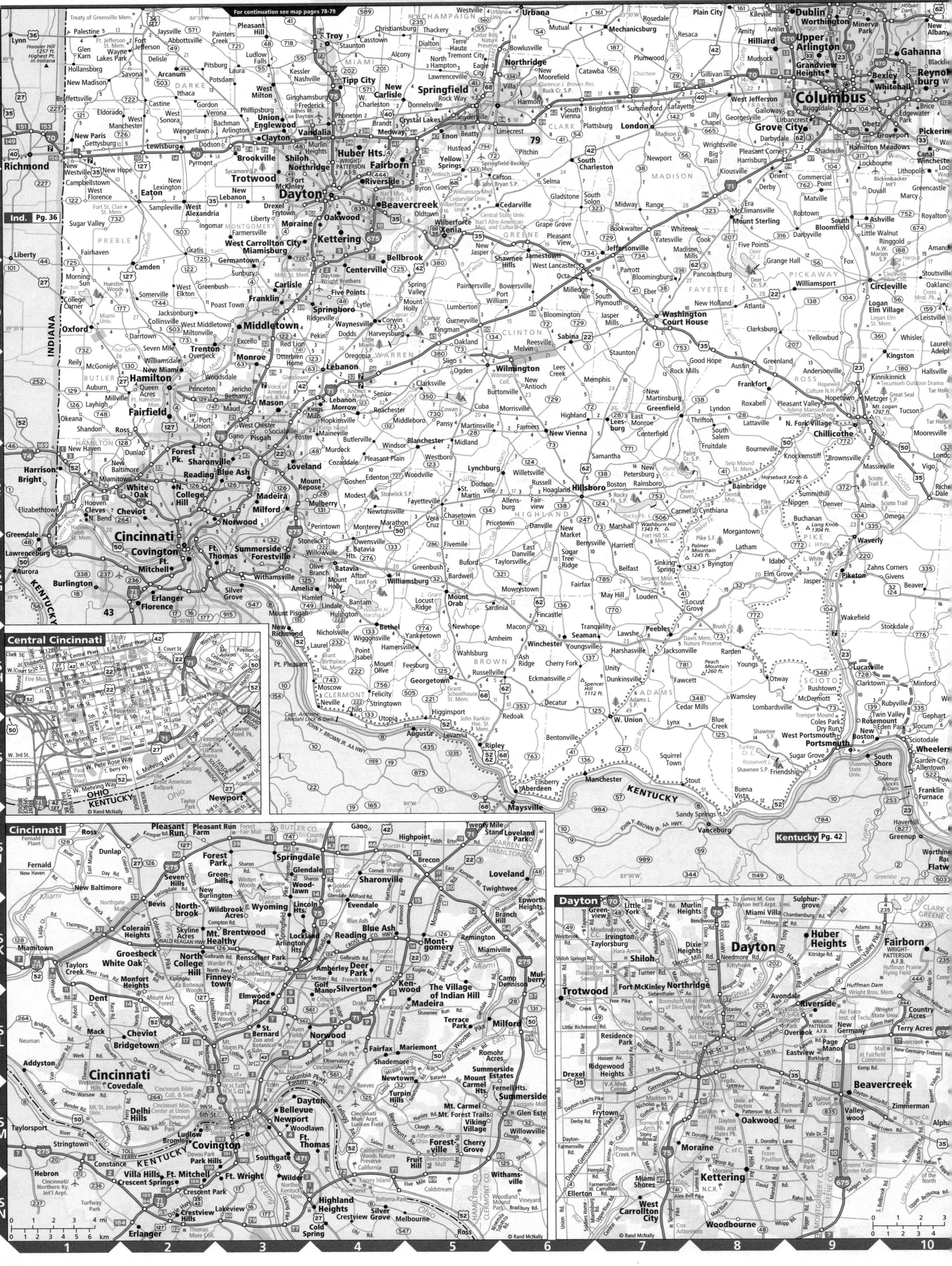

For continuation see map pages 78-79

Ind. Pg. 36

Kentucky Pg. 42

Central Cincinnati

Cincinnati

Dayton

© Rand McNally

Mileages between cities

	Athens	Cambridge	Chillicothe	Cincinnati	Cleveland	Columbus	Dayton	Gallipolis	Huntington, WV	Lancaster	Marietta	Maysville, KY	Portsmouth	Wheeling, WV	Wilmington	Zanesville
Cincinnati	160	183	106		248	106	50	153	148	133	210	61	110	230	51	158
Columbus	74	79	47	106	142		71	106	137	30	124	112	91	126	62	55
Dayton	134	149	77	50	212	71		137	168	101	195	108	122	197	34	126
Gallipolis	42	114	60	153	235	106	137		39	86	66	111	55	162	112	94
Marietta	44	48	104	210	164	124	195	66	106	82		165	128	90	156	69
Portsmouth	81	162	44	110	233	91	122	55	46	80	128	52		210	79	138
Springfield	118	123	69	77	185	45	27	129	160	74	168	102	114	171	38	99
Zanesville	52	24	94	158	145	55	126	94	134	45	69	164	138	72	114	

Total mileages through Ohio

70: 226 miles
75: 211 miles
71: 248 miles
77: 160 miles

More mileages at www.randmcnally.com/MC

Oklahoma

Nickname: The Sooner State
Capital: Oklahoma City, F-13
Land area: 68,667 sq. mi. (rank: 19th)
Population: 3,751,351 (rank: 28th)
Largest city: Oklahoma City, 579,999, F-13

Index of cities Pg. 134

Plan an Oklahoma trip at www.randmcnally.com/OK

Tourism Information
Oklahoma Tourism & Recreation Department: (800) 652-6552; www.travelok.com

Road Conditions & Construction
(877) 403-7623, (405) 425-2385; www.okladot.state.ok.us

Toll Road Information
Oklahoma Turnpike Authority *(PIKEPASS)*: (405) 425-3600; www.pikepass.com

Determining distances along roads

Highway distances (segments of one mile or less not shown):
Cumulative miles (red): the distance between red arrows
Intermediate miles (black): the distance between intersections & places

Interchanges and exit numbers
For most states, the mileage between interchanges may be determined by subtracting one number from the other.

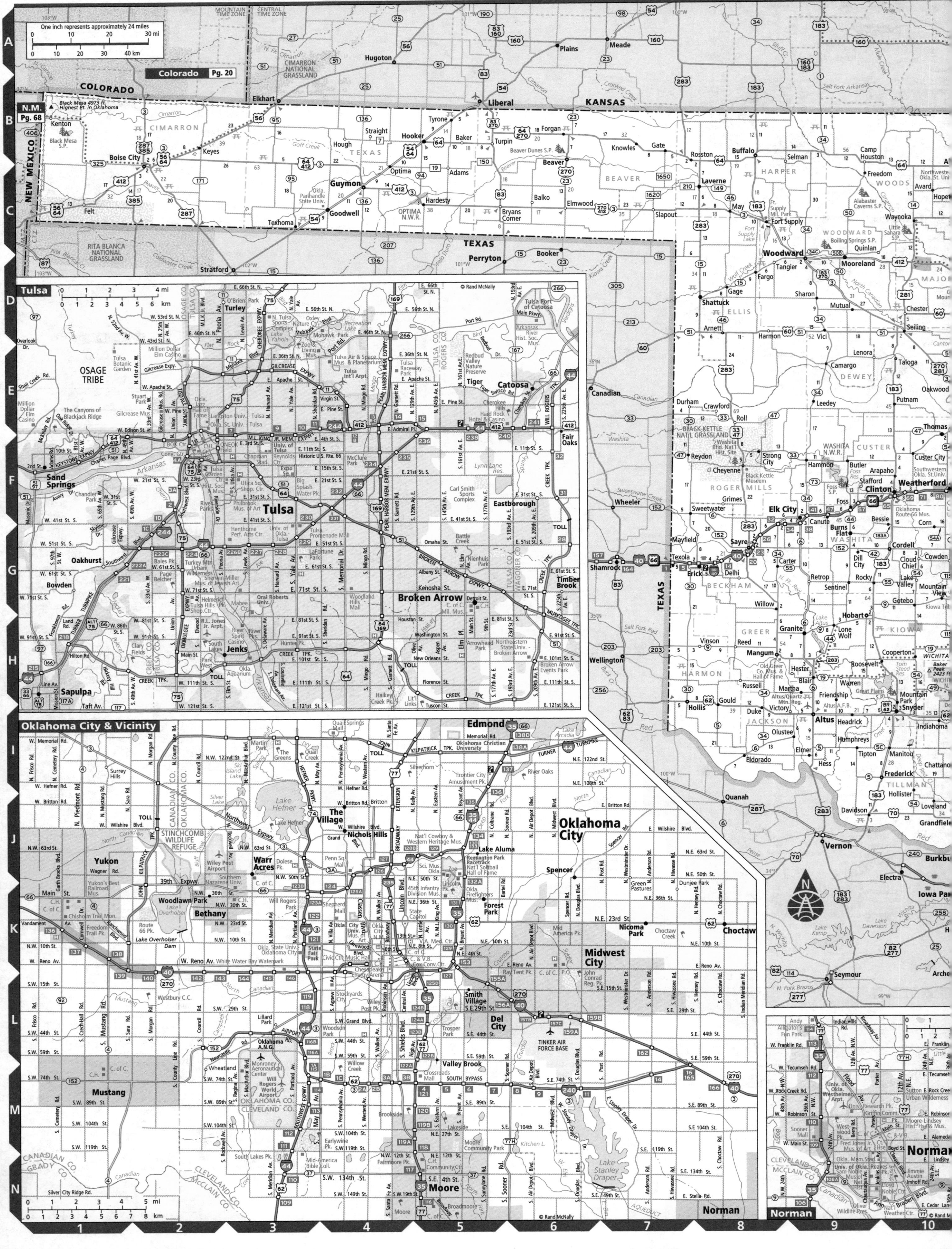

One inch represents approximately 24 miles

Colorado Pg. 20

N.M. Pg. 68

COLORADO

KANSAS

NEW MEXICO

TEXAS

Tulsa

© Rand McNally

Oklahoma City & Vicinity

© Rand McNally

Norman

© Rand McNally

Buffalo

Mileages between cities

	Ardmore	Bartlesville	Dallas, TX	Elk City	Enid	Ft. Smith, AR	Guymon	Joplin, MO	Lawton	McAlester	Muskogee	Oklahoma City	Ponca City	Tulsa	Wichita Falls, TX	Woodward
Ardmore		246	109	208	195	223	360	312	99	116	180	97	200	201	86	236
Elk City	208	260	303		148	292	184	327	108	240	249	112	216	215	143	77
Enid	195	134	302	148		232	211	227	142	204	164	99	67	114	196	87
Guymon	360	344	459	184	211	443		438	294	391	375	263	278	326	317	124
Idabel	149	248	171	352	316	136	504	295	245	116	180	240	293	203	238	380
Muskogee	180	91	236	249	164	70	375	117	218	65		137	142	50	272	251
Oklahoma City	97	149	204	112	99	180	263	216	86	128	137		105	104	140	139
Tulsa	201	45	258	215	114	118	326	113	191	91	50	104	91		244	202

Mileages © Rand McNally

Total mileages through Oklahoma

35 236 miles
44 329 miles
40 331 miles
75 227 miles

More mileages at www.randmcnally.com/MC

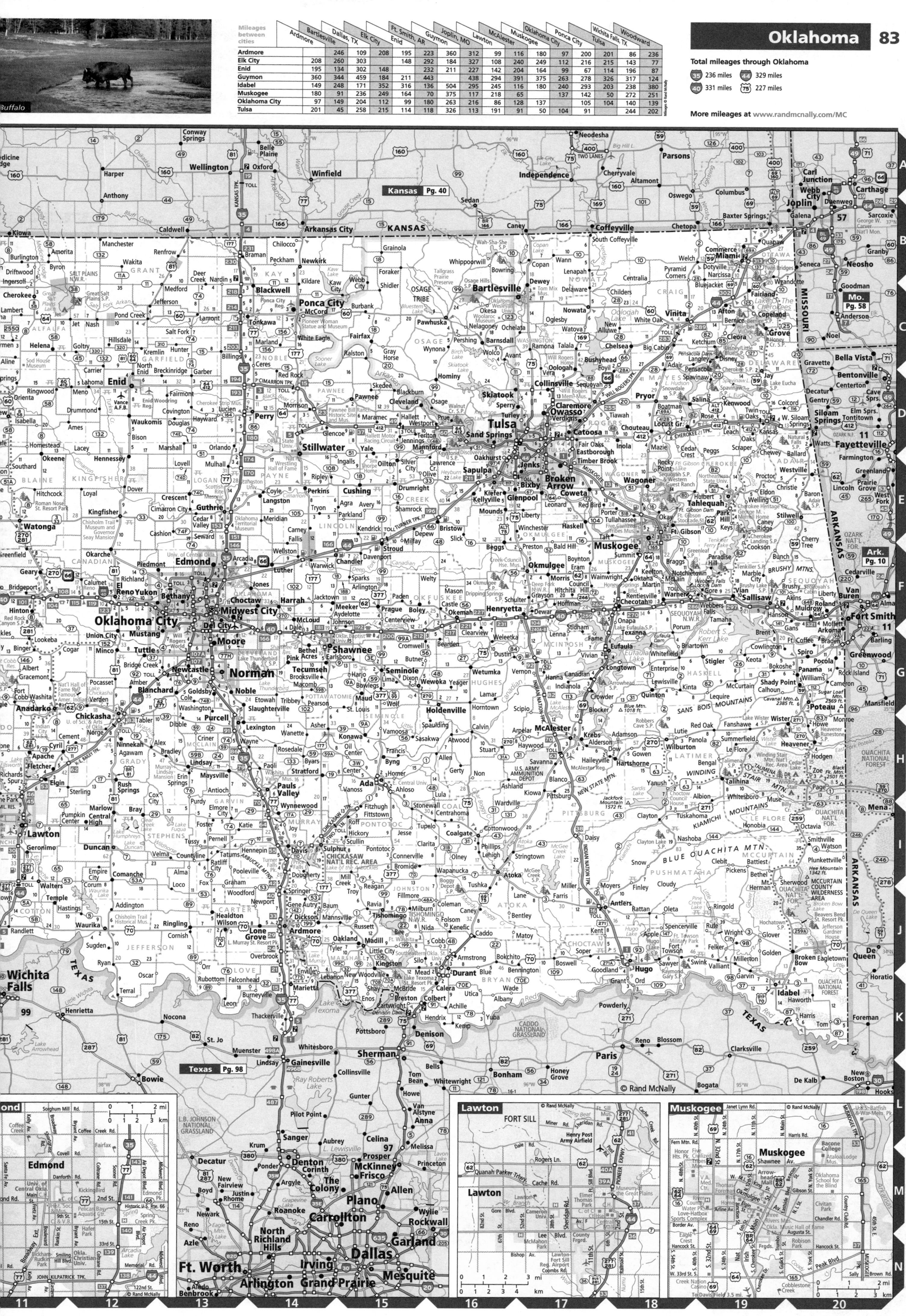

Oregon

Nickname: The Beaver State
Capital: Salem, E-4
Land area: 95,997 sq. mi. (rank: 10th)
Population: 3,831,074 (rank: 27th)
Largest city: Portland, 583,776, C-5

Index of cities Pg. 134

Get more Oregon info at www.randmcnally.com/OR

Tourism Information
Travel Oregon: (800) 547-7842; www.traveloregon.com

Road Conditions & Construction
511, (800) 977-6368, (503) 588-2941; www.oregon.gov/odot, www.tripcheck.com

Toll Road Information
No toll roads

Determining distances along roads

Highway distances (segments of one mile or less not shown):
Cumulative miles (red): the distance between red arrows
Intermediate miles (black): the distance between intersections & places

Interchanges and exit numbers
For most states, the mileage between interchanges may be determined by subtracting one number from the other.

Washington Pg. 108

California Pg. 12

Eugene

© Rand McNally

Mileages between cities

	Astoria	Bend	Brookings	Burns	Coos Bay	Crater Lake N.P.	Eugene	Government Camp	John Day	Lakeview	Medford	Ontario	Pendleton	Portland	Salem	The Dalles
Bend	250		287	130	228	107	115	106	151	175	172	260	242	161	131	129
Corvallis	166	127	280	257	132	187	47	126	260	284	210	387	290	82	37	165
Eugene	193	115	234	245	109	142		154	249	241	166	375	318	110	66	193
McDermitt, NV	525	277	525	147	505	356	392	380	218	222	400	187	354	436	408	405
Medford	356	172	125	305	169	74	166	317	328	171		432	481	273	228	356
Ontario	464	260	547	130	488	367	375	354	131	269	432		167	374	420	291
Pendleton	298	242	550	196	428	349	318	188	126	335	481	167		208	254	125
Portland	96	161	342	281	220	250	110	55	265	336	273	374	208		47	83

Total mileages through Oregon

- 5: 308 miles
- 84: 375 miles
- 82: 11 miles
- 101: 348 miles

More mileages at www.randmcnally.com/MC

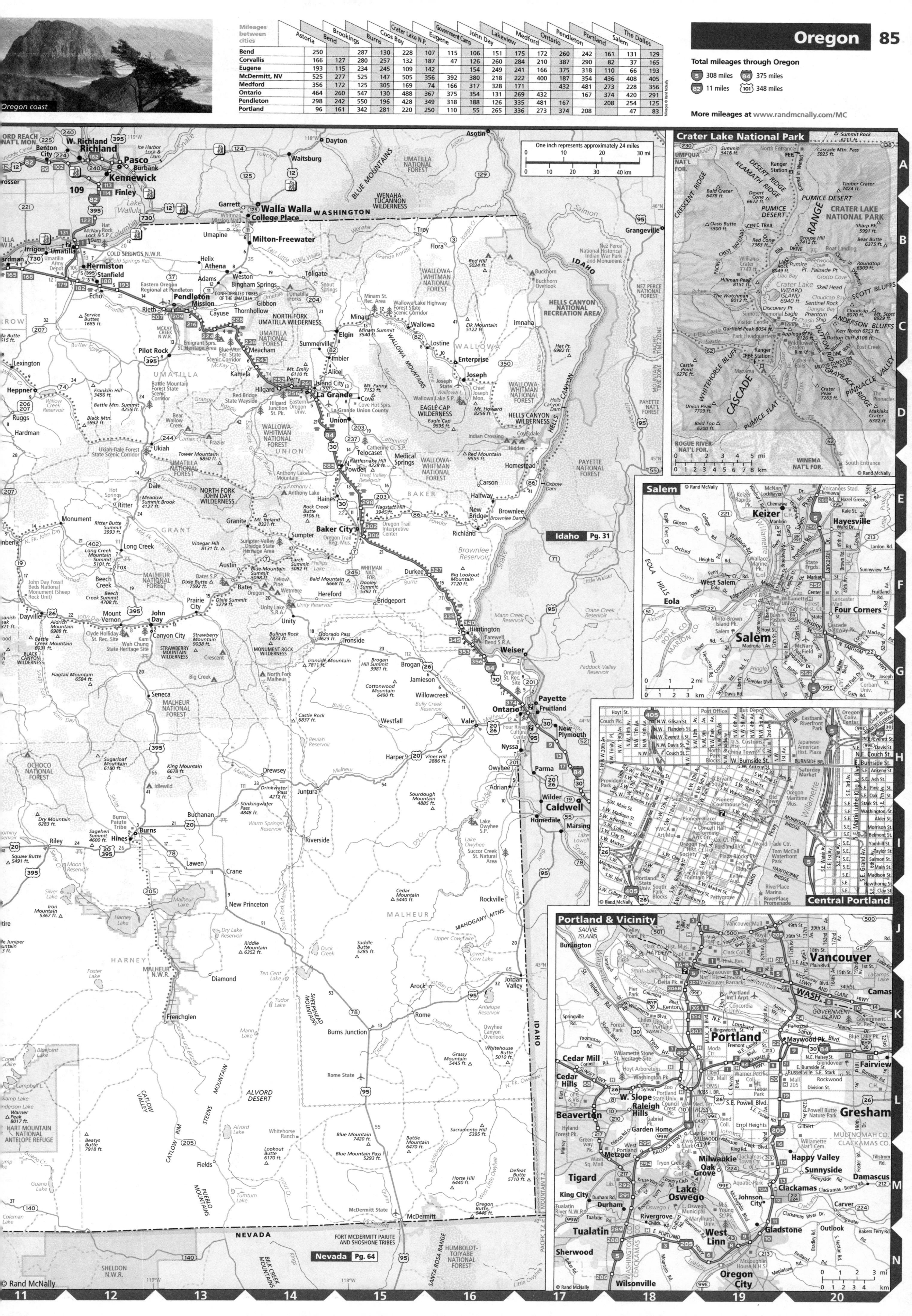

Nickname: The Keystone State
Capital: Harrisburg, EN-4
Land area: 44,817 sq. mi. (rank: 32nd)
Population: 12,702,379 (rank: 6th)
Largest city: Philadelphia, 1,526,006, EP-12

Index of cities Pg. 134

Explore Pennsylvania at www.randmcnally.com/PA

Tourism Information
Pennsylvania Tourism Office:
(800) 847-4872; www.visitpa.com

Road Conditions & Construction
511, (888) 783-6783;
www.dot.state.pa.us

Toll Road Information
Delaware River Port Authority (Phila. area bridges) *(E-ZPass)*: (877) 567-3772; www.drpa.org
Pennsylvania Turnpike Commission *(E-ZPass)*: (800) 331-3414; www.paturnpike.com

Determining distances along roads

Highway distances (segments of one mile or less not shown):
Cumulative miles (red): the distance between red arrows
Intermediate miles (black): the distance between intersections & places

Interchanges and exit numbers
For most states, the mileage between interchanges may be determined by subtracting one number from the other.

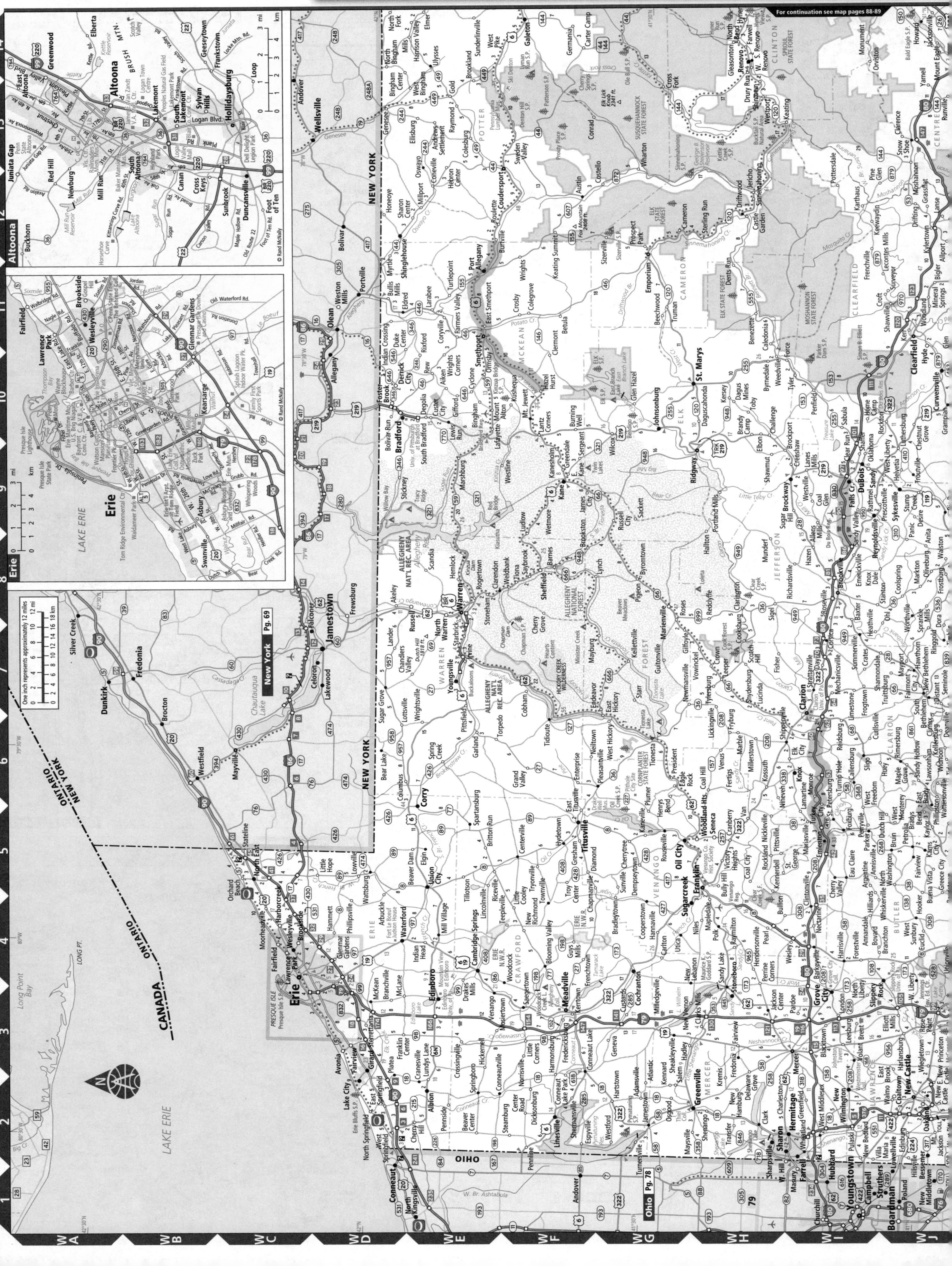

For continuation see map pages 88-89

New York Pg. 69

Ohio Pg. 78

One inch represents approximately 12 miles

Erie

Altoona

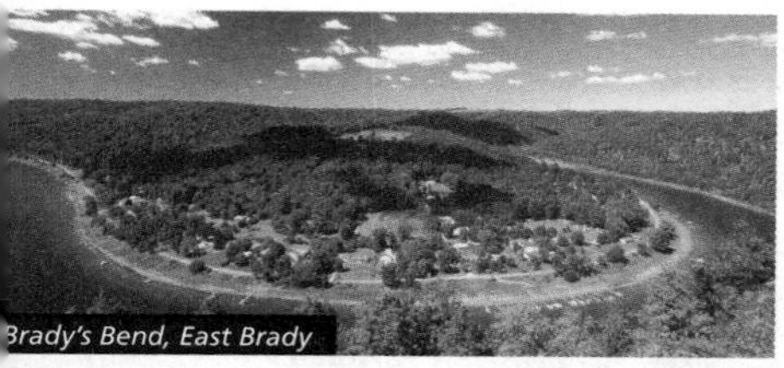

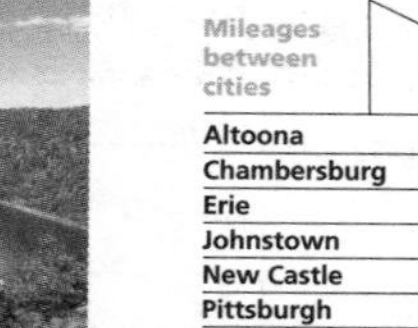

Brady's Bend, East Brady

Mileages between cities

	Altoona	Chambersburg	Cumberland, MD	Du Bois	Erie	Galeton	Harrisburg	Johnstown	Kittanning	Meadville	New Castle	Philadelphia	Pittsburgh	State College	Uniontown	Warren
Altoona		90	66	71	202	135	134	46	79	165	127	234	96	41	112	130
Chambersburg	90		87	153	282	215	54	94	160	246	206	157	160	101	149	218
Erie	202	282	232	148		159	297	177	123	41	88	419	127	208	184	66
Johnstown	46	94	70	77	177	179	137		53	141	102	238	67	85	80	135
New Castle	127	206	156	110	88	197	250	102	48	52		350	52	171	108	120
Pittsburgh	96	160	111	101	127	200	203	67	42	91	52	304		135	51	148
State College	41	101	106	61	208	100	87	85	120	173	171	193	135		152	119
Williamsport	100	132	166	110	257	72	83	146	168	220	219	176	196	63	212	171

Total mileages through Pennsylvania

- 70: 168 miles
- 79: 183 miles
- 80: 311 miles
- 90: 46 miles

More mileages at www.randmcnally.com/MC

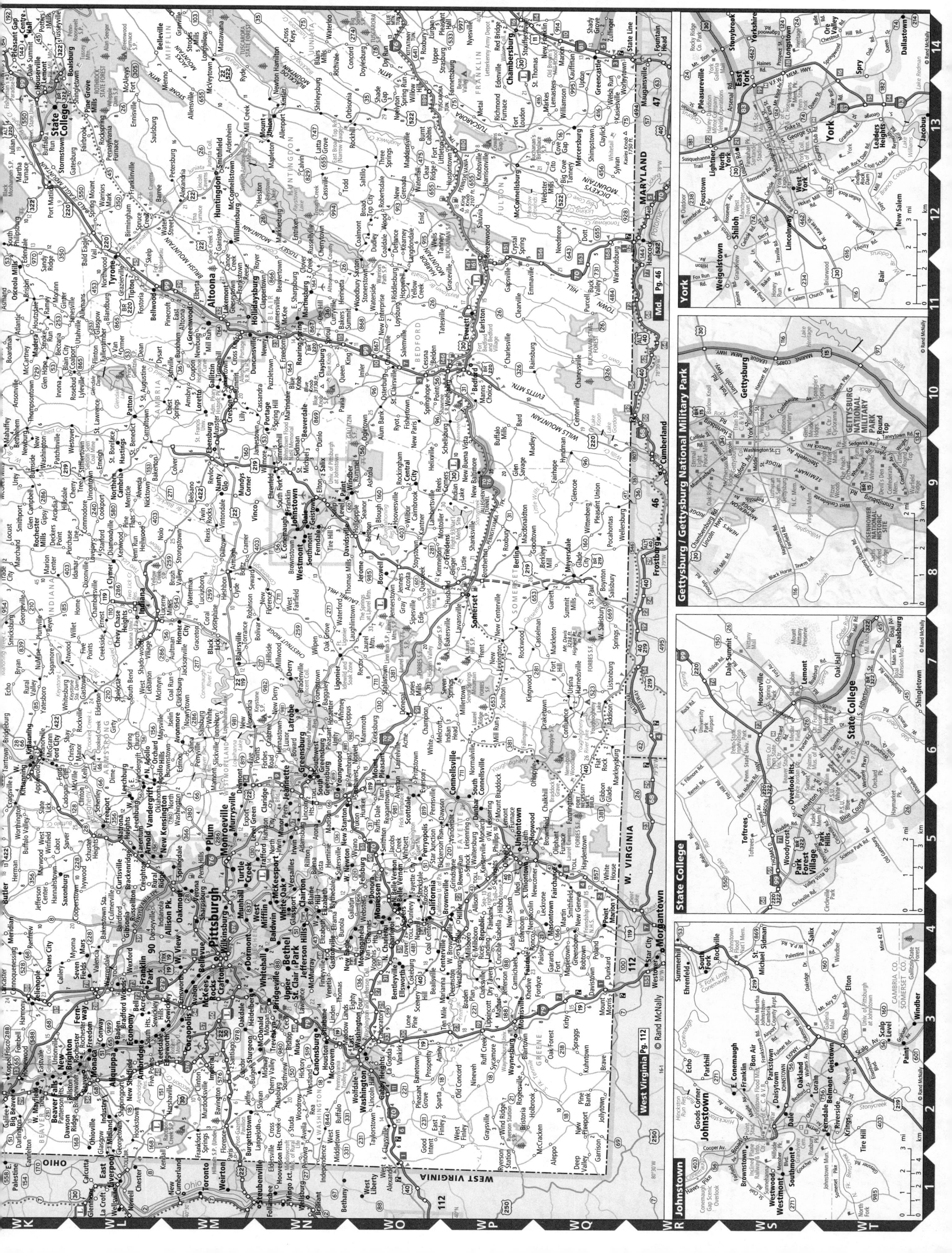

Johnstown

State College

Gettysburg / Gettysburg National Military Park

York

West Virginia Pg. 112

Md. Pg. 46

Nickname: The Keystone State
Capital: Harrisburg, EN-4
Land area: 44,817 sq. mi. (rank: 32nd)
Population: 12,702,379 (rank: 6th)
Largest city: Philadelphia, 1,526,006, EP-12

Index of cities Pg. 134

Explore Pennsylvania at www.randmcnally.com/PA

Tourism Information
Pennsylvania Tourism Office:
(800) 847-4872; www.visitpa.com

Road Conditions & Construction
511, (888) 783-6783;
www.dot.state.pa.us

Toll Road Information
Delaware River Port Authority (Phila. area bridges) *(E-ZPass)*: (877) 567-3772; www.drpa.org
Pennsylvania Turnpike Commission *(E-ZPass)*: (800) 331-3414; www.paturnpike.com

Determining distances along roads
Highway distances (segments of one mile or less not shown):
Cumulative miles (red): the distance between red arrows
Intermediate miles (black): the distance between intersections & places

Interchanges and exit numbers
For most states, the mileage between interchanges may be determined by subtracting one number from the other.

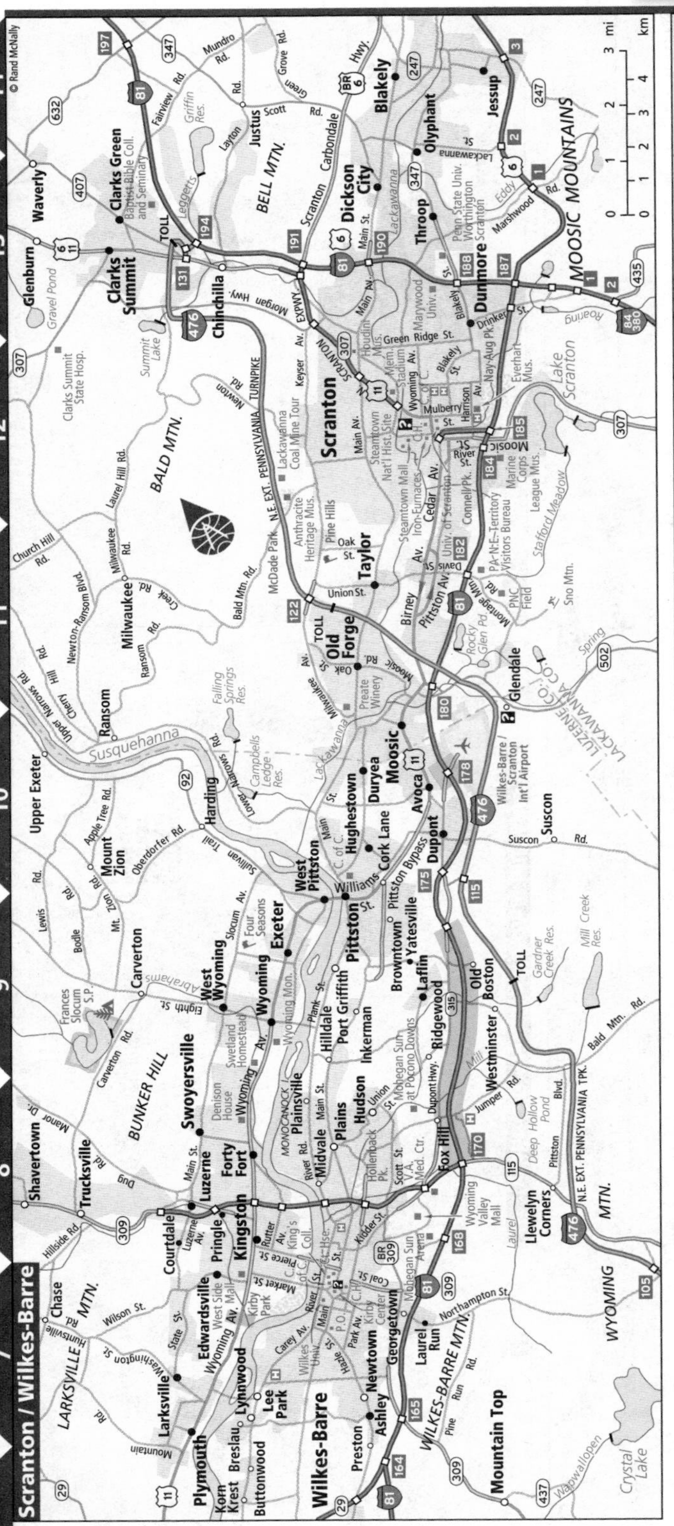

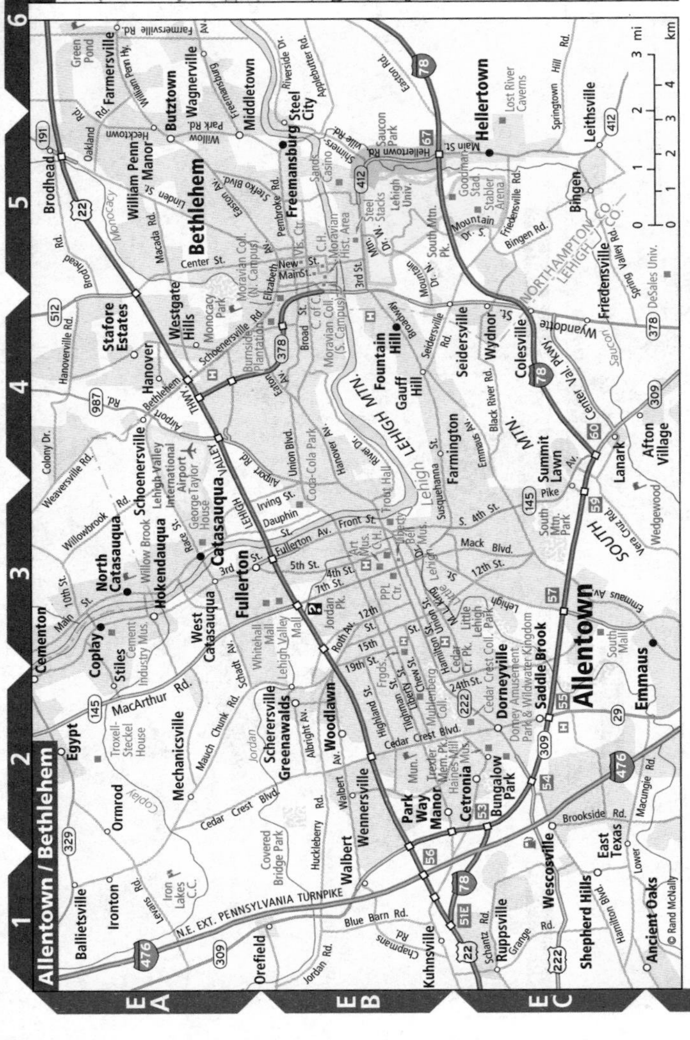

Scranton / Wilkes-Barre

Allentown / Bethlehem

One inch represents approximately 12 miles

For continuation see map pages 86-87

New York Pg. 69

erry rides on the Delaware River

Mileages between cities	Allentown	Gettysburg	Harrisburg	Lancaster	Mansfield	Philadelphia	Pittsburgh	Port Jervis, NY	Scranton	State College	Stroudsburg	Towanda	Trenton, NJ	Wilkes Barre	Williamsport	York
Allentown		121	81	67	177	62	282	81	74	175	40	126	75	60	127	92
Chambersburg	132	25	54	91	182	157	160	227	171	101	170	188	177	154	132	74
Harrisburg	81	38		39	133	107	203	176	120	87	119	139	127	104	83	26
Philadelphia	62	138	107	78	226		304	140	124	193	100	175	32	109	176	101
Reading	37	96	64	34	175	62	261	118	100	150	76	152	82	86	126	56
Scranton	74	160	120	132	102	124	279	59		150	46	64	137	16	101	146
State College	175	129	87	126	107	193	135	205	150		162	134	213	132	63	118
Williamsport	127	126	83	123	50	176	196	157	101	63	113	67	189	84		115

Total mileages through Pennsylvania

- 76: 350 miles
- 80: 311 miles
- 81: 232 miles
- 95: 51 miles

More mileages at www.randmcnally.com/MC

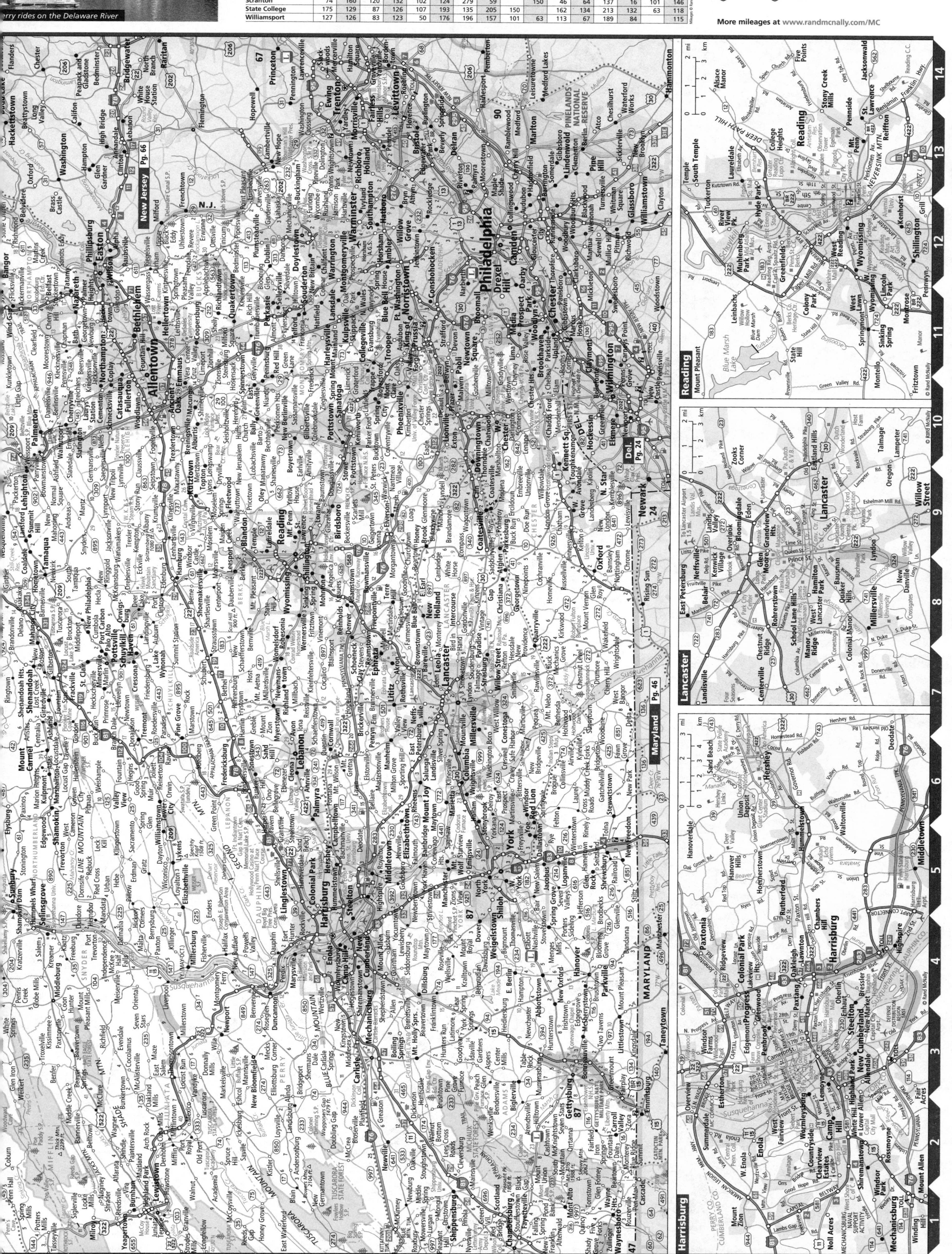

City sights to see

- Adventure Aquarium, Camden, E-5
- The Andy Warhol Museum, Pittsburgh, L-2
- Betsy Ross House, Philadelphia, F-10
- Carnegie Science Center, Pittsburgh, L-1
- Duquesne Incline, Pittsburgh, M-1
- Franklin Institute Science Museum, Philadelphia, F-6
- Independence Hall, Philadelphia, G-9
- Liberty Bell, Philadelphia, G-9
- National Constitution Center, Philadelphia, F-9
- Philadelphia Museum of Art, Philadelphia, E-4
- Point State Park, Pittsburgh, M-1
- The Strip District, Pittsburgh, L-3

Pittsburgh

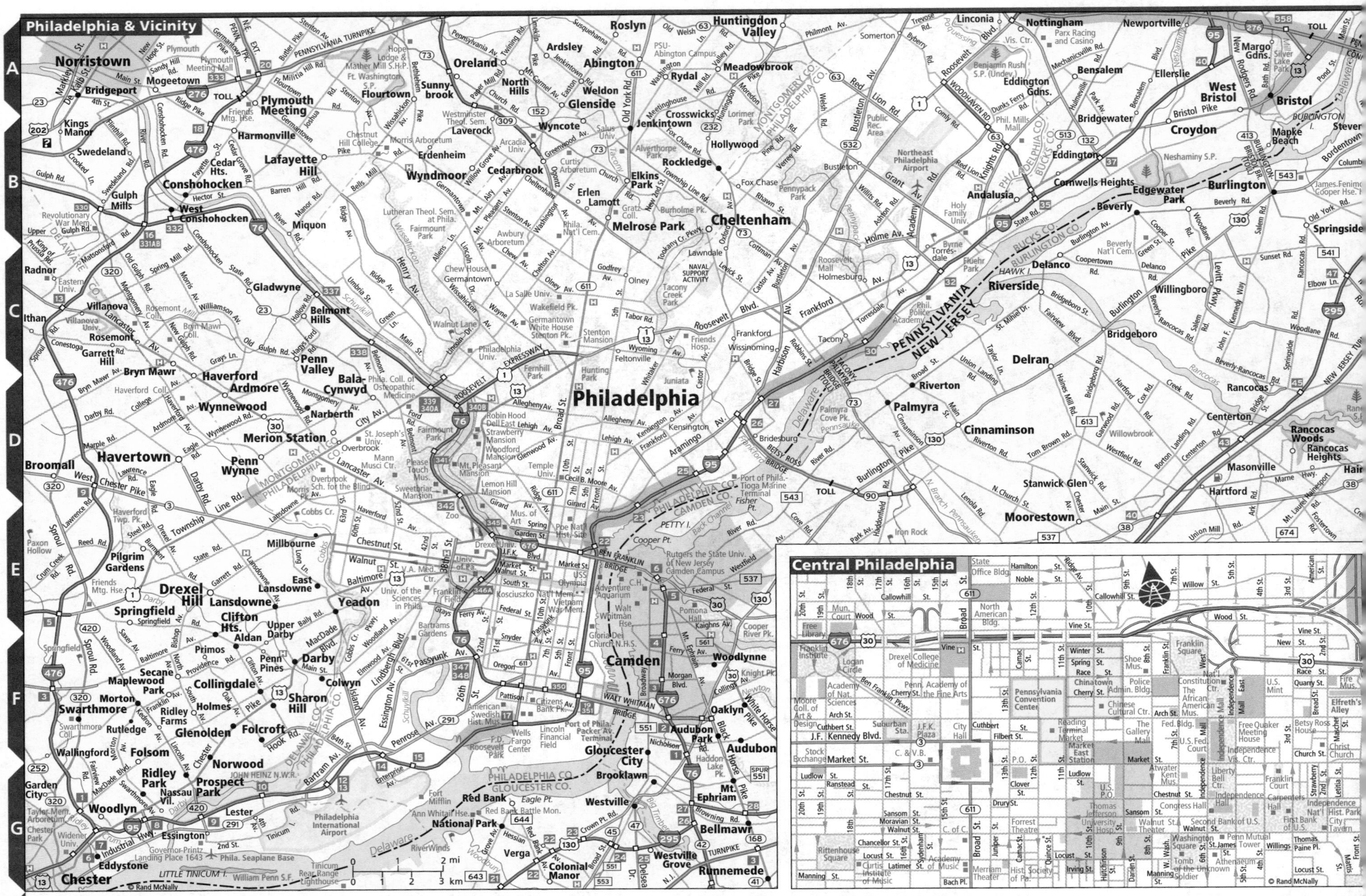

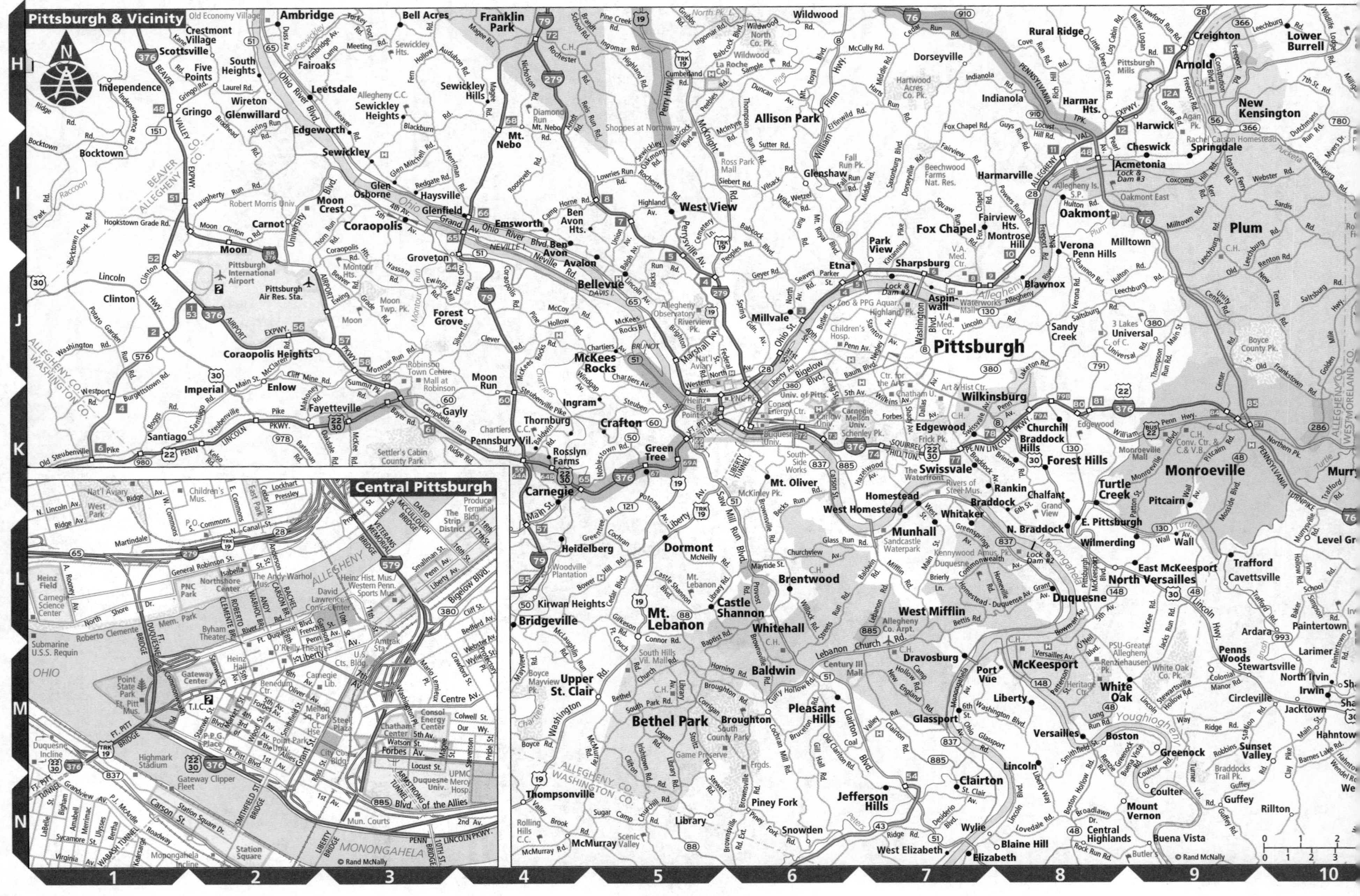

Philadelphia & Vicinity

Central Philadelphia

Pittsburgh & Vicinity

Central Pittsburgh

© Rand McNally

Tourism Information
Rhode Island Tourism Division
(401) 278-9100
www.visitrhodeisland.com

Toll Bridge Info (EZ-Pass)
R.I. Turnpike & Bridge Auth.: (877) 743-9727
www.ritba.org

Road Conditions & Construction
511, (888) 401-4511, (401) 222-2450
www.dot.ri.gov/travel

Determining Distances
(segments of one mile or less not shown)
Cumulative miles (red): the distance between red arrows
Intermediate miles (black): the distance between intersections & places

Total mileages through Rhode Island
95 42 miles
6 31 miles
1 60 miles

More mileages at www.randmcnally.com/MC

Mileages between cities	Fall River, MA	Kingston	Newport	Providence	Warwick	Westerly	Woonsocket	Worcester, MA
Chepachet	35	41	45	19	23	54	13	37
Fall River, MA		35	20	16	25	58	31	56
Newport	20	16		33	26	39	47	72
Providence	16	29	33		10	42	14	40
Warwick	25	23	26	10		37	24	50
Westerly	58	23	39	42	37		56	82
Woonsocket	31	43	47	14	24	56		27
Worcester, MA	56	68	72	40	50	82	27	

Rhode Island

Nickname: The Ocean State
Capital: Providence, D-6
Land area: 1,045 sq. mi. (rank: 50th)
Population: 1,052,567 (rank: 43rd)
Largest city: Providence, 178,042, D-6

Index of cities Pg. 134

Massachusetts Pg. 48

Connecticut Pg. 23

49

MASSACHUSETTS
CONNECTICUT
RHODE ISLAND
Block Island Sound
Rhode Island Sound
ATLANTIC OCEAN

Newport (inset)

Providence (inset)

One inch represents approximately 5.5 miles

South Carolina

Nickname: The Palmetto State
Capital: Columbia, D-7
Land area: 30,110 sq. mi. (rank: 40th)
Population: 4,625,364 (rank: 24th)
Largest city: Columbia, 129,272, D-7

Index of cities Pg. 134

Mileages between cities	Anderson	Augusta, GA	Charleston	Charlotte, NC	Columbia	Hilton Head I.	Myrtle Beach	Spartanburg
Augusta, GA	92		175	160	72	151	216	120
Charleston	238	175		207	112	104	95	201
Charlotte, NC	128	160	207		93	253	176	72
Columbia	117	72	112	93		158	148	93
Florence	206	148	130	104	81	177	67	169
Myrtle Beach	273	216	95	176	148	200		237
Savannah, GA	282	134	106	251	156	34	202	246
Spartanburg	60	120	201	72	93	247	237	

Total mileages through South Carolina

20: 142 miles
85: 106 miles
26: 221 miles
95: 199 miles

More mileages at www.randmcnally.com/MC

Get travel info at www.randmcnally.com/SC

Tourism Information
S.C. Dept. of Parks, Recreation & Tourism:
(803) 734-1700; www.discoversouthcarolina.com

Road Conditions & Construction
511, (877) 511-4672, (855) 467-2368; www.511sc.org, www.dot.state.sc.us

Toll Road Information *(all use Palmetto Pass)*
Cross Island Pkwy. (Hilton Head I.): (843) 342-6718; www.crossislandparkway.org
Southern Connector (Greenville Co.): (866) 725-7277; www.southernconnector.com

Plan a trip at www.randmcnally.com/SD

ourism Information
outh Dakota Department of Tourism:
605) 773-3301; www.travelsd.com

oad Conditions & Construction
11, (866) 697-3511
www.sddot.com, www.safetravelusa.com/sd

Toll Rd. Info
No toll roads

511

Determining Distances
(segments of one mile or less not shown)
Cumulative miles (red): the distance between red arrows
Intermediate miles (black): the distance between intersections & places

Total mileages through South Dakota

29 253 miles
12 317 miles
90 413 miles
83 242 miles

More mileages at
www.randmcnally.com/MC

Mileages between cities	Aberdeen	Mobridge	Pierre	Pine Ridge	Rapid City	Sioux Falls	Watertown	Yankton
Aberdeen		100	160	360	333	203	96	236
Belle Fourche	312	212	206	172	60	403	362	421
Mobridge	100		108	308	243	303	196	332
Pierre	160	108		200	173	224	188	242
Rapid City	333	243	173	111		347	403	365
Sioux City, IA	285	384	305	358	428	85	184	63
Sioux Falls	203	303	224	356	347		103	81
Watertown	96	196	188	415	403	103		155

South Dakota

Nickname: The Mount Rushmore State
Capital: Pierre, D-7
Land area: 75,885 sq. mi. (rank: 16th)
Population: 814,180 (rank: 46th)
Largest city: Sioux Falls, 153,888, F-13

Index of cities Pg. 134

Tennessee

Nickname: The Volunteer State
Capital: Nashville, C-11
Land area: 41,217 sq. mi. (rank: 34th)
Population: 6,346,105 (rank: 17th)
Largest city: Memphis, 646,889, G-2

Index of cities Pg. 134

Explore Tennessee at www.randmcnally.com/TN

Tourism Information
Tennessee Department of Tourist Development: (615) 741-2159; www.tnvacation.com

Road Conditions & Construction
511, (877) 244-0065; www.tn511.com, www.tdot.state.tn.us

Toll Road Information
No toll roads

Determining distances along roads

Highway distances (segments of one mile or less not shown):
Cumulative miles (red): the distance between red arrows
Intermediate miles (black): the distance between intersections & places

Interchanges and exit numbers
For most states, the mileage between interchanges may be determined by subtracting one number from the other.

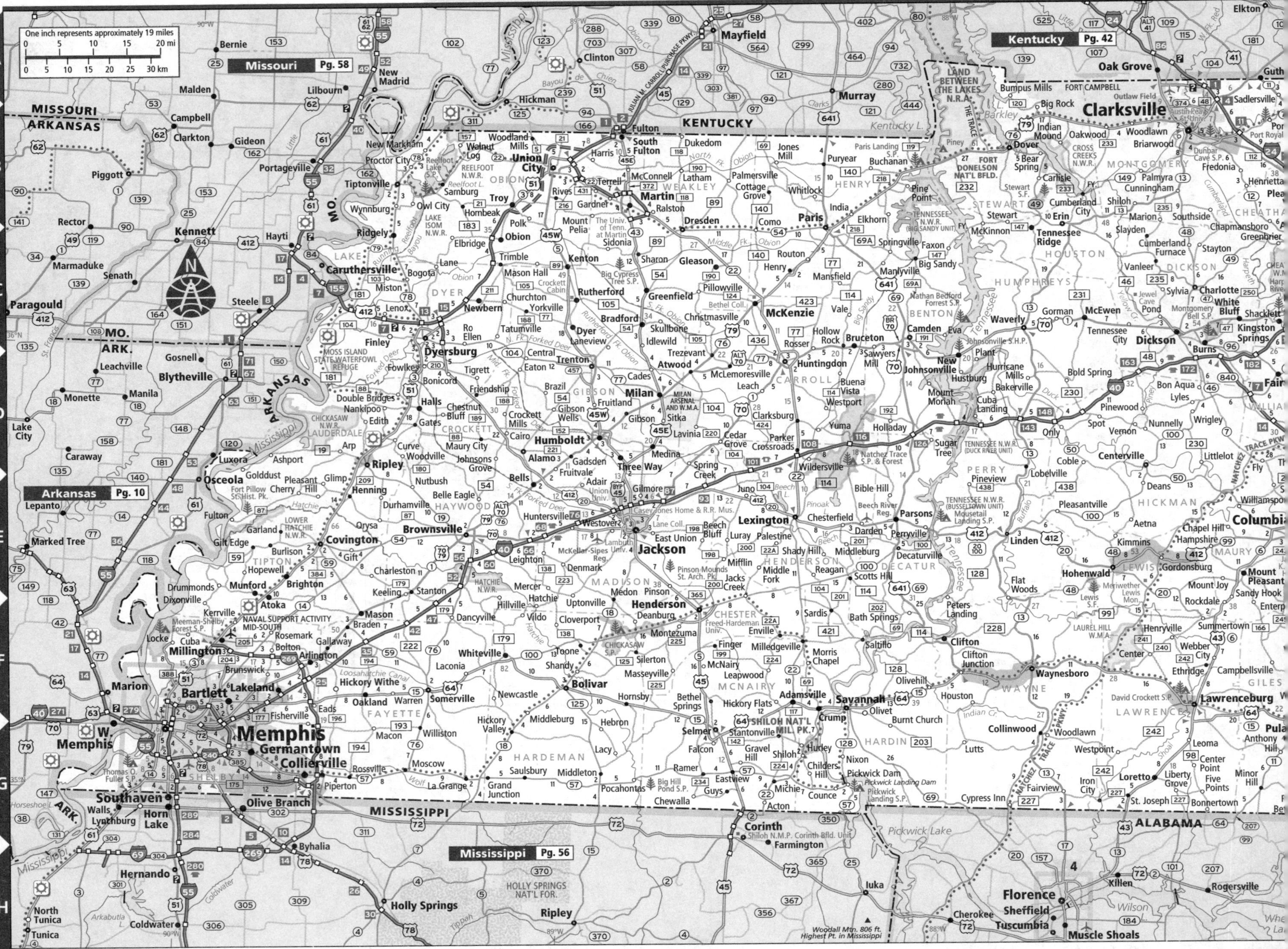

One inch represents approximately 19 miles

Missouri Pg. 58
Kentucky Pg. 42
Arkansas Pg. 10
Mississippi Pg. 56

Memphis & Vicinity

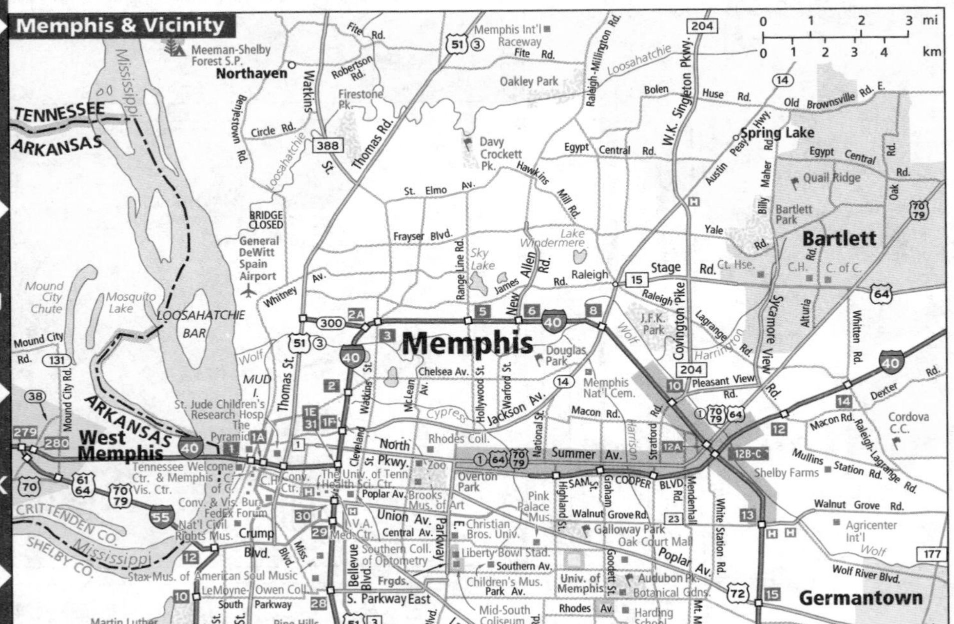

Nashville

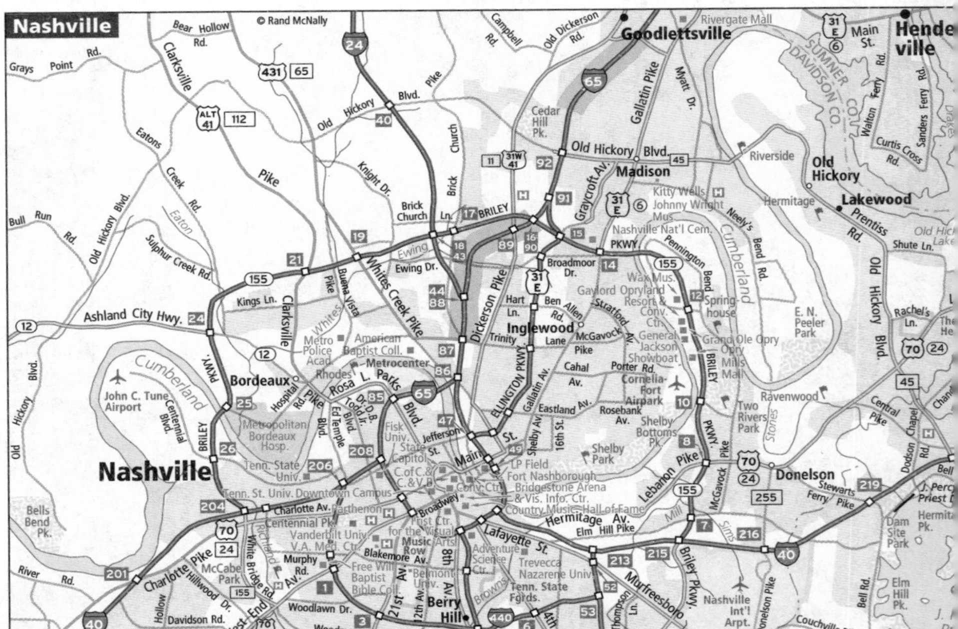

Mileages between cities

	Atlanta, GA	Bristol	Chattanooga	Clarksville	Cookeville	Dyersburg	Fayetteville	Gatlinburg	Jackson	Johnson City	Knoxville	Memphis	Morristown	Nashville	Oak Ridge	Union City
Chattanooga	117	223		177	98	303	94	151	260	215	110	314	158	131	108	311
Clarksville	293	337	177		125	173	136	265	123	329	224	201	271	47	207	138
Dyersburg	418	463	303	173	252		229	392	47	455	351	76	398	172	334	34
Fayetteville	211	317	94	136	109	229		246	167	308	204	243	252	90	189	224
Johnson City	256	24	215	329	206	455	308	106	412		104	495	65	283	128	463
Knoxville	202	113	110	224	102	351	204	41	308	104		390	48	179	24	358
Memphis	380	502	314	201	291	76	243	431	87	495	390		437	212	373	113
Nashville	249	292	131	47	80	172	90	220	129	283	179	212	226		162	168

Total mileages through Tennessee

40 455 miles · 75 161 miles
65 121 miles · 81 76 miles

More mileages at www.randmcnally.com/MC

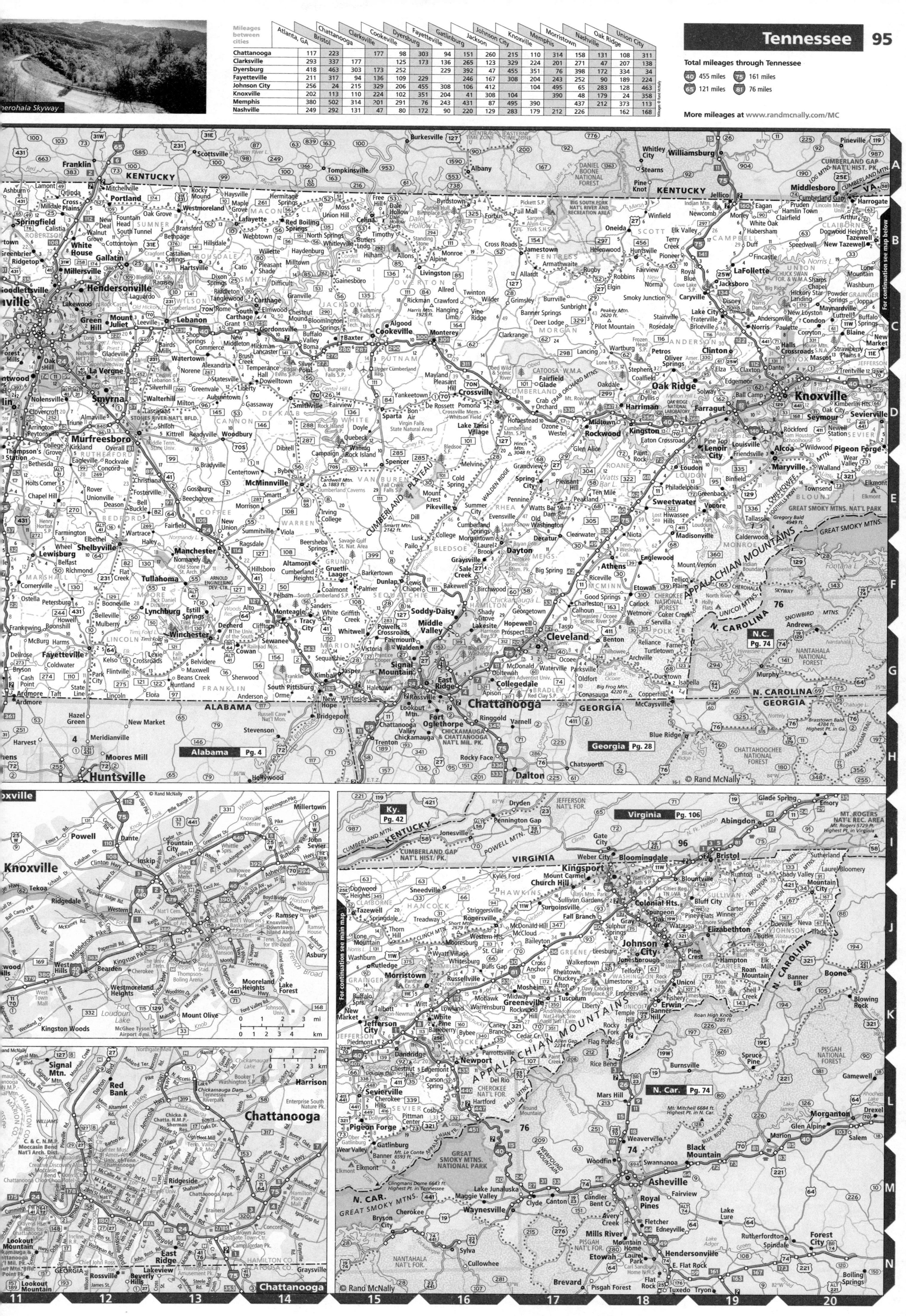

City sights to see

- Appalachian Caverns, Blountville, K-3
- Battleship USS Texas, La Porte, D-9
- Bayou Place, Houston, K-8
- Bristol Caverns, Bristol, J-6
- Bristol Motor Speedway, Bristol, K-4
- Contemporary Arts Museum, Houston, E-5
- Houston Fire Museum, Houston, E-5
- Houston Zoo, Houston, E-5
- Museum of Natural Science, Houston, E-5
- Rocky Mount Museum, Piney Flats, L-3
- Space Center Houston, Houston, G-8
- Wortham Theatre Center, Houston, K-8

Church Circle, Kingsport

Houston & Vicinity

Texas City

Tri-Cities: Johnson City / Kingsport / Bristol

Central Houston

City sights to see

- Dallas Museum of Art, Dallas, B-2
- Dallas Zoo, Dallas, H-10
- Fair Park, Dallas, G-11
- Fort Worth Zoo, Fort Worth, H-4
- Louis Tussaud's Palace of Wax & Ripley's Believe It or Not!, Grand Prairie, G-8
- Old City Park, Dallas, C-3
- The Sixth Floor Museum at Dealey Plaza, Dallas, B-1
- Stockyards Historic District, Fort Worth, G-4
- Sundance Square, Fort Worth, E-1
- Texas Civil War Museum, Fort Worth, G-2

Central Fort Worth

Nickname: The Lone Star State
Capital: Austin, EK-5
Land area: 261,797 sq. mi. (rank: 2nd)
Population: 25,145,561 (rank: 2nd)
Largest city: Houston, 2,099,451, EL-10

Index of cities Pg. 135

Explore Texas at www.randmcnally.com/TX

Tourism Information
Texas Tourism:
(800) 452-9292; www.traveltex.com

Road Conditions & Construction
(800) 452-9292, (512) 463-8588;
www.txdot.gov, www.drivetexas.org

Toll Road Information *(all use TxTag in addition to what is noted below)*
Cameron County Regional Mobility Authority (TX 550, Brownsville): (956) 982-5414; www.cameroncountyrma.org
Central Texas Regional Mobility Authority (TX 183A, Austin): (512) 996-9778; www.mobilityauthority.com
Fort Bend County Toll Road Authority (Houston area) ***(EZTAG)***: (281) 242-9740; www.fbctra.com
Harris County Toll Road Authority (Houston area) ***(EZTAG)***: (281) 875-3279; www.hctra.org
–list continued on following page

(segments of one mile or less not shown)
Cumulative miles (red): the distance between red arrows
Intermediate miles (black): the distance between intersections & places

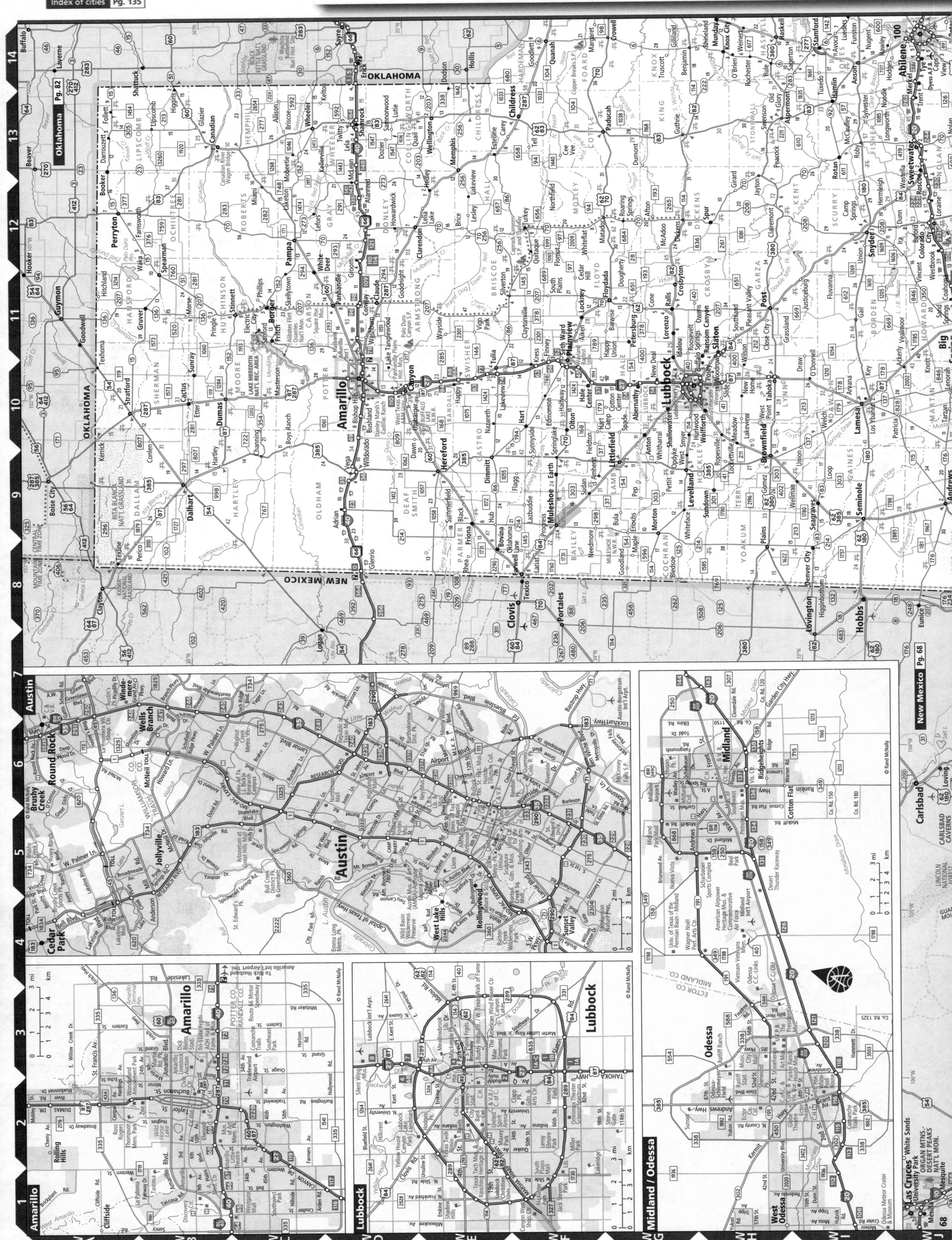

Big Bend National Park

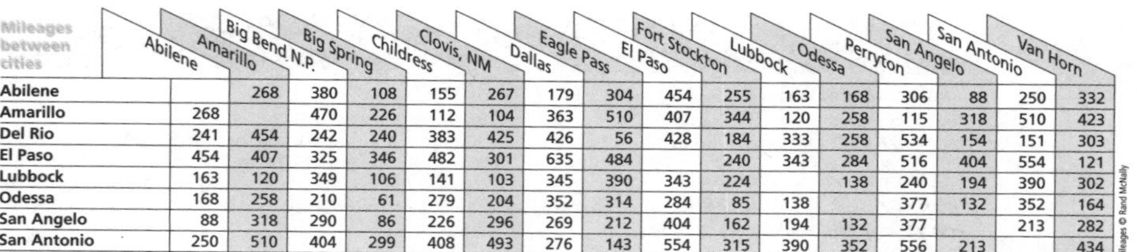

Mileages between cities	Abilene	Amarillo	Big Bend N.P.	Big Spring	Childress	Clovis, NM	Dallas	Eagle Pass	El Paso	Fort Stockton	Lubbock	Odessa	Perryton	San Angelo	San Antonio	Van Horn
Abilene		268	380	108	155	267	179	304	454	255	163	168	306	88	250	332
Amarillo	268		470	226	112	104	363	510	407	344	120	258	115	318	510	423
Del Rio	241	454	242	240	383	425	426	56	428	184	333	258	534	154	151	303
El Paso	454	407	325	346	482	301	635	484		240	343	284	516	404	554	121
Lubbock	163	120	349	106	141	103	345	390	343	224		138	240	194	390	302
Odessa	168	258	210	61	279	204	352	314	284	85	138		377	132	352	164
San Angelo	88	318	290	86	226	296	269	212	404	162	194	132	377		213	282
San Antonio	250	510	404	299	408	493	276	143	554	315	390	352	556	213		434

Total mileages through Texas

10: 881 miles
40: 177 miles
20: 636 miles

More mileages at www.randmcnally.com/MC

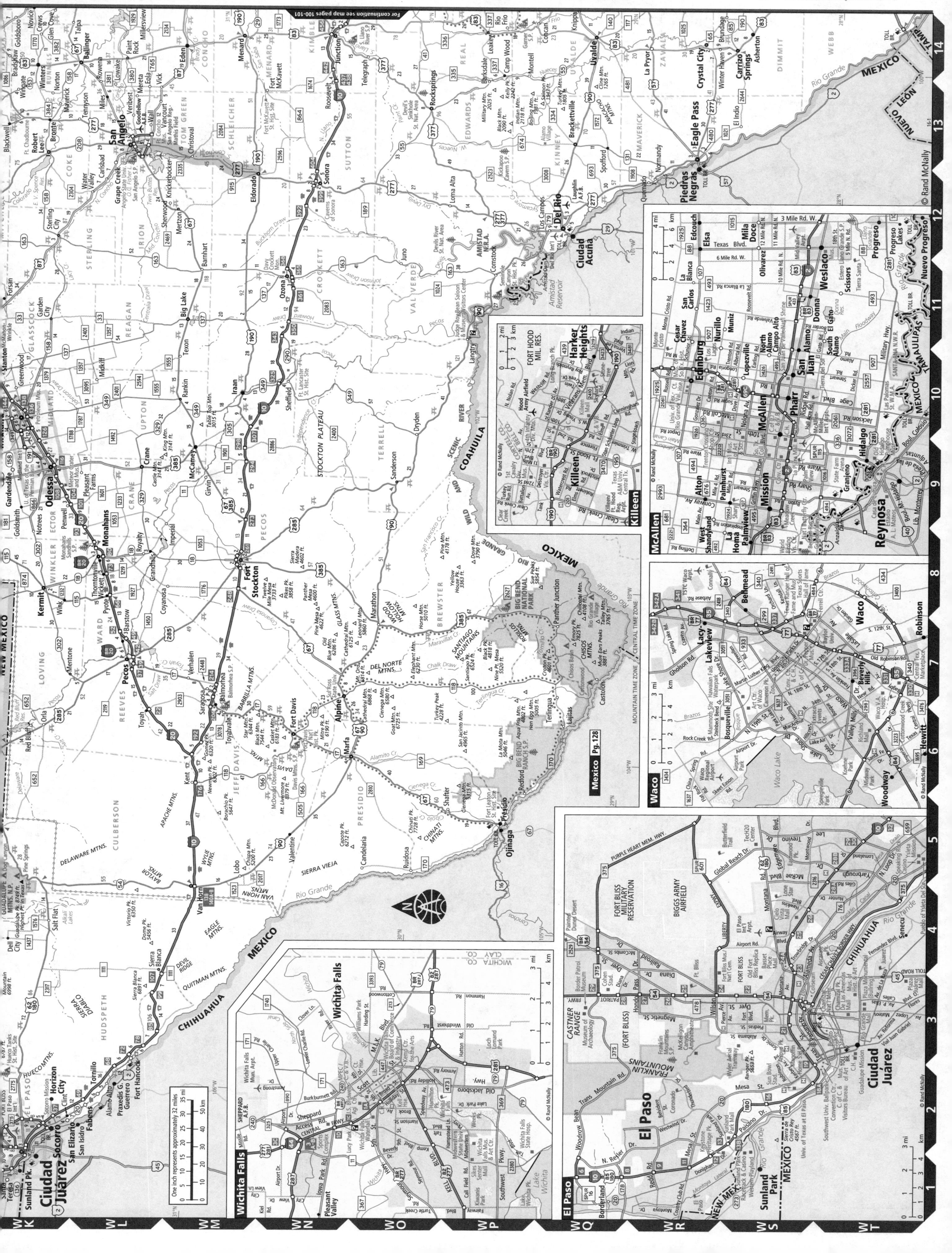

For continuation see map pages 100-101

Mexico Pg. 128

Killeen

McAllen

Waco

Wichita Falls

El Paso

One inch represents approximately 32 miles

Nickname: The Lone Star State
Capital: Austin, EK-5
Land area: 261,797 sq. mi. (rank: 2nd)
Population: 25,145,561 (rank: 2nd)
Largest city: Houston, 2,099,451, EL-10

Index of cities Pg. 135

Explore Texas at www.randmcnally.com/TX

Tourism Information
Texas Tourism:
(800) 452-9292; www.traveltex.com

Road Conditions & Construction
(800) 452-9292, (512) 463-8588;
www.txdot.gov, www.drivetexas.org

Toll Road Information *(all use TxTag in addition to what is noted below)*
–list continued from previous page
North East Regional Mobility Authority (TX 49, Tyler): (903) 594-4834; www.toll49.org
North Texas Tollway Authority (Dallas Metroplex) *(TollTag)*: (972) 818-6882; www.ntta.org
SH 130 Concession Co. (TX 130, Austin): (877) 741-3089; mysh130.com
Texas Department of Transportation (all other toll roads in Texas): (888) 468-9824; www.txtag.org

(segments of one mile or less not shown)
Cumulative miles (red): the distance between red arrows
Intermediate miles (black): the distance between intersections & places

Laredo
Corpus Christi
Tyler
Abilene

For continuation see map pages 98-99

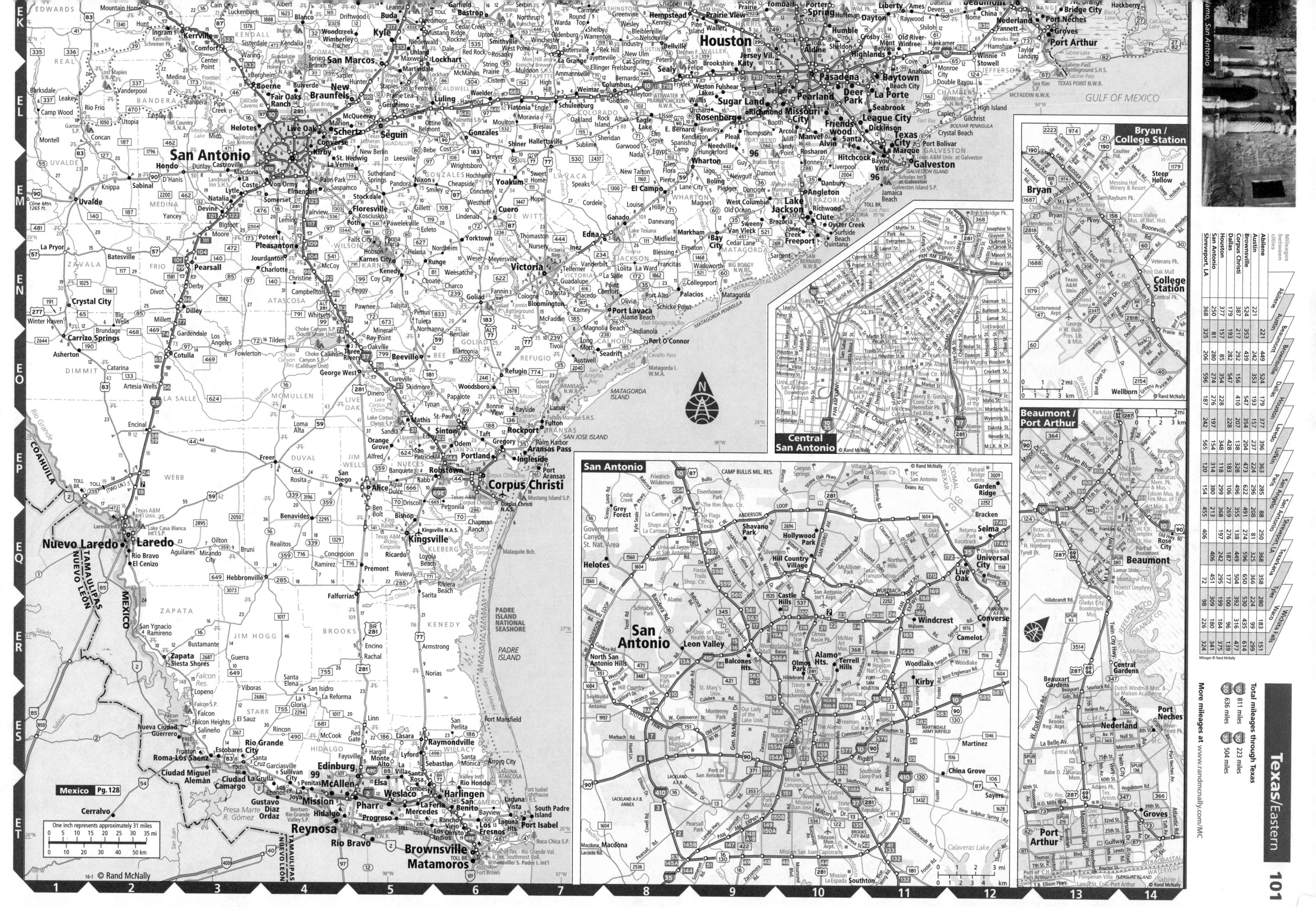

Mileages between cities

	Abilene	Austin	Beaumont	Brownsville	Dallas	Houston	Laredo	Lufkin	Paris	San Angelo	San Antonio	Shreveport, LA	Texarkana	Tyler	Waco	Wichita Falls
Abilene		221	449	524	179	377	396	363	285	88	250	368	358	280	183	151
Austin	221		242	353	193	157	237	224	296	208	81	325	366	224	99	299
Brownsville	524	353	439		547	354	204	473	622	491	274	596	650	530	435	614
Corpus Christi	387	217	292	156	410	207	138	328	496	355	138	449	504	392	316	477
Dallas	179	193	282	547		228	428	183	106	269	276	187	177	100	96	139
Houston	377	157	85	354	228		348	118	299	368	197	242	295	199	184	375
San Antonio	250	81	280	274	276	197	154	314	380	213		406	451	309	180	341
Shreveport, LA	368	325	206	596	187	242	565	120	154	455	406		72	98	226	324

Mileages © Rand McNally

Total mileages through Texas

- I-10: 811 miles
- I-20: 636 miles
- I-30: 223 miles
- I-35: 504 miles

More mileages at www.randmcnally.com/MC

Utah

Nickname: The Beehive State
Capital: Salt Lake City, D-8
Land area: 82,144 sq. mi. (rank: 12th)
Population: 2,763,885 (rank: 34th)
Largest city: Salt Lake City, 186,440, D-8

Index of cities Pg. 135

Plan a Utah trip at www.randmcnally.com/UT

Tourism Information
Utah Office of Tourism: (800) 200-1160, (800) 882-4386, (801) 538-1900; www.utah.com

Road Conditions & Construction
511, (866) 511-8824, (801) 887-3700; www.udot.utah.gov, www.utahcommuterlink.com

Toll Road Information
Adams Av. Pkwy., Inc. (Weber Co.): (801) 475-1909; www.adamsavenueparkway.com

Determining distances along roads

Highway distances (segments of one mile or less not shown):
Cumulative miles (red): the distance between red arrows
Intermediate miles (black): the distance between intersections & places

Interchanges and exit numbers
For most states, the mileage between interchanges may be determined by subtracting one number from the other.

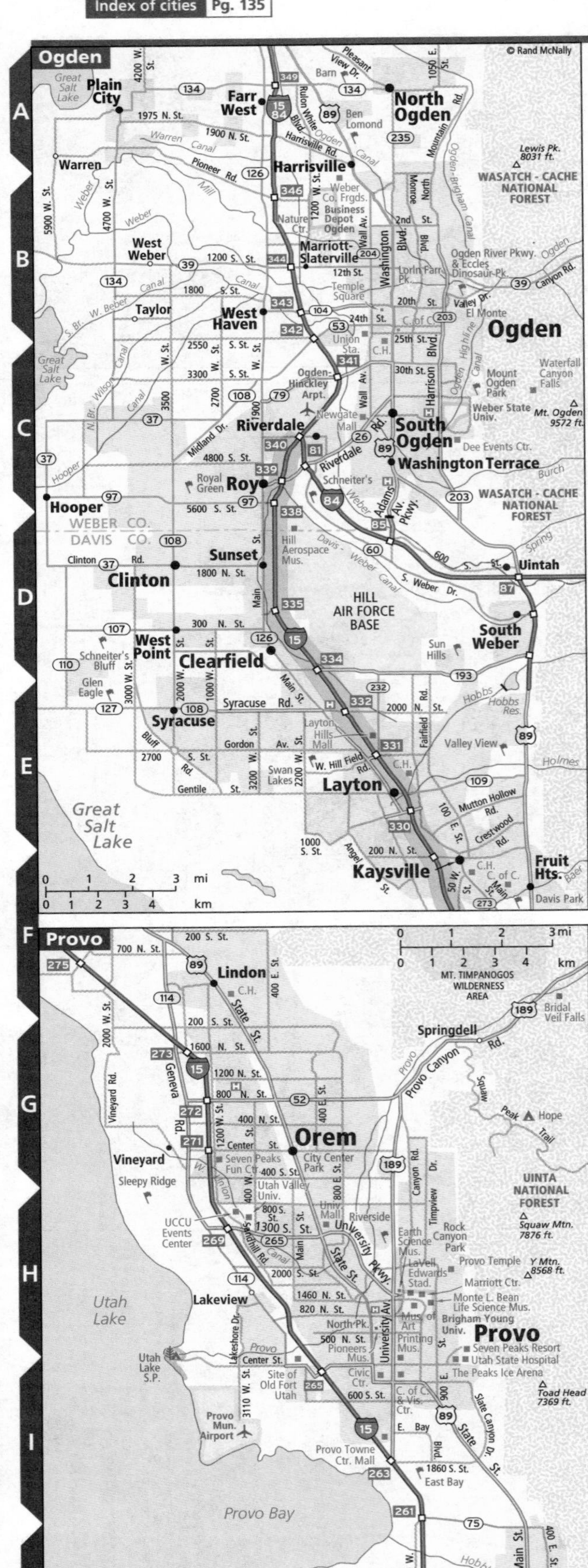

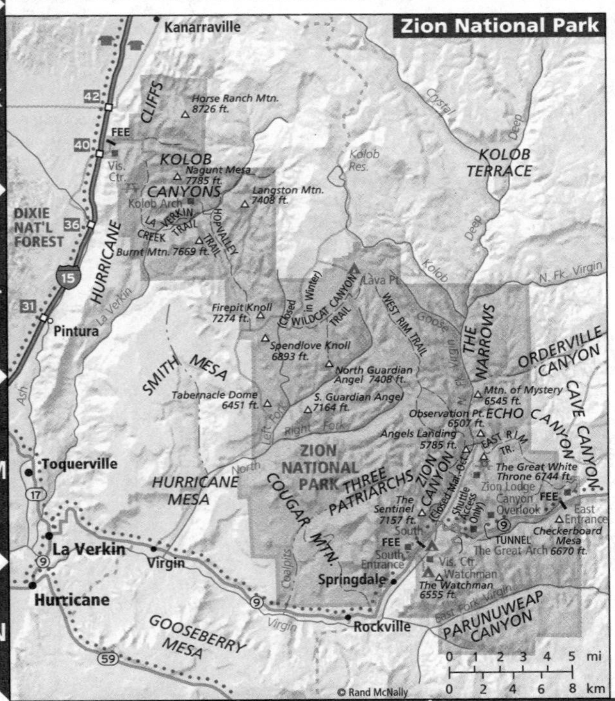

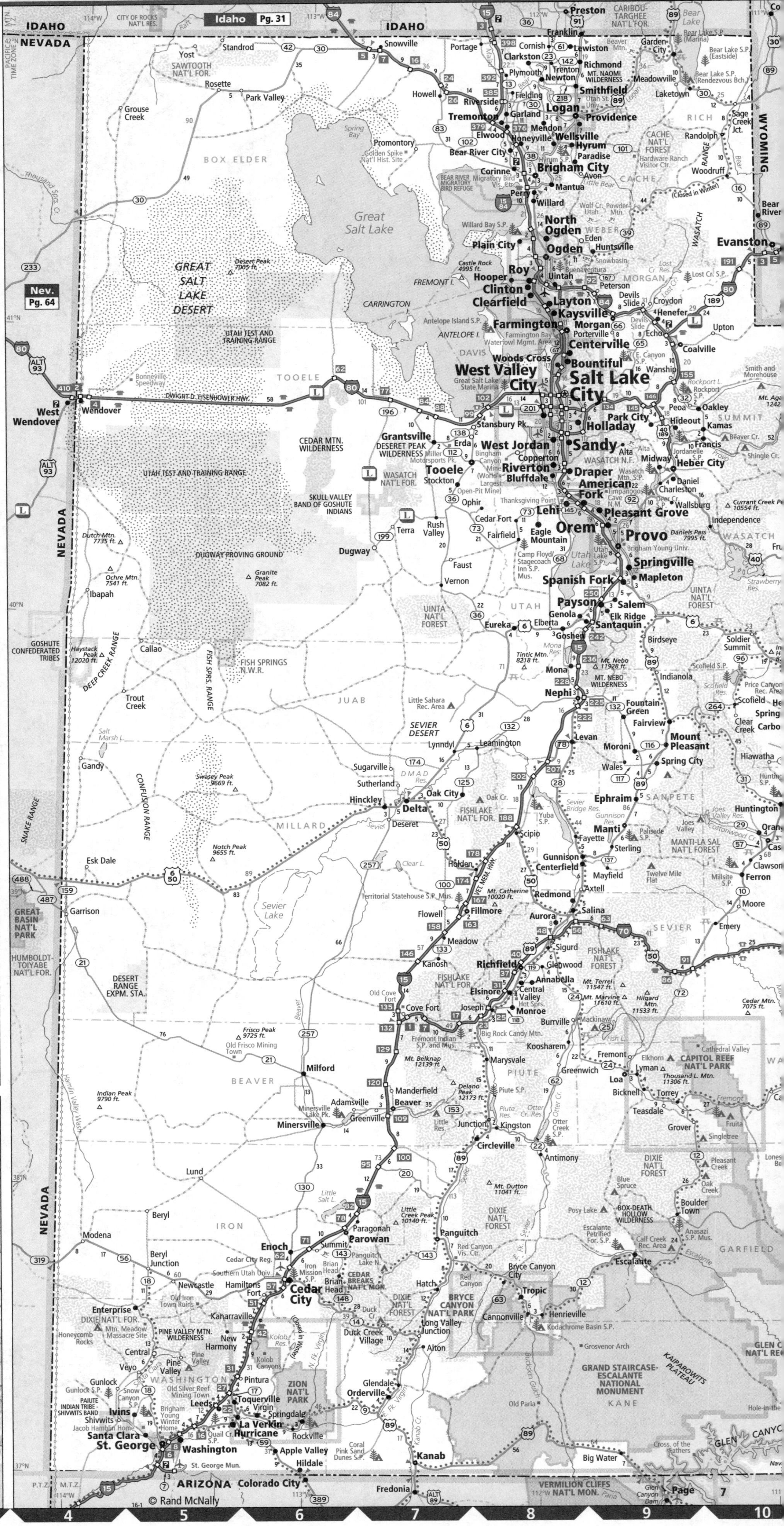

Idaho Pg. 31

Nev. Pg. 64

Mileages between cities

	Blanding	Cedar City	Grand Jct., CO	Las Vegas, NV	Logan	Moab	Ogden	Page, AZ	Park City	Price	Provo	Richfield	St. George	Salt Lake City	Vernal	Wendover
Grand Junction, CO	186	335		506	363	112	319	380	286	164	240	224	389	283	140	401
Logan	388	330	363	499		313	46	457	113	199	124	239	385	82	252	199
Moab	74	287	112	456	313		269	268	238	115	190	174	341	234	207	352
Richfield	249	114	224	282	239	174	194	219	166	121	115		169	159	232	270
St. George	415	55	389	117	385	341	341	154	308	286	261	169		304	401	333
Salt Lake City	308	250	283	419	82	234	37	377	30	119	43	159	304		172	121
Vernal	281	345	140	514	252	207	207	450	145	112	154	232	401	172		291
Wendover	426	317	401	361	199	352	154	503	150	237	161	270	333	121	291	

Total mileages through Utah

- 15: 401 miles
- 70: 232 miles
- 80: 196 miles
- 84: 119 miles

More mileages at www.randmcnally.com/MC

Vermont

Nickname: The Green Mountain State
Capital: Montpelier, E-5
Land area: 9,250 sq. mi. (rank: 43rd)
Population: 625,741 (rank: 49th)
Largest city: Burlington, 42,417, D-2

Index of cities Pg. 135

Mileages between cities

	Albany, NY	Brattleboro	Burlington	Montpelier	Newport	Rutland	St. Johnsbury	White River Jct.
Albany, NY		78	151	156	230	90	187	128
Brattleboro	78		151	115	164	73	121	62
Burlington	151	151		39	76	67	75	90
Montpelier	156	115	39		78	66	37	54
Newport	230	164	76	78		147	43	102
Rutland	90	73	67	66	147		105	45
St. Johnsbury	187	121	75	37	43	105		60
White River Jct.	128	62	90	54	102	45	60	

Total mileages through Vermont

89: 130 miles
93: 11 miles
91: 177 miles
4: 64 miles

More mileages at www.randmcnally.com/MC

Get travel info at www.randmcnally.com/VT

Tourism Information
Vermont Dept. of Tourism and Marketing:
(800) 837-6668, (802) 828-3237; www.vermontvacation.com

Road Conditions & Construction 511 –
511, (800) 429-7623;
www.511vt.com, www.aot.state.vt.us

Toll Rd. Info
No toll roads

Determining Distances

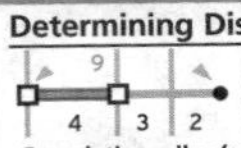
9
4
3
2

(segments of one mile or less not shown)
Cumulative miles (red): the distance between red arrows
Intermediate miles (black): the distance between intersections & places

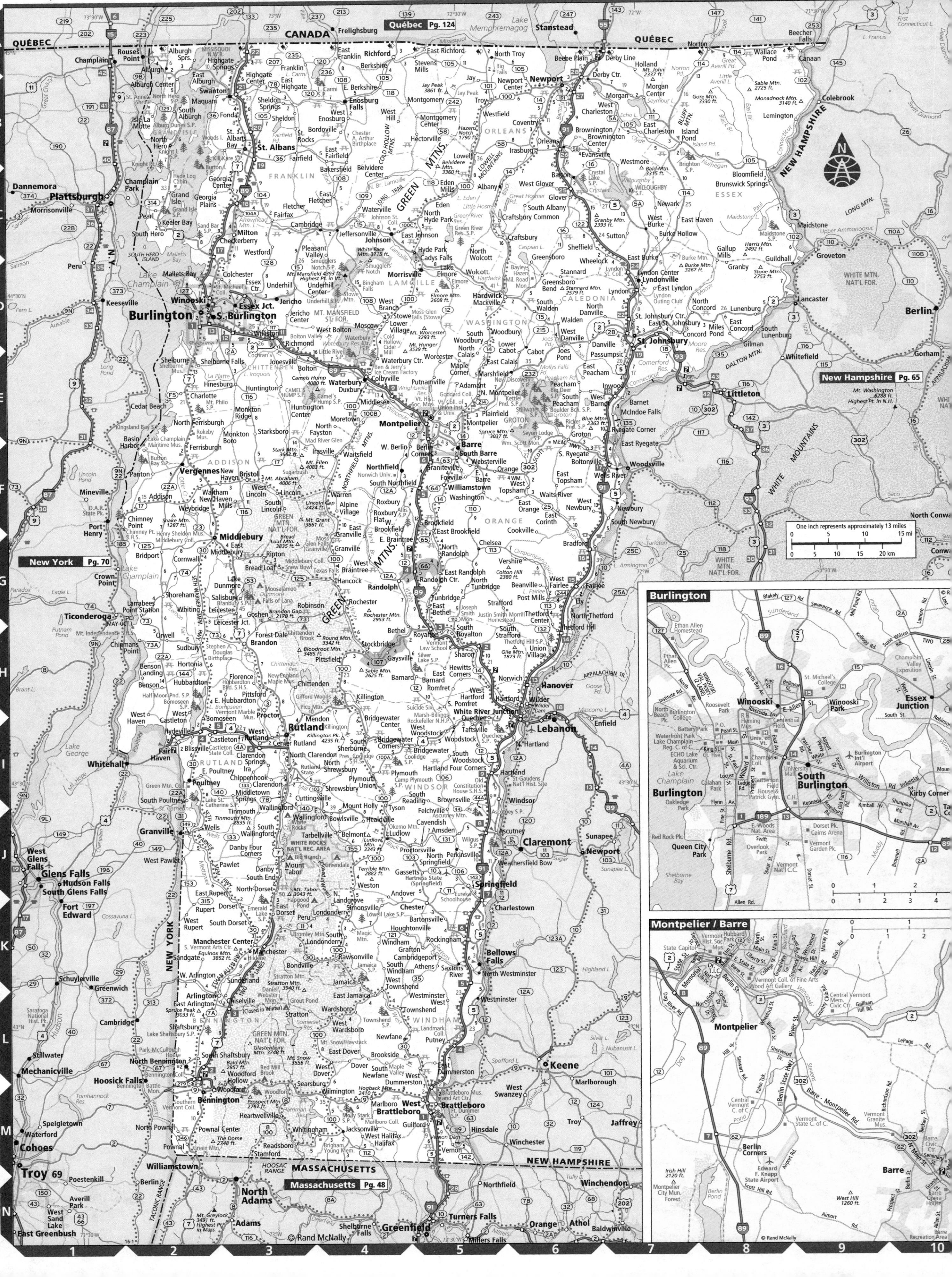
CANADA
QUÉBEC
Québec Pg. 124
New Hampshire Pg. 65
New York Pg. 70
Massachusetts Pg. 48
NEW HAMPSHIRE
NEW YORK
MASSACHUSETTS
Burlington
Montpelier
Rutland
Barre
St. Albans
St. Johnsbury
Newport
Bennington
Brattleboro
Springfield
Middlebury
Lake Champlain
GREEN MTNS.
GREEN MTN. NAT'L FOR.
WHITE MTN. NAT'L FOR.
One inch represents approximately 13 miles
Burlington
Montpelier / Barre
© Rand McNally

storic Downtown Mall, Charlottesville

City sights to see

- Agecroft Hall and Gardens, Richmond, C-7
- Children's Museum of Virginia, Portsmouth, M-6
- Chrysler Museum of Art, Norfolk, L-6
- Colonial Williamsburg, Williamsburg, F-2
- Edgar Allen Poe Museum, Richmond, C-8
- First Landing State Park, Virginia Beach, L-9
- Hermitage Foundation Museum, Norfolk, L-6
- Historic Jamestowne, Williamsburg, G-1
- Nauticus, Norfolk, L-6
- Ocean Breeze Waterpark, Virginia Beach, M-10
- Old Cape Henry Lighthouse, Virginia Beach, K-9
- Three Lakes Nature Center and Aquarium, Richmond, B-8
- Virginia State Capitol, Richmond, C-8

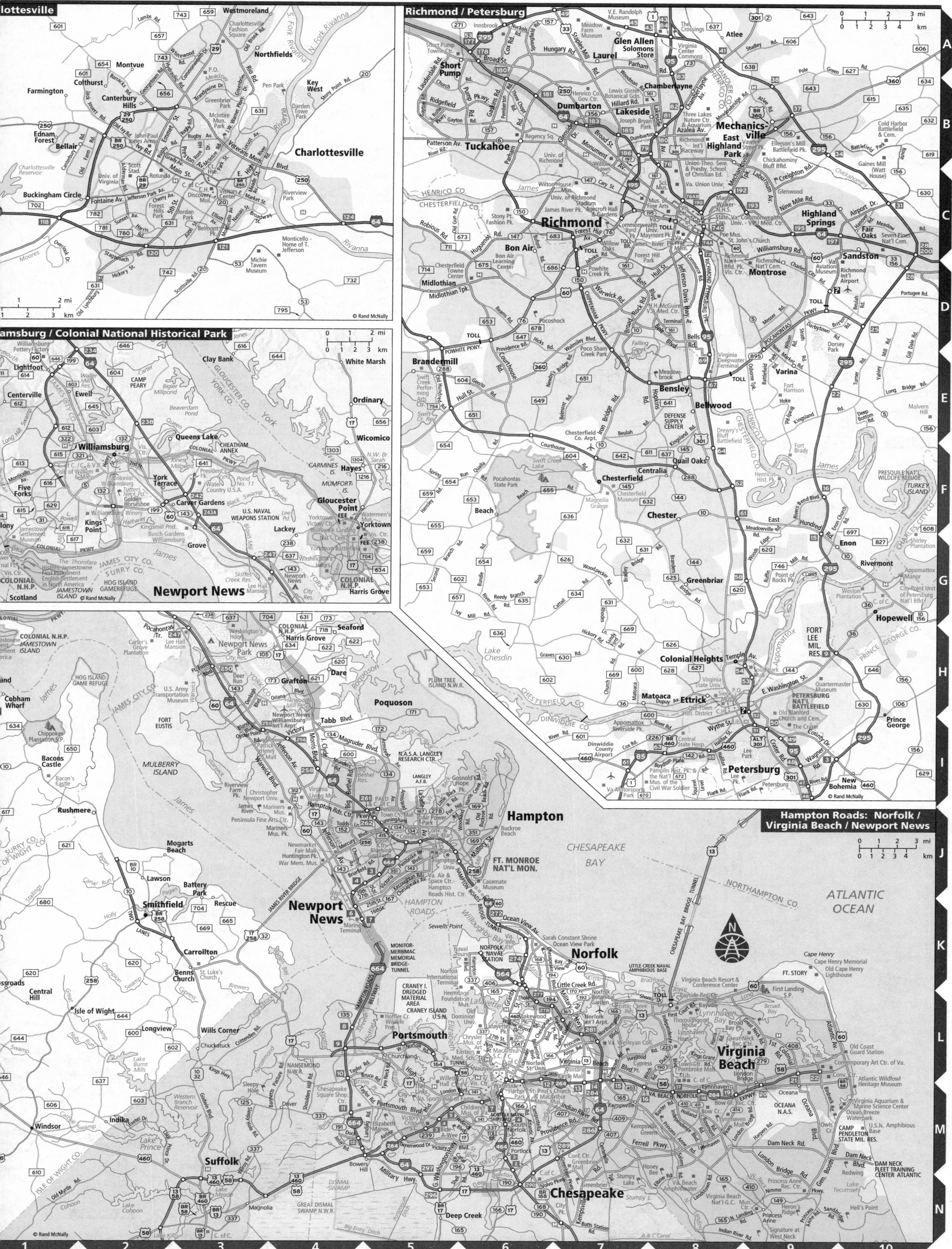

Virginia

Nickname: Old Dominion
Capital: Richmond, J-14
Land area: 39,594 sq. mi. (rank: 37th)
Population: 8,001,024 (rank: 12th)
Largest city: Virginia Beach, 437,994, L-18

Index of cities Pg. 135

Explore Virginia at www.randmcnally.com/VA

Tourism Information
Virginia Tourism Corporation: (800) 847-4882; www.virginia.org

Road Conditions & Construction
511, (800) 578-4111, (800) 367-7623; www.511virginia.org, www.virginiadot.org/travel

Toll Road Information (all use E-ZPass)
Chesapeake Bay Bridge-Tunnel: (757) 331-2960; www.cbbt.com
Chesapeake Expressway (VA 168, in Chesapeake): (757) 204-0100; www.chesapeakeexpressway.com
Dulles Greenway: (703) 707-8870; www.dullesgreenway.com
Metro. Wash. Airports Authority (Dulles Toll Rd.): (877) 762-7824; www.metwashairports.com/tollroad/toll.htm
Richmond Metropolitan Authority (toll rds. within Richmond): (804) 523-3300; www.rmaonline.org
Virginia Dept. of Transportation (all others): (800) 367-7623; www.virginiadot.org/travel/faq-toll.asp

(segments of one mile or less not shown)
Cumulative miles (red): the distance between red arrows
Intermediate miles (black): the distance between intersections & places

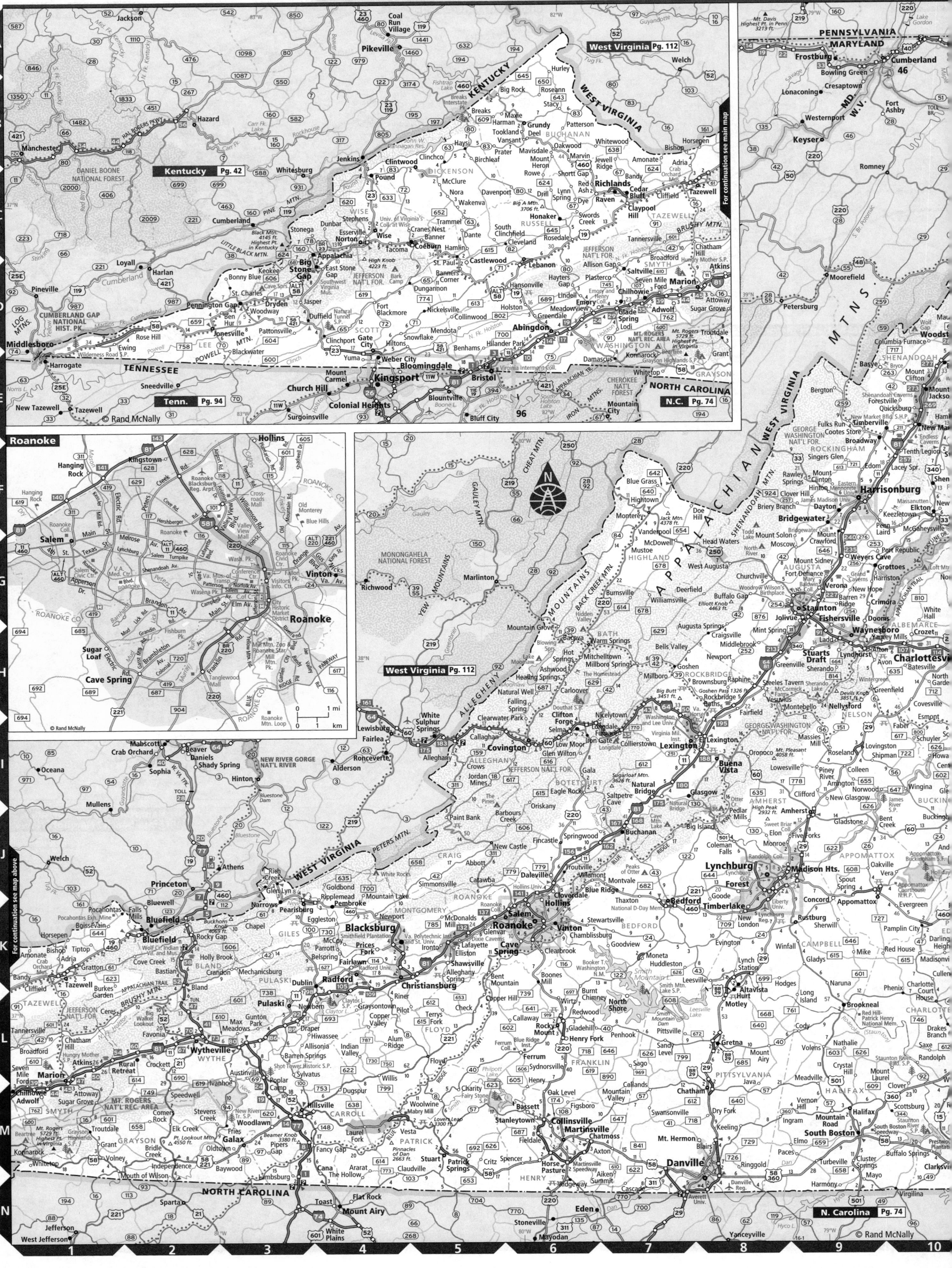

Kentucky Pg. 42
West Virginia Pg. 112
Tenn. Pg. 94
N.C. Pg. 74
For continuation see main map
West Virginia Pg. 112
For continuation see map above
N. Carolina Pg. 74

Roanoke

Mileages between cities	Bristol	Chincoteague	Danville	Emporia	Fredericksburg	Harrisonburg	Lynchburg	Manassas	Norfolk	Richmond	Roanoke	Virginia Beach	Washington, DC	Williamsburg	Winchester	Wytheville
Bristol		510	192	341	323	242	200	347	407	321	145	423	377	370	310	67
Charlottesville	253	260	131	136	66	61	65	81	157	71	117	174	116	121	128	183
Danville	192	300		115	197	163	68	215	191	144	89	206	247	199	230	124
Norfolk	407	104	191	78	139	216	189	177		91	276	17	189	41	222	340
Richmond	321	190	144	66	56	130	114	96	91		187	105	107	50	135	253
Roanoke	145	378	89	176	192	111	53	214	276	187		292	241	238	178	77
Washington, DC	377	168	247	174	53	132	182	32	189	107	241	205		153	76	307
Winchester	310	244	230	200	83	68	164	54	222	135	178	236	76	181		244

Total mileages through Virginia

- 64: 298 miles
- 81: 325 miles
- 85: 69 miles
- 95: 179 miles

More mileages at www.randmcnally.com/MC

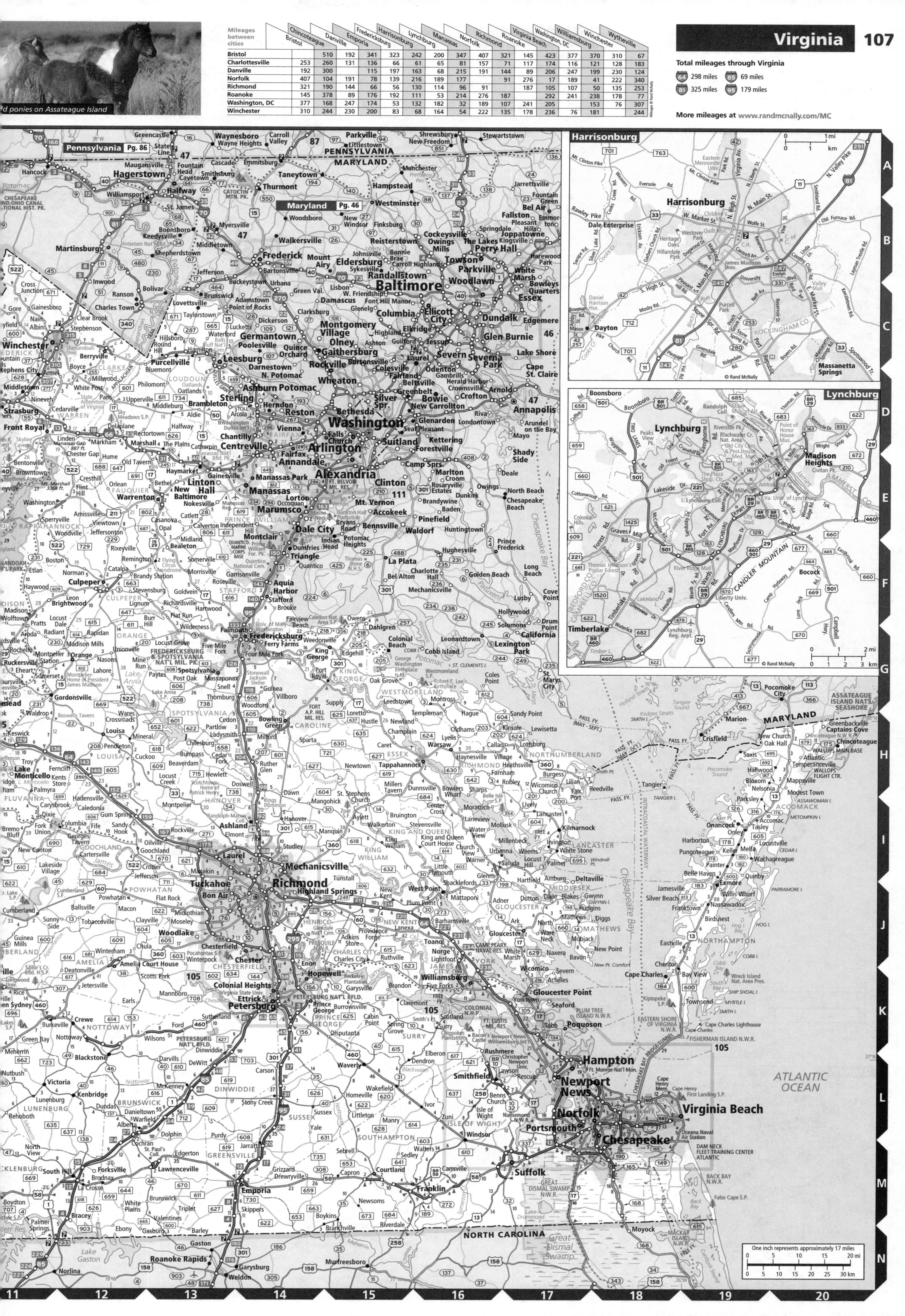

Washington

Nickname: The Evergreen State
Capital: Olympia, H-6
Land area: 66,544 sq. mi. (rank: 20th)
Population: 6,724,540 (rank: 13th)
Largest city: Seattle, 608,660, F-7

Index of cities Pg. 135

Get more Washington info at www.randmcnally.com/WA

Tourism Information
Washington Tourism Alliance: (800) 544-1800; www.experiencewa.com

Road Conditions & Construction
511, (800) 695-7623; www.wsdot.wa.gov/traffic (Good to Go!)

Toll Bridge Information
Wash. St. Dept. of Trans. (Tacoma Narrows Br., SR 520 Br.): (866) 936-8246; www.wsdot.wa.gov/tolling

Determining distances along roads

Highway distances (segments of one mile or less not shown):
Cumulative miles (red): the distance between red arrows
Intermediate miles (black): the distance between intersections & pl

Interchanges and exit numbers
For most states, the mileage between interchanges may be determi
by subtracting one number from the other.

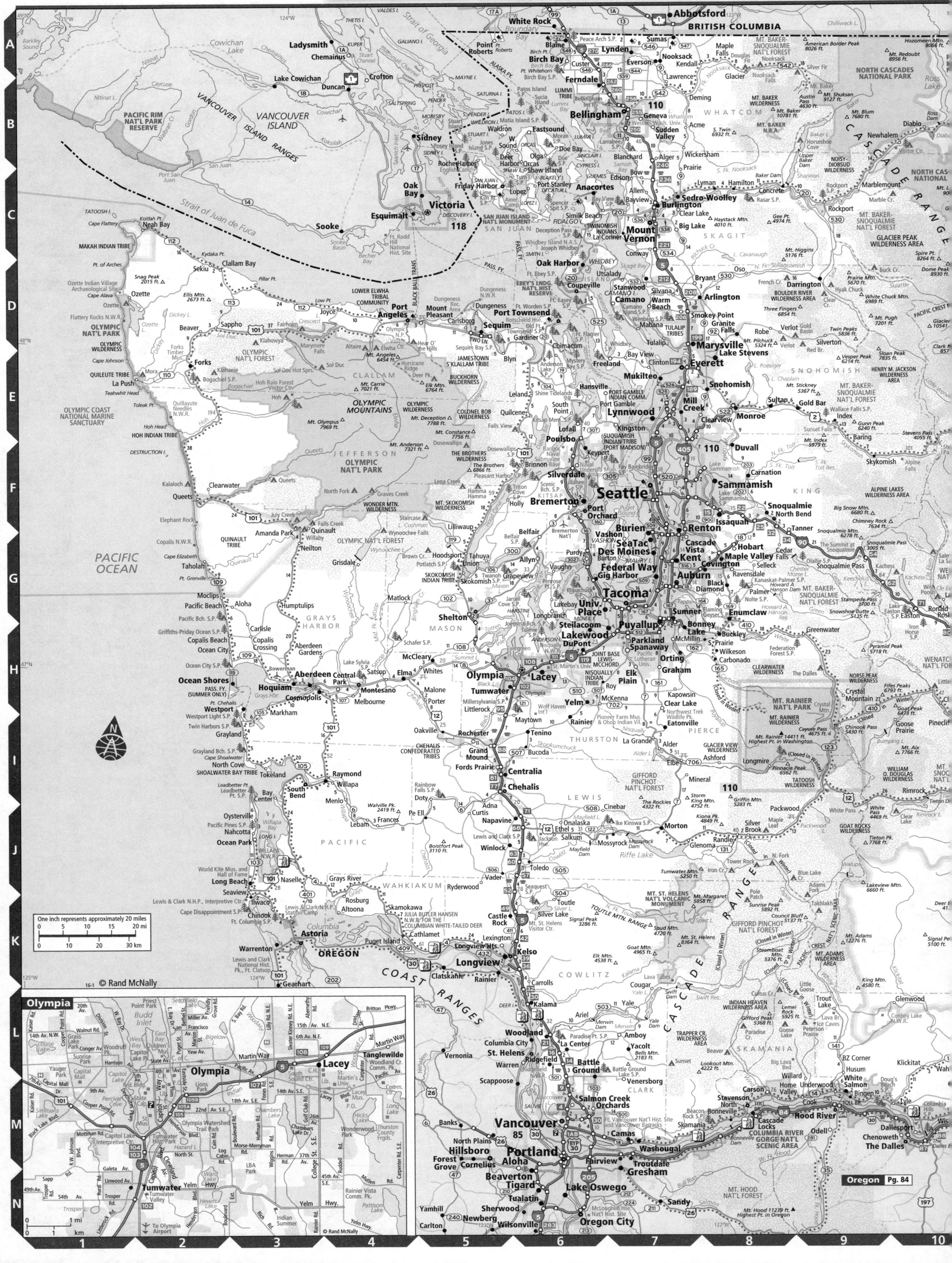

One inch represents approximately 20 miles

Olympia

Oregon Pg. 84

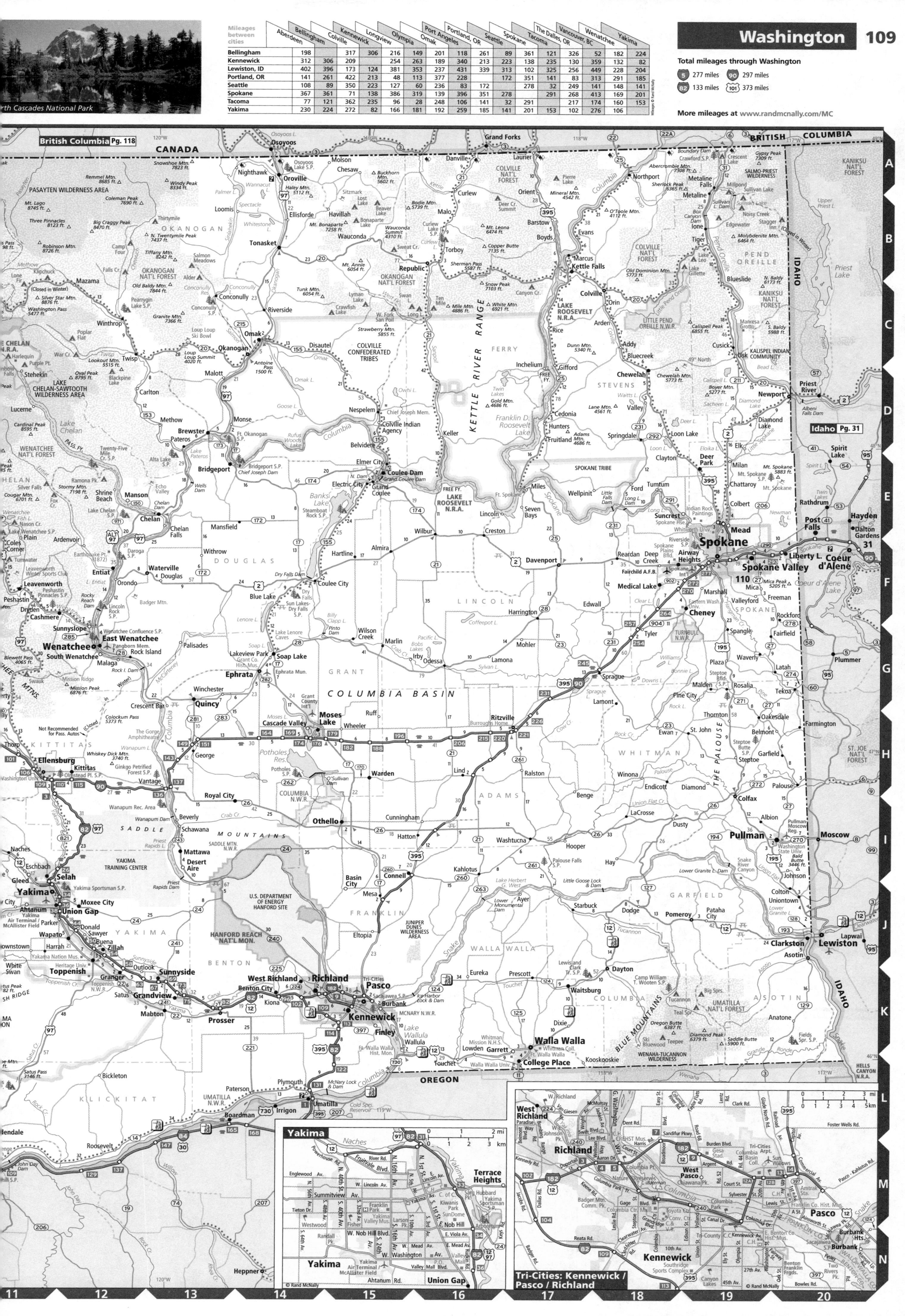

Mileages between cities

	Aberdeen	Bellingham	Colville	Kennewick	Longview	Olympia	Omak	Port Angeles	Portland, OR	Seattle	Spokane	Tacoma	The Dalles, OR	Vancouver, BC	Wenatchee	Yakima
Bellingham	198		317	306	216	149	201	118	261	89	361	121	326	52	182	224
Kennewick	312	306	209		254	263	189	340	213	223	138	235	130	359	132	82
Lewiston, ID	402	396	173	124	381	353	237	431	339	313	102	325	256	449	228	204
Portland, OR	141	261	422	213	48	113	377	228		172	351	141	83	313	291	185
Seattle	108	89	350	223	127	60	236	83	172		278	32	249	141	148	141
Spokane	367	361	71	138	386	319	139	396	351	278		291	268	413	169	201
Tacoma	77	121	362	235	96	28	248	106	141	32	291		217	174	160	153
Yakima	230	224	272	82	166	181	192	259	185	141	201	153	102	276	106	

Total mileages through Washington

- 5: 277 miles
- 90: 297 miles
- 82: 133 miles
- 101: 373 miles

More mileages at www.randmcnally.com/MC

City sights to see

- Experience Music Project, Seattle, H-1
- Frye Art Museum, Seattle, J-3
- Klondike Gold Rush National Historical Park, Seattle, K-2
- Museum of Glass, Tacoma, L-6
- Nordic Heritage Museum, Seattle, C-7
- Pacific Science Center, Seattle, H-1
- Pike Place Market, Seattle, J-2
- Point Defiance Zoo & Aquarium, Tacoma, K-5
- Seattle Aquarium, Seattle, J-1
- Space Needle, Seattle, H-1
- Washington State History Museum, Tacoma, L-6
- Woodland Park Zoo, Seattle, C-7

Elliott Bay, Seattle

Spokane

Bellingham

Central Seattle

Mount Rainier National Park

Seattle / Tacoma & Vicinity

et travel info at www.randmcnally.com/DC

rism Information

tination DC: (800) 422-8644, (202) 789-7000; www.washington.org

d Conditions & Construction

(202) 737-4404, (202) 673-6813; w.ddot.dc.gov

Toll Rd. Info

No toll roads in D.C.; see Maryland and Virginia for toll road information

City sights to see

- Arlington National Cemetery, Arlington, VA, N-1
- Frederick Douglass National Historic Site, G-7
- Freedom Park, Arlington, VA, G-5
- John F. Kennedy Center for the Performing Arts, L-3
- Martin Luther King Jr. Memorial, M-4
- National Arboretum, F-7
- National Mall, M-7
- National Zoological Park, F-6
- Patuxent Research Refuge National Wildlife Visitor Center, Laurel, MD, D-10
- The Pentagon, Arlington, VA, G-6
- Supreme Court of the United States, M-9
- United States Botanic Garden, M-8
- Wolf Trap National Park for the Performing Arts, Vienna, VA, E-2

Washington, D.C.

Land area: 61 sq. mi.
Population: 601,723

ington, D.C. & Vicinity

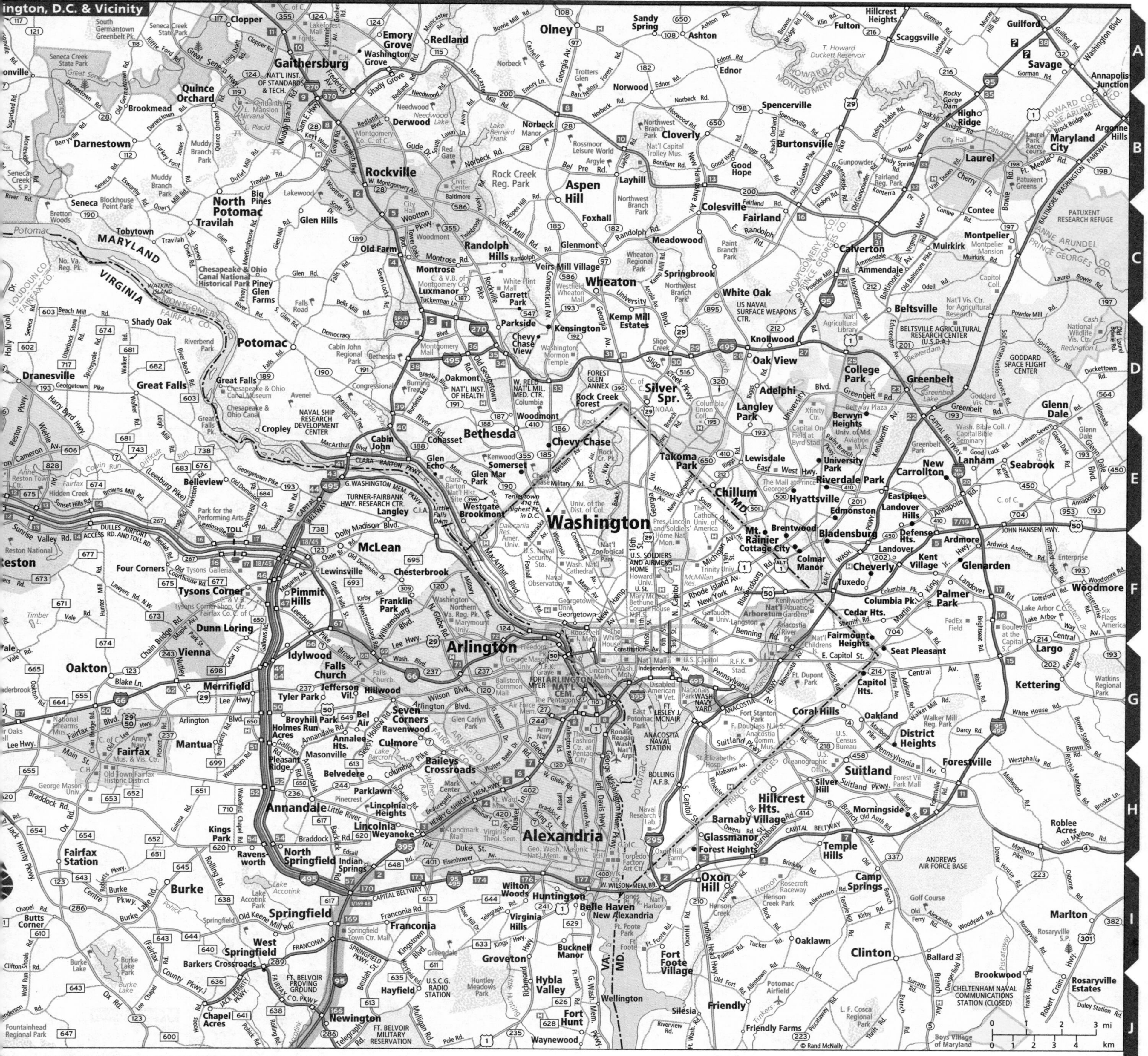

Washington, D.C.

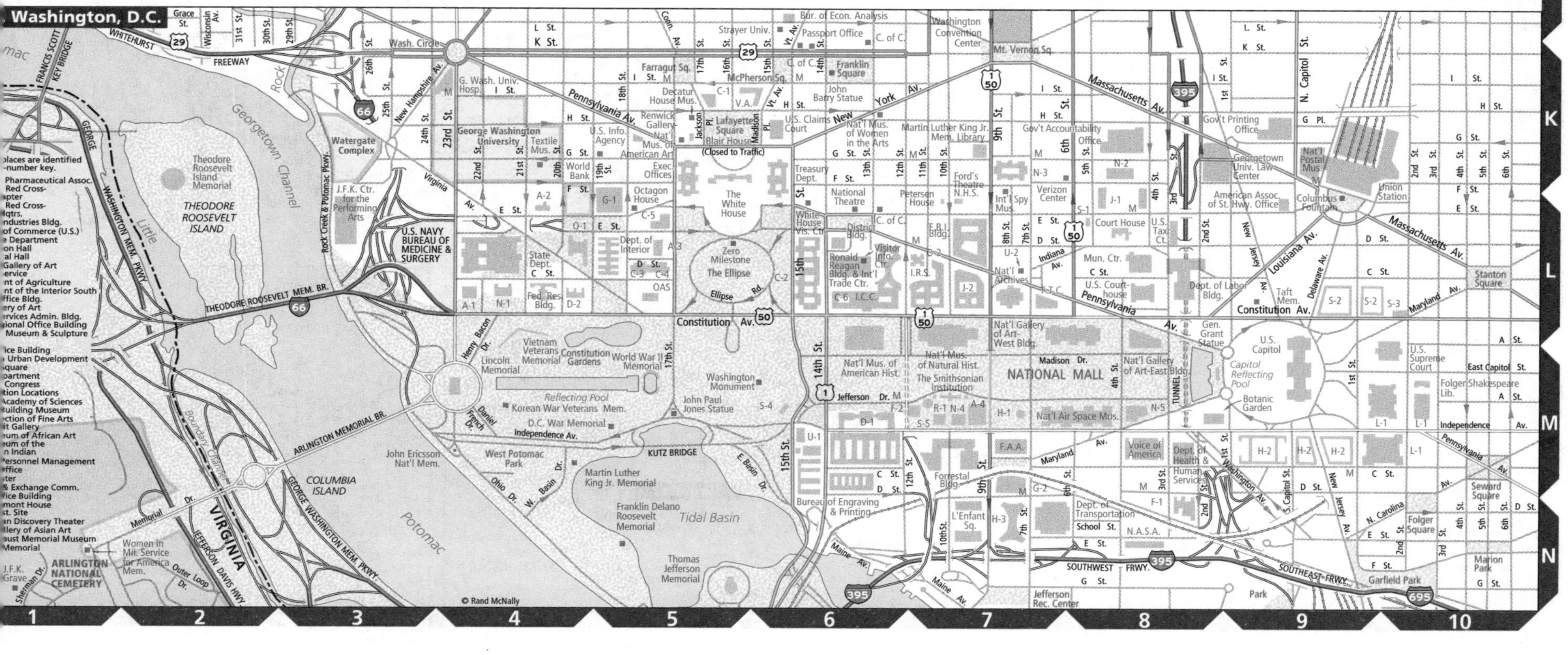

West Virginia

Nickname: The Mountain State
Capital: Charleston, J-3
Land area: 24,078 sq. mi. (rank: 41st)
Population: 1,852,994 (rank: 37th)
Largest city: Charleston, 51,400, J-3

Index of cities Pg. 135

Mileages between cities	Bluefield	Charleston	Clarksburg	Cumberland, MD	Martinsburg	Petersburg	Wheeling	Wh. Sulphur Sprs.
Beckley	50	59	136	239	267	184	236	59
Charleston	106		123	225	304	193	177	120
Cumberland, MD	288	225	109		79	66	155	194
Huntington	158	51	174	276	355	244	228	172
Morgantown	218	154	38	73	151	103	78	187
Parkersburg	183	76	72	181	259	172	104	198
Wheeling	283	177	114	155	225	179		262
Wh. Sulphur Sprs.	79	120	155	194	208	125	262	

Total mileages through West Virginia
64: 189 miles
77: 187 miles
70: 14 miles
79: 161 miles

More mileages at www.randmcnally.com/MC

Plan a trip at www.randmcnally.com/WV

Tourism Information
W.V. Division of Tourism: (800) 225-5982, (304) 558-2200; www.wvtourism.com

Road Conditions & Construction
511, (877) 982-7623; www.wv511org, www.transportation.wv.gov

Toll Road Information *(E-ZPass)*
W.V. Parkways Authority: (304) 926-1900; www.transportation.wv.gov/turnpike

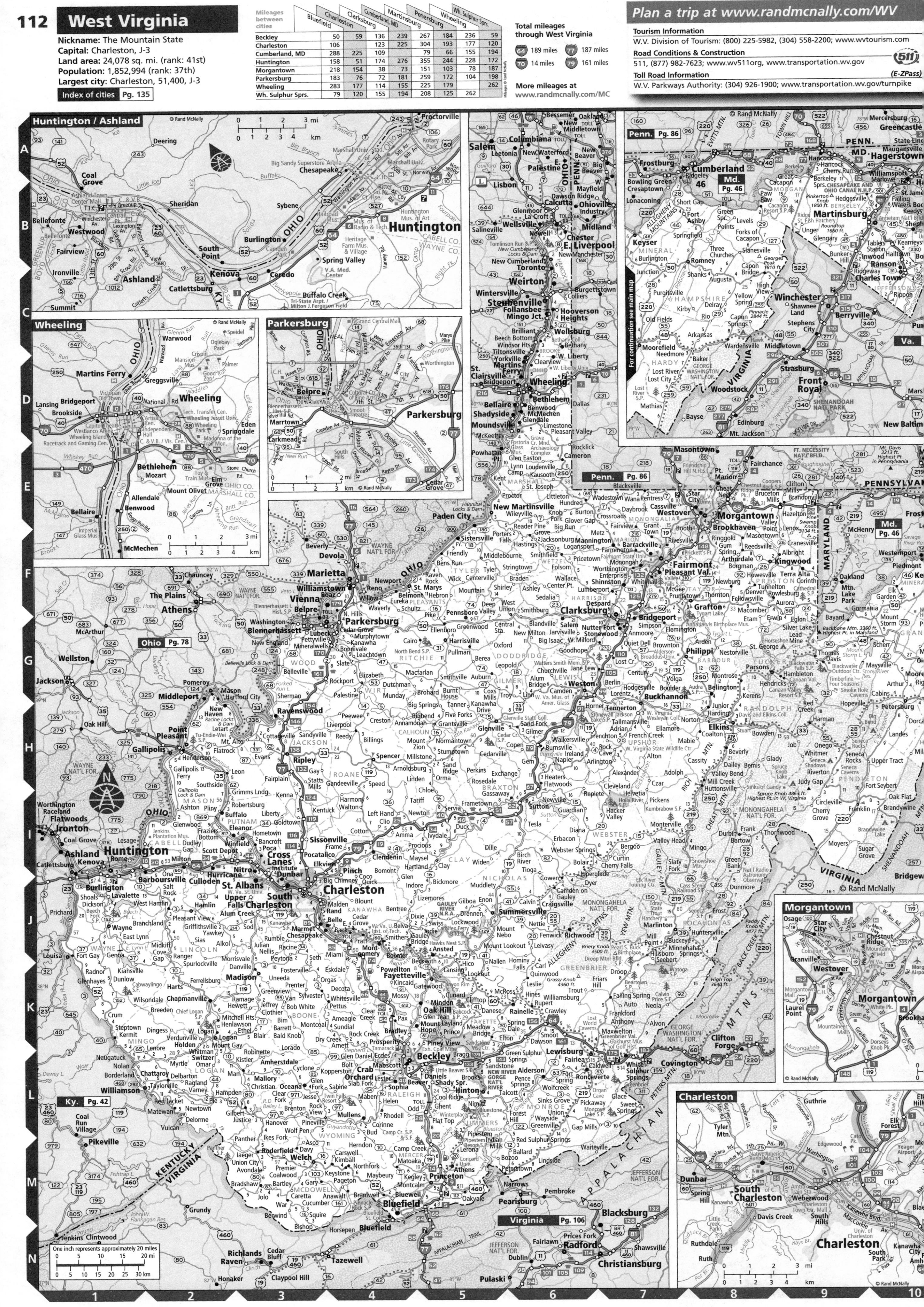

HarborPark promenade, Kenosha

City sights to see

- Angel Museum, Beloit, N-6
- Betty Brinn Children's Museum, Milwaukee, L-3
- Golden Rondelle Theatre, Racine, J-10
- Harley Davidson Museum, Milwaukee, M-2
- Henry Maier Festival Grounds, Milwaukee, M-4
- J.M. Kohler Arts Center, Sheboygan, F-10
- Kenosha History Center, Kenosha, L-10
- Miller Brewery, Milwaukee, E-5
- Milwaukee Art Museum, Milwaukee, L-4
- Milwaukee Public Museum, Milwaukee, L-2
- Mitchell Park Horticultural Conservatory, Milwaukee, F-6

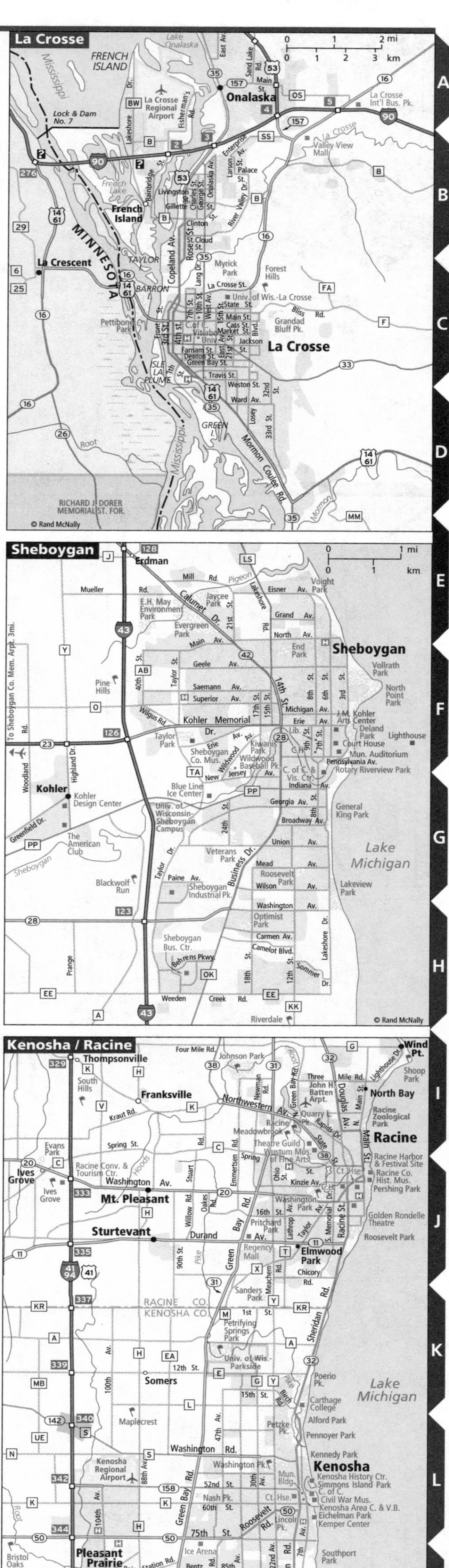

Milwaukee & Vicinity

Milwaukee, Wauwatosa, West Allis, Waukesha, Brookfield, Menomonee Falls, Mequon, Germantown, Greenfield, Franklin, Oak Creek, Cudahy, New Berlin, Muskego, Glendale, Brown Deer, Shorewood, Whitefish Bay, Fox Point, South Milwaukee, St. Francis, Greendale, Hales Corners, Sussex, Pewaukee, Lannon, Butler, Elm Grove, Big Bend

Central Milwaukee

Janesville / Beloit

Janesville, Beloit, Afton, Shopiere

ILLINOIS

© Rand McNally

Wisconsin

Nickname: The Badger State
Capital: Madison, N-9
Land area: 54,310 sq. mi. (rank: 25th)
Population: 5,686,986 (rank: 20th)
Largest city: Milwaukee, 594,833, N-13

Index of cities Pg. 136

Explore Wisconsin at www.randmcnally.com/WI

Tourism Information
Wisconsin Department of Tourism: (800) 432-8747, (608) 266-2161; www.travelwisconsin.com

Road Conditions & Construction
511, (866) 511-9472; www.511wi.gov

Toll Road Information
No toll roads

Determining distances along roads

Highway distances (segments of one mile or less not shown):
Cumulative miles (red): the distance between red arrows
Intermediate miles (black): the distance between intersections & pla

Interchanges and exit numbers
For most states, the mileage between interchanges may be determin
by subtracting one number from the other.

nthouse, Sand Island

Mileages between cities	Beloit	Chicago, IL	Dubuque, IA	Eau Claire	Green Bay	Hayward	La Crosse	Madison	Milwaukee	Oshkosh	Rhinelander	Sheboygan	Sturgeon Bay	Superior	Wausau	Wisconsin Dells
Chicago, IL	96		177	315	206	420	281	146	90	175	338	145	245	462	281	195
Eau Claire	223	315	192		192	106	86	177	243	181	155	228	237	149	98	124
Green Bay	184	206	233	192		283	203	138	116	52	136	64	44	326	96	132
La Crosse	188	281	119	86	203	190		143	209	153	214	195	248	233	170	90
Madison	54	146	93	177	138	282	143		78	87	200	117	185	325	143	57
Milwaukee	74	90	171	243	116	348	209	78		86	244	54	155	390	187	123
Superior	370	462	339	149	326	70	233	325	390	332	182	388	370		232	271
Wausau	189	281	239	98	96	189	170	143	187	103	59	158	141	232		112

Total mileages through Wisconsin

39 182 miles 90 189 miles
43 192 miles 94 341 miles

More mileages at www.randmcnally.com/MC

Nicknames: The Equality State
Capital: Cheyenne, H-13
Land area: 97,100 sq. mi. (rank: 9th)
Population: 563,626 (rank: 50th)
Largest city: Cheyenne, 59,466, H-13

Index of cities Pg. 136

Mileages between cities

	Casper	Cheyenne	Cody	Evanston	Gillette	Laramie	Sheridan	Spearfish, SD
Casper		178	213	325	126	147	148	219
Cheyenne	178		392	357	244	49	324	290
Cody	213	392		376	250	363	148	344
Jackson	283	432	177	190	411	383	325	504
Riverton	119	272	138	238	248	222	213	341
Rock Springs	225	257	278	100	351	207	373	444
Sheridan	148	324	148	473	103	294		196
Spearfish, SD	219	290	344	544	93	296	196	

Total mileages through Wyoming

25: 301 miles
90: 209 miles
80: 403 miles
20: 505 miles

More mileages at www.randmcnally.com/MC

Plan a trip at www.randmcnally.com/WY

Tourism Information
Wyoming Office of Tourism: (800) 225-5996, (307) 777-7777; www.wyomingtourism.org

Road Conditions & Construction
511, (888) 996-7623; www.wyoroad.info

Toll Rd. Info
No toll roads

Determining Distances
(segments of one mile or l[ess] not shown)
Cumulative miles (red): the distance between red arrow[s]
Intermediate miles (black): the distance between intersections & places

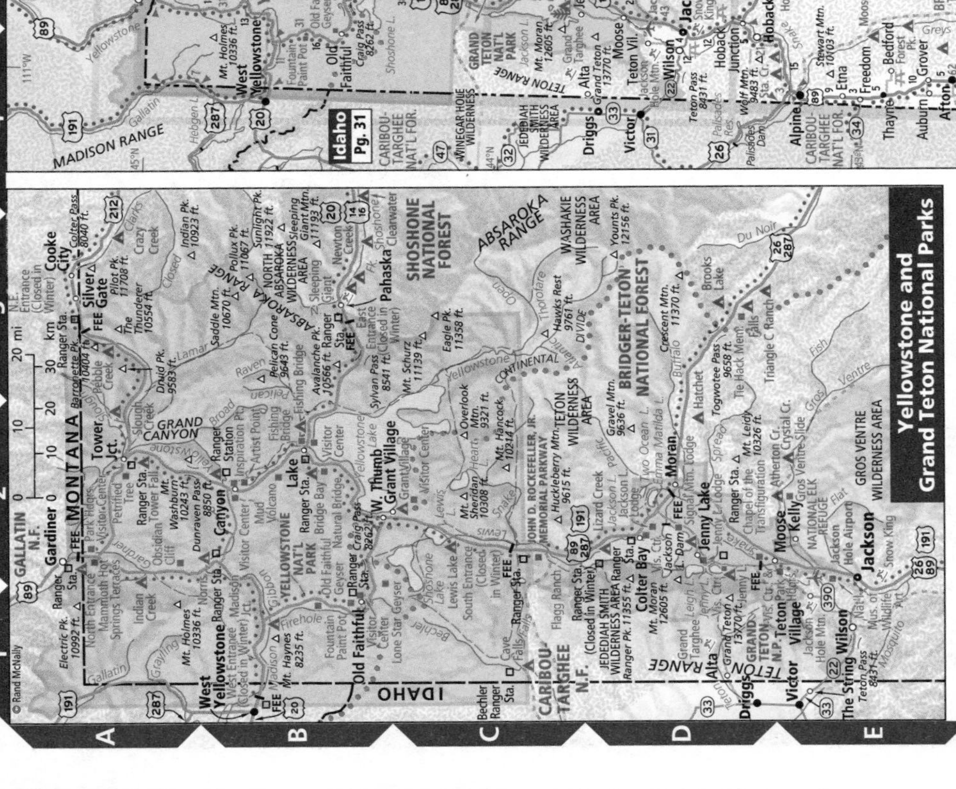

One inch represents: approximately 37 miles

Yellowstone and Grand Teton National Parks

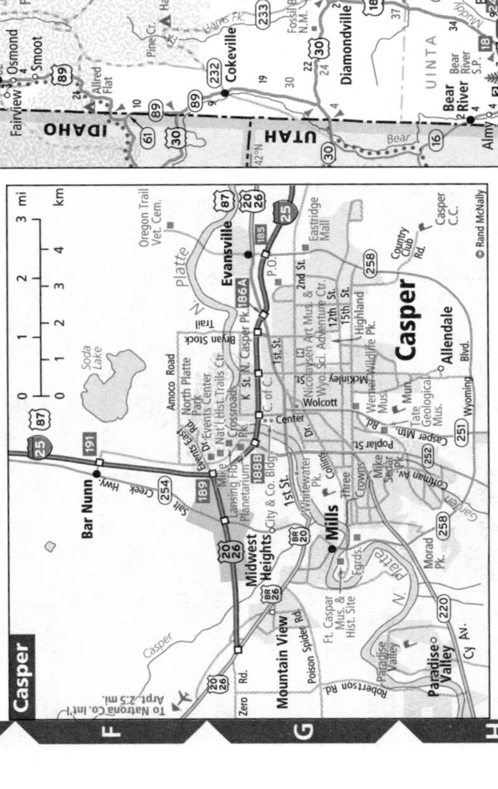

Casper

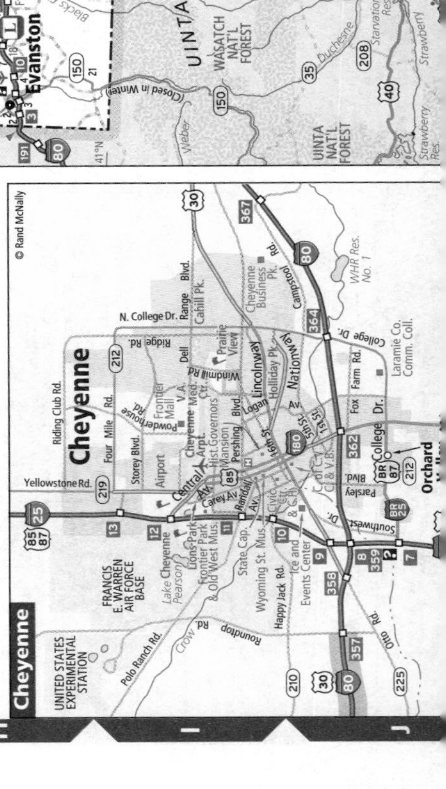

Cheyenne

Selected places of interest

- Banff National Park, G-3
- Cape Breton Highlands National Park, G-13
- Elk Island National Park, F-4
- Fundy National Park, H-12
- Glacier National Park, G-3
- Gros Morne National Park, F-13
- Jasper National Park, F-3
- Kejimkujik National Park, H-12
- Kluane National Park, C-2
- Kootenay National Park, G-3
- Mount Revelstoke National Park, G-3
- Parc Nat. de la Maurice, H-11
- Prince Albert National Park, F-5
- Prince Edward Island National Park, H-12
- Pukaskwa National Park, H-8
- Riding Mountain National Park, H-6
- St. Lawrence Islands National Park, I-10

Capital: Ottawa, I-10
Land area: 3,511,023 sq. mi.
Population: 33,476,688
Largest city: Toronto, 2,615,060

Index of cities Pg. 136

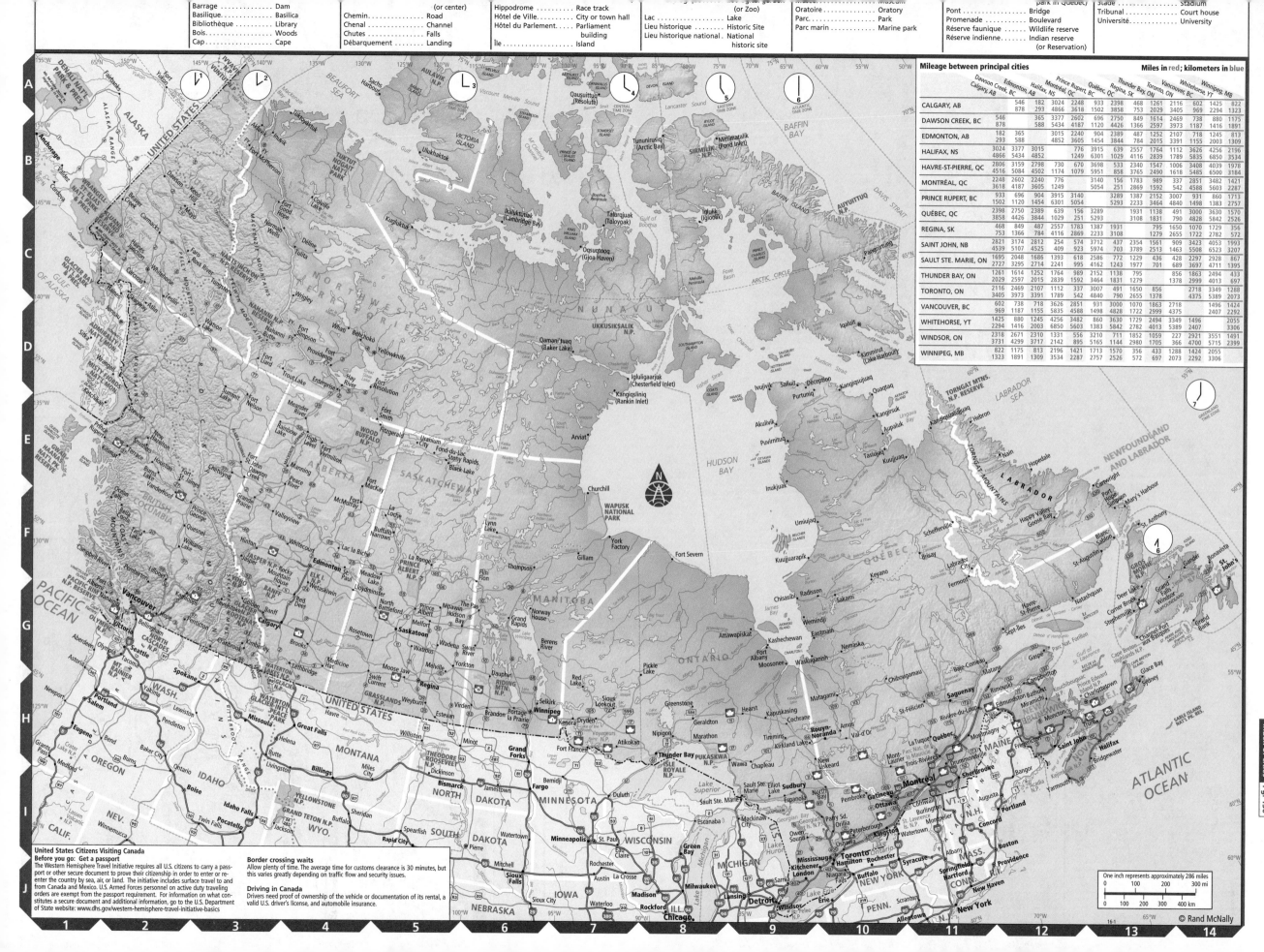

Barrage .... Dam
Basilique .... Basilica
Bibliothèque .... Library
Bois .... Woods
Cap .... Cape
(or center)
Chemin .... Road
Chenal .... Channel
Chutes .... Falls
Débarquement .... Landing
Hippodrome .... Race track
Hôtel de Ville .... City or town hall
Hôtel du Parlement .... Parliament building
Île .... Island
(or Zoo)
Lac .... Lake
Lieu historique .... Historic Site
Lieu historique national .... National historic site
Oratoire .... Oratory
Parc .... Park
Parc marin .... Marine park
Pont .... Bridge
Promenade .... Boulevard
Réserve faunique .... Wildlife reserve
Réserve indienne .... Indian reserve (or Reservation)
Tribunal .... Court house
Université .... University

Mileage between principal cities — Miles in red; kilometers in blue

	Calgary, AB	Dawson Creek, BC	Edmonton, AB	Halifax, NS	Montréal, QC	Prince Rupert, BC	Québec, QC	Regina, SK	Thunder Bay, ON	Toronto, ON	Vancouver, BC	Whitehorse, YT	Winnipeg, MB
CALGARY, AB		546 878	182 293	3024 4866	2248 3618	933 1502	2398 3858	468 753	1261 2029	2116 3405	602 969	1425 2294	822 1323
DAWSON CREEK, BC	546 878		365 588	3377 5434	2602 4187	696 1120	2750 4426	849 1366	1614 2597	2469 3973	738 1187	880 1416	1175 1891
EDMONTON, AB	182 293	365 588		3015 4852	2240 3605	904 1454	2389 3844	487 784	1252 2015	2107 3391	718 1155	1245 2003	813 1309
HALIFAX, NS	3024 4866	3377 5434	3015 4852		776 1249	3915 6301	639 1029	2557 4116	1764 2839	1112 1789	3626 5835	4256 6850	2196 3534
HAVRE-ST-PIERRE, QC	2806 4516	3159 5084	2798 4502	730 1174	670 1079	3698 5951	533 858	2340 3765	1547 2490	1006 1618	3408 5485	4039 6500	1978 3184
MONTRÉAL, QC	2248 3618	2602 4187	2240 3605	776 1249		3140 5054	156 251	1783 2869	989 1592	337 542	2851 4588	3482 5603	1421 2287
PRINCE RUPERT, BC	933 1502	696 1120	904 1454	3915 6301	3140 5054		3289 5293	1387 2233	2152 3464	3007 4840	931 1498	860 1383	1713 2757
QUÉBEC, QC	2398 3858	2750 4426	2389 3844	639 1029	156 251	3289 5293		1931 3108	1138 1831	491 790	3000 4828	3630 5842	1570 2526
REGINA, SK	468 753	849 1366	487 784	2557 4116	1783 2869	1387 2233	1931 3108		795 1279	1650 2655	1070 1722	1729 2782	356 572
SAINT JOHN, NB	2821 4539	3174 5107	2812 4525	254 409	574 923	3712 5974	437 703	2354 3789	1561 2513	909 1463	3423 5508	4053 6523	1993 3207
SAULT STE. MARIE, ON	1695 2727	2048 3295	1686 2714	1393 2241	618 995	2586 4162	772 1243	1229 1977	436 701	428 689	2297 3697	2928 4711	867 1395
THUNDER BAY, ON	1261 2029	1614 2597	1252 2015	1764 2839	989 1592	2152 3464	1138 1831	795 1279		856 1378	1863 2999	2494 4013	433 697
TORONTO, ON	2116 3405	2469 3973	2107 3391	1112 1789	337 542	3007 4840	491 790	1650 2655	856 1378		2718 4375	3349 5389	1288 2073
VANCOUVER, BC	602 969	738 1187	718 1155	3626 5835	2851 4588	931 1498	3000 4828	1070 1722	1863 2999	2718 4375		1496 2407	1424 2292
WHITEHORSE, YT	1425 2294	880 1416	1245 2003	4256 6850	3482 5603	860 1383	3630 5842	1729 2782	2494 4013	3349 5389	1496 2407		2055 3306
WINDSOR, ON	2318 3731	2671 4299	2310 3717	1331 2142	556 895	3210 5165	711 1144	1852 2980	1059 1705	227 366	2921 4700	3551 5715	1491 2399
WINNIPEG, MB	822 1323	1175 1891	813 1309	2196 3534	1421 2287	1713 2757	1570 2526	356 572	433 697	1288 2073	1424 2292	2055 3306	

United States Citizens Visiting Canada

Before you go: Get a passport
The Western Hemisphere Travel Initiative requires all U.S. citizens to carry a passport or other secure document to prove their citizenship in order to enter or re-enter the country by sea, air, or land. The initiative includes surface travel to and from Canada and Mexico. U.S. Armed Forces personnel on active duty traveling orders are exempt from the passport requirement. For information on what constitutes a secure document and additional information, go to the U.S. Department of State website: www.dhs.gov/western-hemisphere-travel-initiative-basics

Border crossing waits
Allow plenty of time. The average time for customs clearance is 30 minutes, but this varies greatly depending on traffic flow and security issues.

Driving in Canada
Drivers need proof of ownership of the vehicle or documentation of its rental, a valid U.S. driver's license, and automobile insurance.

One inch represents approximately 286 miles

British Columbia
Capital: Victoria, M-7
Land area: 357,216 sq. mi. (rank: 4th)
Population: 4,400,057 (rank: 3rd)
Largest city: Vancouver, 603,502, L-7

Index of cities Pg. 136

Mileages between cities	Banff, AB	Dawson Creek	Jasper, AB	Port Hardy	Prince Rupert	Vancouver	Victoria	Williams Lake
Banff, AB		503	178	808*	855	524	578*	483
Cranbrook	173	638	312	806*	989	521	575*	553
Dawson Creek	503		326	1022*	696	738	791*	399
Kamloops	307	576	275	502*	769	217	271*	177
Kelowna	299	671	376	526*	865	242	295*	272
Prince George	408	250	231	772*	447	488	542*	149
Prince Rupert	855	696	677	307*		931	985*	592
Vancouver	524	738	492	285*	931		72*	339

*Via ferry

Mileages © Rand McNally

Total mileages through British Columbia
1: 538 miles
16: 658 miles

More mileages at www.randmcnally.com/MC

Get travel info at www.randmcnally.com/BC

Tourism Information
Destination British Columbia: (604) 660-2861; www.hellobc.com

Road Conditions & Construction
(800) 550-4997; www.drivebc.ca

Toll Bridges
TransLink (Golden Ears Bridge, Vancouver) (*QuickPass*): (877) 299-0599; www.translink.ca
TreO: (Port Mann Bridge, Vancouver): (604) 516-8736; www.treo.ca

Mileages between cities	Calgary	Dawson Creek, BC	Edmonton	Fort McMurray	Grande Prairie	Jasper	Lethbridge	Red Deer
Banff	78	503	260	544	423	178	217	167
Calgary		546	182	465	463	256	139	89
Grande Prairie	463	82	283	467		246	602	376
Edmonton	182	365		281	283	226	321	95
Lethbridge	139	684	321	604	602	395		227
Medicine Hat	178	724	360	563	641	434	102	267
Peace River	480	146	299	421	123	354	618	392
Vermilion	299	481	120	321	399	342	338	211

Saskatchewan
Capital: Regina, K-8
Land area: 228,445 sq. mi. (rank: 7th)
Population: 1,033,381 (rank: 6th)
Largest city: Saskatoon, 222,189, G-6

Index of cities Pg. 136

Mileages between cities	La Loche	La Ronge	Medicine Hat, AB	N. Battleford	Prince Albert	Regina	Saskatoon	Yorkton
Estevan	668	498	391	371	350	125	285	159
Lloydminster	331	347	289	85	214	331	171	375
Meadow Lake	217	232	370	98	162	343	183	388
Prince Albert	318	148	365	129		225	88	233
Regina	543	373	289	246	225		160	116
Saskatoon	379	236	277	86	88	160		205
Swift Current	505	403	139	190	255	151	167	266
Yorkton	551	382	405	290	233	116	205	

Total mileages through Saskatchewan
1: 413 miles
16: 437 miles

More mileages at www.randmcnally.com/MC

Get travel info at www.randmcnally.com/SK

Tourism Information
Tourism Saskatchewan:
(877) 237-2273, (306) 787-2300; www.sasktourism.com

Road Conditions & Construction
(888) 335-7623, Saskatoon: (306) 933-8333, Regina area: (306) 787-7623
www.highways.gov.sk.ca/road-conditions

Toll Rd. Info
No toll roads

Determining Distances
(segments of one mile or less not shown)
Cumulative miles (red), km (blue): the distance between red arrows
Intermediate miles (black): the distance between intersections & places

Manitoba

Capital: Winnipeg, L-17
Land area: 213,729 sq. mi. (rank: 8th)
Population: 1,208,268 (rank: 5th)
Largest city: Winnipeg, 663,617, L-17

Index of cities Pg. 136

urism Information
vel Manitoba: (800) 665-0040,
4) 927-7838; www.travelmanitoba.com

ad Conditions & Construction
, (877) 627-6237, (204) 945-3704;
w.manitoba.ca/roadinfo, www.manitoba.ca

Toll Rd. Info
No toll roads

Determining Distances
(segments of one mile or less not shown)
Cumulative miles (red), km (blue): the distance between red arrows
Intermediate miles (black): the distance between intersections & places

Total mileages through Manitoba
1: 306 miles
16: 166 miles

More mileages at www.randmcnally.com/MC

Mileages between cities	Ashern	Brandon	Dauphin	Flin Flon	Grand Rapids	Pine Falls	Thompson	Winnipeg
Brandon	200		104	444	355	217	558	134
Dauphin	127	104		342	282	267	485	198
Flin Flon	368	444	342		255	546	244	483
Morden	184	129	216	552	338	167	542	87
Portage la Prairie	119	80	144	485	274	136	477	53
Swan River	233	208	106	236	211	372	385	303
Virden	245	47	148	419	399	262	568	178
Winnipeg	114	134	198	483	269	81	472	

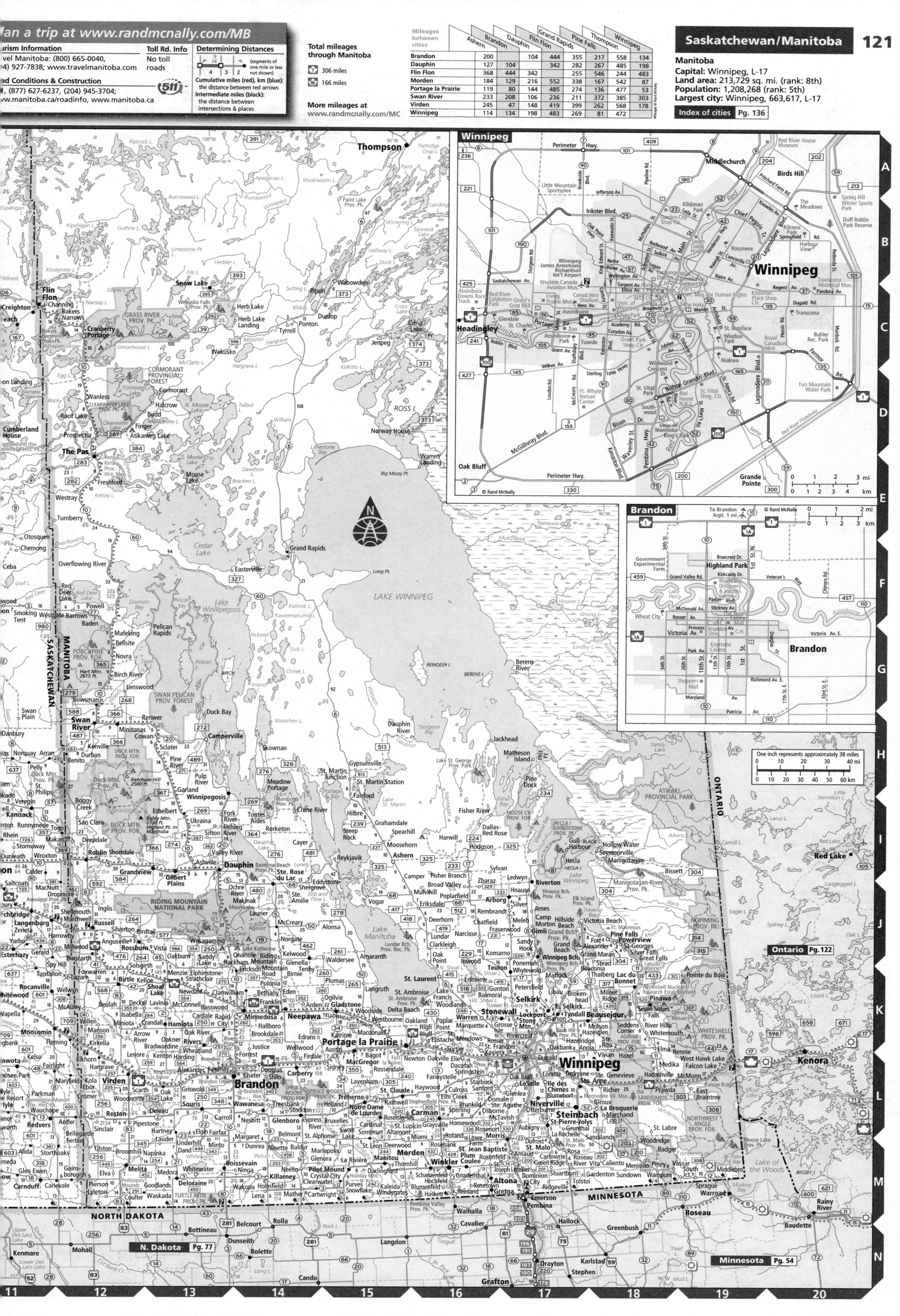

Ontario
Capital: Toronto, I-10
Land area: 354,342 sq. mi. (rank: 5th)
Population: 12,851,821 (rank: 1st)
Largest city: Toronto, 2,615,060, I-10

Index of cities Pg. 136

For a glossary of common French terms, see page 117.

Explore Ontario at www.randmcnally.com/ON

Tourism Information
Ontario Tourism Marketing Partnership Corp.: (800) 668-2746; www.ontariotravel.net

Road Conditions & Construction
511, In ON: (800) 268-4686
Toronto area: (416) 235-4686; www.mto.gov.on.ca/english/traveller

Toll Road Information:
407 ETR (Toronto): (888) 407-0407; www.407etr.com

Ontario–Michigan Toll Bridge Information:
Ambassador Bridge (Detroit): www.ambassadorbridge.com
Mich. Dept. of Transportation (all other bridges): (517) 373-2090; www.michigan.gov/mdot
see Michigan page for Detroit-Windsor tunnel info

Ontario–New York Toll Bridge Information:
Buffalo & Ft. Erie Public Br. Auth. (Peace Br.) (*E-ZPass*): (716) 884-674 www.peacebridge.com
Niagara Falls Bridge Comm. (*ExpressPass or NEXUS*): (716) 285-6322 (905) 354-5641; www.niagarafallsbridges.com
Ogdensburg Br. & Port Auth. (Prescott): (315) 393-4080; www.ogdensport.co
Seaway Int'l Bridge Corp. (Cornwall): (613) 932-6601; www.sibc.ca
Thousand Islands Br. Auth. (Lansdowne): (315) 482-2501; www.tibridge.com

For continuation see map at lower right

Toronto

Central Toronto

Mich. Pg. 50

Ohio Pg. 78

Penn. Pg. 86

Mileages between cities	Bracebridge	Hamilton	Kenora	Kingston	Montréal, QC	Niagara Falls	Ottawa	Owen Sound	Pembroke	Sarnia	Sault Ste. Marie	Sudbury	Thunder Bay	Timmins	Toronto	Windsor
Kingston	223	204	1285		180	243	120	269	154	335	555	369	983	509	161	381
London	213	81	1255	274	450	127	360	143	360	68	525	339	953	535	121	116
Niagara Falls	185	47	1227	243	419		329	163	328	188	497	311	925	507	83	233
Ottawa	237	290	1207	120	124	329		338	91	421	494	300	905	445	247	467
Sudbury	153	272	925	369	424	311	300	238	209	401	195		623	182	242	446
Thunder Bay	767	886	303	983	989	925	905	852	814	1015	436	623		517	856	1060
Toronto	116	44	1158	161	337	83	247	118	246	182	428	242	856	438		227
Windsor	319	187	1361	381	556	233	467	259	466	96	631	445	1059	641	227	

Mileages © Rand McNally

Total mileages through Ontario

69 & 400 & QEW 323 miles   401 513 miles

17 & 417 1358 miles

More mileages at www.randmcnally.com/MC

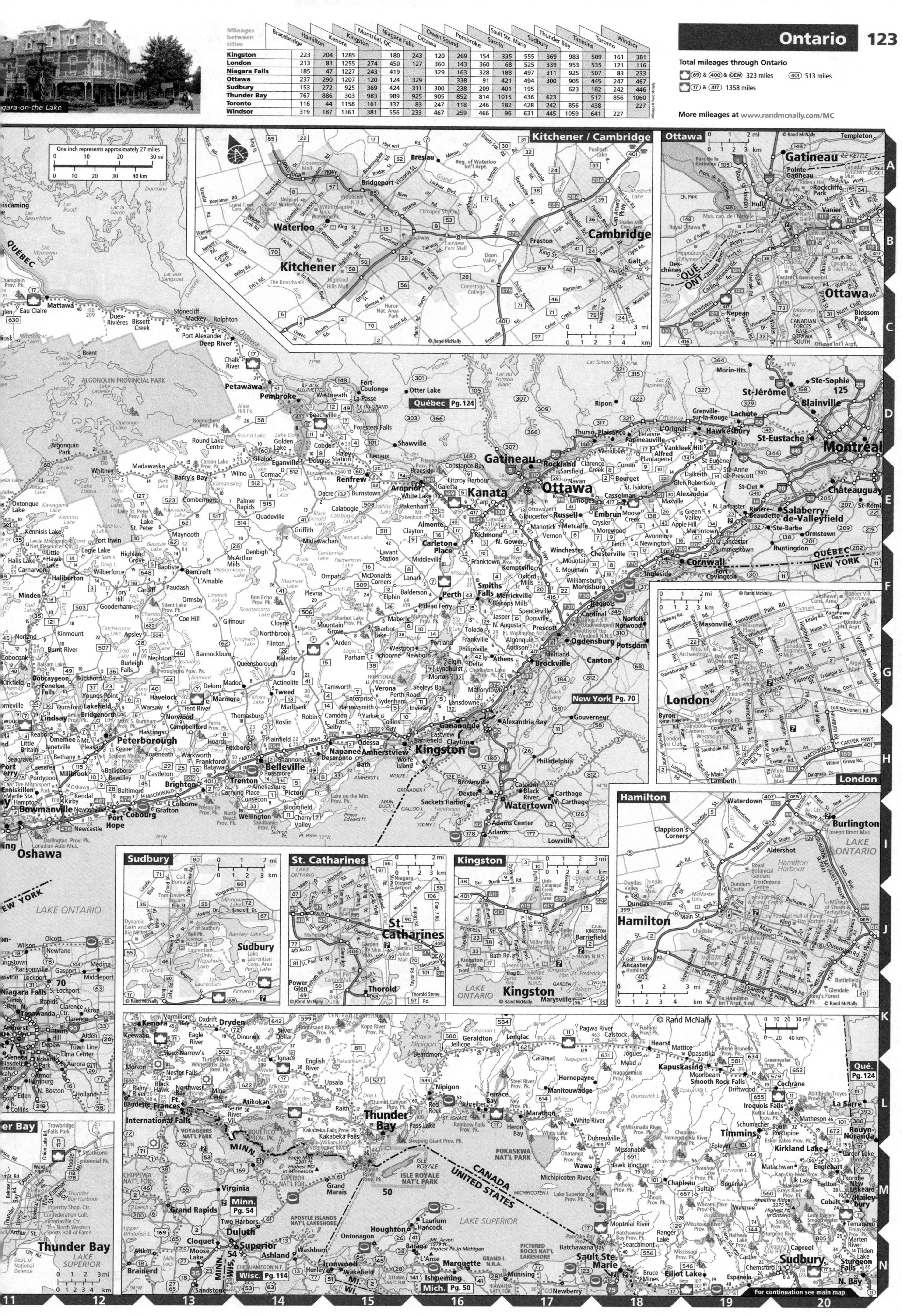

Québec
Capital: Québec, J-11
Land area: 527,079 sq. mi. (rank: 2nd)
Population: 7,903,001 (rank: 2nd)
Largest city: Montréal, 1,649,519, M-8

Index of cities Pg. 136

For a glossary of common French terms, see page 117.

Get more Québec info at www.randmcnally.com/QC

Tourism Information
Tourisme Québec: (877) 266-5687, (514) 873-2015; www.bonjourquebec.com

Road Conditions & Construction
511, (888) 355-0511,
In QC: (877) 393-2363;
www.quebec511.gouv.qc.ca/en

Toll Road Information
Concession A25 (Pont Olivier-Charbonneau, Montréal): (855) 766-8225, (514) 766-8225; www.a25.com
A30Express (near Montréal): (514) 782-0800; www.a30express.com

Determining distances along roads
Highway distances (segments of one mile or less not shown):
Cumulative miles (red): the distance between red arrows
Cumulative kilometers (blue): the distance between red arrows
Intermediate miles (black): the distance between intersections & pla

Comparative distance: 1 mile = 1.609 kilometers 1 kilometer = 0.621 mile

Trois-Rivières

Québec

Central Montréal

Sherbrooke

Ontario Pg. 122

New York Pg. 70

Vermont Pg. 104

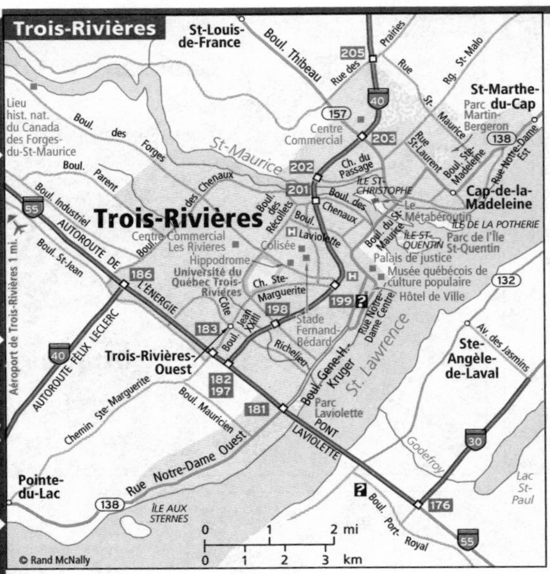

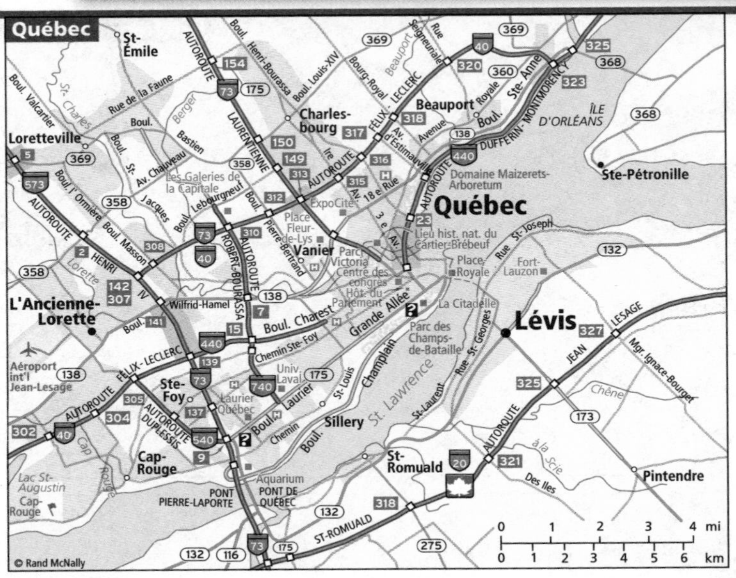

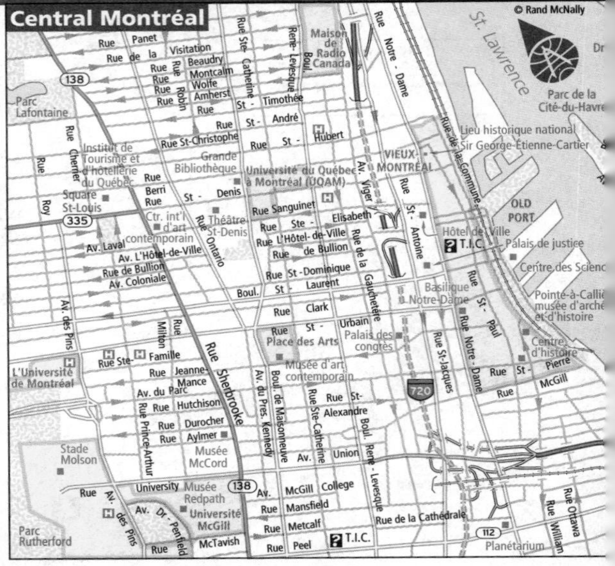

Mileages between cities	Baie-Comeau	Edmundston, NB	Gaspé	Mont-Laurier	Montréal	North Bay, ON	Ottawa, ON	Québec	Rimouski	Rivière-du-Loup	Rouyn-Noranda	Saguenay	Sept-Îles	Sherbrooke	Thetford Mines	Trois-Rivières
Montréal	410	336	566	145		346	124	156	331	266	389	289	534*	93	143	88
Ottawa, ON	533	459	689	122	124	222		279	454	389	323	411	657*	213	266	205
Québec	253	199	429	294	156	501	279		195	129	537	135	397*	146	72	78
Rouyn-Noranda	706	723	953	243	389	181	323	537	719	653		517	921*	481	530	461
Saguenay	196	186*	390*	427	289	634	411	135	156*	108*	517		339	279	205	211
Sept-Îles	143	306*	319*	678*	534*	879*	657*	397*	206*	268*	921*	339		524*	450*	465*
Sherbrooke	400	326	556	237	93	435	213	146	321	256	481	279	524*		65	94
Trois-Rivières	342	268	497	217	89	427	205	78	263	197	461	211	465*	94	88	

*Via ferry

Mileages © Rand McNally

Total mileages through Québec

20 132: 937 miles; 40 138: 765 miles; 15 117: 412 miles

More mileages at www.randmcnally.com/MC

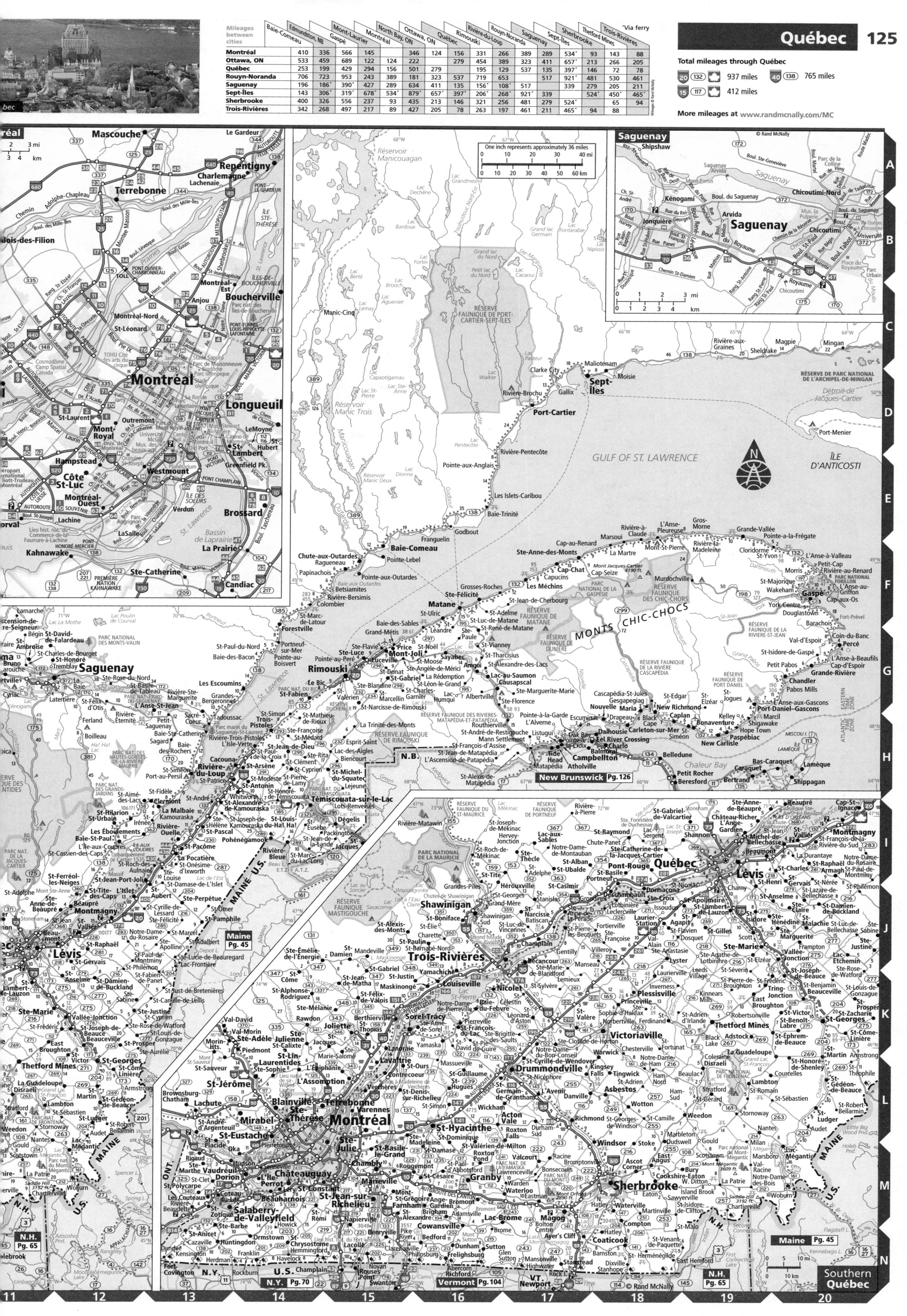

New Brunswick
Capital: Fredericton, H-4
Land area: 27,587 sq. mi. (rank: 11th)
Population: 751,171 (rank: 8th)
Largest city: Saint John, 70,063, J-5

Index of cities Pg. 136

Explore the Atlantic Provinces at www.randmcnally.com/Canada

Tourism Information

Tourism New Brunswick: (800) 561-0123; www.tourismnewbrunswick.ca

Nova Scotia Tourism Agency: (800) 565-0000, (902) 424-5000; www.novascotia.com

Prince Edward Island Tourism: (800) 463-4734; www.tourismpei.com

Newfoundland & Labrador Tourism: (800) 563-6353, (709) 729-2830; www.newfoundlandlabrador.com

Road Conditions & Construction

New Brunswick: 511, (800) 561-4063, (506) 459-3939; www.gnb.ca/roads

Nova Scotia: 511, (888) 780-4440, (902) 424-3933; 511.gov.ns.ca/map

Prince Edward Island: 511, (902) 368-4770 In Canada: (855) 241-2680 www.gov.pe.ca/roadconditions

Newfoundland & Labrador: Avalon: (709) 729-2382, Eastern: (709) 466-4120, Central: (709) 292-4300, Western: (709) 635-4217, Labrador: (709) 896-7840; www.roads.gov.nl.ca

Toll Road Information

Confederation Bridge *(StraitPass)*: (888) 437-6565; www.confederationbridge

Cobequid Pass: (TransCanada 104, Nova Sc

(877) 727-7104; www.cobequidpass.com

Halifax Harbor Bridges (Halifax): *(MACPAS*

(902) 463-2800; www.hdbc.ca

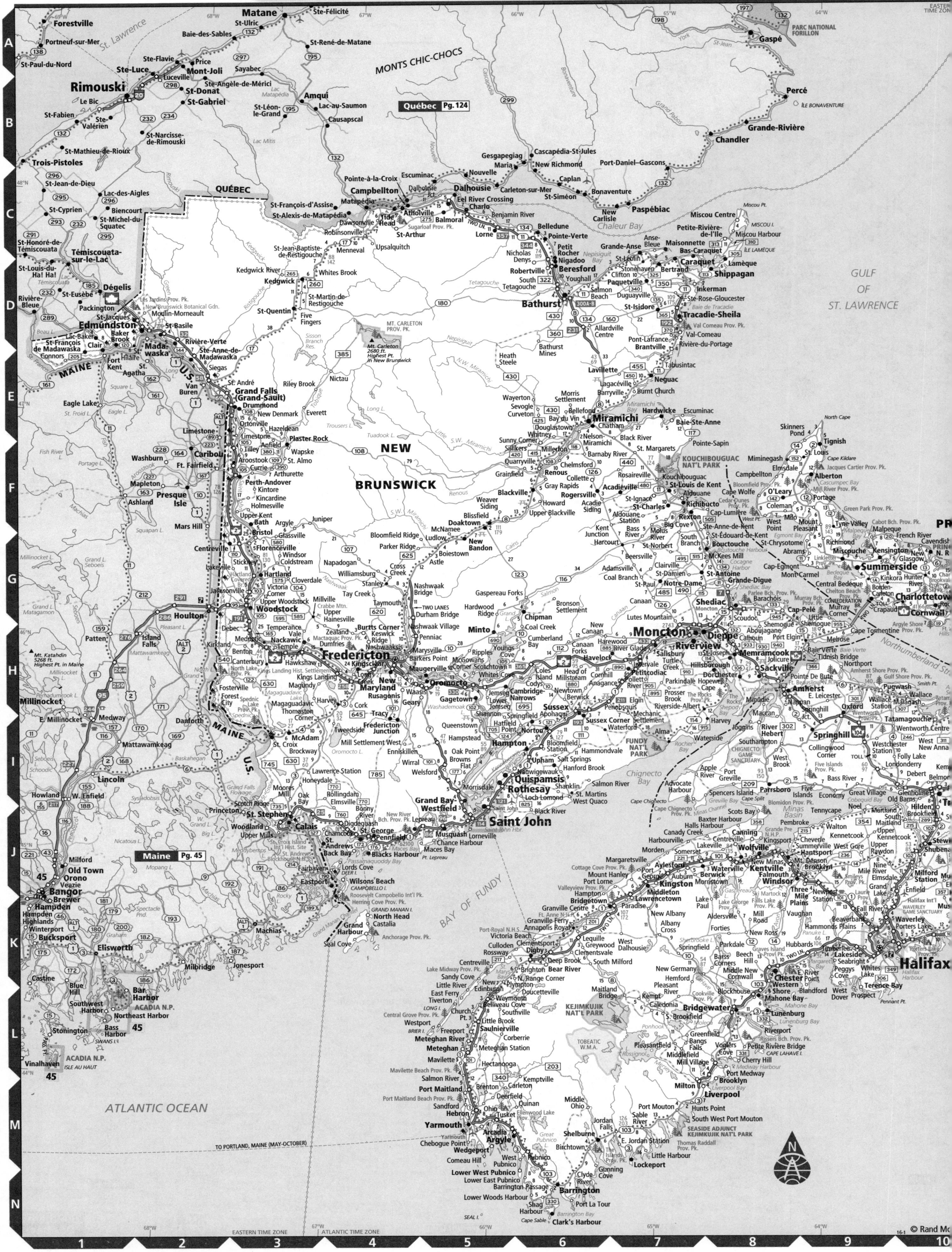

Québec Pg. 124

Maine Pg. 45

NEW BRUNSWICK

GULF OF ST. LAWRENCE

BAY OF FUNDY

ATLANTIC OCEAN

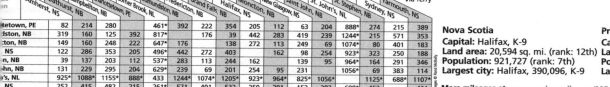

	Amherst, NS	Bathurst, NB	Campbellton, NB	Charlottetown, PE	Corner Brook, NL	Edmundston, NB	Fredericton, NB	Grand Falls, NB	Halifax, NS	Moncton, NB	New Glasgow, NS	Saint John, NB	St. John's, NL	St. Stephen, NB	Sydney, NS	Yarmouth, NS
tetown, PE	82	214	280		461*	392	222	354	205	112	63	204	888*	274	215	389
dston, NB	319	160	125	392	817*		176	39	442	283	419	239	1244*	215	571	353
cton, NB	149	160	248	222	647*	176		138	272	113	249	69	1074*	80	401	183
NS	122	286	353	205	496*	442	272	403		162	98	254	923*	323	250	188
n, NB	39	137	203	112	537*	283	113	244	162		139	95	964*	164	291	346
hn, NB	131	229	295	204	629*	239	69	201	254	95	231		1056*	69	383	114
's, NL	925*	1088*	1155*	888*	433	1244*	1074*	1205*	923*	964*	825*	1056*		1125*	688*	1107*
NS	252	415	482	215	261*	571	401	532	250	291	152	383	688*	452		434

*Via ferry

Mileages © Rand McNally

More mileages at www.randmcnally.com/MC

Nova Scotia
Capital: Halifax, K-9
Land area: 20,594 sq. mi. (rank: 12th)
Population: 921,727 (rank: 7th)
Largest city: Halifax, 390,096, K-9

Prince Edward Island
Capital: Charlottetown, G-10
Land area: 2,185 sq. mi. (rank: 13th)
Population: 140,204 (rank: 10th)
Largest city: Charlottetown, 34,562, G-10

Newfoundland & Labrador
Capital: St. John's, F-20
Land area: 144,353 sq. mi. (rank: 10th)
Population: 514,536 (rank: 9th)
Largest city: St. John's, 106,172, F-20

For a glossary of common French terms, see page 117.

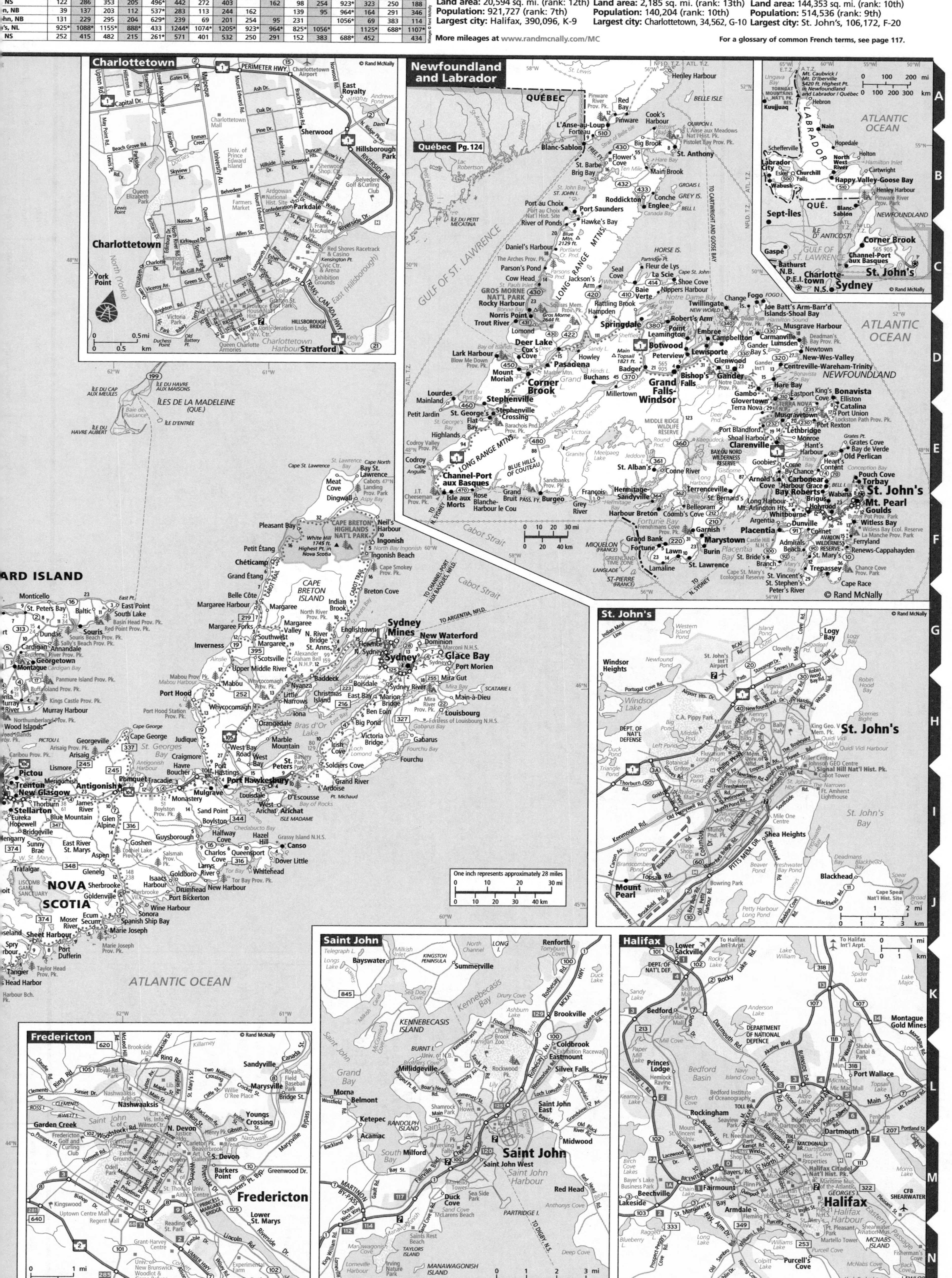

Mexico
Capital: Mexico City, G-8
Land area: 758,450 sq. mi.
Population: 112,336,538
Largest city: Mexico City, 8,851,080, G-8

Puerto Rico (U.S.)
Capital: San Juan, A-13
Land area: 3,425 sq. mi.
Population: 3,725,789
Largest city: San Juan, 381,931, A-13

Index of cities Mexico: Pg. 136; P.R.: Pg. 134

Selected places of interest
- Bahía Fosforescente (P.R.), B-10
- Barranca del Cobre, C-4
- Catarata de la Mina (P.R.), A-14
- Castillo del Morró (P.R.), A-13
- Chichen Itza Ruinas, G-13
- Grutas de Cacahuamilpa, H-8
- Monte Albán Ruinas, H-9
- Museo de Arte de Ponce (P.R.), B-11
- Palenque Ruinas, H-12
- Parque Ecológico de Xochimilco, I-3
- Parque Internacional del Rio Bravo, C-7
- Plaza de la Constitucion, G-2
- Submarine Gardens (P.R.), A-13
- Teotihuacán Ruinas, G-8
- Tulum Ruinas, G-14
- Uxmal Ruinas, G-12

Explore at www.randmcnally.com

Mexico Tourism Information
Mexico Tourism Board:
(800) 446-3942;
www.visitmexico.com/en
Mexico Toll Information, Road Conditions, & Construction
www.sct.gob.mx/carreteras (Spanish)

Puerto Rico Tourism Information
Tourism Company of Puerto Rico
(800) 866-7827;
www.puertorico.com
Puerto Rico Toll Information, Road Conditions, & Construction
www.dtop.gov.pr/carretera

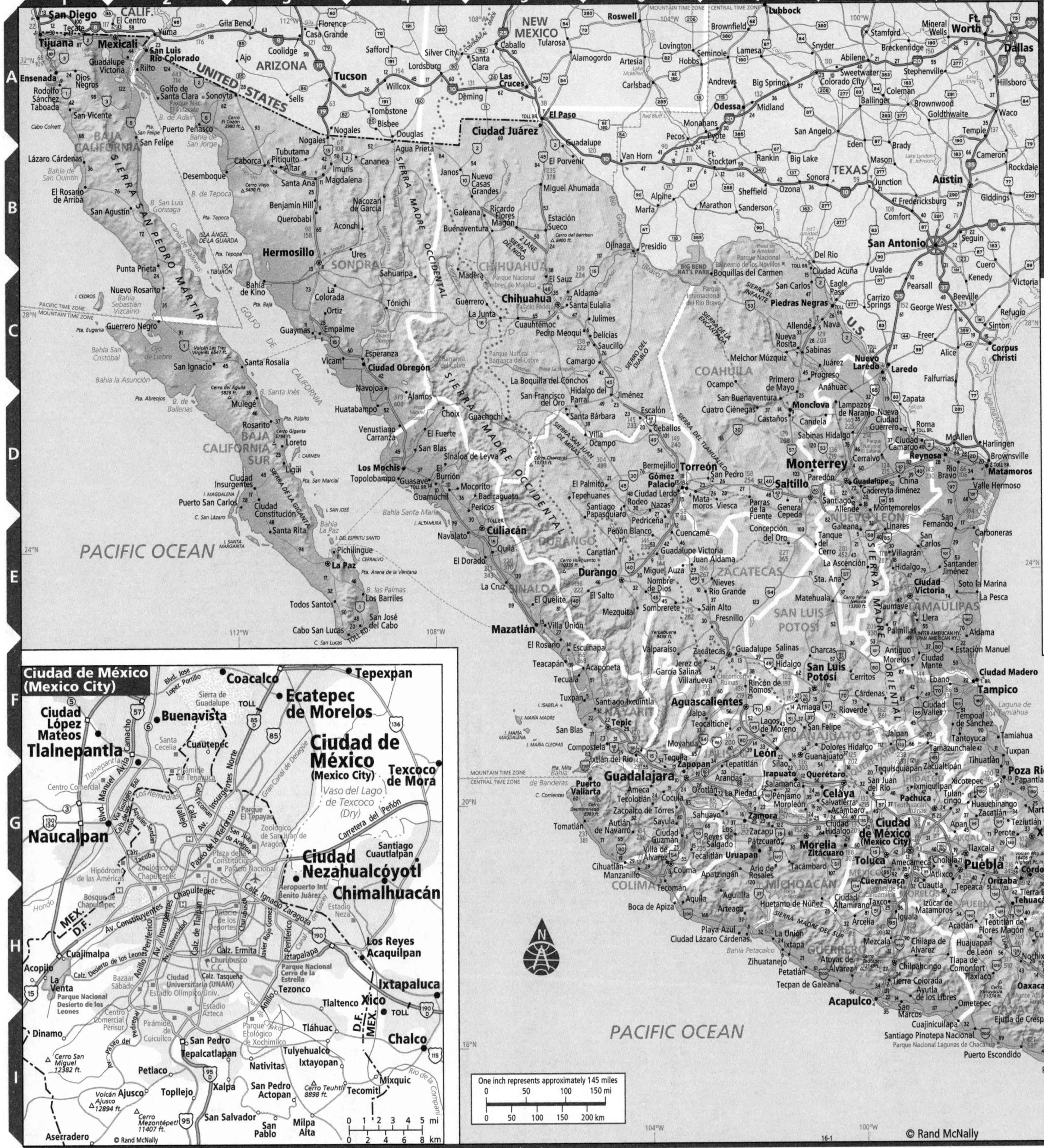

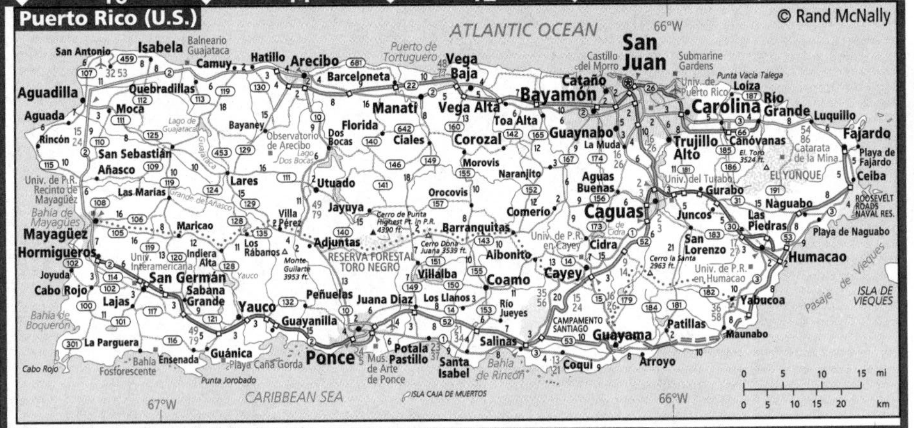

Puerto Rico (U.S.)

Ciudad de México (Mexico City)

United States Citizens Visiting Mexico

Before you go: Get a passport
The Western Hemisphere Travel Initiative requires all U.S. citizens to carry a passport or other secure document to prove their citizenship in order to enter or re-enter the country by sea, air, or land. The initiative includes surface travel to and from Canada and Mexico. U.S. Armed Forces personnel on active duty traveling orders are exempt from the passport requirement. For information on what constitutes a secure document and additional information, go to the U.S. Department of State website: www.dhs.gov/western-hemisphere-travel-initiative-basics

Border crossing waits
Allow plenty of time. The average time for customs clearance is 30 minutes, but this varies greatly depending on traffic flow and security issues.

Driving in Mexico
According to the U.S. Department of State, tourists traveling beyond the border zone must obtain a temporary import permit or risk having their car confiscated by Mexican customs officials. To acquire a permit, submit evidence of citizenship, title for the car, a car registration certificate, driver's license, and a processing fee to either a Banjercito (Mexican Army Bank) branch located at a Mexican Customs office at the port of entry, or at one of the Mexican consulates in the U.S. Mexican law also requires posting a bond at a Banjercito office to guarantee departure of the car from Mexico within a period determined at the time of application. Carry proof of car ownership (the current registration card or a letter of authorization from the finance or leasing company). Auto insurance policies, other than Mexican, are not valid in Mexico. A short-term liability policy is obtainable at the border.

Tourist cards
Tourist cards are valid up to six months, require a fee, and are required for all persons, regardless of age, to visit the interior of Mexico. Cards may be obtained from Mexican border authorities, Consuls of Mexico, or Federal Delegates in major cities. Cards are also distributed to passengers en route to Mexico by air.

Mileage between principal cities

Miles in red; kilometers in blue

	Acapulco, GR	Chihuahua, CH	Cuidad Juárez, CH	Guadalajara, JA	Hermosillo, SO	La Paz, BS	Matamoros, TM	Mazatlan, SI	Mérida, YU	Mexico City, DF	Monterrey, NL	Nogales, SO	Nuevo Laredo, TM	Oaxaca, OA	San Luis Potosí, SL	Tampico, TM	Tijuana, BC	Torreón, CO	Tuxtlas Gutierrez, CS	Veracruz, VE
CUIDAD JUÁREZ, CH	1323 2129	233 375		910 1465	468 753	988 1590	933 1502	807 1299	1943 3127	1121 1804	739 1188	374 602	874 1406	1394 2243	855 1375	1058 1703	782 1259	518 834	1700 2735	1357 2183
GUADALAJARA, JA	509 819	678 1090	910 1465		864 1391	587 945	612 985	301 484	1140 1834	318 511	457 735	1034 1664	592 952	590 950	207 333	429 691	1392 2240	409 658	896 1442	553 891
MÉRIDA, YU	1027 1652	1710 2752	1943 3127	1140 1834	2004 3225	1727 2779	1255 2020	1440 2318		822 1323	1270 2044	2174 3499	1409 2268	691 1111	1088 1751	947 1525	2529 4070	1442 2320	486 782	649 1045
MEXICO CITY, DF	217 349	888 1429	1121 1804	318 511	1182 1902	905 1457	568 914	618 995	822 1323		551 887	1352 2176	678 1091	273 439	266 429	260 419	1710 2752	620 997	579 931	236 379
MONTERREY, NL	768 1236	506 814	739 1188	457 735	882 1419	813 1308	195 314	526 846	1270 2044	551 887		979 1576	135 218	790 1272	336 541	323 520	1387 2232	220 355	1027 1653	621 1000
TIJUANA, BC	1872 3013	882 1419	782 1259	1392 2240	528 850	891 1434	1582 2546	1092 1757	2529 4070	1710 2752	1387 2232	484 779	1522 2449	1981 3188	1503 2419	1726 2778		1167 1878	2284 3676	1943 3127
TUXTLAS GUTIERREZ, CS	560 901	1467 2360	1700 2735	896 1442	1760 2833	1484 2388	1012 1628	1197 1926	486 782	579 931	1027 1653	1931 3107	1166 1876	303 487	845 1360	704 1133	2284 3676	1198 1928		406 653

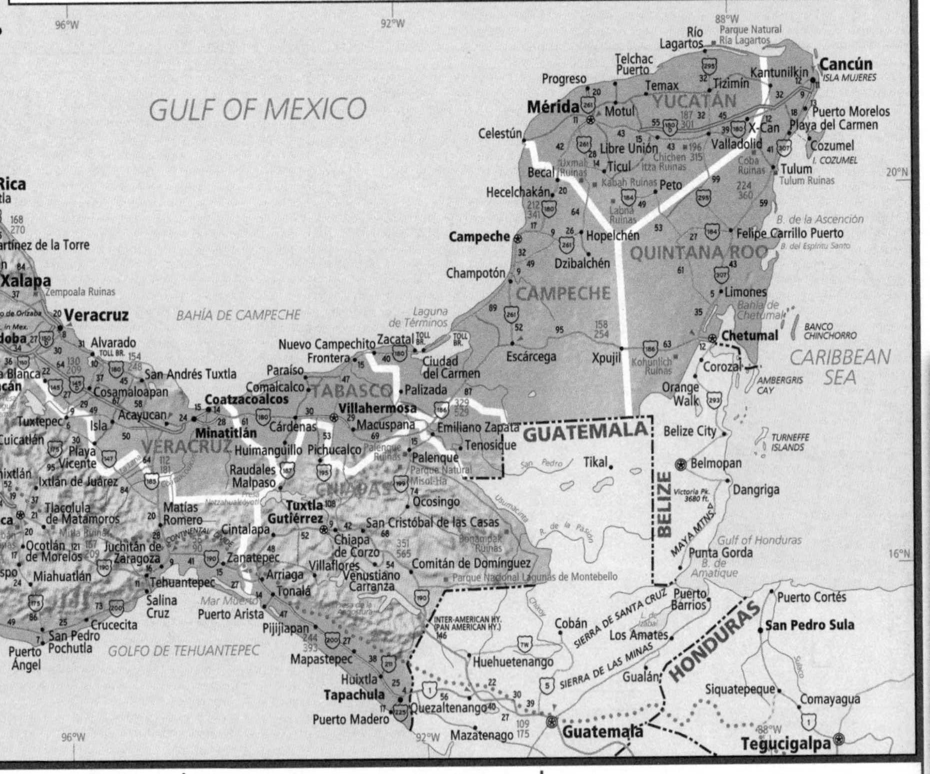

One inch represents approximately 145 miles

Glossary of Spanish terms

Avenida (Av.) ... Avenue	Canal ... Canal, strait	Cerro ... Mountain	Grutas ... Caves	Parque Nacional (Nac.) ... National park	Presa ... Reservoir
Bahía (B.) ... Bay	Carretera ... Highway	Ciudad ... City	Hipódromo ... Race track	Parque Natural ... Wildlife park	Punta (Pta.) ... Point, headland
Barranca ... Canyon	Castillo ... Fort	Deportes ... Sports	Isla (I.) ... Island		Sierra ... Mountain

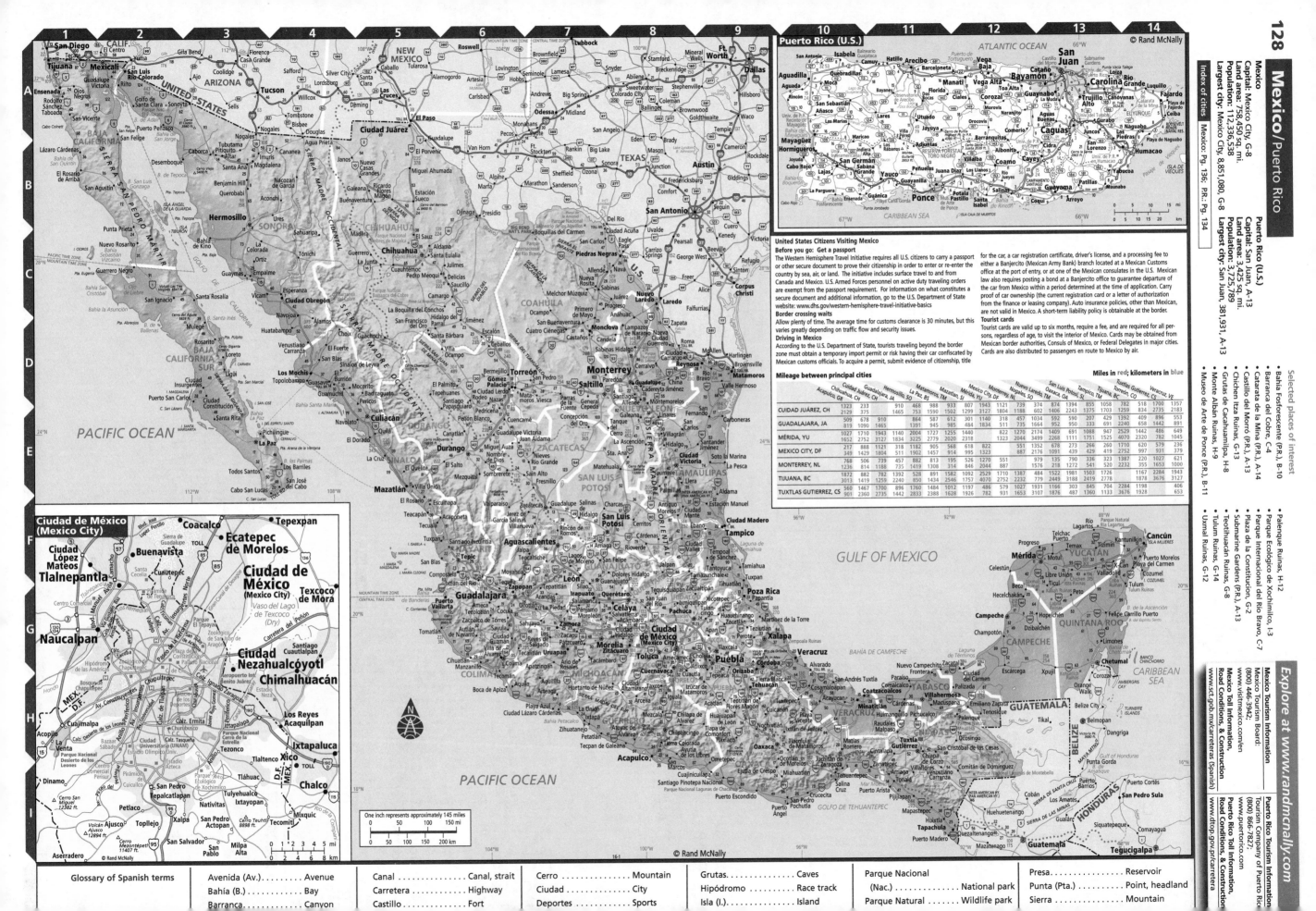

[In]dex

[Uni]ted States Counties, cities, towns & places

[Popula]tions are from the 2010 U.S. Census or Rand McNally estimates

[For] Canada and Mexico cities and towns, page 136

[Al]abama

[Ma]p pp. 4 – 5

Alaska

Map p. 6

Arizona

Map pp. 8 – 9

* City keyed to p. 7

Arkansas

Map pp. 10 – 11

California

Map pp. 12 – 15

Map keys	Atlas pages
NA – NN	12 – 13
SA – SN	14 – 15

* City keyed to p. 16
† City keyed to p. 17
‡ City keyed to pp. 18 – 19

Colorado

Map pp. 20 – 21

* City keyed to p. 22

Connecticut

Map p. 23

Delaware

Map p. 24

District of Columbia

Map p. 111

Florida

Map pp. 26 – 27

* City keyed to p. 24
† City keyed to p. 25

*, †, ‡, § See explanation under state title in this index. County and parish names are listed in capital letters and in boldface type. Independent cities (not in any county) are shown in italics.

*, †, ‡, § See explanation under state title in this index. County and parish names are listed in capital letters and in boldface type. Independent cities (not in any county) are shown in italics.

*, †, ‡, § See explanation under state title in this index. County and parish names are listed in capital letters and in boldface type. Independent cities (not in any county) are shown in italics.

New Mexico

Map p. 68

New York

Map pp. 69 – 71

Map keys	Atlas pages
NA – NN	70 – 71
SA – SJ	69

* City keyed to pp. 72 – 73

North Carolina

Map pp. 74 – 75

* City keyed to p. 76

North Dakota

Map p. 77

Ohio

Map pp. 78 – 81

Map keys	Atlas pages
NA – NN	78 – 79
SA – SN	80 – 81

* City keyed to p. 112

Oklahoma

Map pp. 82 – 83

Oregon

Map pp. 84 – 85

Pennsylvania

Map pp. 86 – 89

Map keys	Atlas pages
EA – ET	88 – 89
WA – WT	86 – 87

* City keyed to p. 24
† City keyed to p. 67
‡ City keyed to p. 90

Puerto Rico

Map p. 128

Rhode Island

Map p. 91

South Carolina

Map p. 92

* City keyed to p. 28

South Dakota

Map p. 93

Tenne...

Map pp...

† City keyed to...

*, †, ‡, § See explanation under state title in this index. County and parish names are listed in capital letters and in boldface type. Independent cities (not in any county) are shown in italics.

*, †, ‡, § See explanation under state title in this index. County and parish names are listed in capital letters and in boldface type. Independent cities (not in any county) are shown in italics.

Belle, 1260 I-4
Belmont, 903 F-4
Benwood, 1420 D-6
BERKELEY CO., 104169 B-9
Berkeley Sprs., 624 B-9
Bethany, 1036 C-6
Bethlehem, 2499 D-6
Beverly, 702 I-8
Blennerhassett, 3089 G-3
Bluefield, 10447 M-4
Bluewell, 2184 M-4
Boaz, 1297 F-4
Bolivar, 1045 C-10
BOONE CO., 24629 K-3
Bradley, 2040 K-4
BRAXTON CO., 14523 H-5
Bridgeport, 8149 G-7
BROOKE CO., 24069 C-6
Brookhaven, 5171 K-10
Buckhannon, 5639 H-7
Buffalo, 1236 I-2
Buffalo Creek, 900 L-4
Bunker Hill, 700 B-9
CABELL CO., 96319 I-2
CALHOUN CO., 7627 H-4

Wisconsin

Map pp. 114 – 115

† City keyed to p. 113

Wyoming

Map p. 116

Canada Cities and Towns

Populations are from latest available census or are Rand McNally estimates

Alberta

Map pp. 118 – 119

* City keyed to p. 117

Acme, 653 H-16
Airdrie, 42564 H-16
Alberta Bch., 865 E-15
Alix, 830 G-17
Athabasca, 2990 E-16
Banff, 7584 I-15

British Columbia

Map pp. 118 – 119

* City keyed to p. 117

Manitoba

Map p. 121

* City keyed to p. 117

New Brunswick

Map pp. 126 – 127

Nunavut

Map p. 117

Northwest Territories

Map p. 117

Nova Scotia

Map pp. 126 – 127

Newfoundland & Labrador

Map p. 127

Ontario

Map pp. 122 – 123

Québec

Map pp. 124 – 125

* City keyed to p. 117

Prince Edward Island

Map pp. 126 – 127

Saskatchewan

Map p. 120

* City keyed to p. 117

Yukon

Map p. 117

Mexico Cities and Towns (map p. 128)

Populations are from 2010 Mexican Census or are Rand McNally estimates

Aguascalientes

Aguascalientes, 722250 F-7
Rincón de Romos, 27988 F-7

Baja California

Baja California Sur

Campeche

Chiapas

Chihuahua

Coahuila

Colima

Distrito Federal

Durango

Guanajuato

Guerrero

Hidalgo

Jalisco

México

Michoacán

Morelos

Nayarit

Nuevo León

Oaxaca

Puebla

Querétaro

Quintana Roo

San Luis Potosí

Sinaloa

Sonora

Tabasco

Tamaulipas

Tlaxcala

Veracruz

Yucatán

Zacatecas

*, †, ‡, § See explanation under state title in this index. County and parish names are listed in capital letters and in boldface type. Independent cities (not in any county) are shown in italics.